DINOSAURS

GARLAND REFERENCE LIBRARY
OF THE HUMANITIES
(VOL. 1196)

Saurornithoides faces the primitive opossum *Didelphis*. From *Archosauria: A New Look at the Old Dinosaur* by John C. McLoughlin. Copyright © 1979 by John C. McLoughlin. Used by permission of Viking Penguin, a division of Penguin Books USA Inc.

DINOSAURS
A Guide to Research

Bruce Edward Fleury

GARLAND PUBLISHING, INC. • NEW YORK & LONDON
1992

© 1992 Bruce Edward Fleury
All rights reserved

Library of Congress Cataloging-in-Publication Data

Fleury, Bruce E.
    Dinosaurs : a guide to research / Bruce Edward Fleury.
      p.   cm. — (Garland reference library of the humanities ; vol. 1196)
    Includes bibliographical references and index.
    ISBN 0–8240–5344–3 (alk. paper)
    1. Dinosaurs—Bibliography. I. Title. II. Series.
Z6033.D55F54   1992
[QE862.D5]
016.5679'7—dc20   92–232
                                                                                   CIP

Printed on acid-free, 250-year-life paper
Manufactured in the United States of America

This book is dedicated to my son Benjamin, who is just beginning to play with his father's dinosaurs.

CONTENTS

Illustrations	ix
Preface	xi
Introduction	xiii

1. Return of the Dinosaurs — 3

Bibliographies	5
Reference Works	7
General Works	9
Primary Journals	21

2. Dinosaur Hunters — 23

First Discoveries	27
The Victorian Dinosaur	28
The American West	32
Battles Over Bones	37
General Works	43

3. The World of the Dinosaurs — 45

Geology	50
Climate	58
Biogeography	64
The Origin of Angiosperms	72

4. The Dinosaurs — 85

General Works	88

5. Warm-Blooded Dinosaurs — 127

Endotherm or Ectotherm	132
Predator/Prey Ratios	142
Stance, Gait, and Speed	144
Trackways	156
Brain Size and Intelligence	162
Bone Tissue	166
Thermoregulation of Modern Reptiles	171

6. Dinosaur Ecology — 181

Ecology of Dinosaurs	189
Herbivores	201
Carnivores	216
Ecology of Modern Animals	220
Social Behavior	232
Nests, Eggs, and Juveniles	241

7. Dinosaur Evolution — 257

The Evolution of Dinosaurs	262
Origin of Dinosaurs	266
Taxonomy and Phylogeny	271

8. Dinosaurs and Birds — 287

Archaeopteryx	291
Dinosaurs and Birds	299
Phylogeny and Evolution of Birds	305
Flight	315

9. Death of the Dinosaurs — 321

Catastrophic Extinction	326
Gradual Decline	336
Asteroids, Comets, and Meteors	345
Nemesis, the Death Star	366
Supernovae	368
Climate and Vegetation	370
Volcanos	379

Appendices

Mesozoic Time Chart	387
Stratigraphic Correlations	388
Glossary	389
Classification of Dinosaurs	398

Index

Index of Curricular Materials	401
Author Index	403
Subject Index	417

Illustrations

Saurornithoides faces the primitive opposum *Didelphis*	ii
Diplopdocus rears on its hind legs to feed	xii
"Hey.... Since the kids are in bed, what say we run out and kill ourselves a couple of plant-eaters." (*The Far Side*)	2
"However, there was no question that, on the south side of the river, the land was ruled by the awesome *Tyrannosaurus mex.*" (*The Far Side*)	84
Iguanodon may have used its spiked thumbs to defend itself against predators.	126
"It's roughage, and that's about it." (*The Far Side*)	180
Variation in ceratopsian horn and frill morphology	256
Archaeopteryx lithographica pursues its prey	286

PREFACE

Most young boys and many young girls play with dinosaurs. Most outgrow it, but fortunately for us all, some do not. They fan the spark of dinosaur fever, and develop into the next generation of vertebrate paleontologists.

If this book helps smooth the path of embryonic paleontologists, or reduces the time that students or scientists need to penetrate the dense tangle of dinosaur literature, then the work will have been worthwhile. I wish to thank all the many faculty, students and friends who encouraged me to complete this herculean task. Special thanks go to my wife Mary Ellen, for coping with a husband turned word-processor troglodyte. I am also grateful to the staff of Howard-Tilton Library's Interlibrary Loan Department, for their assistance in unearthing a lengthy list of articles and books to feed my insatiable bibliographic appetite. I wish to thank Viking/Penguin for permission to use several illustrations from John McLoughlin's *Archosauria*. And last, but far from least, a big thank you to Gary Larson and Universal Press Syndicate, for permission to reprint several "Far Side" cartoons.

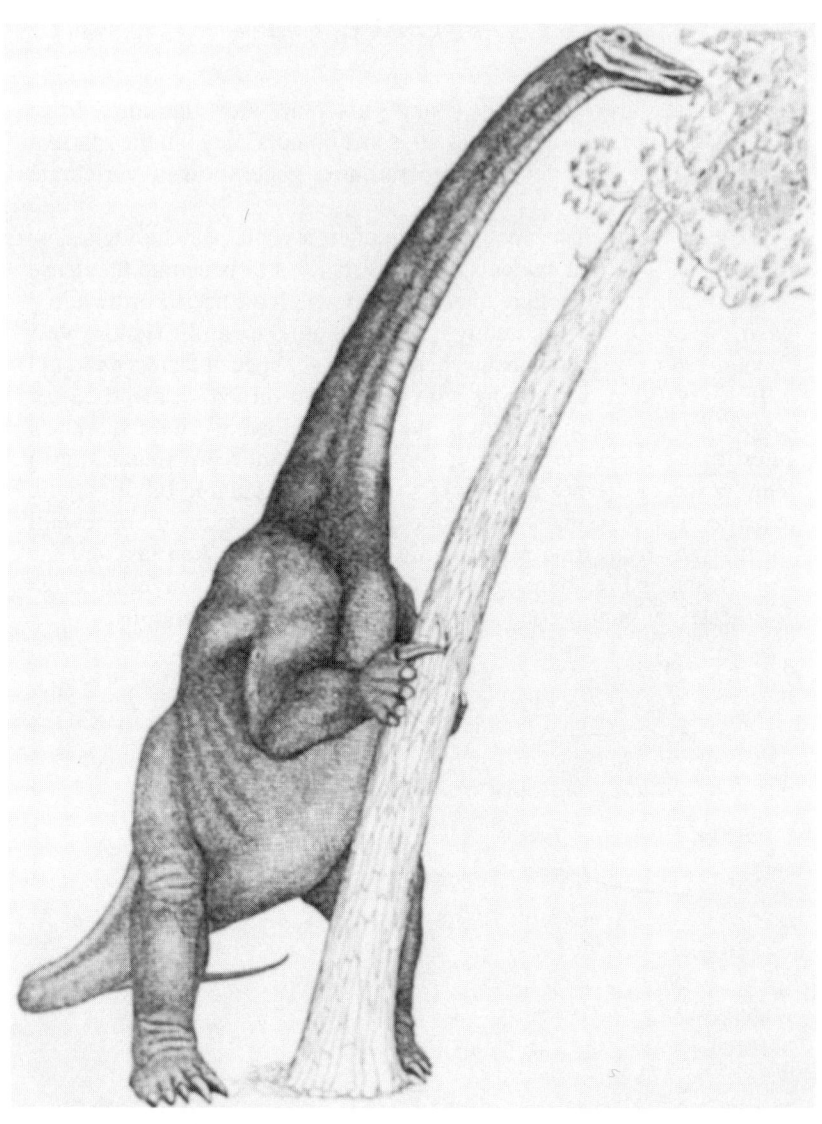

Diplodocus rears on its hind legs to feed. From *Archosauria: A New Look at the Old Dinosaur* by John C. McLoughlin. Copyright © 1979 by John C. McLoughlin. Used by permission of Viking Penguin, a division of Penguin Books USA Inc.

Introduction

The scientific literature on dinosaurs is as vast and ponderous as its subject. It is difficult to encapsulate a literature that sprawls over two hundred years, and may approach 15,000 or more references, in a mere 1,150 citations. By so doing, however, I hope to leave a comfortable path for students and researchers seeking to know more about these vanished titans, and the world they inhabited.

What function does the traditional annotated bibliography fulfill in the age of readily available computerized literature retrieval? Computer searches of *Biological Abstracts*, *Zoological Record*, or the *Bibliography and Index of Geology*, offer easy keyword access to a mountain of scientific literature. Computerized literature searches, however, are expensive. Searching for basic topics in online databases is like buying textbooks printed on gold leaf instead of paper. Online bibliographic files are so heavily indexed that a phrase like "dinosaur ecology" can retrieve hundreds of citations. While computerized databases are excellent for compiling a reference list on a narrow topic, such as a particular species of dinosaur or the works of an individual author, they are not an efficient or practical means of acquiring an introduction to the literature as a whole.

Vertebrate paleontology is fortunate to have a long-running printed index, the *Bibliography of Fossil Vertebrates*, which in various formats dates back to the turn of the century [*See* 1–5]. This index covers the dinosaur literature, but embeds it in the much larger literature on fossil vertebrates in general. A manual search through this towering stack of index volumes would produce a good reference list, but the cost would be eyestrain and backache from interminable hours of patient sifting.

My intent is to provide a well-blazed trail into the heart of the literature on, or related to, dinosaurs. Most of the literature surveyed is readily available from most university libraries. With the exception of several articles from the distinguished and well-written *New Scientist*, *American Scientist*, and *Scientific American*, the scope is limited to research publications, including journal articles, books, conference papers, and a few useful letters and news notes from scholarly journals.

The introductory chapter departs from the overall scope, and surveys the general literature with an emphasis on titles suitable for acquisition by both public and academic libraries. Some works of fiction are included that will be of general interest to dinosaur buffs. This chapter also includes several titles of interest to professors seeking appropriate textbooks or introductory readings for undergraduate courses. Given the growing number of dinosaur courses sprouting in the groves of academe, I have appended a separate "Index of Curricular Materials". This list draws heavily on articles from *New Scientist*, *Scientific American*, and review articles from a variety of publications. These works are also integrated into the full subject index. The index heading "illustration sources" includes several works with excellent graphics suitable for preparing slides for lectures, and recommended textbooks for an undergraduate course are listed under "suggested texts".

I have devoted the second chapter to historical events. The Victorian conception of the dinosaur is a fascinating portrait of the effect that social and political forces can have on the nature of the scientific enterprise. A clearer understanding of this formative period also helps us appreciate the nature of the modern renaissance in dinosaur studies.

The famous fossil feud of Cope and Marsh also receives its due. It provides a remarkable insight into the humanity of research scientists, and a rare glimpse into how science should and should not be done. It is not only interesting as a topic for student research, but useful as a springboard for a classroom lecture or discussion on the nature of the scientific enterprise.

Most of the work, however, is devoted to the ecology, evolution, and extinction of the former masters of our primeval globe, the dinosaurs. As a biologist concerned mainly with the ecology and evolution of modern communities, I have sought to bring a somewhat different perspective to the topic than might be provided by a geologist or paleontologist.

Just as modern organisms can only be fully understood and appreciated in the context of their environment, so are dinosaurs best considered in their own ecological element. One of the most significant evolutionary events during the long reign of the dinosaur, for example, was the evolution of flowering plants. The incredible success of both dinosaurs and flowering plants may have been inextricably intertwined.

Introduction

I have, therefore, devoted much space to a review of early plant evolution, as well as climatic change, the origin and evolution of birds, and other topics designed to give a basic picture of the Mesozoic world through which dinosaurs roamed unchallenged.

Other chapters reflect the most recent discoveries relating to dinosaur biology, including the ongoing warm-blooded dinosaur debate, dinosaur social behavior, and the competing theories of dinosaur extinction. I hope that these topics will convey the overall scope and direction of the multi-faceted field of dinosaur research.

The book should prove useful to teachers developing undergraduate or high-school courses, and for students at all levels, from advanced high school through graduate school. As a working librarian and perpetual graduate student, I am keenly aware of the need to locate solid references that are also available without the necessarily prolonged wait for interlibrary loans.

Most articles and books date from 1960 through August of 1991, with the obvious exception of historical topics. This period represents the modern emergence of dinosaur biology. The sources are exclusively English language, which, though unforgivably parochial, was necessary to restrain length, as well as maximize the usefulness of this bibliography for smaller library collections. In keeping with this latter goal, I have also drawn most heavily on titles like *Science*, *Nature*, *Ecology*, *Evolution*, and so forth, which most college or research libraries will possess. A list of these primary titles will be found at the end of Chapter One.

Each chapter is prefaced by a brief bibliographic essay which charts the broad dimensions of the literature. References in bibliographic essays, as well as cross references within annotations, are indicated in standard scientific format (author date), supplemented by citation numbers in square brackets for quick location of these references, for example: (Cox 1988 [8]; Colbert 1986 [162]). Some adjacent or multiple cross references are shown simply as [*See* 34–37]. Where several papers have been cross linked to lead the reader to alternate hypotheses, lengthy lists of cross references have been confined to a single core paper, usually a critical review or a recent and readily obtainable article. Other relevant citations refer back to this core paper for additional cross references. Finding any individual citation on these topics of special interest will thus lead the reader to the best additional material for or against the particular hypothesis.

DINOSAURS

THE FAR SIDE — By GARY LARSON

"Hey.... Since the kids are in bed, what say we run out and kill ourselves a couple of plant-eaters."

The Far Side, copyright 1988 & 1991 Universal Press Syndicate. Reprinted with permission. All rights reserved.

Chapter One

Return of the Dinosaurs

This chapter departs somewhat from the scope of the remaining work. Included with the more scholarly works are a number of basic books suitable for developing library collections for public or college libraries. Fleury 1988 [34] provides a bibliographic essay for building a basic college library collection.

I have specifically recommended several books for use as classroom texts or for developing curricular materials on dinosaurs for all educational levels. A separate index of suggested course materials will be found at the end of this volume. Works with particularly good graphics, useful for creating lecture slides, are indexed under the heading "illustration sources".

For the best curricular materials, I strongly recommend Norman 1985 [14]; Weishampel et al. 1990 [16]; Charig 1983 [23]; Chure 1989 [24]; Colbert 1983 [28]; Farlow 1989 [33]; McGowan 1991 [50]; McLoughlin 1979 [51]; Padian and Chure 1989a [56]; 1989b [57]; Russell 1989 [66]; Wilford 1985 [75]; Zipko 1981 [78].)

Several basic texts are recommended for a general introduction to vertebrate osteology and paleontology (Behrensmeyer and Hill 1980 [18]; Benton 1990 [19]; Briggs and Crowther 1990 [21]; Carroll 1988 [22]; Romer 1956 [61]; Romer 1966 [62]; Romer 1968 [63]). At the end of the chapter I have listed the primary journals from which most of the citations in this bibliography were taken. This list should prove useful for those seeking to keep abreast of this rapidly changing field.

I have included several references regarding the use of dinosaurs by creationists as an argument against evolution (Gish 1977 [36]; Hastings 1987 [40]; Milne and Schafersman 1983 [52]; Stokes 1989 [71]). Creationists argue that men and dinosaurs were contemporary, and claim to have the footprints to prove it! A recent catalog of materials available from the Institute for Creation Research includes an amazing array of books, videos, tee-shirts, and other items aimed at taking advantage of young children's interest in dinosaurs to turn them against the science of evolution.

You will also find a few works of poetry and fiction (Bradbury 1983 [20]; Crichton 1990 [29]; Learner 1985a [45]; 1985b [46]; Mash 1983 [48]; Silverberg et al. 1982 [69]). Even the most assiduous student or professor of dinosaur biology needs to relax, and what better way to do so than with a good book about dinosaurs?

BIBLIOGRAPHIES

1. Hay, O.P., ed. 1902. *Bibliography and Catalogue of the Fossil Vertebrates of North America. U.S. Geological Survey Bulletin* no. 179; Hay. O.P., ed. 1929–1930. *Second Bibliography and Catalogue of the Fossil Vertebrates of North America.* 2 vols. *Carnegie Institution Publication* no. 390.

   This long-running serial set, continued under various editors and publishers as the *Bibliography of Fossil Vertebrates*, forms a fairly complete literature index to dinosaurs, mammals, and other fossil vertebrates. Published under several variant titles, it has been issued as a government document, a series of *G.S.A. Memoirs*, and an annual publication of the Society of Vertebrate Paleontologists [*See* 2–5]. It includes author, site location, rock formation, species and subject indexes. This series is the mother lode for references in vertebrate paleontology.

2. *Bibliography of Fossil Vertebrates.* 1928–1973. Geological Society of America.

   Continues O.P. Hay's bibliography [*See* 1]. Volumes for 1928–1933 through 1964–1968 edited by C.L. Camp et al.; 1969–1972 edited by J.T. Gregory et al.; 1928–1933, 1934–1938 issued as *Special Papers of the Geological Society of America* nos. 27, 42; volumes for 1939–1943, 1944–1948, 1949–1953, 1954–1958, 1959–1963, 1964–1968, 1969–1972, issued as *Geological Society of America Memoirs* nos. 37, 57, 84, 92, 117, 134, and 141. Continued and supplemented by various publications [*See* 3–5].

3. *Bibliography of Fossil Vertebrates* 1973–1977. ed. J.A. Bacskai et al. American Geological Institute, 1983.

   A continuation of the *Bibliography of Fossil Vertebrates*, published until 1973 by the Geological Society of America [*See* 2]. The indexing is continued from 1978 to date as an annual publication of the Society of Vertebrate Paleontologists [*See* 4].

4. *Bibliography of Fossil Vertebrates.* 1978 to date. ed. J.T. Gregory et al. American Geological Institute, Society of Vertebrate Paleontology.

   This annual index continues the monographic series published by the Geological Society of America from 1928–1973 [*See* 3]. Volumes from 1978–1980 were published by the American Geological Institute, and volumes from 1981 to date were published by the Society of Vertebrate Paleontology.

5. *Bibliography of Fossil Vertebrates, Exclusive of North America 1509–1927.* ed. A.S. Romer et al. *Geological Society of America Memoir* no. 87, 1962.

   Complements the scope of earlier volumes by O.P. Hay to complete this unbroken, though very complex, series of index volumes [*See* 1–4].

6. Chure, D.J., and J.S. McIntosh. 1989. *A Bibliography of the Dinosauria (Exclusive of the Aves) 1677–1986. Museum of Western Colorado Paleontology Series* no. 1, Grand Junction: Museum of Western Colorado.

   Covering the literature through 1986, this has been (until now) the only comprehensive single volume index to dinosaur literature. Entries are not annotated, and are listed alphabetically by author, with a complex and unwieldy ichnotaxonomic index best suited to specialists. Its scope is poorly defined; newspaper accounts and anonymous citations are mixed with popular articles, scholarly books and journal articles. Despite its flaws as a reference work, it is a useful volume for assembling a comprehensive list of works by a particular paleontologist, and for locating older references.

7. Kues, B.S., and S.A. Northrop. 1981. *Bibliography of New Mexico Paleontology.* Albuquerque: University of New Mexico Press.

   A useful reference list for an area rich in fossil finds. Lists 2,031 citations on New Mexico's geology and paleontology, arranged alphabetically by author. Entries are not annotated, and the book includes a broad subject index.

REFERENCE WORKS

8. Cox, B., R.J.G. Savage, B. Gardner, and D. Dixon, eds. 1988. *Macmillan Illustrated Encyclopedia of Dinosaurs and Prehistoric Animals.* London: Macmillan.
    This British publication is hard to get (now out of print) but worth the effort to acquire. It covers early reptiles, mammals and dinosaurs. The combination of authoritative writing and lavish illustration makes this an appealing and informative reference book.

9. Fairbridge, R.W., and D. Jablonski. 1979. *The Encyclopedia of Paleontology.* New York: Academic Press.
    The *Encyclopedia of Earth Sciences* series consists of encyclopedic dictionaries covering various aspects of geology. The articles are extensively referenced. Though a little dated, the work is still very useful.

10. Kuhn, O., et al. 1969–1988. *Handbuch der Paläoherpetologie (Encyclopedia of Palaoherpetology).* 19 vols. Stuttgart: G. Fischer.
    This is a standard reference for dinosaur taxonomy, covering fossil amphibians and reptiles. Illustrated essays on each major taxa are followed by detailed systematic descriptions. Entries include synonyms, holotypes, and references to the taxonomic literature.

11. Kuhn-Schnyder, E., H. Rieber, and E. Kucera. 1986. *Handbook of Paleozoology.* Baltimore: Johns Hopkins.
    Arranged in taxonomic order, this handbook provides a guide to the often bewildering taxonomic classification of extinct animals. Extensive black and white line drawings accompany the brief taxonomic descriptions, and the work includes an index to genera and species.

12. Lambert, D. 1983. *A Field Guide to Dinosaurs.* New York: Avon Books.

Most suitable for the general reader or undergraduate student, this profusely illustrated "field guide" offers brief descriptions of typical species in each major taxa, along with a map showing the locations of major fossil finds. Several short articles on miscellaneous topics related to dinosaur biology are interspersed with the species accounts. Includes a lengthy list of museum displays.

13. Lambert, D. 1985. *The Field Guide to Prehistoric Life*. New York: Facts on File.

   Forms a good complementary volume to the author's dinosaur guide, covering extinct plants, invertebrates, and fossil vertebrates other than dinosaurs. Like the earlier work, it also contains a list of museum displays.

14. Norman, D. 1985. *The Illustrated Encyclopedia of Dinosaurs: An Original and Compelling Insight Into Life in the Dinosaur Kingdom*. New York: Crescent Books.

   Perhaps the best book ever written about dinosaurs for the general reader or undergraduate, Norman's work has been frequently used as a textbook for undergraduate courses on dinosaurs. It is remarkably well written, beautifully illustrated, authoritative, and relatively inexpensive. The species accounts include both skeletal reconstructions and first-rate color drawings, along with a time line and silhouettes for judging comparative sizes.

15. Steel, R., and A.P. Harvey. 1979. *The Encyclopedia of Prehistoric Life*. New York: McGraw-Hill.

   This indexed encyclopedic dictionary features signed articles by eminent British paleontologists. It covers plants, vertebrates and invertebrates.

16. Weishampel, D.B, P. Dodson, and H. Osmólska, eds. 1990. *The Dinosauria*. Berkeley: University of California Press.

   The single most important book on dinosaurs. Following three introductory essays on dinosaur origins, paleobiology, and distribution, are twenty-six authoritative articles covering each major taxa. Review articles cover anatomy, taxonomy, phylogeny, evolution taphonomy and paleoecology.

GENERAL WORKS

17. Averett, W.R., ed. 1987. *Paleontology and Geology of the Dinosaur Triangle*. Grand Junction: Museum of Western Colorado.
    Eighteen articles describe various fossil sites and exhibits in the Dinosaur Triangle. Three road logs chart geological field trips through the area, focusing on the Jurassic Morrison Formation. The Dinosaur Triangle is roughly bounded by Grand Junction Colorado, Price, Utah and Vernal, Utah.

18. Behrensmeyer, A.K., and A.P. Hill. 1980. *Fossils in the Making: Vertebrate Taphonomy and Paleoecology*. Chicago: University of Chicago Press.
    The fifteen articles in this collection describe taphonomic processes in a variety of modern environments, including contributions from archaeological studies of human remains.

19. Benton, M.J. 1990. *Vertebrate Palaeontology*. London: Unwin Hyman.
    A good current review of vertebrate paleontology, less thorough than Carroll (1988 [22]), but well suited for undergraduates or general readers. Includes a chapter on Triassic reptiles, a chapter on dinosaurs and other Mesozoic reptiles, and a chapter on the origin and evolution of birds.

20. Bradbury, R. 1983. *Dinosaur Tales*. New York: Bantam Press.
    A delightful compendium of dinosaurian prose, including five short stories and a poem, lovingly rendered from the hands of a modern master of speculative fiction.

21. Briggs, D.E., and P.R. Crowther, eds. 1990. *Palaeobiology: A Synthesis*. Cambridge, Mass.: Blackwell Scientific.

An encyclopedic survey of the field, with a superb list of contributors. Covers evolutionary theory and life history, paleoecology, and the taxonomy and taphonomy of extinct organisms. Includes information on core journals, museums, and organizations of interest to paleobiologists.

22. Carroll, R.L. 1988. *Vertebrate Paleontology and Evolution.* New York: W.H. Freeman.

    A thorough and up to date introduction to vertebrate paleontology. This is the most significant new textbook on the subject in decades. The chapters on dinosaur biology offer an informed and readable introduction at an advanced undergraduate level. Thorough reference lists accompany each chapter.

23. Charig, A.J. 1983. *New Look at the Dinosaurs.* New York: Facts on File.

    A good general introduction, suitable for an undergraduate textbook or for supplementary reading. Covers basic paleontology, the history of dinosaur research, and all aspects of dinosaur biology.

24. Chure, D.J. 1989. Quo vadis *Tyrannosaurus*?: the future of dinosaur studies. In *The Age of Dinosaurs*, ed. K. Padian and D.J. Chure, 1–6. *Geological Society of America Short Courses in Paleontology* no. 2. Knoxville: The Paleontological Society.

    Discusses the prognosis for the future of dinosaur studies, and predicts major advances in phylogeny and paleobiology. Recommends framing hypotheses so that they can be rigorously tested.

25. Cloudsley-Thompson, J.L. 1984. The success of the dinosaurs. *New Scientist*, 24 May, 13–17.

    Dinosaur buffs should shed their inferiority complex. The author makes a strong case for the complete superiority of dinosaurs in their prehistoric environment, based on a variety of evolutionary adaptations and other evidence. The fittest do not always survive.

26. Colbert, E.H. 1945. *The Dinosaur Book: The Ruling Reptiles and Their Relatives*. New York: American Museum of Natural History.

   Though very dated in parts, this primer from the American Museum of Natural History probably helped launch more than one paleontological career.

27. Colbert, E.H. 1961. *Dinosaurs: Their Discovery and Their World*. New York: Dutton.

   A well-written general introduction to the reptilian fauna of the Mesozoic, including several chapters on dinosaurs.

28. Colbert, E.H. 1983. *Dinosaurs, an Illustrated History*. Maplewood, NJ: Hammond.

   The author's most comprehensive introduction to dinosaurs, including chapters on dinosaur endothermy, behavior, and extinction. Readable, authoritative, extensively illustrated and highly recommended for the general reader and for classroom use.

29. Crichton, M. 1990. *Jurassic Park*. New York: Knopf.

   This rousing tale of modern dinosaurs, brought back to life through genetic engineering and placed in a prehistoric theme park, is perhaps the liveliest and most engaging fictional work ever devoted to dinosaurs. Crichton's well-researched thriller is a "must read" for any dinosaur devotee, and will soon be made into a major motion picture.

30. Czerkas, S., and E.C. Olson, eds. 1987. *Dinosaurs Past and Present*. 2 vols. Los Angeles: Natural History Museum of Los Angeles County.

   The unusual combination of a dinosaur art show and a scientific symposium led to these lavishly illustrated conference proceedings. Many of the articles in this highly recommended work are annotated in this bibliography.

31. De Camp, L.S., and C.C. De Camp. 1968. *The Day of the Dinosaur*. Garden City, NY: Doubleday.

The author brings much stylistic grace to this weighty subject. In addition to chapters on basic dinosaur biology (a little dated in spots) and Mesozoic geography, De Camp includes material on Mesozoic flora and fauna, and the Cope-Marsh feud. Out of print, but worth looking for.

32. Dixon, D. 1988. *The New Dinosaurs: An Alternative Evolution.* Topsfield, Ma.: Salem House.

    A whimsical look at what types of dinosaurs might have evolved if they had not vanished from the Earth. The engaging speculations are based on sound biogeographical and evolutionary reasoning.

33. Farlow, J.O., ed. 1989. *Paleobiology of the Dinosaurs. Geological Society of America Special Paper* no. 238.

    An excellent short monograph with authoritative articles on various aspects of dinosaur ecology and behavior. Most of the papers included are annotated in later chapters of this bibliography.

34. Fleury, B.E. 1988. Dinosaurs. *Choice* 26:609–620.

    This bibliographic essay, written for the American Library Association, includes 67 books recommended for developing an undergraduate library collection on dinosaurs.

35. Frey, R.W., ed. 1975. *The Study of Trace Fossils: A Synthesis of Principles, Problems and Procedures in Ichnology.* New York: Springer-Verlag.

    Twenty-three essays cover invertebrate and vertebrate ichnology. Ichnology is the study of trace fossils, such as tracks, coprolites, and eggshells.

36. Gish, D. 1977. *Dinosaurs: Those Terrible Lizards.* El Cajon, Ca.: Master Books.

    In its various editions, this book summarizes the curious creationist claim that dinosaurs coexisted with humans. An interesting secondary reading for classroom discussion. (*See also* Hastings 1987 [40]; Milne and Schafersman 1983 [52]; Stokes 1989 [71].)

37. Glut, D.F. 1980. *The Dinosaur Scrapbook.* Secaucus, NJ: Citadel Press.

    This marvelous compendium is a browser's delight. Presents dinosaur illustrations from comic books, movies, card sets, television, pulp fiction and a host of other sources. Glut has assembled the definitive work on how dinosaurs have been visually portrayed in popular culture.

38. Glut, D.F. 1982. *The New Dinosaur Dictionary.* Secaucus, NJ: Citadel Press.

    A good encyclopedic dictionary with fine black and white illustrations and a separate illustration index.

39. Halstead, L.B., and J. Halstead. 1981. *Dinosaurs.* Dorset: Blandford Press.

    A solid general introduction which describes and illustrates over 100 species of dinosaurs.

40. Hastings, R.J. 1987. New observations on Paluxy tracks confirm their dinosaurian origin. *Journal of Geological Education* 35:4–15.

    A scientific analysis of the so-called human footprints in Mesozoic strata reveals that they are actually dinosaur tracks. Creationists have frequently cited these tracks as evidence that cavemen were contemporary with dinosaurs. (*See also* Gish 1977 [36]; Milne and Schafersman 1983 [52]; Stokes 1989 [71].)

41. Horner, J.R., and J. Gorman. 1988. *Digging Dinosaurs.* New York: Workman.

    Describes Horner's revolutionary work in unveiling multiple dinosaur nest sites. A good book for acquiring the feel of a modern dinosaur dig, as well as an absorbing account of dinosaur reproductive biology.

42. Jacobs, L.L., ed. 1980. *Aspects of Vertebrate History: Essays in Honor of Edwin Harris Colbert.* Flagstaff: Museum of Northern Arizona Press.

Twenty-six distinguished contributions comprise this tribute to E.H. Colbert on his seventy-fifth birthday. The work includes a comprehensive bibliography of Colbert's work, and a short testimonial by G.G. Simpson.

43. Jordan, W.H. jr. 1989. They move, they roar: dinosaurs are here once more. *Smithsonian*, August, 46–57.

    Dinamation has fueled the public's continuing fascination with dinosaurs. The author shows how the complex models are designed and manufactured.

44. Kurtén, B. 1968. *The Age of Dinosaurs*. New York: McGraw-Hill.

    A good general introduction, dated but well written and comprehensive.

45. Learner, R.J. 1985a. Dinosaur ditties. *Earth Science* 38 (4):18–19.

    A light-hearted tribute to the Mesozoic masters, including nonsense verse and ballads to ease the pains of long hours of field and laboratory investigation. [*See* 46].

46. Learner, R.J. 1985b. Odes to dinosaurs. *Earth Science* 38 (1):16–18.

    More dinosaurian verse [*See* 45].

47. Lucas, S.G., J.K. Rigby, and B.S. Kues, eds. 1981. *Advances in San Juan Basin Paleontology*. Albuquerque: University of New Mexico Press.

    The Cretaceous-Tertiary Boundary is of critical concern to paleontologists. Work in the San Juan Basin has been a benchmark for studies of Late Cretaceous and Early Tertiary vertebrates. Several of these contributions are analyzed in this bibliography.

48. Mash, R. *How to Keep Dinosaurs*. 1983. New York: Viking Press.

    This whimsical work is perfect for overworked paleontologists looking for the lighter side of dinosaurs. If dinosaurs had survived, how would we have used them in our daily lives? How do you house train an *Apatosaurus*? The illustrations are priceless, especially the snarling *Deinonychus* harnessed as a "police dog".

49. McGowan, C. 1983. *The Successful Dragons: A Natural History of Extinct Reptiles*. Toronto: Samuel Stevens.
    Topics covered in this excellent general introduction include evolution, the fossil record, the implications of dinosaur anatomy for skeletal reconstruction, the complexity of dinosaur behavior, and the warm-blooded hypothesis (which the author cautiously accepts). The work concludes with a survey of ichthyosaurs and pterosaurs, and the relationship between dinosaurs and birds. (*See* [50] for a revised edition.)

50. McGowan, C. 1991. *Dinosaurs, Spitfires and Sea Dragons*. Cambridge Mass.: Harvard University Press.
    Unlike most general introductions, this work emphasizes understanding dinosaurs through an understanding of modern animals, a theme also stressed throughout this bibliography. (An updated and revised version of [49]).

51. McLoughlin, J.C. 1979. *Archosauria, A New Look at the Old Dinosaur*. New York: Viking Press.
    This beautifully illustrated volume provides a good summation of current theories. The author subscribes to the "warm-blooded" school of thought, which is reflected in the excellent black and white illustrations. Highly recommended for general readers and undergraduate students.

52. Milne, D.H., and S.D. Schafersman. 1983. Dinosaur tracks, erosion marks and midnight chisel work (but no human footprints) in the Cretaceous limestone of the Paluxy River Bed, Texas. *Journal of Geological Education* 31:111–123.
    Creationists have repeatedly tried to prove that humans and dinosaurs were contemporaries. This controversy has centered on the trackways of the Paluxy River. An analysis of these Cretaceous "footprints" reveals that they are not human,

and that some have been altered by modern chisels to render them better creationist evidence. (*See also* Gish 1977 [36]; Hastings 1987 [40]; Stokes 1989 [71]).

53. *North American Paleontological Convention. Proceedings.* 1970–1988. Various publishers.

    This important series, while not analyzed further in this bibliography, offers a good source for a variety of paleontological literature, much of it related to dinosaurs. The first convention proceedings were published in 1970 (Lawrence, Ka.: Allen Press). The second and third appeared as supplements to the *Journal of Paleontology* (v.51, no.2, 1977, v.56 no.2, 1982). The fourth convention, held in 1988, is the most recent meeting, with the conference title *The Golden Age of Dinosaurs: the Mid-Mesozoic Terrestrial Ecosystems of North America*.

54. Moody, R. 1977. *A Natural History of Dinosaurs*. London: Hamlyn.

    Following a brief introduction to dinosaur biology, the bulk of the work consists of a series of full-page plates on typical Dinosauria, each plate accompanied by a full page of text describing the species and its habits and habitat.

55. Olson, E.C. 1985. Vertebrate paleoecology; a current perspective. *Palaeogeography, Palaeoclimatology, Palaeoecology* 50:83–106.

    Taphonomy is a rapidly growing concern in vertebrate paleoecology. Hominid studies, mass extinction, physiological ecology, behavior, and the structure and evolution of communities are particularly active areas of research.

56. Padian, K., and D.J. Chure, eds. 1989a. *The Age of Dinosaurs. Geological Society of America Short Courses in Paleontology* no. 2. Knoxville: The Paleontological Society.

    Provides a good scholarly survey of the entire field, including contributions on Mesozoic flora, major dinosaur taxa, the origin of flight, other contemporary vertebrates, and extinction. Many of the individual papers are annotated in this bibliography.

57. Padian, K., and D.J. Chure. 1989b. Organizing and teaching a dinosaur course. In *The Age of Dinosaurs*, ed. K. Padian and D.J. Chure, 1-6. *Geological Society of America Short Courses in Paleontology* no. 2. Knoxville: The Paleontological Society.

    Includes several practical suggestions for organizing course materials and requirements for an undergraduate course on dinosaurs. Recommends several textbooks for such a course.

58. Preiss, B. 1981. *The Dinosaurs*. New York: Bantam.

    Sumptuous art nouveau illustrations set this unusual book apart from the herd of general works on dinosaurs. The text furnishes "eye witness" accounts that effectively convey the drama of dinosaur daily life. Though out of print, this volume is definitely worth searching for.

59. Ratkevitch, R.P. 1976. *Dinosaurs of the Southwest*. New Mexico: University of New Mexico Press.

    Surveys the Mesozoic in New Mexico, Arizona, Texas, Utah, Colorado, Oklahoma, Nevada and California, with an appendix listing museum displays in the southwest.

60. Ritchie, A. 1983. Reptiles of the mind—the fascination of dinosaurs. *Medical Journal of Australia* 2:631–636.

    A general article on dinosaurs which focuses on selected species featured in the exhibit "Dinosaurs from China". (*See also* Smith 1982 [70], Zhiming 1988 [77].)

61. Romer, A.S. 1956. *Osteology of the Reptiles*. Chicago: University of Chicago Press.

    A classic volume, updating and extending Williston's (1925 [76]) earlier magnum opus.

62. Romer, A.S. 1966. *Vertebrate Paleontology*. 3d ed. Chicago: University of Chicago Press.

Still one of the best volumes available for an introduction to the subject. The reader should also consult Carroll (1988 [22]) for the latest word on this material.

63. Romer, A.S. 1968. *Notes and Comments on Vertebrate Paleontology.* 3d ed. Chicago: University of Chicago Press.

    Much interesting material was omitted from Romer 1966 [62]) to keep the length reasonable. Extends the earlier work's discussion of several topics, including some controversial areas. The chapters on dinosaurs and birds are of particular interest.

64. Russell, D.A. 1977. A *Vanished World: The Dinosaurs of Western Canada.* Ottawa: National Museum of Natural Sciences (Canada).

    Western Canada was a critical habitat for dinosaurs. The inland sea created a warm coastal environment during the Cretaceous. Russell evokes the vanished habitats with photographs of modern Gulf Coast habitats.

65. Russell, D.A. 1980. Reflections on the dinosaurian world. In *Aspects of Vertebrate History: Essays in Honor of Edwin Harris Colbert,* ed. L.L. Jacobs, 257–265. Flagstaff: Museum of Northern Arizona Press.

    A good general summary of dinosaur ecology, morphology, and evolution. Russell concludes that "an appreciation of the dinosaurian world lends a certain fullness to one's appreciation of life."

66. Russell, D.A. 1989. *An Odyssey in Time: The Dinosaurs of North America.* Minocqua, WI: NorthWord Press (Published simultaneously by the University of Toronto Press).

    The noted Canadian paleontologist takes us on a chronological voyage through the Mesozoic. Russell's detailed analysis of Mesozoic geology and ecology is supported by numerous color photographs depicting modern environments that most resemble ancient environments. Highly recommended.

67. Sarjeant, W.A.S. 1975. Fossil tracks and impressions of vertebrates. In *The Study of Trace Fossils: A Synthesis of Principles, Problems and Procedures in Ichnology*, ed. R.W. Frey, 283–324. New York: Springer-Verlag.

    Discusses problems of preservation, problems in the interpretation of trackways, and the use of footprints in classification.

68. Sattler, H.R., and A. Rao. 1981. *Dinosaurs of North America*. New York: Lothrop, Lee & Shepard.

    This well-written text is aimed at a young adult audience. The book won the Golden Kite Award from the Society of Children's Book Writers. Of chief interest here are the numerous first-rate sepia-tone illustrations by Anthony Rao. A good source for teachers building a slide collection for illustrating lectures. (Additional sources for good illustrations can be found in the index under the heading "illustration sources.")

69. Silverberg, R., C.G. Waugh, and M.H. Greenberg, eds. 1982. *The Science Fictional Dinosaur*. New York: Avon Books.

    Features nine stories from the pen of such luminaries as Isaac Asimov, Poul Anderson, and Harry Harrison. Hard-core dinosaur lovers will enjoy the rebirth of dinosaurs in Robert Silverberg's *Our Lady of the Sauropods*, which anticipates Michael Crichton's *Jurassic Park* (Crichton 1990 [29]).

70. Smith, B.J. 1982. *Dinosaurs From China, Including a Catalogue to the Exhibition in the National Museum of Victoria and the Australian Museum, Sydney*. Melbourne: Council of the National Museum of Victoria.

    A short work cataloging the dinosaurs from this historic traveling exhibit. (*See also* Ritchie 1983 [60]; Zhiming 1988 [77].)

71. Stokes, W.L. 1989. Creationism and the dinosaur boom. *Journal of Geological Education* 37:24–26.

    Addresses the difficulty of reconciling fundamentalist beliefs and dinosaur facts. Creationists have promulgated many false ideas about dinosaurs, many of which find their way into Sunday-school classes. Details many of the creationist arguments (did dinosaurs travel on Noah's Ark, did cavemen share the planet with dinosaurs, etc.) and briefly refutes them. (*See also* Gish 1977 [36]; Hastings 1987 [40]; Milne and Schafersman 1983 [52].)

72. Swinton, W.E. 1970. *The Dinosaurs*. New York: Wiley-Interscience.

    The latest edition of Swinton's classic work is especially popular in Britain. Though predating the "dinosaur renaissance", it is written clearly and with great authority.

73. Tweedie, M.W.F. 1979. *The World of Dinosaurs*. New York: Morrow.

    Distinguished by the author's illustrations, this introductory work has a good account of the "warm-blooded" controversy.

74. Weigelt, J. 1989. *Recent Vertebrate Carcasses and their Paleobiological Implications*. Translated by J. Schaefer. Chicago: University of Chicago Press.

    A classic study, recently reprinted. This is the definitive work on taphonomy, written before the word was even coined. The author examines the fate of the remains of modern animals that died under a wide variety of environmental conditions.

75. Wilford, J.N. 1985. *The Riddle of the Dinosaur*. New York: Knopf.

    This is one of the best general introductions in print. Starting with the discovery of geologic time, Wilford proceeds through the historic early explorations, including the Cope-Marsh feud and the Gobi desert expedition. He discusses the revival of interest in dinosaurs, the warm-blooded debate, and the latest theories regarding extinction. The book is distinguished for its in-depth survey of the social, intellectual, and historical forces shaping modern theories.

76. Williston, S.W. 1925. *The Osteology of the Reptiles.* Cambridge, Ma.: Harvard University Press.
    One of the first major works on the subject, and still a useful reference from the leading American authority of his day. Also available as a 1971 reprint volume from the Society for the Study of Amphibians and Reptiles.

77. Zhiming, D. 1988. *Dinosaurs From China.* London: British Museum of Natural History.
    A copiously illustrated description of dinosaurs and digs from China. The book was written as a guide to a traveling exhibit of Chinese dinosaurs. China is particularly rich in Mid-Jurassic fossil beds, a layer often missing from other sites. (*See also* Ritchie 1983 [60]; Smith 1982 [70].)

78. Zipko, S.J. 1981. An interdisciplinary approach to dinosaur fossils, morphology, ethology, and energetics. *American Biology Teacher* 43:430–439.
    Presents suggestions and background material for a ten-day to twenty–day interdisciplinary course in dinosaur biology at the junior high or freshman high school level. A good review for anyone starting basic classroom instruction on this topic at any level. Many of the suggestions could be readily reworked for undergraduate courses.

PRIMARY JOURNALS

The following serials are recommended for scanning the current literature for papers on dinosaur biology and related topics. The list is by no means comprehensive, but contains the serials which comprise most of this bibliography.

Acta Palaeontologica Polonica
Alcheringa
American Museum of Natural History (Bulletin, Novitates)
American Naturalist
American Zoologist

Annals of the Carnegie Museum
Annual Review of Earth and Planetary Sciences
Annual Review of Ecology and Systematics
Biological Journal of the Linnean Society
Canadian Journal of Earth Sciences
Copeia
Cretaceous Research
Ecological Monographs
Ecology
Evolution
Geobios
Geological Magazine
Geological Society of America (Bulletin, Memoirs)
Herpetologica
Journal of Herpetology
Journal of Paleontology
Journal of Vertebrate Paleontology
Journal of Zoology (London)
Lethaia
National Geographic Research
Nature
New Scientist
Oecologica
Palaeontologia Polonica
Palaeontology
Palaeogeography, Palaeoclimatology, Palaeoecology
Paleobiology
Paleontological Journal
Physiological Zoology
Quarterly Review of Biology
Royal Society of London (Proceedings, Transactions)
Science
Scientific American
Terra Nova
Zoological Journal of the Linnean Society

Chapter Two

Dinosaur Hunters

The earliest discovery of dinosaur bones is lost in the mists of prehistoric time. No doubt cavemen created legends to explain the huge bones unearthed by flood and weather. The Chinese believed they were unearthing the bones of dragons. The more sophisticated Europeans, however, knew that the bones were actually the bones of giants. As the Bible claimed, "there were giants in those days" (Buffetaut 1987 [151]).

Several papers in the *Philosophical Transactions of the Royal Society of London* during the late Eighteenth and early Nineteenth Century discuss fossil finds that may have been dinosaur bones. As yet, no knowledge of their true nature existed; in fact, most scientists had little conception of the existence of past eras or the true immensity of geologic time.

Before dinosaurs could be conceived, prehistoric time itself had to be invented. Toulmin and Goodfield (1982 [83]) examine the process through which scientists gradually became aware of the extent of the Earth's life history. The 4,000 year-old Earth of Bishop Usher's chronology gradually gave way to a planet that had nurtured life for hundreds of millions of years.

The time was ripe for Gideon Mantell and William Buckland to announce their momentous discoveries of the bones of *Iguanodon* and *Megalosaurus* (Buckland 1824 [79]; Mantell 1825 [81]; Swinton 1951 [82]; Delair and Sarjeant 1975 [152]). The classic tale of Dr. Mantell's discovery is apocryphal. Mrs. Mantell actually found the *Iguanodon* teeth, while waiting for her husband to complete a house call.

Georges Cuvier had earlier identified a large skull as that of a gigantic prehistoric lizard, similar to modern monitor lizards. Following the lead of the respected Cuvier, Buckland and Mantell reconstructed their dinosaurs as gigantic lizards, similar in form and function to modern reptiles.

Richard Owen reconstructed his dinosaurs with more mammalian proportions. Owen's squat pachyderms reflected his desire to show the Age of Reptiles as the peak of reptilian creation, thus refuting the Lamarckian notion that modern reptiles were more highly evolved (Desmond 1979 [87]). The intense debate over the true nature of extinct creatures was often dominated by Owen, who christened the Dinosauria, and T.H. Huxley, the ardent evolutionist (Owen 1842 [93]; Desmond 1984 [88]; McLeod 1965 [92]).

The historic and social forces that shaped the Victorian model of the dinosaur are an excellent example of how scientific theory can be influenced by social context. Rudwick (1985A [95], 1985B [96]) and Bowler (1976 [86]) provide a good scholarly analysis of how early paleontological and evolutionary theories were shaped by peer pressure and religious beliefs as well as by fossil evidence.

The existence of a lost age ruled by monstrous reptiles weighed heavily on the minds of Victorian scientists, most of whom were devout Christians. If the Creator was perfect then his creation, by definition, must also be perfect. But how could a perfect creator allow any part of this perfection to become extinct?

They found the solution in a catastrophic scheme of successive waves of creation, each wave more advanced than the preceding one. An Age of Fish was followed by an Age of Reptiles, replaced in its turn by an Age of Mammals. The whole series led ever upward, to culminate (naturally) in the ultimate creation of man himself.

The savage cold-blooded reptiles molded by Victorian beliefs quickly found a prominent place in the public's imagination. Books like Hutchinson's *Extinct Monsters* and Seely's *Dragons of the Air* fed the public's thirst for information about the lost age (Hutchinson 1893 [90]; Seeley 1901 [98]).

The grounds of the Crystal Palace during the Great Exhibition featured several dinosaurs, the work of sculptor Benjamin Waterhouse Hawkins. This Victorian exhibit, like our modern-day Dinamation, was viewed by thousands of people and kindled a continuing love affair between dinosaurs and the general public. The elephantine models of *Iguanodon* and *Megalosaurus* shaped an image of dinosaurs that continued to influence paleontological thought until the early 1960's.

There were a few flashes of brilliance in early reconstructions. Richard Owen's ideas were more advanced than is generally credited. T.H. Huxley was aware of the advanced design and evolutionary importance of *Archaeopteryx* (Huxley 1870 [91]; Bibby 1972 [85]; DiGregorio 1982 [89]). O.C. Marsh offered perceptive reconstructions along the lines of more modern views. Charles Knight's many wonderful paintings for the American Museum of Natural History, like his duelling *Dryptosaurus*, were also reminiscent of the more agile dinosaurs reconstructed today (Knight 1947 [336]).

But with the passing of the Victorian era, most modernistic voices were silenced, and the image of the ponderous lizard prevailed. Charles Gilmore, O.P. Hay and other influential paleontologists of the early 1900's set the dinosaur's feet firmly back on the ground, where they remained until the early 1970's (Bakker 1987 [464]).

Desmond gives a particularly clear and entertaining account of how many of the first dinosaurs were reconstructed (Desmond 1976 [425], 1979 [87], 1984 [88]). Good bones were forced to fit bad models. Poor *Diplodocus* was reconstructed in 1910 by Oliver P. Hay as a giant crocodile. Its belly would have hung so low that someone would have needed to precede the unfortunate animal and dig a trench so it could walk about.

During the first half of the Twentieth Century, the focus of discovery shifted from the Old World to the New World. The wealth of fossil remains discovered with the opening of the American West drew many notable paleontologists. They often endured great hardships to exhume the vanished past from the still untamed land.

There were many prominent fossil hunters in this turbulent period. Men like Barnum Brown, Joseph Leidy, C.W. Gilmore, L.S. Russell, S.W. Williston and C.H. Sternberg brought the past to life for a new generation to witness [*See* 99–123]. Among these dinosaur hunters were two scientists whose bitter personal feud created an outstanding clash of egos, as if *Allosaurus* had met *Megalosaurus* in the distant Jurassic.

Othniel Charles Marsh and Edward Drinker Cope were both competent and dedicated men in their own right, though each branded the other as a charlatan and a thief. By the end of their respective careers their constant warfare almost overshadowed their many important discoveries. Shor (1974 [150]), Lanham (1973 [137]) and Plate (1964 [146]) all give good accounts of the Cope-Marsh feud.

Their fossil feud was a war of words, fought in the newspapers and various scholarly journals, primarily the *American Journal of Science* and the *American Naturalist*. [*See* 124–150]. It was also a war of bullets, claim-jumping and espionage, fought in the forbidding western badlands as each side sought to lay claim to vast stretches of rich fossil beds.

For additional information about the many colorful personalities that shaped the early history of geology and paleontology, start with Sarjeant's five-volume bibliographic index (Sarjeant 1980 [156]). Standard reference works that should also prove helpful include the *Dictionary of Scientific Biography*, the *Isis Cumulative Bibliography*, the *Dictionary of American Biography*, and the *Dictionary of National Biography*. *American Men and Women of Science* provides brief but useful information on current researchers.

FIRST DISCOVERIES

79. Buckland, W. 1824. Notice on the *Megalosaurus*, or great fossil lizard of Stonesfield. *Geological Society of London Transactions* 2:390–396.

    One of the first significant dinosaur finds. Presents several loosely associated bones probably derived from several specimens of *Megalosaurus*. The specimens are from the Stonesfield quarry near Oxford. The bones are incorrectly identified as "probably an amphibious animal," though later study will correctly place the specimen within the Dinosauria, which would not be so named until 1842. The plates include a dramatic sketch of the formidable lower jaw.

80. Curwen, E.C. 1940. *The Journal of Gideon Mantell*. London: Oxford University Press.

    Mantell kept a journal from 1815 to 1852. About half of the original journal is presented in this abridgement. The journal shows Mantell to be an energetic researcher with wide-ranging interests. His journal reveals much about the intellectual climate and personalities of the times, and witnesses the unfolding of geological knowledge and the growing awareness of past eras.

81. Mantell, G.A. 1825. On the teeth of the *Iguanodon*, a newly-discovered fossil herbivorous reptile. *Philosophical Transactions of the Royal Society of London* 115:179–186.

    The classic paper presenting Gideon Mantell's discovery of the first known dinosaur. The actual find was made by Mrs. Mantell in 1822. Buckland and Cuvier misidentified the teeth as mammalian (rhinoceros) or perhaps belonging to some giant fish, and Mantell includes Cuvier's gracious admission of error.

82. Swinton, W.E. 1951. Gideon Mantell and the Maidstone *Iguanodon*. *Royal Society of London Notes and Records* 8:261–276.

A thorough study of this critical discovery. The Maidstone quarry specimen was the first *Iguanodon* find that consisted of more than isolated teeth and fragments. It was purchased by Mantell for the princely sum of 25 pounds, and included in Owen's classic Report on British Fossil Reptiles (Owen 1842 [93]). It is still regarded as the type specimen for this species.

83. Toulmin, S.E., and J. Goodfield. 1982. *The Discovery of Time*. Chicago: University of Chicago Press (originally N.Y.: Harper & Row, 1965).

    Before dinosaurs could be discovered, the concept of geological time had to be formulated. Extinct animals could not be recognized if the past ages that contained them were inconceivable. The authors survey the growing intellectual awareness of earth history, and its implications for the development of biology and geology.

THE VICTORIAN DINOSAUR

84. Benton, M.J. 1982. Progressionism in the 1850's: Lyell, Owen, Mantell and the Elgin fossil reptile *Leptopleuron (Telerpeton)*. *Archives of Natural History* 11:123–136.

    This specimen was first used to argue against progressionism, and later used to demonstrate it. Owen, Lyell, and Mantell were involved in a bitter dispute over its interpretation. Provides a good window on the dispute between Owen and Mantell, and the development of progressionism.

85. Bibby, C. 1972. *Scientist Extraordinary: The Life and Scientific Work of Thomas Henry Huxley 1825–1895*. New York: St. Martin's Press.

    Concentrates on Huxley's later years. Includes a selected bibliography of Huxley's works, and an annotated glossary of his contemporaries.

86. Bowler, P.J. 1976. *Fossils and Progress: Paleontology and the Idea of Progressive Evolution in the Nineteenth Century*. New York: *Science* History Publications.

   Progressionism dominated much of the scientific debate in biology and geology in the mid-Nineteenth century. The nature and significance of fossils was a major intellectual problem in light of widespread religious fundamentalism and competing schools of evolutionary thought. The idea of progression by natural selection from simpler to more complex forms competed with the dogma of instant creation. Darwin's evolutionary theory actually contradicted both schools of thought.

87. Desmond, A.J. 1979. Designing the dinosaur—Richard Owen. Response to Robert Edmond Grant. *Isis* 70:224–234.

   The author contends that Owen's concept of the dinosaur was radically different from the creature conceived by his predecessors. Owen correctly deduced the dominance of the Dinosauria from only three known species. Rather than reconstruct them as super-lizards, Owen assigned mammalian proportions, creating the stout-limbed pachydermal creatures that later graced the grounds of the Crystal Palace. His motive in presenting dinosaurs as the peak of reptilian creation was to argue against progressionism. If dinosaurs were more like mammals than reptiles, then modern reptiles must be degenerate rather than more progressive.

88. Desmond, A.J. 1984. *Archetypes and Ancestors: Palaeontology in Victorian London, 1850–1875*. Chicago: University of Chicago Press.

   Already a classic, and currently available in paperback, the book describes the relationship between Huxley and Owen. Desmond focuses on the shift in the scientific balance of power from the "romantic" Owen to "professionalisers" like Huxley. Explores how the debates over evolution and dinosaur biology were shaped by their cultural and social context. (*See also* Desmond 1976 [425].)

89. Di Gregorio, M.A. 1982. The dinosaur connection: a reinterpretation of T.H. Huxley's evolutionary view. *Journal of the History of Biology* 15:397–418.

   The author contends that Huxley was not an instant convert to evolutionary thought. His progress towards full acceptance of evolution parallels that of his German contemporaries, especially Haeckel. Huxley was not entirely convinced of the key role of natural selection in evolution. Much of the discussion centers on Huxley's developing views on the relationship between birds and dinosaurs.

90. Hutchinson, H.N. 1893. *Extinct Monsters: A Popular Account of Some of the Larger Forms of Ancient Animal Life*. London: Chapman and Hall.

   The aftermath of Cope and Marsh's spectacular discoveries was a great upsurge in interest in prehistoric animals and in natural history museums in general. It also spawned several popular books, of which this is a first-rate example. Includes three chapters on dinosaurs.

91. Huxley, T.H. 1870. Contributions to the anatomy and taxonomy of the Dinosauria. *Quarterly Journal of the Geological Society of London* 26:3–50.

   A series of short notes, including material on *Hypsilophodon foxii*, the relationship between dinosaurs and birds, dinosaur taxonomy, and Triassic dinosaurs.

92. McLeod, R.M. 1965. Evolutionism and Richard Owen, 1830–1868: an episode in Darwin's century. *Isis* 56:259–280.

   Discusses the parallels between Owen's rise and fall and the passing of "German idealism and Cuvierian teleology." Traces the development of Owen's evolutionary thinking, leading up to his rejection of natural selection and the Darwinian school. His philosophical outlook, his acidic personality and his extreme professional self-interest combined to bring about his downfall.

93. Owen, R. 1842. Report on British fossil reptiles, part 2. *British Association for the Advancement of Science Report* 1841:60–204.

    Proposes the new taxon Dinosauria, based on three species (*Iguanodon, Megalosaurus, and Hylaeosaurus*), and provides a detailed description of each. Also describes a number of other fossil reptiles, including various crocodilians and thecodonts.

94. Owen, R.S. 1894. *The Life of Richard Owen.* 2 vols. New York: D. Appleton & Co.

    A thorough and sympathetic biography of Owen, written by his grandson. Balances the negative publicity surrounding much of Owen's distinguished career. The author says "I can but repeat the unfailing testimony of his friends in regard to his charm of manner, his genial courtesy, and his kindness of heart." One wonders if this is the same Richard Owen!

95. Rudwick, M.J.S. 1985a. *The Meaning of Fossils: Episodes in the History of Palaeontology.* 2d ed. Chicago: University of Chicago Press.

    Rudwick helps unravel the tangled skein of the human history of paleontology. This well-received work is based on a series of lectures at Cambridge, and traces the gradual realization of the nature and importance of fossils from the Sixteenth through the Nineteenth Century.

96. Rudwick, M.J.S. 1985b. *The Great Devonian Controversy: The Shaping of Knowledge Among Gentlemanly Specialists.* Chicago: University of Chicago Press.

    Though not directly concerned with dinosaur biology, this valuable and interesting work surveys the background of a great geological controversy that shaped the thinking of key players in the late Nineteenth Century revolutions in geology and paleontology. The dispute over strata in Devon that led to the establishment of the Devonian period dramatically demonstrated the great age of the earth and the long history of life.

97. Seeley, H.G. 1887. On the classification of the fossil animals commonly named Dinosauria. *Proceedings of the Royal Society of London* 43:165–171.

    Seeley devised the basic division of the Dinosauria into two orders, Ornithischia and Saurischia, based on differences in their pelvic structure. Although this astute observation has withstood the test of time, it was generally ignored when first published. Later work by von Huene utilized Seeley's classification scheme and furthered its acceptance.

98. Seeley, H.G. 1901. *Dragons of the Air*. London: Methuen (Reprinted Dover, 1967).

    Still a useful and interesting work on the spectacular flying reptiles of the Mesozoic. A classic in the same vein as Hutchinson (1893 [90]), it also served to introduce the general public to the dramatic forms of extinct animal life.

THE AMERICAN WEST

99. Bartlett, R.A. 1962. *Great Surveys of the American West*. Norman: University of Oklahoma Press.

    A narrative history of four western expeditions under Clarence King, George Montague Wheeler, Ferdinand Vandeveer Hayden and John W. Powell. Their voluminous reports, collectively called the "Great Surveys", helped open the rich bone beds of the west to a generation of dinosaur hunters (including Cope and Marsh), and provided the first detailed survey of the natural history and geology of the western territories.

100. Bird, R.T. 1985. *Bones for Barnum Brown: Adventures of a Dinosaur Hunter*. Fort Worth: Texas Christian University Press.

     Roland Thaxter Bird was Barnum Brown's main assistant. Their hunt for new specimens for the American Museum of Natural History uncovered many significant fossils, including Bird's sauropod footprints from the Texas Cretaceous. The author describes his adventures and gives a unique perspective on the career of Barnum Brown, one of the most important dinosaur collectors. The introduction by James Farlow is a good brief account of American dinosaurs and the men who hunted them.

101. Brown, B. 1935. Sinclair dinosaur expedition, 1934. *Natural History*, June, 3–15.

Describes Brown's excavation of Jurassic dinosaurs in Wyoming, including the 1934 Sinclair Expedition. Among his key discoveries was a wealth of skin impressions. Includes several photographs of the Howe Quarry dig.

102. Brown, B. 1941a. The age of sauropod dinosaurs. *Science* 93:594–595.

A short note regarding a debate about the age of the Morrison Formation. Bird's discovery of Cretaceous sauropod footprints led Brown to revise his opinion that sauropods did not survive beyond the Jurassic.

103. Brown, B. 1941b. The last dinosaurs. *Natural History*, December, 290–295.

A general discussion of dinosaurs, including the puzzling absence of juveniles (an issue still under debate), discoveries of skin impressions, gizzard stones, and a short review of the prevailing extinction theories.

104. Colbert, E.H. 1984. *The Great Dinosaur Hunters and Their Discoveries*. New York: Dover.

An excellent historical narrative of the quest for dinosaurs, starting with Mantell and Buckland and covering through Barnum Brown and the Sternbergs. Also notable for two chapters on the Mongolian, African, and Patagonian expeditions. Originally published by Dutton in 1968 as *Men and Dinosaurs: The Search in Field and Laboratory*.

105. Colbert, E.H. 1980. *A Fossil-Hunter's Notebook: My Life With Dinosaurs and Other Friends*. New York: Dutton.

An intimate look at the world of a notable dinosaur hunter. Focuses on Colbert's important field work.

106. Colbert, E.H. 1989. *Digging Into the Past: An Autobiography*. New York: Dembner (Dist. by Norton).

    The life and times of one of our most famous and influential paleontologists. Includes several photographs.

107. Darrah, W.C. 1951. *Powell of the Colorado*. Princeton: Princeton University Press.

    Chronicles one of the greatest explorers of the American west, known to most of his contemporaries as "the Major". John Wesley Powell's survey helped open the fossil beds of the west.

108. Gregory, J.T. 1979. North American vertebrate paleontology, 1776–1976. In *Two Hundred Years of Geology in America: Proceedings of the New Hampshire Bicentennial Conference on the History of Geology*, ed. C.J. Schneer, 303–335. Hanover, N.H.: University Press of New England.

    A brief survey which mentions a number of lesser lights in addition to the usual luminaries who have collected dinosaur remains. Cites the trend from merely descriptive work towards functional morphology and paleoecology. The accompanying notes cite a large number of useful historical works.

109. Howard, R.W. 1975. *The Dawnseekers: The First History of American Paleontology*. New York: Harcourt Brace Jovanovich.

    From Amos Eaton's fossil discoveries, made while digging the Erie Canal, through the inspired malice of Cope and Marsh, the author provides a sketchy but well-written and interesting overview of American paleontology.

110. Leidy, J. 1873. Description of remains of reptiles and fishes from the Cretaceous formation of the interior of the United States. In *Report of the United States Geological Survey of the*

Territories. Part 1. *Contributions to the Extinct Vertebrate Fauna of the Western Territories*. Washington: USGPO.

Not much dinosaur content (*Poicilopleuron valens* is the lone species described), but a good cross-section of such Mesozoic fauna as fish, turtles, and mosasaurs. Leidy was a key figure in early American paleontology. (*See* Osborn 1913 [113].)

111. Lewis, G.E. 1964. Memorial to Barnum Brown (1873–1963). *Geological Society of America Bulletin* 75:P19–P27.

    A brief tribute to Barnum Brown which includes a three page bibliography of his work.

112. McGinnis, H.J. 1982. *Carnegie's Dinosaurs: A Comprehensive Guide to Dinosaur Hall at Carnegie Museum of Natural History, Carnegie Institute*. Pittsburgh: Carnegie Institute.

    A good survey of the collection in the Carnegie Museum, along with a nice introduction to dinosaurs and their contemporaries.

113. Osborn, H.F. 1913. Biographical memoir of Joseph Leidy, 1823–1891. *Biographical Memoirs of the National Academy of Sciences* 7:339–396.

    Surveys Leidy's career, and includes a lengthy bibliography of his many contributions to the field of paleontology. (*See* Leidy 1873 [110].)

114. Osborn, H.F. 1924. Joseph Leidy, Founder of Vertebrate *Palaeontology* in America. In *Impressions of Great Naturalists*, 130–148. New York: Scribners.

    This tribute includes an interesting comparison of Leidy's temperament with that of Cope and Marsh, as well as a discussion of the intellectual environment Leidy flourished in. Includes a photograph.

115. Russell, L.S. 1966. Dinosaur hunting in western Canada. *Royal Ontario Museum Life Sciences Contributions* no. 70:1–37.

Describes the exploration of the Red Deer River badlands in Alberta and Saskatchewan, focusing on the work of C.M. Sternberg. Includes several photographs and a bibliography.

116. Schuchert, C. 1905. John Bell Hatcher. *American Geologist* 35:131–141.

    A summary of Hatcher's life and career. Hatcher is best known for his fossil hunting forays to Patagonia, and was a significant figure in osteology and vertebrate stratigraphy. Includes a photograph.

117. Scott, W.B. 1939. *Some Memories of a Paleontologist.* Princeton: Princeton University Press.

    A lengthy autobiography of one of the more important Patagonian explorers and a key collector of early mammals. Lacks a bibliography.

118. Simpson, G.G. 1942. The beginnings of vertebrate paleontology in North America. *Proceedings of the American Philosophical Society* 86:130–188.

    An extensive survey of early work from the 1500's to the 1840's.

119. Simpson, G.G. 1943. The discovery of fossil vertebrates in North America. *Journal of Paleontology* 17:26–38.

    The first fossil discovery in America is credited to Charles Le Moyne, who found the remains of a mastodon in 1739. Simpson describes the discovery and attempts to pinpoint the locality of the find.

120. Simpson, G.G. 1981. History of vertebrate paleontology in the San Juan Basin. In *Advances in San Juan Basin Paleontology*, ed. S.G. Lucas, K. Rigby, and B. Kues, 3–25. Albuquerque: University of New Mexico Press.

    Relates the human history of work in the San Juan Basin. E.D. Cope made the first scientific discoveries of fossil vertebrates in the Basin, followed later by David Baldwin. Baldwin collected for Marsh, but later switched allegiance to Cope. The move was made just before Baldwin's important

Dinosaur Hunters

discovery of a major Paleocene mammalian fauna. Barnum Brown and C.H. Sternberg collected dinosaur bones in the Basin, though the most significant finds in the Basin have been mammalian fossils. (*See also* Lucas et al. 1981 [47] for modern work in the San Juan Basin.)

121. Sternberg, C.H. 1909. *The Life of a Fossil Hunter.* New York: Henry Holt.

    Chronicles Sternberg's early life and career, during which he collected in Wyoming, Kansas and Texas. Followed by Sternberg (1985 [122]) which covers the author's later career and Canadian explorations.

122. Sternberg, C.H. 1985. *Hunting Dinosaurs in the Bad Lands of the Red Deer River, Alberta, Canada.* Canada: NeWest Press.

    Originally published in 1917 by the author (San Diego, CA., also 2d edition 1932), this volume is a sequel to the earlier *The Life of a Fossil Hunter* (1909 [121]). Like its predecessor, it follows Sternberg through the wilds of Alberta in search of Cretaceous fossils.

123. Wilkins, T. 1988. *Clarence King: A Biography.* Albuquerque: University of New Mexico Press. (revised and enlarged, originally New York: Macmillan, 1958).

    The first director of the U.S. Geological Survey, King was intimately involved with early western exploration.

BATTLES OVER BONES

124. Baur, G. 1890. A review of the charges against the paleontological department of the U.S. Geological Survey, and of the defence made by Prof. O.C. Marsh. *American Naturalist* 24:298-304.

    A defense of Marsh made by a former assistant. Refutes several of Cope's charges, including the accusation that most of Marsh's work was done by his assistants.

125. Beecher, C.E. 1899. Othniel Charles Marsh. *American Journal of Science*. 4th ser. 7:403–428.

Summarizes Marsh's life and career, including a photograph and thorough bibliography.

126. Bowler, P.J. 1977. Edward Drinker Cope and the changing structure of evolutionary theory. *Isis* 68:249–265.

Cope promulgated the "law of acceleration", in which evolution was seen as the gradual unfolding of a plan that was ultimately Divine in origin. His later views were neo-Lamarckian.

127. Case, E.C. 1940. Cope—the man. *Copeia* 1940 (2):61–65.

An interesting analysis and apologia of Cope's temperament, discussed in terms of his "peaceful" Quaker heritage. Includes a photograph and a droll two-page doggerel *The Scientific Scrap* in the manner of Bret Harte.

128. Cohen, I.B., ed. 1980. *The Life and Scientific Work of Othniel Charles Marsh*. N.Y.: Arno Press.

A valuable reprint volume containing four of Marsh's most important publications:

1) Fossil horses in North America. *American Naturalist* vol.8, 1874.
2) Odontornithes: A Monograph on the Extinct Toothed Birds of North America. *United States Geological Exploration of the Fortieth Parallel*, vol.7, Washington D.C., 1880.
3) The Dinosaurs of North America. *Sixteenth Annual Report of the U.S. Geological Survey to the Secretary of the Interior 1894–1895, Part I*, Washington, D.C., 1896. (*See also* 141.)
4) Vertebrate Fossils. *Monographs of the United States Geological Survey*, vol. 27, Washington D.C., 1896.

129. Cope, E.D. 1869. Specimens of extinct reptiles. *Nature* 1:121–122.

A brief summary of material presented by Cope at a meeting of the Academy of Natural Sciences, including remains of a large dinosaur he named *Ornithotarsus immanis*.

130. Cope, E.D. 1873. On some of Professor Marsh's criticisms. *American Naturalist* 7:290–299.

A scathing response to criticism of some of Cope's work on Eocene mammals. Includes the famous quote: "To sum up the matter, it is plain that most of Prof. Marsh's criticisms are misrepresentations, his systematic innovations are untenable, and his statements as to the dates of my papers are either criminally ambiguous or untrue."

131. Cope, E.D. 1878. On the saurians recently discovered in the Dakota beds of Colorado. *American Naturalist* 12:71–85.

Discusses several dinosaur specimens from the Lower Cretaceous Dakota Formation.

132. Cope, E.D. 1878. The principal characters of American Cretaceous dinosaurs. *American Naturalist* 12:811–812.

A short but cutting reply to Marsh's paper on the Sauropoda, challenging several of his taxonomic criteria and stating that "Prof. Marsh does not deviate from his usual habit of ignoring the work of contemporary naturalists." Cope claims that this "new" division was previously described by Owen, among others, under a different name, and that several of Marsh's "new" genera have also been previously described.

133. Cope, E.D. 1882. Marsh on the classification of the Dinosauria. *American Naturalist* 16:253–255.

Takes issue with Marsh's suggestion that Dinosauria is a sub-class, and adds a few personal swipes. Marsh is accused of "failure to characterize his genera on first publishing them . . . failure to recognize the labors of others, except to point out supposed errors . . . failure to credit others with their discoveries, and permission of the inference that they are his own."

134. Cope, E.D. 1884. Marsh on *Diplodocus*. *American Naturalist* 18:526.

A brief note on *Diplodocus*, arguing that the animal was aquatic, walking on the bottom sediments, rather than terrestrial as Marsh had claimed.

135. Cope, E.D. 1885. Marsh on the Jurassic Dinosauria, Part VIII. *American Naturalist* 19:67–68.

   A short diatribe, one of a long series of same, attacking Marsh's reports on the Jurassic dinosaurs. "As usual, Professor Marsh omits the customary reference to facts already determined by others."

136. Gill, T. 1897. Edward Drinker Cope, naturalist: a chapter in the history of science. *American Naturalist* 31:831–863.

   A sympathetic summation of Cope's life and work, including the last known photograph of Cope. No bibliography.

137. Lanham, U. 1973. *The Bone Hunters*. New York: Columbia University Press.

   An excellent study of the famous feud in all its livid detail, readable and informative. Though lacking a bibliography of Cope and Marsh, it has a good bibliography of secondary sources.

138. McIntosh, J.S., and D.S. Berman. 1975. Description of the palate and lower jaw of the sauropod dinosaur *Diplodocus* (Reptilia: Saurischia) with remarks on the nature of the skull of *Apatosaurus*. *Journal of Paleontology* 49:187–199

   Reviews the controversy over O.C. Marsh's use of the wrong skull in his restoration of *Apatosaurus* (=*Brontosaurus*) in light of new evidence. Includes an unpublished plate by Marsh of the palate of *Diplodocus*. *Apatosaurus* skulls are very similar to *Diplodocus* skulls, and several skulls identified as *Diplodocus* may actually belong to *Apatosaurus*. (*See also* Berman and McIntosh 1978 [277].)

139. Marsh, O.C. 1878. Principal characters of American Jurassic dinosaurs. Part I. *American Journal of Science* 3d ser. 16:411–416.

   The first of a continuing series in this journal (*See* [140] for other entries). The series consisted of short articles describing various groups of Jurassic dinosaurs, later collected and enlarged in Marsh (1896 [141]). The first article covers *Morosaurus*, *Diplodocus*, and *Laosaurus*.

140. Marsh, O.C. 1879. Principal characters of American Jurassic dinosaurs. Part II. *American Journal of Science* 3d ser. 17:86–92.

    Part 2 of the series covers *Apatosaurus*, *Atlantosaurus*, and *Allosaurus*. *See also* Part 1 (Marsh 1878 [139]), and the collected work (Marsh 1896 [141]). Other contributions to this series include Pt.3, 1880, 3d ser. 19:253–259; Pt.4 (*Stegosaurus*), 1881, 3d ser. 21:167–170; Pt.5, 1881, 3d ser. 21:417–423; Pt.6 (*Brontosaurus*), 1883, 3d ser. 26:81–85; Pt.7 (*Diplodocus*), 1884, 3d ser. 27:160–167; Pt.8 (Theropoda), 1884, 3d ser. 27:329–340, Pt.9 (*Stegosaurus* again), 1887, 3d ser. 34:413–417.

141. Marsh, O.C. 1896. The Dinosaurs of North America. *U.S. Geological Survey Annual Report* 16:133–244.

    This is Marsh's major work on the Jurassic dinosaurs, originally appearing as a series of short articles in the *American Journal of Science* [*See* 139–140]. This government document is complete with extensive plates that are lacking in the abbreviated journal series. (*See* the Cohen 1980 [128] reprint, generally easier to obtain than the original document in smaller libraries.)

142. Nield, T. 1985. Sticks, stones and broken bones. *New Scientist*, 19 December, 64–67.

    A popular account of the feud, suitable for classroom discussion, especially for non-science majors.

143. Osborn, H.F. 1924. Edward Drinker Cope. In *Impressions of Great Naturalists*, 148–164. New York: Scribners.

    This biographical sketch has a good analysis of Cope's personality, and summarizes his contributions to science.

144. Osborn, H.F. 1931. *Cope, Master Naturalist*. N.Y.: Arno Press (originally Princeton University Press, 1931).

A lengthy and sympathetic biography of Cope, together with an exhaustive bibliography of his works.

145. Ostrom, J.H., and J.S. McIntosh. 1966. *Marsh's Dinosaurs: The Collections From Como Bluff.*
    Marsh's extensive collections from Como Bluff formed the nucleus of the collections in Yale's Peabody Museum and the National Museum in Washington, D.C. The work consists primarily of 150 lithographs of stegosaurs and sauropods, prepared for Marsh's publication. Most of these plates are published here for the first time.

146. Plate, R. 1964. *The Dinosaur Hunters: Othniel C. Marsh and Edward D. Cope.* New York: D. McKay.
    An engaging analysis of the feud and its combatants, of whom Plate says "When they started, almost nothing was known of dinosaurs, but they made 'dinosaur' a household word." The author emphasizes the human side of the conflict, with a sympathetic portrayal of both Cope and Marsh.

147. Romer, A.S. 1964. Cope versus Marsh. *Systematic Zoology* 13:201–207.
    A terse summary of the feud, with a photographs of the two combatants. No bibliography.

148. Schuchert, C. 1939. Biographical memoir of Othniel C. Marsh 1831–1899. *Biographical Memoirs of the National Academy of Sciences* 20:1–78.
    A summary of Marsh's life and a detailed description of his career and contributions. Includes a comprehensive bibliography.

149. Schuchert, C., and C.M. LeVene. 1940. *O.C. Marsh: Pioneer in Paleontology.* New Haven: Yale University Press.
    A brief survey of Marsh's life and a thorough study of his career. Contains several photographs, a list of genera described by Marsh, and a comprehensive bibliography.

150. Shor, E.N. 1974. *The Fossil Feud Between E.D. Cope and O.C. Marsh.* Hicksville, NY: Exposition Press.

   This treatment of the feud is especially valuable for its copious extracts from contemporary newspaper accounts in the *New York Herald,* which occupy the bulk of the text. The last hundred pages are a biographical dictionary of the eminent scientists and other personalities mentioned in the *Herald'*s coverage.

GENERAL WORKS

151. Buffetaut, E. 1987. *A Short History of Vertebrate Palaeontology.* London: Croom Helm.

   The author emphasizes European discoveries and the influence of fossil finds on the revolutions in geology and biology. Buffetaut skips over the Cope-Marsh feud and similar episodes covered in depth elsewhere, making the work a good supplement to other studies. The author surveys the history of the discipline from the "pre-scientific" period (during which fossils were known but their true nature not appreciated) to about World War I.

152. Delair, J.B., and W.A.S. Sarjeant. 1975. The earliest discoveries of dinosaurs. *Isis* 66:5–25.

   A careful reexamination of early discoveries, considering new evidence on the priority of discovery of *Megalosaurus* and *Iguanodon.* Buckland apparently found *Iguanodon* bones before Mantell, but failed to appreciate their true significance. Buckland's *Megalosaurus* also predates Mantell's *Iguanodon,* but Mantell was the first to publish a scientific paper correctly attributing such remains to extinct reptiles.

153. Dunbar, C.O. 1959. A half century of paleontology. *Journal of Paleontology* 33:909–914.

   A short retrospective of the first fifty years of American Twentieth Century paleontology. Discusses the difficulty of the species concept in paleontology and the growth of systematics.

154. Gerstner, P.A. 1970. Vertebrate paleontology, an early Nineteenth Century transatlantic science. *Journal of the History of Biology* 3:137–148.

   Concludes that American studies were respected and used by European colleagues in the early Nineteenth Century, despite a prevailing skeptical attitude toward American "fossil collectors." Richard Harlan was an important influence in gaining respect for American paleontologists.

155. Kielan-Jaworowska, Z. 1969. *Hunting for Dinosaurs.* Cambridge: MIT Press.

   A narrative account of the Polish Mongolian expedition to the Gobi Desert from 1963 to 1965. Gives a good feel for the perils of paleontological forays into the outback.

156. Sarjeant, W.A.S. 1980. *Geologists and the History of Geology: An International Bibliography From the Origin to 1978.* 5 vols. New York: Arno Press.

   An impressive and thorough bibliography of the history of geology up to about 1978. Volumes 2 and 3 are of greatest interest, comprising an alphabetic list of individual geologists. Entries include a paragraph summarizing their contributions and a chronological bibliography of their work.

157. Weishampel, D.B., and W.E. Reif. 1984. The work of Franz Baron Nopcsa (1877–1933); dinosaurs, evolution and theoretical tectonics. *Jahrbuch der Geologischen Bundesanstalt Wien* 127:187–203.

   Summarizes the work of one of Europe's most influential early dinosaur hunters. Nopcsa is best known for generating interest in sexual dimporphism in dinosaurs, the subject of one of his few papers in English. Though incorrect as stated, his sexual dimorphism hypothesis may ultimately be proven essentially correct by future discoveries.

Chapter Three

The World of the Dinosaurs

At the beginning of the Mesozoic the world bore little resemblance to the world we know today. By its close, the world had assumed its familiar modern geography. Open shrubland of palms, cycads, and exotic gymnosperms had been replaced by a wealth of herbaceous angiosperms. Towering forests of pines and flowering trees shaded early forms of familiar birds and mammals. The voice of the dinosaur was heard no more.

We cannot appreciate the ecology or evolution of dinosaurs without an understanding of the world they inhabited. What was the earth like under their enormous feet? How did they adapt to changing climates and diverse habitats? What affect did the rise of flowering plants have on the massive herbivores that roamed the Mesozoic?

During the early evolution of the dinosaurs in the Triassic, the land masses were still pushed close together. Triassic continents were so closely joined that they are usually considered a single land mass called Pangea (Barron 1987 [161]). The northern supercontinent of Laurasia was flanked by the southern supercontinent of Gondwanaland. Between them stretched a narrow band of water called the Tethys Sea. Animals and plants could readily disperse from one continent to the other as Pangea gradually tore itself apart (Parrish 1987 [201]; Colbert 1985 [219]; Cox 1980 [220]).

Although Laurasia remained essentially intact, with a substantial Jurassic connection between North America and Europe, Gondwanaland fragmented into enormous blocks, pushed apart by rifting between the tectonic plates. North and South America drifted west as the South Atlantic Ocean grew. South America was nearly isolated from North America, while the other continents retained tenuous connections with one another (Bonaparte 1984 [210]; Chatterjee 1986 [217], 1987 [218]; Hallam 1983 [223]).

At the dawn of the Triassic the therapsids dominated Gondwanaland, while thecodonts ruled supreme in Laurasia. The thecodonts were early archosaurs that would later give rise to dinosaurs. Between the middle and Late Triassic a great faunal transition took place. The once successful therapsids, or mammal-like reptiles, were completely replaced by the better adapted thecodonts, who were in turn displaced by the newly radiating dinosaurs. The old Permian ecological web of labyrinthodont amphibians, phytosaurs, cotylosaurs, and therapsids, was replaced by ancestral forms of our modern crocodiles, turtles, lizards, and frogs, and by the new masters of the planet, the dinosaurs.

Some authorities claim that this faunal replacement was competitive (Bonaparte 1982 [209]; Charig 1984 [586]; Charig 1980 [794]; Bonaparte 1969 [805]), but others maintain that the older faunas died out before the dinosaurs radiated into their ecological niches (Benton 1979 [580]; Benton 1983 [581]; Crompton and Attridge 1986 [617]; Benton 1984b [804]). Amidst this turbulent era evolved the small mammals that would skulk around the ecological fringes of the later Mesozoic.

The geological and ecological transition from the Triassic to the Jurassic is not sharply defined, though the end of the Triassic witnessed widespread faunal changes and the beginning of the breakup of Pangea. (Colbert 1985 [219], 1986 [162]). The Lower Jurassic is poorly represented in the terrestrial fossil record. Much of the continental land masses were covered by shallow inland seas, and the remaining patches of land are known from relatively few fossil sites. The Upper Jurassic offers a more favorable taphonomic environment, with shallow lakes and braided rivers contributing vast stretches of sand and mud for quick burial and preservation of organisms.

Four regions stand out as meccas for Jurassic dinosaur hunters. The western North America Morrison Formation, the Tendaguru beds in Tanzania, several sites in western Europe (especially England), and various sites in China have yielded a wealth of Upper Jurassic dinosaurs. There are many similarities between faunas from these widespread locations, mute evidence of the broad pathways open for dispersing Jurassic vertebrates (Charig 1973 [216]; Galton 1974a [309]; Galton and Jensen 1975 [317]; Galton and Powell 1980 [318]).

The Cretaceous marks the transition to the modern world. While the dinosaurs rose to their evolutionary peak, the seeds of the next world were literally being set in place. The early evolution of mammals and birds, the growing importance of angiosperms, and the continuing separation of continental land masses formed the backdrop to the zenith of dinosaurian power.

The Jurassic-Cretaceous boundary was not marked by the wholesale faunal replacements that characterized the transition from the Cretaceous to the Tertiary. Stegosaurs disappeared in the early Cretaceous, along with most sauropods, some crocodilians and some pterosaurs, but there were no dramatic geological events or mass extinctions at the boundary itself. The new faunas were dominated by increasingly sophisticated ornithopod herbivores and savage carnosaurs like the tyrannosaurids.

The oceans invaded continental interiors at least six times during the Cretaceous, dividing North America and Eurasia in half. Such synchronous global changes in sea level are called eustacy. Eustatic cycles probably resulted from sea-floor spreading, which reduced the volume of ocean basins and displaced water onto the continents. Seas rose and fell by as much as 150 to 250 meters (Cooper 1977 [192]; Hallam 1978 [196]; Hays and Pittman 1973 [198]; Schlanger 1986 [205]; Weishampel and Horner 1987 [803]).

Yet the remaining land surface was vast and varied, and interconnected by land bridges. Western North America was attached to Eurasia, while eastern North America was linked to western Europe, and India was joined to Africa and Madagascar (Hallam 1983 [223]; Sahni 1984 [227]; Sues 1980 [229]; Currie 1989 [295]; Weishampel and Bjork 1989 [409]). During the Cretaceous we can finally see the broad outlines of our familiar modern continents, now separated by small but ever-growing oceans.

Eustacy may have directly affected evolution. Rising sea levels would have favored rapid speciation, with increased migration and radiation, while regressions would have led to more extreme climates and habitat deterioration, with lower speciation rates, and increased levels of endemism and extinction (Cooper 1977 [192]; Hallam 1978 [196]; Cox 1980 [220]). The early radiation and geographic dispersal of flowering plants was closely linked to cycles of sea-level change (Hallam 1984 [197]; Parrish 1987 [201]; Axelrod 1970 [232]; Retallack and Dilcher 1986 [259]).

The Upper Cretaceous was also a time of active mountain building. Great modern mountain ranges like the Alps, the Rocky Mountains, the Himalayas, Carpathians, Caucasus, and parts of the Andes were all upthrust during this period.

The Lower Cretaceous Wealden fauna from southern England, the North American Cloverly Formation, and similar faunas from Mongolia and China give us a good ecological picture of the Lower Cretaceous. North American fossil beds have yielded an incredible treasure of Upper Cretaceous dinosaurs, exhumed from the Lance, Hell Creek, Edmonton, Kirtland, Fruitland, Oldman, Judith River, Two Medicine and Mesa Verde Formations. The Lameta Group in India and the Patagonian and Mongolian fossil beds extend our picture of the Late Cretaceous world.

The biogeography of the Mesozoic is a challenging subject. The distribution of animals preserved in the fossil record provides clues to supplement our reconstruction of global paleogeography (Cox 1980 [220]). For example, faunal similarities suggest that India was accessible to North American dinosaurs during the Late Triassic (Chatterjee 1986 [217], 1987 [218]). The geographic distribution of Jurassic dinosaurs indicates that Laurasia and Gondwanaland were still physically connected in the Upper Jurassic (Galton 1977 [221], 1980 [222]). The Americas were connected for at least part of the Late Cretaceous, based on the fossil evidence of a great faunal interchange at that time, rivaling in importance the later faunal interchange of the Pleistocene (Bonaparte 1980 [208], 1984 [210]; Brett-Surman and Paul 1985 [213]; Buffetaut 1989 [214]; Bonaparte 1979 [280]; Brett-Surman 1979 [829]).

Mesozoic climates were generally warm and dry, with subtropical conditions prevailing over much of the planet (Barron and Washington 1982 [190]; Frakes 1986 [194]; Srivastava 1970 [206]). There is evidence for periods of aridity throughout the Mesozoic (Buffetaut and Martin 1984 [191]; Hallam 1984 [197]; Tucker and Benton 1982 [801]). There is no evidence for glaciation, although there are indications of seasonal ice at higher latitudes. Triassic climates continued the warming trend begun in the Permian, with climates dominated by the effects of low sea levels. Jurassic climates continued warm, and fluctuations were minimal throughout this period. This long-term warming reaches its peak in the Cretaceous, but a pronounced cooling trend is evident in the Late Cretaceous (Crowley et al. 1986 [193]; Hays and Pittman 1973 [198]; Savin 1977 [204]).

Among the many great transitions of the Cretaceous, the rise of the angiosperms stands out as a major evolutionary event. The origin of angiosperms has been a hotly disputed topic for decades. Charles

Darwin called the problem "an abominable mystery." Recent discoveries have greatly enriched our knowledge of the fossil record, and a clearer picture of the nature and radiation of the first angiosperms is finally starting to emerge (Doyle 1978 [242]).

The first flowering plants were humble herbaceous weeds, probably adapted to colonize the disturbed habitats that giant herbivores left in their wake, and to invade the endless new shores and backwater habitats created by the ebbing and rising inland seas (Crane 1987 [237]; Doyle and Hickey 1976 [244]; Hickey and Doyle 1977 [247]; Retallack and Dilcher 1986 [259]).

Dinosaurs and angiosperms, Mesozoic herbivores and the plants they consumed, were inextricably linked in an ecological and evolutionary web. The effects of the angiosperms on the dinosaurs, and their effect in turn on flowering plants, are discussed in detail in Chapter Six ("Herbivores"). For now, we will be content to set the stage for the great ecological challenge faced by herbivorous dinosaurs in the closing days of the Cretaceous.

The old gymnosperm floras were declining (Crane 1987 [237]; Lidgard and Crane 1988 [252], 1990 [253]; Tiffney 1981 [264]). The angiosperms that replaced them were armed with potent new chemical defenses, secondary compounds that rendered them inedible and perhaps even toxic to some herbivores. Closed forests replaced open scrub, creating new opportunities for some animals, and closing ecological doors for others.

In the vanished world of the Mesozoic the dinosaurs flourished. Their domination of the Earth's surface was complete. Ichthyosaurs, plesiosaurs and mosasaurs held sway in the oceans, but dinosaurs ruled the land.

GEOLOGY

158. Anderson, T.H., and V.A. Schmidt. 1983. The evolution of Middle America and the Gulf of Mexico-Caribbean Sea region during Mesozoic time. *Geological Society of America Bulletin* 94:941–966.

    Discusses a new tectonic model of the Gulf of Mexico. Mexico and Central America were sheared into several microplates by severe faulting as North America split away from the other continents. This split formed a Mediterranean type sea which was the precursor for the modern Gulf of Mexico.

159. Averett, W.R., M.E. Averett, E.S. McReynolds, and D.G. Wolny. 1987. Mid-Mesozoic paleontology of the Rabbit Valley area, western Colorado. In *Paleontology and Geology of the Dinosaur Triangle*, ed. W.R. Averett, 37–44. Grand Junction: Museum of Western Colorado.

    Rabbit Valley is associated with a monocline created by the Uncompahgre Uplift. This short paper relates the history of digs in the area.

160. Armstrong, H.J., and E.S. McReynolds. 1987. Paleontological significance of the Dinosaur Triangle. In *Paleontology and Geology of the Dinosaur Triangle*, ed. W.R. Averett, 1–4. Grand Junction: Museum of Western Colorado.

    Describes and maps the numerous fossil sites in the Dinosaur Triangle, and notes their historical importance to paleontology.

161. Barron, E.J., ed. 1987. Cretaceous Paleogeography. *Palaeogeography, Palaeoclimatology, Palaeoecology* 59 (1–3):1–214.

    This special issue is devoted to a series of articles outlining the paleogeography of the Cretaceous, touching on every continent except North America. It provides an invaluable review of the physical outline of the Cretaceous world.

162. Colbert, E.H. 1986. Historical aspects of the Triassic-Jurassic boundary problem. In *The Beginning of The Age of Dinosaurs; Faunal Changes Across the Triassic-Jurassic Boundary*, ed. K. Padian, 9–19. Cambridge: Cambridge University Press.

It is difficult to draw a sharp line between the geological and ecological continuum of the Triassic and Jurassic. Colbert reviews the boundary worldwide, and concludes that both the stratigraphic and paleontological picture is unclear. The boundary problem is "a story filled with unresolved problems."

163. Cole, R.D. 1987. Cretaceous rocks of the Dinosaur Triangle. In *Paleontology and Geology of the Dinosaur Triangle*, ed. W.R. Averett, 21–36. Grand Junction: Museum of Western Colorado.

Describes ten major geological events in the formation of the Cretaceous beds in the Triangle. The geological history of the area is dominated by repeated incursions of the Western Interior Seaway.

164. Dodson, P. 1971. Sedimentology and taphonomy of the Oldman Formation (Campian), Dinosaur Provincial Park, Alberta (Canada). *Palaeogeography, Palaeoclimatology, Palaeoecology* 10:21–74.

The Oldman Formation was a floodplain crossed by meandering and braided fluvial channels. The seasonal climate was warm and temperate. Highly articulated dinosaur skeletons, found mainly in channel sediments, indicate that the dinosaurs (hadrosaurs and ceratopsians) spent a great deal of their time in the water, and could probably swim. Hadrosaurs and ceratopsians occur together in swampy lowland habitats. Juveniles are rare.

165. Dodson, P., A.K. Behrensmeyer, and R.T. Bakker. 1980. Taphonomy of the Morrison Formation (Kimmeridgian-Portlandian) and Cloverly Formation (Aptian-Albian) of the western United States. *Mémoires de la Société Géologique de France* 139:87–93.

Single quarries from the limestones, sandstones and mudstones of the Morrison Formation have produced over 10,000 bones. Plant fossils are unfortunately rare, due to a shortage of coal seams in the formation. Stegosaurs and other large herbivores were common; sauropods were found throughout the formation, though aquatic habitats were sparse. Conditions ranged from arid, or semiarid, to poorly drained emergent habitats. The Cloverly Formation was deposited after a 40 million year gap. There were no stegosaurs in its fauna, and sauropods were rare. Ornithopods dominated the herbivorous niche. The Cloverly Formation yields mainly single, well-articulated skeletons, contrasting with the massive jumbled bone deposits in the Morrison. Although the Cloverly environment may have been somewhat wetter, it did not differ substantially from that of the Morrison. Perhaps the mode of life of the Cloverly fauna was more important in the pattern of their preservation than differences in environmental conditions.

166. Ethridge, F.G., R.M. Flores, and M.D. Harvey, eds. 1987. Recent Developments in Fluvial Sedimentology. *Society of Economic Paleontologists and Mineralogists Special Publication* no. 39. Tulsa: Society of Economic Paleontologists and Mineralogists.

Fluvial sediments are critically important in the preservation of dinosaur remains. Many important finds are made in river channel, deltaic, and floodplain sediments, which offer an ideal environment for rapid burial and preservation. Geologists have made significant recent advances in fluvial sedimentology. This volume contains papers presented at the Third International Fluvial Sedimentology Conference. Other volumes in this series include: *1st International Symposium on Fluvial Sedimentology* (1978), published as *Canadian Society of Petroleum Geologists Memoir* no. 5; *2nd International Conference on Fluvial Sediments* (1981), abstracts published by the University of Keele (U.K.); and, most recently, *4th International Conference on Fluvial Sedimentology* (1989– Abstracts and Programme), held in Barcelona.

167. Fastovsky, D.E. 1989. Dinosaurs in space and time: the geological setting. In *The Age of Dinosaurs*, ed. K. Padian and D.J. Chure, 22–33. *Geological Society of America Short Courses in Paleontology* no. 2. Knoxville: The Paleontological Society.

Examines the paleogeography and paleoclimate of the Mesozoic, and discusses major geological formations containing dinosaur remains. Fluvial channels and their associated flood plains were the most important sites for dinosaur preservation.

168. Goodwin, M.B., and A.L. Deino. 1989. The first radiometric ages from the Judith River Formation (Upper Cretaceous), Hill County, Montana. *Canadian Journal of Earth Sciences* 26:1384–1391.

K-Ar dating and $^{40}Ar/^{39}Ar$ dating give an age of 78 million years ago for the Judith River Formation. The formation encapsulates a period of about five million years, and is roughly correlated with the late Campanian of the Western Interior.

169. Grigorescu, D. 1983. A stratigraphic, taphonomic, and paleoecologic approach to a "forgotten land": the dinosaur-bearing deposits from the Hateg Basin (Transylvania-Romania). In *Second International Symposium on Mesozoic Terrestrial Ecosystems*, ed. Z. Kielan-Jaworska and H. Osmólska, p.103–121, *Acta Palaeontologica Polonica* 28 (1/2).

Dinosaurs in Transylvania? Extends the work of Baron Nopcsa on the important dinosaur fauna from the Hateg Basin in Transylvania. The sandstone beds were probably formed by a braided river system on the slope of a mountain piedmont area. 70% of known remains belong to three genera, *Rhabdodon* (Iguanodontidae), *Orthomerus* (Hadrosauridae), and *Titanosaurus*, and 20% are Chelonia remains. Most bones are well preserved but disarticulated. Biotopes included alluvial islands, swamps, flood plains, and drier upland areas. The flora was most likely tropical or subtropical, and dominated by palms.

170. Hallam, A. 1975. *Jurassic Environments*. Cambridge: Cambridge University Press.

   A complete survey of Jurassic geology, emphasizing Europe, North America, and North Africa. Includes chapters on stratigraphy, tectonic history, eustacy, paleoclimates, and the biogeography of marine invertebrates.

171. Howell, D.G., and K.A. McDougall, eds. 1978. *Mesozoic Paleogeography of the Western United States. Pacific Coast Paleogeography Symposium* no. 2. Los Angeles: Society of Economic Paleontologists and Mineralogists.

   Forty articles survey western U.S. stratigraphy, tectonics, and paleogeography.

172. Jacobs, L.L., D.A. Winkler, Z.M. Kaufulu, and W.R. Downs. 1990. The dinosaur beds of Northern Malawi, Africa. *National Geographic Research* 6:196–204.

   Thirteen vertebrate taxa have been found in the Lake Malawi beds, including several species of dinosaurs. Describes the stratigraphy of the beds. Some specimens suggest that the beds are Late Jurassic, like the Tendaguru beds of Tanzania, while other species resemble West African Early Cretaceous fauna. The latter age is more likely, considering the crocodilian and turtle remains.

173. Kauffman, E.G. 1977. Cretaceous Facies, Faunas, and Paleoenvironments Across the Western Interior Basin. *Mountain Geologist* 14 (3/4):75–274.

   This combined issue of *Mountain Geologist* is a monograph outlining a five-day field trip through the Western Interior Basin, site of the great Cretaceous Seaway. It includes several articles on the area's geology and road logs for field trips.

174. Lucas, S.G., G. Basabilvazo, and T.F Lawton. 1990. Late Cretaceous dinosaurs from the Ringbone Formation, southwestern New Mexico, U.S.A. *Cretaceous Research* 11:343–349.

Laramide deposits of uncertain age lie atop Lower Cretaceous sediments in southwestern New Mexico. Dinosaur remains in the Ringbone Formation suggest that the Laramide sediments are Late Cretaceous. Much of southwestern New Mexico, northern Mexico and southeastern Arizona show the same nonmarine lacustrine and fluvial sediments in the latest Cretaceous.

175. Moullade, M., and A.E.M. Nairn, eds. 1978. *The Phanerozoic Geology of the World II: The Mesozoic, Volumes A and B.* Amsterdam: Elsevier.

    This two-volume compendium includes twenty-five articles describing global geology during the Mesozoic.

176. Nelson, M.E., and D.M. Crooks. 1987. Stratigraphy and paleontology of the Cedar Mountain Formation (Lower Cretaceous). In *Paleontology and Geology of the Dinosaur Triangle*, ed. W.R. Averett, 55–64. Grand Junction: Museum of Western Colorado.

    The formation consists of two facies, the Buckhorn Conglomerate and an unnamed mudstone and sandstone layer. Many fragmentary dinosaur teeth and eggs have been recovered from this formation.

177. Ostrom, J.H. 1970. Stratigraphy and paleontology of the Cloverly Formation (Lower Cretaceous) of the Bighorn Basin area, Wyoming and Montana. *Peabody Museum of Natural History Bulletin* 35:1–234.

    The Cloverly Formation is an important source of scarce Lower Cretaceous fossils in the western interior. Surveys the stratigraphy of the Cloverly Formation in south-central Montana and north-central Wyoming, and lists then known fossil specimens from the Formation. Includes 27 plates, numerous fold-out maps, and two larger maps in an attached pocket.

178. Reyment, R.A., and P. Bengston. 1981. *Aspects of Mid-Cretaceous Regional Geology.* New York: Academic Press.

Ten contributions survey the mid-Cretaceous geology (Aptian to Coniacian) of Russia, Germany, Lebanon, West Africa, Mozambique, Colombia, Venezuela, New Zealand and Antarctica.

179. Reynolds, M.W., and E.D. Dolly. 1983. *Mesozoic Paleogeography of the West-Central United States.* Denver: Society of Economic Paleontologists and Mineralogists.

    The published proceedings of the Second Rocky Mountain Paleogeography Symposium includes eighteen articles on western geology and paleogeography.

180. Riccardi, A.C. 1988. The Cretaceous System of Southern South America. *Geological Society of America Memoir* no. 168.

    Reviews South American Cretaceous geology. The Cretaceous climate in southern South America was warm and very dry north of 43° south latitude, and humid and temperate to the south of this arid zone.

181. Schlanger, S.O., and M.B. Cita. 1982. *Nature and Origin of Cretaceous Carbon-rich Facies.* New York: Academic Press.

    Ten papers discuss aspects of Cretaceous climate and oceanic conditions, and the formation of organic-rich rocks.

182. Sill, W.D. 1982. The tetrapod-bearing continental Triassic sediments of South America. *American Journal of Science* 267:805–821.

    Documentation of the Triassic faunal transition has been difficult due to the scarcity of sediments spanning this period. Describes new finds in western Argentina, which, together with other South American sites, preserve large sections of the Middle and Upper Triassic.

183. Stott, D.F., and D.J. Glass, eds. 1984. The Mesozoic of Middle North America. *Canadian Society of Petroleum Geologists Memoir* no. 9: 1–556.

    Presents 32 papers from a CSPG conference in Alberta on the Mesozoic geology of Canada and the northern U.S. The emphasis is on economic geology, with many basic papers on Mesozoic stratigraphy and sedimentology.

184. Thomas, R.G., D.A. Eberth, A.L. Deino, and D. Robinson. 1990. Composition, radioisotopic ages, and potential significance of an altered volcanic ash (bentonite) from the Upper Cretaceous Judith River Formation, Dinosaur Provincial Park, southern Alberta, Canada. *Cretaceous Research* 11:125–162.

    The bentonite (Plateau Tuff) represents volcanic ash deposited in a shallow floodplain lake. The eruption probably occurred in Montana's Elkhorn Mountains. Detailed data on the bentonite's age and geochemistry should help to date and correlate the stratigraphy of this important formation, which has produced an abundance of dinosaur remains.

185. Ventress, W.P.S., D.G. Bebout, B.F. Perkins, and C.H. Moore, eds. 1984. *The Jurassic of the Gulf Rim.* Austin: Earth Enterprises.

    Twenty-three papers discuss the Jurassic geology of the Gulf coastal states.

186. Weijermars, R. 1989. Global tectonics since the breakup of Pangea 180 million years ago: evolution maps and lithospheric budget. *Earth Science Reviews* 26:113–162.

    Charts the tectonic evolution of the planet, using two sets of assumptions. The initial series shows a consistently increasing rate of ocean lithospheric production rate for the past 140 million years. Revising the assumptions generates a chart series with a constant production rate.

187. Wood, J.M., R.G. Thomas, and J. Visser. 1988. Fluvial processes and vertebrate taphonomy: the Upper Cretaceous Judith River Formation, South-Central Dinosaur Provincial Park, Alberta, Canada. *Palaeogeography, Palaeoclimatology, Palaeoecology* 66:127–143.

    Presents a detailed depositional model for the upper 60 meters of the Judith River Formation. Three types of bonebeds can be distinguished: high diversity (macrovertebrate) beds, representing lag deposits buried by migrating dune trains; low diversity (macrovertebrate) beds, which probably represent mass deaths of ceratopsian herds crossing a river; and microvertebrate beds, which represent mechanically resistant bones sorted together by their similar hydrodynamic behavior.

188. Young, R.G. 1987. Triassic and Jurassic rocks in the Dinosaur Triangle. In *Paleontology and Geology of the Dinosaur Triangle*, ed. W.R. Averett, 5–20. Grand Junction: Museum of Western Colorado.

Describes and maps the Triassic and Jurassic strata; neither is completely represented in the Triangle. Volcanic ash and pyroclastic fragments, intermixed with erosional debris from the Rocky Mountains, combined to create the Late Triassic Chinle Formation. The fluvial-lacustrine sediments of the Morrison Formation were laid down in the Late Jurassic.

CLIMATE

189. Barron, E.J., and W.H. Peterson. 1989. Model simulation of the Cretaceous ocean circulation. *Science* 244:684–686.

Computer models of the Tethys Sea show an eastward current, contrary to the westward global equatorial current previously predicted. The eastward flow hypothesis also explains the biogeographical evidence traditionally advanced to support a westward flow [*See* 190].

190. Barron, E.J., and W.M. Washington. 1982. Cretaceous climate: a comparison of atmospheric simulations with the geological record. *Palaeogeography, Palaeoclimatology, Palaeoecology* 40:103–133.

A computer simulation of Cretaceous climate, based on Cretaceous geography, agrees fairly well with oceanic paleotemperature data. Oceanic temperatures were more uniform in the Cretaceous, with tropical temperatures about 1–2°C above present temperatures. The model also predicts strong polar easterlies, contradicting the standard assumption of polar westerlies [*See* 189].

191. Buffetaut, E., and M. Martin. 1984. Continental vertebrate distribution, faunal zonation and climate in the Late Triassic. In *Third Symposium on Mesozoic Terrestrial Ecosystems, Short Papers*, ed. W.E. Reif and F. Westphal, 25–29. Tübingen: ATTEMPTO-Verlag.

    The Late Triassic is often depicted as arid and semiarid (Tucker and Benton 1982 [801]). In reality, Triassic climates probably varied between alternating arid and mesic periods. The global presence of phytosaurs and other aquatic vertebrates contradicts the hypothesis of an arid Late Triassic.

192. Cooper, M.R. 1977. Eustacy during the Cretaceous; its implications and importance. *Palaeogeography, Palaeoclimatology, Palaeoecology* 22:1–60.

    Thirteen episodes of eustacy occurred during the Cretaceous. These cycles were short in duration, rarely lasting more than two million years. Waters advanced rapidly, and receded slowly. The transgressions were related to sea-floor spreading from the expansion of the mid-oceanic ridges. Episodes of eustacy were apparently correlated with continental margin volcanism. Regressions tended to produce more arid and seasonally extreme climates, while exposing land bridges for faunal migration. Transgressions favored more stable and warmer climates, with greater precipitation and lush vegetation. Regression would have led to deterioration of habitat, phyletic gradualism and higher rates of extinction. Transgression would have favored more rapid speciation. Plate tectonics thus influenced the pattern of biological evolution. (*See also* Hallam 1978 [196]; Horner 1983 [328]; Weishampel and Horner 1987 [803].)

193. Crowley, T.J., D.A. Short, J.G. Mengel, and G.R. North. 1986. Role of seasonality in the evolution of climate during the last 100 million years. *Science* 231:579–584.

    Computer modeling demonstrates that seasonality plays a critical role in long-term climatic patterns. Ice-free periods may be due to high summer temperatures balancing low winter temperatures, rather than an indication of year-round warm temperatures. The Late Cretaceous high latitudes experienced very cold temperatures, with sufficient summer warmth to support mixed conifer-hardwood forests.

194. Frakes, L.A. 1986. Mesozoic-Cenozoic climatic history and causes of the glaciation. In *Mesozoic and Cenozoic Oceans*, ed. K. Hsü, 33–48. Washington: AGU.

    Mesozoic temperatures were anomalously warm. Frakes reviews changes in climate from the Triassic to the present, and relates these changes to variations in atmospheric carbon dioxide. Temperatures rose throughout the Mesozoic, until a period of cooling began in the Late Cretaceous. This cool period is at odds with temperature predictions based on estimated Late Cretaceous carbon dioxide curves. Decreased sea-floor spreading, changes in sea level, changes in planetary albedo, and outgassing of carbon dioxide from volcanic eruptions were all involved in Mesozoic climatic patterns.

195. De Graciansky, P.C., G. Deroo, J.P. Herbin, L. Montadert, C. Müller, A. Schaaf, and J. Sigal. 1984. Ocean-wide stagnation episode in the Late Cretaceous. *Nature* 308:346–349.

    Layers of carbonaceous shale occur in Late Cretaceous sediments that contain unoxidized marine organic matter. This Cenomanian-Turonian Black Shale Horizon indicates a widespread anoxic ocean event. The disconformity coincides with a global marine transgression. The causes of this unusual event are unknown.

196. Hallam, A. 1978. Eustatic cycles in the Jurassic. *Palaeogeography, Palaeoclimatology, Palaeoecology* 23:1–32.

    Northwest European shallow-water marine sediments show local changes that are correlated with global sea-level changes. Presents five eustatic models. The best model predicts a rapid rise in sea level, a prolonged interim period, and a rapid sea-level fall. Sea-level rise is accompanied by a widespread migration and radiation of marine fauna. Regression is characterized by high levels of endemism. (*See* Cooper

1977 [192]; Horner 1983 [328]; Weishampel and Horner 1987 [803].)

197. Hallam, A. 1984. Continental humid and arid zones during the Jurassic and Cretaceous. *Palaeogeography, Palaeoclimatology, Palaeoecology* 47:195–223.

An arid zone in the western Pangean tropics at low to mid-latitudes spread northward in the Late Jurassic to cover most of southern Eurasia. Humid conditions returned in the Early Cretaceous. By the Late Cretaceous the tropical arid zone had substantially contracted. Regional aridity may have influenced the early evolution of angiosperms. Many angiosperm traits could be interpreted as adaptations to arid conditions.

198. Hays, J.D., and W.C. Pittman III. 1973. Lithospheric plate motion, sea level changes and climatic and ecological consequences. *Nature* 246:18–22.

Upper Cretaceous eustacy was caused by a pulse of rapid sea-floor spreading that greatly increased the overall volume of the global mid-oceanic ridge system. This increase in ridge volume displaced water in oceanic basins, leading to a global rise in sea-level. Upper Cretaceous climates were warm and moderate during the transgression. Later Cretaceous climates, when the waters abated, were more seasonal and cooler at high latitudes.

199. Kitchell, J.A., and D.L. Clark. 1982. Late Cretaceous–Paleogene paleogeography and paleocirculation: evidence of north polar upwelling. *Palaeogeography, Palaeoclimatology, Palaeoecology* 40:135–165.

Evidence of polar upwelling in the Late Cretaceous comes from the measurement of biogenic silica in deep-sea cores from the Arctic Ocean. Discusses the geological history of the north polar region during the Late Cretaceous.

200. Lloyd, C.R. 1982. The mid-Cretaceous earth: paleogeography; ocean circulation and temperature; atmospheric circulation. *Journal of Geology* 90:393–413.

A map of the late Albian-early Cenomanian period is used to reconstruct mid-Cretaceous oceanic and atmospheric circulation patterns. These predictions compare well with other independent data on paleoclimate. The predictions include low wind speeds in the mid-latitude westerlies, enhanced north-south wind patterns over the continents, with sharp seasonal reversals, very hot summers and cold winters over continental interiors at mid-latitudes, and a tropical circulation similar to the present, with vigorous monsoons.

201. Parrish, J.T. 1987. Global paleogeography and paleoclimate of the Late Cretaceous and Early Tertiary. In *The Origins of Angiosperms and their Biological Consequences*, ed. E.M. Friis et al., 51–73. Cambridge: Cambridge University Press.

    Angiosperms evolved during a period of climatic and geological stability. Parrish discusses methodological problems of determining paleoclimates, and reviews Cretaceous paleogeography. Temperature differentials were relatively slight, and posed no barrier to angiosperm dispersal. Several possible land bridges between continents could have aided in the dispersal of primitive angiosperms.

202. Parrish, J.T., and R.L. Curtis. 1982. Atmospheric circulation, upwelling, and organic-rich rocks in the Mesozoic and Cenozoic eras. *Palaeogeography, Palaeoclimatology, Palaeoecology* 40:31–66.

    One of eleven articles in a special issue devoted to paleogeography and climate. (*See also* Kitchell and Clark 1982 [199]; Barron and Washington 1982 [190].) Computer modeling of paleoatmospheres can be used to generate maps of wind patterns. These maps can be used to predict areas of oceanic upwelling. Maps are presented for seven selected geological periods from the Mesozoic and Cenozoic. The predicted pattern of upwelling corresponds to areas of organic-rich rock in three periods, including two in the Mesozoic. Anoxic events and marine transgressions also affect deposition of organic-rich rocks.

203. Roth, P.H. 1989. Ocean circulation and calcareous nanoplankton evolution during the Jurassic and Cretaceous. *Palaeogeography, Palaeoclimatology, Palaeoecology* 74:111–126.

Cretaceous oceanic circulation can be reconstructed using calcareous nanoplankton data. Oceanic and atmospheric conditions affect the spatial and temporal evolution of planktonic species, as well as their rate of evolution. Fischer cycles, fluctuations in ocean-atmosphere circulation patterns caused by tectonic events, are the ultimate force behind nanoplankton evolution. Milankovitch cycles affect the circulation of the upper ocean and relative abundance patterns. Speciation rates are highest during anoxic events.

204. Savin, S. 1977. The history of the earth's surface temperature during the past 100 million years. *Annual Review of Earth and Planetary Sciences* 5:319–355.

Reviews paleoclimatic reconstruction using indicator species and oxygen isotope ratios. Summarizes the climatic record of the Upper Cretaceous and the Cenozoic. Temperatures were especially warm during the Albian in Northern Europe and the tropical Pacific. Temperatures dropped during the Albian or Cenomanian, rose again during the Turonian or Coniacian, then dropped sharply, reaching their lowest level well before the Cretaceous-Tertiary boundary. A net global cooling occurred between the Albian and the end of the Cretaceous, as much as 8–10°C in Northern Europe and the tropical Pacific.

205. Schlanger, S.O. 1986. High frequency sea-level fluctuations in Cretaceous time: an emerging geophysical problem. In *Mesozoic and Cenozoic Oceans*, ed. K. Hsü, 61–74. Washington: AGU.

The Cretaceous is characterized by eustacy, with six major marine transgressions from the Albian through the Maastrichtian. The lack of glaciation in the Cretaceous makes it difficult to determine a cause for these cyclic changes in global sea level. No known rate of sea-floor spreading can explain the magnitude of sea-level changes in the Cretaceous

(150–250 meter amplitudes). Nor do any other known geological factors explain this eustatic cycle.

206. Srivastava, S.K. 1970. Pollen biostratigraphy and paleoecology of the Edmonton Formation (Maestrichtian), Alberta, Canada. *Palaeogeography, Palaeoclimatology, Palaeoecology* 7:221-276.

The Upper Cretaceous Edmonton Formation shows a series of pollen assemblages that allow us to reconstruct floral changes in the Upper Cretaceous. The Bearpaw Sea supported a tropical to subtropical climate with rain forest vegetation. This climate gave way to a warm, humid, subtropical to temperate climate, with a corresponding increase in ferns and gymnosperms. Cooler climates followed, supporting savanna-type vegetation, which was in turn replaced by a warm-temperate flood plain habitat.

207. Sundquist, E.T., and W.S. Broecker, eds. 1985. The Carbon Cycle and Atmospheric CO_2: Natural Variations Archean to Present. *Geophysical Monograph* no. 32.

Includes eleven articles relevant to Phanerozoic climates and the global carbon cycle. (*See also* Hsü and McKenzie 1985 [117].)

BIOGEOGRAPHY

208. Bonaparte, J.F. 1980. Jurassic tetrapods from South America and dispersal routes. In *Aspects of Vertebrate History: Essays in Honor of Edwin Harris Colbert,* ed. L.L. Jacobs, 73-98. Flagstaff: Museum of Northern Arizona Press.

Jurassic tetrapods in South America were poorly known until the 1960's. Several assemblages have since been discovered, including a rich mid-Jurassic fauna in Patagonia. The author reviews five major fauna (Roca Blanca, Cerra Cóndor, Laguna Manantiales, Araraquara, Neugén) and other isolated discoveries. South American Jurassic fauna show affinities with Gondwana and Euroamerican fauna.

209. Bonaparte, J.F. 1982. Faunal replacement in the Triassic of South America. *Journal of Vertebrate Paleontology* 2:362–371.

Therapsid extinction in the Triassic was due to improved locomotion in the radiating archosaurs, increases in body size by archosaurs, competitive pressures by rhynchosaurs on medium-sized therapsids, and the evolution of competitive archosaurian herbivores in the Late Triassic. The replacement in South America was coincident with the development of a rich Dicroidium flora, which stimulated a great radiation of archosaurs and therapsids. (*See also* Bonaparte 1984 [210]; Bonaparte 1979 [280]. *See* Benton 1983 [581] for a review and additional cross references.)

210. Bonaparte, J.F. 1984. Late Cretaceous faunal interchange of terrestrial vertebrates between the Americas. In *Third Symposium on Mesozoic Terrestrial Ecosystems, Short Papers*, ed. W.E. Reif and F. Westphal, 19–24. Tübingen: ATTEMPTO-Verlag.

Discoveries in Patagonia document the faunal interchange between North and South America in the Late Cretaceous. The presence of the southern titanosaurid *Alamosaurus sanjuanensis* in the southwestern United States, and the presence of northern hadrosaurs and ceratopsians in Patagonia, indicates a significant faunal interchange. This migration was as important to American biogeography as the more famous faunal interchange of the Pleistocene. (*See also* Bonaparte 1982 [209]; Bonaparte 1979 [280].)

211. Bonaparte, J.F., and Z. Kielan-Jaworowska. 1987. Late Cretaceous dinosaur and mammal faunas of Laurasia and Gondwana. In *Fourth Symposium on Mesozoic Terrestrial Ecosystems, Short Papers*, ed. P.J. Currie and E. Koster, 24–29. Drumheller, Alta.: Tyrell Museum of Paleontology.

A comparison of Late Cretaceous dinosaur and mammalian faunas from Laurasia and Gondwanaland reveals many differences at the generic and family level, despite superficial similarities. They probably evolved as vicariant types, in isolation from one another. Laurasian dinosaur faunas were dominated by ornithischians and tyrannosaurids, while Gondwanaland faunas were dominated by titanosaurid sauropods and Abelisauridae and Spinosauridae carnivores.

212. Bonaparte, J.F., and J.E. Powell. 1980. A continental assemblage of tetrapods from the Upper Cretaceous beds of El Brete, northwestern Argentina (Sauropoda-Coelurosauria-Carnosauria-Aves). *Mémoires de la Société Géologique de France* 139:19–28.

    El Brete, in northwestern Argentina, was probably a flood plain forest near the sea in the Upper Cretaceous. Reports on a diverse group of birds and dinosaurs from El Brete, including a new titanosaurid, *Saltasaurus loricatus*, and a new coelurosaur, *Noasaurus leali*.

213. Brett-Surman, M.K., and G.S. Paul. 1985. A new family of bird-like dinosaurs linking Laurasia and Gondwanaland. *Journal of Vertebrate Paleontology* 5:133–138.

    Describes a new theropod species, *Avisaurus archibaldi*, and a new family, Avisauridae, based on metatarsi from the Hell Creek Formation and the Lecho Formation of Argentina. The new species supports a hypothesized Late Cretaceous land bridge between North and South America (Brett-Surman 1979 [829]).

214. Buffetaut, E. 1989. Archosaurian reptiles with Gondwanan affinities in the Upper Cretaceous of Europe. *Terra Nova* 1:69–74.

    Gondwanaland archosaurs, such as titanosaurid sauropods and abelisaurid theropods, give Late Cretaceous European faunas a distinctive difference from North American and Central Asian faunas. Low sea levels may have allowed a faunal interchange across the Tethys Sea in the Late Cretaceous, possibly by island hopping across the Apulian or Alboran plates.

215. Buffetaut, E., N. Sattayarak, and V. Suteethorn. 1989. A psittacosaurid dinosaur from the Cretaceous of Thailand and

its implications for the palaeogeographical history of Asia. *Terra Nova* 1:370–373.

Discovery of psittacosaurid jaws in the Early Cretaceous Khorat Plateau's Khok Kruat suggests that the poorly known southeast Asian fauna may be similar to that of northern and central Asia. Their presence shows that the Indochina block was a part of the Asian mainland at this time, contrary to earlier paleogeographical reconstructions.

216. Charig, A.J. 1973. Jurassic and Cretaceous dinosaurs. In *Atlas of Palaeobiogeography*, ed. A. Hallam, 339–352. Amsterdam: Elsevier.

A useful early review of the global biogeography of Jurassic and Cretaceous dinosaurs. Many families appear to have a cosmopolitan distribution. In the Late Cretaceous there were no major barriers to migration between Asia, North America and South America. Migration from Europe to Africa, and from there through Asia and across the North Atlantic to North America, was possible but more difficult. The South Atlantic Ocean, however, formed a formidable barrier to migration.

217. Chatterjee, S. 1986. The Late Triassic Dockum vertebrates: their stratigraphic and paleobiogeographic significance. In *The Beginning of The Age of Dinosaurs; Faunal Changes Across the Triassic-Jurassic Boundary*, ed. K. Padian, 139–150. Cambridge: Cambridge University Press.

The Dockum Formation in western Texas and eastern New Mexico is difficult to date accurately. Chatterjee proposes several parasuchid "biozones" to divide the Late Triassic beds, and correlate them with similar zones in Germany. Dockum vertebrates suggest a land connection between North America and Africa during the Late Triassic. The biotic evidence also suggests that South America was isolated from North America at this time.

218. Chatterjee, S. 1987. A new theropod dinosaur from India with remarks on the Gondwana-Laurasia connection in the Late Triassic. *Geophysical Monograph* 41:183–189.

Describes a new theropod genus and species, *Walkeria maleriensis*, from the Late Triassic of India. A member of the family Podekosauridae, this new taxon, along with other animals from the Maleri Formation, establishes a close faunal link between the Maleri Formation and the North American Dockum Formation. The faunal similarities between the two formations suggest a Late Triassic Gondwana-Laurasia land bridge between India and North America, perhaps by way of northern Africa.

219. Colbert, E.H. 1985. *Wandering Lands and Animals: The Story of Continental Drift and Animal Populations.* New York: Dover (orig. Dutton, 1973).

    An excellent and readable introduction to the geography and biogeography of the prehistoric world. While the dinosaur content is minimal, this clearly written and well illustrated book reveals the essential geological and biological context of the dinosaurs' reign.

220. Cox, C.B. 1980. An outline of the biogeography of the Mesozoic world. *Mémoires de la Société Géologique de France* 139:75–79.

    Tectonic movements during the Mesozoic set the modern patterns of faunal distributions. Summarizes the biogeography of angiosperms, dinosaurs and mammals in the Mesozoic. Angiosperms and dinosaurs show different biogeographic patterns, explained by their different geographic origins and differences in their ability to disperse across oceanic barriers.

221. Galton, P.M. 1977. The ornithopod dinosaur *Dryosaurus* and a Laurasia-Gondwanaland connection in the Upper Jurassic. *Nature* 268:230–232.

    Laurasia and Gondwanaland were joined by a land bridge at some point in the Upper Jurassic. Reviews the faunal evidence for this land bridge, and reassigns *Dysalotosaurus lettow-vorbecki,* from the African Tendaguru Beds, to the genus *Dryosaurus.* The presence of *Dryosaurus* in the American Morrison Formation and the Tanzanian Tendaguru Beds is further evidence for the postulated Jurassic land bridge. (*See* Galton 1980 [222] for discussion of a data error in this article. For additional articles on the Jurassic connection between North America and Europe *See also* Galton 1974a [309]; Galton and Jensen 1975 [317]; Galton and Powell 1980 [318].)

222. Galton, P.M. 1980. *Dryosaurus* and *Camptosaurus*, intercontinental genera of Upper Jurassic ornithopod dinosaurs. *Mémoires de la Société Géologique de France* 139:103–108.

   A land bridge in the Upper Jurassic between Laurasia and Gondwanaland is indicated by the presence of *Camptosaurus* and *Dryosaurus* in western North America, eastern Africa, and western Europe. Corrects a serious error in tabular data presented in Galton (1977 [221]). (*See* Galton 1977 [221] for additional articles on Jurassic land bridges.)

223. Hallam, A. 1983. Early and mid-Jurassic molluscan biogeography and the establishment of the Central Atlantic Seaway. *Palaeogeography, Palaeoclimatology, Palaeoecology* 43:181–193.

   Sea-level changes were an important factor in Jurassic faunal distributions. Molluscan bivalve fossils from North America, South America and Europe demonstrate that although intermigration between Europe and the Americas was possible for part of the mid-Jurassic, the seaway was shallow and migration was restricted. Large areas of the epicontinental sea between North America and Europe dried up completely during major oceanic regressions. Late Jurassic terrestrial vertebrates, including dinosaurs, are very similar in North America and Europe, supporting the conclusion that the Atlantic did not open between these two continents until late in the Jurassic. (*See also* Galton 1974a [309]; Galton and Jensen 1975 [317]; Galton and Powell 1980 [318].)

224. Lillegraven, J.A.,et al. 1979. Paleogeography of the world of the Mesozoic. In *Mesozoic Mammals*, ed. J.A. Lillegraven, M.J. Kraus, and T.M. Brown, 277–308. Berkeley: University of California Press.

Summarizes Mesozoic climate, geography and mammalian faunas, and briefly discusses the coevolution of mammals and angiosperms.

225. Milner, A.R., and D.B. Norman. 1984. The biogeography of advanced ornithopod dinosaurs (Archosauria: Ornithischia): a cladistic-vicariance model. In *Third Symposium on Mesozoic Terrestrial Ecosystems, Short Papers*, ed. W. Reif and F. Westphal, 145–150. Tübingen: Tübingen University Press.

Examines the biogeographic implications of Norman's cladistic analysis of the ornithopods (Norman 1984 [855]). The model offers several predictions for late Mesozoic ornithopod biogeography. The distribution of Hadrosauridae and Iguanodontidae can be explained by a single event which isolated the two families in the mid-Jurassic. This isolation broke down twice, leading to the expansion of their ranges during the Cretaceous.

226. Nicholls, E.L., and A.P. Russell. 1990. Paleobiogeography of the Cretaceous Western Interior Seaway of North America: the vertebrate evidence. *Palaeogeography, Palaeoclimatology, Palaeoecology* 79:149–169.

Analyzes the distribution of marine vertebrates from the Western Interior Seaway during the Lower Campanian, using relative abundance data. The Northern Interior Subprovince shows a low diversity of vertebrates, while the Southern Interior Subprovince shows a high diversity of vertebrates. The data support cool water temperatures in the northern Seaway and warm-temperate to subtropical water temperatures in the southern Seaway.

227. Sahni, A. 1984. Cretaceous-Paleocene terrestrial faunas of India: lack of endemism during rifting of the Indian plate. *Science* 226:441–443.

Cretaceous vertebrates from India, Madagascar and Africa show many similarities. A dispersal corridor must have connected these areas in the Upper Cretaceous, about 80 million years ago. Geophysical models usually depict India as a separate land mass prior to its collision with the Tibetan block.

228. Scott, R.W. 1986. Biogeographic influences on Early Cretaceous paleocommunities, western interior. *Journal of Paleontology* 60:197–207.

Reconstructs late Albian environments of the western interior, and examines physical and biological factors affecting marine invertebrate communities. Comparison of Caribbean Province and Southern Western Interior Province communities shows that some communities in both provinces shared component species, with different dominant species, while others showed a high degree of endemism. Marine community patterns are related to variations in substrate and salinity.

229. Sues, H.D. 1980. A Pachycephalosaurid dinosaur from the Upper Cretaceous of Madagascar and its paleobiogeographical implications. *Journal of Paleontology* 54:954–962.

Reports the first discovery from the Southern Hemisphere of the Laurasian pachycephalosaurids. Describes the Madagascar species *Majungatholus atopus* from a partial skull, and its relation to other dinosaurs in the Majunga District fauna. The specimen suggests the existence of a land bridge between Gondwanaland and Laurasia during part of the Cretaceous.

230. Weishampel, D.B., and J.B. Weishampel. 1983. Annotated localities of ornithopod dinosaurs; implications to Mesozoic paleobiogeography. *The Mosasaur* 1:43–87.

Annotates the ornithopod fossil record with information on locality, horizon, literature references, and species diversity of known ornithopods. Includes a discussion of ornithopod biogeography.

THE ORIGIN OF ANGIOSPERMS

231. Ash, S.R. 1986. Fossil plants and the Triassic-Jurassic boundary. In *The Beginning of The Age of Dinosaurs; Faunal Changes Across the Triassic-Jurassic Boundary*, ed. K. Padian, 21–30. Cambridge: Cambridge University Press.

    With a few cautionary words for vertebrate paleontologists unfamiliar with fossil plants, Ash systematically reviews Upper Triassic and Lower Jurassic plant megafossils. This period experienced luxuriant growth compared to the impoverished floras of the Upper Paleozoic. There is a smooth floral transition between the two periods. The flora suggests that the climate was warm to hot; humid areas were intermixed with slightly higher and drier areas. Fossils of more xeric plants, like conifers, are fragmentary. They were probably transported from relatively arid upland areas. Besides new species of lycopods, horsetails, ferns and seed ferns, many new species of cycads, Voltziales, Coniferales and the new order Bennettitales enter the fossil record in the Upper Jurassic.

232. Axelrod, D.I. 1970. Mesozoic paleogeography and early Angiosperm history. *Botanical Review* 36:277–319.

    Global sea-level changes in the Early Cretaceous led to warm and stable climates, which aided the angiosperm invasion of the lowlands. Angiosperms originated in "mild uplands at low latitudes" during the Late Triassic. Increasing diversity arose as floras drifted farther apart from ocean-floor spreading. (*See also* Brenner 1976 [236]; Spicer et al. 1989 [260]).

233. Axelrod, D.I. 1984. An interpretation of Cretaceous and Tertiary biota in polar regions. *Palaeogeography, Palaeoclimatology, Palaeoecology* 45:105–147.

    We don't need to postulate a change in the tilt of the Earth's axis to explain how polar floras could survive extended periods of darkness. (*See* Douglas and Williams 1982 [241].) The "old problem" of polar forests is explicable in terms of the normal physiological adaptations to low light levels seen in many modern plant species. Many species grow beyond the Arctic Circle. Polar dinosaurs probably coped with extended darkness by undergoing seasonal migrations.

234. Batten, D.J., and W.L. Kovach, eds. 1990. Catalog of Mesozoic and Tertiary Megaspores. *American Association of Stratigraphic Palynologists Contribution Series* 24:1–227.

A thorough taxonomic and nomenclatural index of Mesozoic palynomorphs, covering published reports on pollen grains and spores in the fossil record. Over 3,200 species are listed alphabetically by genus, and the information will eventually be available on IBM-compatible computer disks.

235. Beck, C.B. 1976. *Origin and Early Evolution of Angiosperms*. New York: Columbia University Press.

A useful collection of ten articles, several of which are summarized in this section. (*See* Doyle and Hickey 1976 [244]; Stebbins 1976 [261]; Brenner 1976 [236]. *See* Beck 1988 [612] for a similar work on gymnosperms.)

236. Brenner, G.J. 1976. Middle Cretaceous floral provinces and early migrations of angiosperms. In *Origin and Early Evolution of Angiosperms*, ed. C.B. Beck, 23–47. New York: Columbia University Press.

Various routes have been proposed for the dispersal of the first angiosperms. The tricolpate pollen fossil data support Axelrod's hypothesis that angiosperms originated in the tropics and spread northward (Axelrod 1970 [232]), but contradict his hypothesis of pre-Cretaceous angiosperms. (*See also* Spicer et al. 1987 [260].)

237. Crane, P.R. 1987. Vegetational consequences of the angiosperm diversification. In *The Origins of Angiosperms and Their Biological Consequences*, ed. E.M. Friis et al., 107–144. Cambridge: Cambridge University Press.

Angiosperms came to dominate plant communities in the mid-Cretaceous. They first developed from weedy colonizing plants into early successional forms, and later (by the Late

Cretaceous) into canopy trees. Conifers continued to dominate many areas. They were the only major group of land plants to successfully compete with the angiosperms. Reviews the floras of each age of the Cretaceous.

238. Crane, P.R., M.J. Donoghue, J.A. Doyle, E.M. Friis, W.H. Li, M. Gouy, K.H. Wolfe, P.M. Sharp, W. Martin, A. Gierl, and H. Saedler. 1989. Angiosperm origins. *Nature* 342:131–132.

    This series of three letters debates Martin et al.'s (1989 [255]) attempt to date primitive angiosperms by molecular clock methods. The phylogenetic evidence contradicts Martin's conclusion. Martin also fails to include other seed plant groups in his analysis. Includes a rebuttal by Martin. (*See also* Wolfe et al. 1989 [269].)

239. Crepet, W.L., and E.M. Friis. 1987. The evolution of insect pollination in the angiosperms. In *The Origins of Angiosperms and Their Biological Consequences*, ed. E.M. Friis et al., 181–202. Cambridge: Cambridge University Press.

    Angiosperm evolution is characterized by coevolution between flowers and their insect pollinators. Explores pollination in the early angiosperms and other early land plants. Primitive pollination syndromes may date back to the Late Carboniferous. Discusses the time of appearance of major pollinating taxa. Bees, wasps, various Lepidoptera, and other pollinators important in modern floras evolved in the Late Cretaceous.

240. Dilcher, D.L. 1979. Early angiosperm reproduction: an introductory report. *Review of Paleobotany and Palynology* 27:291–328.

    Our model of the primitive angiosperm was formulated before the angiosperm fossil record was well known. Extant flowers thought to be primitive, like the Magnoliales, do not necessarily resemble the actual ancestral angiosperm. (*See also* Hughes 1976 [248]; Taylor and Hickey 1990 [262].) Dilcher reviews fossil angiosperms and discusses the evolution of pollination. Selective pressures from presumed insect pollinators shaped the lineage of extant angiosperms.

Angiosperms radiated extremely rapidly in the early Cretaceous.

241. Douglas, J.G., and G.E. Williams. 1982. Southern polar forests: the Early Cretaceous floras of Victoria and their paleoclimatic significance. *Palaeogeography, Palaeoclimatology, Palaeoecology* 39:171–185.

Victorian floras are typical of other Early Cretaceous floras. Coniferous forests, with an evergreen and deciduous understory, dominated the landscape. Both the flora and the dinosaur fauna suggest a moderately seasonal, warm to cool-temperate climate. This does not agree with the climate predicted from the latitudes Australia is believed to have occupied at that time. The flora could not have survived the two to five-month polar nights. Perhaps we need to reconsider the hypothesis that the Earth's axial tilt was different at that time. (*See also* Axelrod 1984 [233].)

242. Doyle, J.A. 1978. Origin of angiosperms. *Annual Review of Ecology and Systematics* 9:365–392.

Claims for pre-Cretaceous angiosperms are dubious. The real fossil record begins in the Cretaceous. Although the question of monophylesis is still unsettled, angiosperms are most likely monophyletic, originating by progenesis from the seed ferns near the Jurassic-Cretaceous boundary. The first angiosperms were small "weedy immigrants from semiarid areas," adapted to disturbed habitats.

243. Doyle, J.A., and M.J. Donoghue. 1980. The origin of angiosperms: a cladistic approach. In *The Origins of Angiosperms and Their Biological Consequences*, ed. E.M. Friis et al., 17–49. Cambridge: Cambridge University Press.

Presents a cladistic analysis of seed plants, and discusses alternate cladograms for angiosperms.

244. Doyle, J.A., and L.J. Hickey. 1976. Pollen and leaves from the mid-Cretaceous Potomac Group and their bearing on early angiosperm evolution. In *Origin and Early Evolution of*

Angiosperms, ed. C.B. Beck, 139–206. New York: Columbia University Press.

Charts trends in mid-Cretaceous leaf and pollen evolution. Angiosperms were weedy colonizers, adapted to unstable and disturbed environments. They initially invaded forests as understory shrubs.

245. Friis, E.M., and W.L. Crepet. 1987. Time of appearance of floral features. In *The Origins of Angiosperms and Their Biological Consequences*, ed. E.M. Friis et al., 145–179. Cambridge: Cambridge University Press.

Reviews the appearance of floral features and major types of fruit in the Cretaceous. Early fossil fruits from the Albian and Cenomanian are dry, and show no obvious adaptation for dispersal. Fleshy fruits appear in the Campanian, and berries in the late Maastrichtian.

246. Gottsberger G., and G.T. Prance. 1990. Reproductive Biology and Evolution of Tropical Woody Angiosperms. *Memoirs of the New York Botanical Garden* 55:1–195.

Thirteen articles comprise the proceedings of a symposium from the 14th International Botanical Congress. The earliest angiosperms were tropical or subtropical woody plants. Most modern woody angiosperms are still tropical species, but little is known about the evolution of such plants. Covers the evolution of breeding systems, the morphology of primitive reproductive structures, and the evolution of pollination syndromes.

247. Hickey, L.J., and J.A. Doyle. 1977. Early Cretaceous fossil evidence for angiosperm evolution. *Botanical Review* 43:3–104.

The Early Cretaceous Potomac Group shows a monophyletic origin for angiosperms just before the Barremian. The first angiosperms were small-leafed shrubs in seasonally arid habitats. These invaded riparian areas as weedy colonizers, and radiated into aquatic and later successional stage vegetations. (*See also* Doyle and Hickey 1976 [244].)

248. Hughes, N.F. 1976. *Palaeobiology of Angiosperm Origins: Problems of Mesozoic Seed-Plant Evolution.* Cambridge: Cambridge University Press.

In a somewhat radical departure, Hughes objects to traditional phylogenetic hypotheses concerning the origin of the angiosperms. They are all based on insufficient evidence, and once formulated they constrain the objective analysis of new fossil finds. (*See also* Dilcher 1979 [240]; Taylor and Hickey 1990 [262].) Hughes attempts an objective review of the fossil record, disdaining "unprofitable lines of enquiry such as imaginary 'upland' fossil floras."

249. Kosanke, R.M., ed. 1970. Symposium on Palynology of the Late Cretaceous and Early Tertiary. *Geological Society of America Special Paper* no. 127.

This GSA symposium includes seven papers focused on Late Cretaceous palynology in the U.S. and Canada.

250. Krassilov, V.A. 1977. The origin of angiosperms. *Botanical Review* 43:143–176.

Angiosperms are not a monophyletic group. Three different groups of Mesozoic seed plants, the Caytoniales, Czekanowskiales, and Dirhopalostachyaceae, may be "proangiosperms" [*See* 251].

251. Krassilov, V.A. 1984. New paleobotanical data on origin and early evolution of angiospermy. *Annals of the Missouri Botanical Garden* 71:577–592.

A refinement of earlier work, based on new specimens from Mongolia and other sites. The new fossils affirm a polyphyletic origin for angiosperms. "Not long ago," bemoans Krassilov, "the origin of angiosperms seemed mysterious because there were no acceptable candidates for ancestors. Now the problem is that there are too many of them." (*See* Doyle 1978 [242]; Doyle and Donoghue 1980 [243]; Hickey and Doyle 1977 [247] for a contrasting view supporting monophylesis.)

252. Lidgard, S., and P.R. Crane. 1988. Quantitative analysis of the early angiosperm radiation. *Nature* 331:344–346.

Data from 197 floras and over 3,500 megafossils suggests a competitive displacement of cycadophytes and pteridophytes by angiosperms. By about 90 million years ago angiosperms completely dominated Northern Hemisphere floras. Conifer diversity shows only a slight decline during this angiosperm radiation. The authors caution that "complex changes in floral composition" may have preceded the angiosperm radiation. Angiosperms may have accelerated, rather than caused, the observed decline in other groups [*See* 253].

253. Lidgard, S., and P.R. Crane. 1990. Angiosperm diversification and Cretaceous floral trends: a comparison of palynofloras and leaf macrofloras. *Paleobiology* 16:77–93.

Leaves and palynomorphs (pollen and spores) constitute two parallel and independent sources of data in the plant fossil record. Despite different sources of bias in their respective fossil record, both data sets are largely in agreement. Angiosperms underwent a dramatic increase in diversity in the mid-Cretaceous; the leaf record shows a more rapid rise than the pollen record. Conifer diversity stayed relatively stable in the face of the angiosperm radiation, but other seed plants and free-sporing plants declined in diversity [*See* [252].

254. Mc Clammer, J.U. jr., and D.R. Crabtree. 1989. Post-Barremian (Early Cretaceous) to Paleocene paleobotanical collections in the western interior of North America. *Review of Palaeobotany and Palynology* 57:221–232.

Presents a thoroughly referenced list of paleobotanical collections from locations in the western U.S. This record includes the most complete existing sample of Cretaceous angiosperms.

255. Martin, W., A. Gierl, and H. Saedler. 1989. Molecular evidence for pre-Cretaceous angiosperm origins. *Nature* 339:46–48.

DNA sequencing (molecular clock method) of a glycolytic enzyme produces an estimated date for angiosperm origins of about 300 million years ago, supporting a pre-Cretaceous angiosperm origin. (*See* Crane et al. 1989 [238] for a critique, with a rebuttal by Martin. *See also* Wolfe et al. 1989 [269]).

256. Raven, P.H. 1977. A suggestion concerning the Cretaceous rise to dominance of the angiosperms. *Evolution* 31:451–452.

    Insect pollination enabled angiosperms to exist as widely dispersed populations, giving them a competitive edge in tropical habitats over wind-pollinated plants. Angiosperms became dominant in the tropical lowlands during a period of global warming.

257. Regal, P.J. 1977. Ecology and evolution of flowering plant dominance. *Science* 196:622–629.

    Birds and mammals contributed to the success of insect-pollinated plants, by dispersing seeds and by adapting to the insectivorous and frugivorous niches opened up by the radiation of angiosperms. Angiosperms could maintain scattered populations because they relied on animal vectors for pollination. Gymnosperm populations were diluted to the point where wind pollination became a liability.

258. Retallack, G.J., and D.L. Dilcher. 1981. A coastal hypothesis for the dispersal and rise to dominance of flowering plants. In *Paleobotany, Paleoecology, and Evolution*, Vol. 2, ed. K.J. Niklas, 27–78. New York: Praeger.

    Prior speculation about the origin of the angiosperms has relied on inferences from living taxa. The authors agree with Hickey and Doyle's general concept of early angiosperms, but reject the hypotheses that they originated in upland areas, and somewhat resembled modern Magnolias. (*See* Dilcher 1979 [240]; Doyle 1978 [242]; Doyle and Hickey 1976 [244]; Hickey and Doyle 1977 [247].) The Upper Cretaceous Dakota Formation (lower Cenomanian) represents a critical juncture in the early evolution of angiosperms. These angiosperms were generalists, adapted to unstable coastal depositional environments, and were probably small woody perennials, whose reproduction was like that of modern early successional plants. They thrived in the coastal habitats made so abundant by the retreat and return of the Cretaceous inland seas.

259. Retallack, G.J., and D.L. Dilcher. 1986. Cretaceous angiosperm invasion of North America. *Cretaceous Research* 7:227–252.

While gymnosperms continued to dominate upland habitats, angiosperms rapidly invaded coastal and fluvial depositional habitats in the late Barremian. These colonizing species were quickly dispersed by the ebb and invasion of inland seas. They thrived in disturbed open habitats, and favored generalist strategies of pollination and seed dispersal.

260. Spicer, R.A., J.A. Wolfe, and D.J. Nichols. 1987. Alaskan Cretaceous-Tertiary floras and Arctic origins. *Paleobiology* 13:73–83.

A review of Alaskan Cretaceous floras refutes the hypothesis that angiosperms spread from the poles towards the equator, and supports Axelrod's hypothesis of a poleward migration (Axelrod 1970 [232], 1984 [233]; Brenner 1976 [236]). Angiosperms moved northward through disturbed streamside habitats. Following their initial invasion, angiosperm diversity decreased as Alaska moved into higher latitudes and global temperatures dropped.

261. Stebbins, G.L. 1976. Seeds, seedlings, and the origin of angiosperms. In *Origin and Early Evolution of Angiosperms*, ed. C.B. Beck, 300–311. New York: Columbia University Press.

Angiosperms probably evolved in tropical and subtropical areas which experienced seasonal drought. Many of their adaptations are related to growth in unstable habitats such as stream banks. The most important traits setting angiosperms apart from gymnosperms are reproductive traits. Modern angiosperms which are considered primitive are not actually ancestral, but represent secondary adaptations to more stable habitats, such as flood plains.

262. Taylor, D.W., and L.J. Hickey. 1990. An Aptian plant with attached leaves and flowers: implications for angiosperm origin. *Science* 247:702–704.

Ancient angiosperm fossils from Australia suggest a new hypothesis for the nature of the first angiosperms. The plant is similar to living Magnoliidae and basal monocots. The ancestral angiosperm was a small rhizomatous perennial, with small reproductive structures. The small size of the specimen explains the lack of pre-Albian angiosperm wood, and calls for a corrected "search image" in the continuing hunt for ancient angiosperms. (*See also* Dilcher 1979 [240].)

263. Tidwell, W.T., S.R. Ash, and L.R. Parker. 1980. Cretaceous and Tertiary floras of the San Juan Basin. In *Advances in San Juan Basin Paleontology*, ed. S.G. Lucas, J.K. Rigby, and B.S. Kues, 307–336. Albuquerque: University of New Mexico Press.

The San Juan Basin offers a good record of Late Cretaceous to Eocene floras. Most studies have been floral lists compiled for stratigraphic purposes. The Fruitland and Kirtland Formation floras are dominated by dicots, which grew in and around narrow coastal swamps. The basin flora in the Fruitland gave way to an impoverished upland flora, suggesting an uplift in late Kirtland times.

264. Tiffney, B.H. 1981. Diversity and major events in the evolution of land plants. In *Paleobotany, Paleoecology, and Evolution*, Vol. 2, ed. K.J. Niklas, 193–230. New York: Praeger.

A review of the evolution and diversification of all land plants. Angiosperm success can be attributed to their "r-strategy" life history. They are opportunistic, and can rapidly colonize disturbed areas. The first weedy angiosperms lived in unstable stream and riverside environments. While retaining the essential nature of their reproductive system, they increased in size (Cope's Rule) and adopted an arborescent habit. While angiosperms dominated lowland habitats, gymnosperms continued to dominate upland habitats.

265. Tiffney, B.H. 1989. Plant life in the age of the dinosaurs. In *The Age of Dinosaurs*, ed. K. Padian and D.J. Chure, 34–47. *Geological Society of America Short Courses in Paleontology* no. 2. Knoxville: The Paleontological Society.

Reviews the major flora of the Mesozoic, including pteridophytes, gymnosperms, and angiosperms. Discusses their evolutionary trends and the interaction between plants and herbivorous dinosaurs. Includes suggested sources for illustrations for teaching about Mesozoic plant life.

266. Upchurch, G.R. jr., and J.A. Wolfe. 1987. Mid-Cretaceous to Early Tertiary vegetation and climate: evidence from fossil leaves and woods. In *The Origins of Angiosperms and Their Biological Consequences*, ed. E.M. Friis et al., 75–105. Cambridge: Cambridge University Press.

Plant megafossils can fill the gap in knowledge about Cretaceous climates. The fossil record shows that a major change in climate accompanied, and probably influenced, early angiosperm evolution. Late Cretaceous angiosperms are adapted to aseasonal dryness. True closed-canopy stratified rain forests did not appear until precipitation increased at the Cretaceous-Tertiary boundary. Discusses the climatic implications of leaf shape and pollination.

267. Wesley, A. 1973. Jurassic plants. In *Atlas of Palaeobiogeography*, ed. A. Hallam, 329–338. Amsterdam: Elsevier.

Gymnosperms dominated Jurassic floras, with conifers, cycadophytes and ginkgophytes all reaching their evolutionary peaks. Horsetails and ferns were common, but the other pteridophytes and the lycopods were much reduced from their former importance.

268. Whitehead, D.R. 1983. Wind pollination: some ecological and evolutionary perspectives. In *Pollination Biology*, ed. L. Real, 97–109. New York: Academic Press.

Wind pollination favors closely spaced individuals in areas of low rainfall. Discusses physical and biological factors in the ecology of wind-pollinated plants.

269. Wolfe, K.H., M. Gouy, Y.W. Yang, P.M. Sharp, and W.H. Li. 1989. Date of the monocot-dicot divergence estimated from chloroplast DNA sequence data. *Proceedings of the National Academy of Sciences* 86:6201–6205.

The divergence of the two main types of modern angiosperms, the monocots (one seed leaf) and dicots (two seed leaves) is one of the most important events in early angiosperm evolution. There are no fossils to document this step, but DNA sequencing of chloroplast DNA give an estimated time of 200 million years ago for the divergence (late Triassic). This implies that the angiosperms originated in Jurassic-Triassic times, well in advance of their appearance in the fossil record. (*See also* Martin et al. 1989 [255]; Crane et al. 1989 [238].)

THE FAR SIDE   By GARY LARSON

However, there was no question that, on the south side of the river, the land was ruled by the awesome *Tyrannosaurus Mex.*

The Far Side, copyright 1988 & 1991 Universal Press Syndicate. Reprinted with permission. All rights reserved.

Chapter Four

The Dinosaurs

We first encounter dinosaurs in the fossil record of the mid-Triassic. Even the very earliest dinosaurs, like *Staurikosaurus* and *Heterodontosaurus*, represent a significant evolutionary step. Some were bipeds, some were quadrupeds, but all possessed the ability to move efficiently through their world, seeking prey, escaping predators, and finding mates.

The sprawling gait of the therapsids and the somewhat improved stance of the thecodonts was soon to be swept away by animals that held their legs straight under their bodies, moving them in the forward-backward motion that announced their conquest of the terrestrial world.

We recognize two broad groups of dinosaurs, the Saurischia and the Ornithischia, separated primarily by differences in their pelvic structure. *Staurikosaurus* and *Heterodontosaurus* are problematic, and may predate the split into two main orders (Brinkman and Sues 1988 [282]).

Did the two orders of dinosaurs evolve from separate groups of thecodonts, or did they stem from a common ancestor as yet undiscovered? The question is far from settled, but as we will see in Chapter Seven there is mounting evidence that dinosaurs are a monophyletic group, united in the dim Triassic past by a common thecodont ancestor.

Within the Saurischia we can distinguish two major groups, the bipedal carnivorous theropods, and the mainly quadrupedal herbivorous sauropods. We can further subdivide the theropods into the large carnosaurs and the smaller coelurosaurs.

The Ornithischia are a more complex group, harder to separate into neat categories. The primitive fabrosaurids are often split off into their own lineage, as are the stegosaurs. By the Jurassic, the ornithischian line had led to the hypsilophodonts, medium sized cursorial bipeds who would in turn give rise to the more advanced iguanodontids and hadrosaurids. Fabrosaurids, hypsilophodonts, iguanodontids and hadrosaurids are usually placed together in the suborder Ornithopoda.

From somewhere near the base of this assemblage of ornithopods evolved several diverse groups of herbivores, including the ceratopsians, or horned dinosaurs, the ankylosaurs, or armored dinosaurs, and the dome-headed pachycephalosaurs.

While a complete review of the many taxa of dinosaurs is well beyond the scope of this bibliography, an Appendix is included for the reader's convenience which summarizes the major taxa, together with typical genera.

Included in this chapter are those works on individual taxa which do not readily fall under other topical headings. These works are primarily reports of discoveries of new fossil material, reports on new taxa, or reexamination of known specimens.

If all of the literally hundreds of research papers proclaiming "I found a jawbone in Montana," or words to that effect, had been included in this bibliography it would rival the Manhattan telephone book in thickness. Despite the importance of such works in establishing a complete picture of dinosaur diversity, I have had to be very selective, focusing on those papers readily available in most mid-sized research libraries, and concentrating on the most important and current literature available.

The subject index will serve to pull together the works on individual taxa that are scattered throughout the topical chapters. As always, the best place to start is with the reference lists from the most up-to-date available research papers discussing that taxon.

For each major taxon, Weishampel et al. (1990 [16]) is highly recommended as a starting point for research. The long-running *Bibliography of Fossil Vertebrates* [See 1–5] is also an invaluable research tool for locating articles on individual taxa.

The indexing journal *Zoological Record* can also help locate articles and books indexed under species, genera, family, or other taxonomic name, for both living and fossil reptiles. *Zoological Record* is arranged taxonomically; each separate volume has a complete set of indexes for all articles in a given year. You will need to use the annual volumes covering the Class Reptilia to locate articles on dinosaurs, pterosaurs, or other archosaurian reptiles.

Zoological Record is also recommended as a starting point for any research on modern animals such as birds, extant reptiles, and mammals, for comparison with dinosaurs. It is available online, through DIALOG and other computer search services, but is especially easy to use in its printed form, far easier than its counterpart *Biological Abstracts*.

The novice reader may be disappointed to discover that many animals traditionally discussed under the popular rubric "dinosaur", are not treated in this bibliography. This includes the pterosaurs, winged rulers of the Mesozoic skies, the ichthyosaurs and mosasaurs that dominated the oceans, and the sail-backed pelycosaurs, such as *Dimetrodon*, which are actually Permian reptiles not contemporary with dinosaurs.

GENERAL WORKS

270. Adams, D. 1987. The bigger they are the harder they fall: implications of ischial curvature in ceratopsian dinosaurs. In *Fourth Symposium on Mesozoic Terrestrial Ecosystems, Short Papers*, ed. P.J. Currie and E. Koster, 1–6. Drumheller, Alta.: Tyrell Museum of Paleontology.

    Ischial curvature in ceratopsians suggests that the animals were very vulnerable to clever predators. Ceratopsian species range from having little or no ischial curvature to showing strong curvature. Skull length and horn placement are both correlated with ischial curvature. The curvature functioned in a "tension circle" as a structural support mechanism. If a predator severed the ventral abdominal muscles, however, the head would have dropped, making the horns useless in defense.

271. Armstrong, W.G., L.B. Halstead, F.B. Reed, and L. Wood. 1983. Fossil proteins in vertebrate calcified tissues. *Philosophical Transactions of the Royal Society of London B* 301:301–343.

    An amino acid assay of several fossils from a variety of geological periods showed little intact collagen in Mesozoic fossils (including two dinosaurs). Racemization techniques were used to identify modern contaminants in the specimens. Concludes that "There seems little hope that direct study of the evolution of proteins based on fossil material can be achieved from analysis of the amino acid patterns alone."

272. Attridge, J.A., A.W. Crompton, and F. Jenkins. 1985. The southern African Liassic prosauropod dinosaur *Massospondylus* in North America. *Journal of Vertebrate Paleontology* 5:128–132.

    A skull of the prosauropod *Massospondylus*, discovered in the Kayenta Formation of the Glen Canyon Group (Arizona) is compared with that of *Plateosaurus*. The teeth confirm a herbivorous diet. *Massospondylus* was previously known only from Africa.

273. Barsbold, R. 1974. Saurornithoididae, a new family of small theropod dinosaurs from Central Asia and North America. *Palaeontologia Polonica* 30:5–22.

Proposes a new theropod family Saurornithidae for the genera *Saurornithoides* and *Stenonychosaurus*. These genera are removed from the Troödontidae; this family is of uncertain validity. Describes *Saurornithoides junior*, a new species which is somewhat larger than *S. mongoliensis*.

274. Barsbold, R. 1979. Opisthopubic pelvis in the carnivorous dinosaurs. *Nature* 279:792–793.

A short paper reporting on an opisthopubic pelvis (pubis parallel to the ischium) in some theropods. This condition is traditionally used to separate ornithischians and saurischians. This type is found in segnosaurids, dromaeosaurids and a new undescribed Mongolian theropod (possibly representing a new theropod family). Not strictly saurischian, this pelvic type supports dinosaur monophyly, and may have evolved several times in the early evolution of dinosaurs and birds.

275. Barsbold, R. 1988. A new Late Cretaceous ornithomimid from the Mongolian People's Republic. *Paleontological Journal* 22:124–127.

Describes *Anserimimus planinychus*, a new genus and species of Late Cretaceous ornithomimid from Mongolia. The unguals of the forelimb are flattened, a condition not typical of theropods. Mongolian ornithomimids are more anatomically and ecologically diverse than their American counterparts.

276. Barsbold, R., and A. Perle. 1980. Segnosauria, a new infraorder of carnivorous dinosaurs. *Acta Palaeontologica Polonica* 25:187–195.

Describes a new genus and species, *Erlikosaurus andrewsi*, from the Late Cretaceous of Mongolia. Together with *Segnosaurus galbinensis* and an indeterminate specimen of segnosaur, this new species defines a new infraorder of theropods called Segnosauria. The infraorder includes the single family Segnosauridae. Their morphology suggests a life style unlike that of typical bipedal predatory theropods. They lacked the usual theropod armament, and may have fed on fish.

277. Berman, D.S., and J.S. McIntosh. 1978. Skull and relationships of the Upper Jurassic sauropod *Apatosaurus* (Reptilia, Saurischia). *Carnegie Museum of Natural History Bulletin* 8:1–35.

The skull of *Apatosaurus* is similar to that of *Diplodocus*, and the two are closely related. The two genera are more closely related to one another than either is related to *Camarasaurus*. Discusses the history of the specimens, including Marsh's errors in restoration of *Apatosaurus*. *Apatosaurus*, *Diplodocus*, *Barosaurus*, *Cetiosaurus*, *Mamenchisaurus*, *Dicraeosaurus* and *Nemegtosaurus* are grouped together in a revised definition of the family Diplodocidae (*See also* McIntosh and Berman 1975 [138]).

278. Berman, D.S., and J.S. McIntosh. 1986. Description of the lower jaw of *Stegosaurus* (Reptilia, Ornithischia). *Annals of the Carnegie Museum* 55:29–40.

Describes a well-preserved lower jaw of *Stegosaurus*. Cranial remains of this species are relatively rare. The jaw represents a very primitive ornithischian grade.

279. Blows, W.T. 1988. The armoured dinosaur *Polacanthus foxi* from the Lower Cretaceous of the Isle of Wight. *Palaeontology* 30:557–580.

A new specimen of *Polacanthus foxi* from the Wealden Formation is a sub-adult, very similar in skeletal morphology to *Stegosaurus*. The genus *Polacanthus* is not synonymous with *Hylaeosaurus*, as previously suggested. *Polacanthoides ponderosus* is no longer a valid taxa. *P. foxi* is closely related to the American species *Hoplitosaurus marshi*, and the two species are probably synonymous. This would add to the growing list of Wealden fauna also found in the American Lakota Formation.

280. Bonaparte, J.F. 1979. Dinosaurs: a Jurassic assemblage from Patagonia. *Science* 205:1377–1379.

Reports an early discovery of South American dinosaurs. The Callovian-Oxfordian beds include *Piatnitzkysaurus floresi*, a new species of Megalosauridae related to *Allosaurus*, and two new species of sauropods, *Patagosaurus fariasi* and *Volkheimeria chubutensis*. This assemblage suggests a faunal interchange during the Jurassic between South American and other continents. (*See also* Bonaparte 1982 [209]; Bonaparte 1984 [210].)

281. Bonaparte, J.F. 1985. A horned Cretaceous carnosaur from Patagonia. *National Geographic Research* 1:149–151.

    A short note describing a nearly complete articulated skeleton of *Carnatosaurus sastrei*, a new Cretaceous carnosaur from northern Patagonia. This new species of Abelisauridae, with its prominent supraorbital horns, is very different from the Tyrannosauridae. Both families of predators probably evolved separately during the Cretaceous, after North and South America became separated at the end of the Jurassic.

282. Brinkman, D.B., and H.D Sues. 1988. A staurikosaurid dinosaur from the Upper Triassic Ischigualasto Formation of Argentina and the relationships of the Staurikosauridae. *Palaeontology* 30:493–503.

    A partial skeleton of *Staurikosaurus*, a very primitive dinosaur, is reported from Argentina's Ischigualasto Formation. Reviews the classification of the staurikosaurids, and presents a revised cladogram with *Staurikosaurus* and *Herrerasaurus* as sister taxa to the remaining ornithischians and saurischians.

283. Bryan, J.R., D.L. Frederick, D.R. Schwimmer, and W.G. Seisser. 1991. First dinosaur record from Tennessee: a Campanian dinosaur. *Journal of Paleontology* 65:696–697.

    Describes five bones from an adult hadrosaur. Though not diagnostic, even at the family level, they are the first dinosaur specimens identified from Tennessee.

284. Buffetaut, E. 1983. Mesozoic vertebrates from Thailand. In *Second International Symposium on Mesozoic Terrestrial Ecosystems*, ed. Z. Kielan-Jaworska and H. Osmólska, 43–53. *Acta Palaeontologica Polonica* 28 (1/2).

Reviews Mesozoic localities in Thailand, including fragmentary dinosaur material from the Khorat Group in northeastern Thailand.

285. Carpenter, K. 1982. Skeletal and dermal armor reconstruction of *Euoplocephalus tutus* (Ornithischia: Ankylosauridae) from the Late Cretaceous Oldman Formation of Alberta. *Canadian Journal of Earth Sciences* 19:689–697.

A restoration of the armor of *Euoplocephalus tutti* contradicts earlier restorations which show uniform rows of keeled plates. *Euoplocephalus* and the sympatric *Panoplosaurus* (Nodosauridae) show differences in muzzle shape that suggest partitioning of food resources, analogous to modern ungulates.

286. Carpenter, K. 1984. Skeletal reconstruction and life restoration of *Sauropelta* (Ankylosauridae: Nodosauridae) from the Cretaceous of North America. *Canadian Journal of Earth Sciences* 21:1491–1498.

A composite restoration of the Early Cretaceous nodosaurid *Sauropelta edwardsi* is based on several partial skeletons from the Cloverly Formation. Reviews earlier attempts at nodosaurid reconstruction. The feet of *Sauropelta* match those of the British Columbian species *Tetrapodosaurus borealis*, previously described as a ceratopsian but actually synonymous with *Sauropelta*. Bloating of the body after death could be the cause of the inverted position in which ankylosaurs are usually found. This position is rarely seen in Mongolian specimens, which are usually buried in dune deposits. Observations of road-killed armadillos in Mississippi support this hypothesis.

287. Charig, A.J., and A.C. Milner. 1986. *Baryonyx*, a remarkable new theropod dinosaur. *Nature* 324:359–361.

Describes *Baryonyx walkeri*, a rare Lower Cretaceous theropod from the Wealden Beds. (*See* also Galton 1973 [308].) It represents a new genus and a new family (Baryonychidae). A formidable 30 cm. claw associated with the skeleton may belong on either the forelimb or hindlimb. The predator may have weighed a ton or more.

288. Chatterjee, S. 1978. *Indosuchus* and *Indosaurus*, Cretaceous carnosaurs from India. *Journal of Paleontology* 52:570–580.

    Indosuchus raptorius is confirmed as a tyrannosaur; *Indosaurus matleyi* is a megalosaur. Both occur in the Lameta Group, and new material of *I. raptorius* is described. Three structural grades can be defined in tyrannosaurid evolution: the primitive grade (*Indosuchus*), the intermediate grade (*Albertosaurus* and *Daspletosaurus*), and the advanced grade, (*Tyrannosaurus* and *Tarbosaurus*).

289. Cobabe, E.A., and D.E. Fastovsky. 1987. *Ugrosaurus olsoni*, a new ceratopsian (Reptilia: Ornithischia) from the Hell Creek Formation of eastern Montana. *Journal of Paleontology* 61:148–154.

    A new ceratopsian, *Ugrosaurus olsoni*, is described from fragmentary remains. Several unique features of the snout establish it as a new genus of ceratopsian.

290. Colbert, E.H. 1970. A saurischian dinosaur from the Triassic of Brazil. *American Museum Novitates* 2405:1–39.

    A new genus and species of an early saurischian, *Staurikosaurus pricei*, is described from the Upper Triassic of Brazil. It is a small biped with sharp thecodontian teeth, which suggest an active predatory lifestyle. The genus is placed in the suborder Paleopoda. The infraorder Palaeosauria is renamed Teratosauria, and includes the families Ammosauridae, Teratosauridae, and Palaeosaurischidae (formerly Palaeosauridae).

291. Colbert, E.H., and D.A. Russell. 1969. The small dinosaur *Dromaeosaurus*. *American Museum Novitates* 2380:1–49.

Examines the type specimens of *Dromaeosaurus albertensis*, a small theropod from the Upper Cretaceous of Alberta. The species is placed in the new family Dromaeosauridae, which also includes *Velociraptor* and *Deinonychus*. The family is assigned to the infraorder Deinonychosauria, a new taxon intermediate between the infraorders Coelurosauria and Carnosauria.

292. Coombs, W.P. jr. 1978. Forelimb muscles of the Ankylosauria (Reptilia, Ornithischia). *Journal of Paleontology* 52:642–657.

    The forelimb muscles of *Euoplocephalus* are similar to those of modern crocodiles. *Sauropelta* has a relatively short forelimb moment arm, compared with other ankylosaurs. A fossorial habit is suggested for the ankylosaurs.

293. Coombs, W.P. jr. 1979. Osteology and myology of the hindlimb in the Ankylosauria (Reptilia, Ornithischia). *Journal of Paleontology* 53:666–684.

    Compares Ankylosaur pelvic morphology with that of several other ornithischians. Ankylosaurs had an unusual pelvic structure, in some respects more primitive than that of other ornithischians. It was unlike *Stegosaurus*, but shared some features with the pelvic structure of the pachycephalosaurid *Homalocephale*. Ossified tendons and well-developed tail musculature were used to swing the defensive bony tail club. Ankylosaurs were probably sluggish herbivores, and were possibly fossorial.

294. Crompton, A.W., and A.J. Charig. 1962. A new ornithischian from the Upper Triassic of South Africa. *Nature* 196:1074–1077.

    Describes *Heterodontosaurus tucki*, a new species from South Africa, and discusses its similarities to other primitive ornithischians.

295. Currie, P.J. 1989. The first records of *Elmisaurus* (Saurischia, Theropoda) from North America. *Canadian Journal of Earth Sciences* 26:1319–1324.

Elmisaurus elegans is described from the Upper Cretaceous of Dinosaur Provincial Park. The genus was previously known only from Mongolia. The holotype, originally designated *Ornithomimus elegans*, is redescribed as *E. elegans*. The specimen indicates that faunal interchange between Mongolia and North America was still occurring in the Late Cretaceous [*See* 296].

296. Currie, P.J., and D.A. Russell. 1988. Osteology and relationships of *Chirostenotes pergracilis* (Saurischia, Theropoda) from the Judith River (Oldman) Formation of Alberta, Canada. *Canadian Journal of Earth Sciences* 25:972–986.

    A new discovery of *Chirostenotes pergracilis* shows it to be synonymous with *Macrophalangia canadensis* and *Ornithomimus elegans* [*See* 295]. The genus is similar to *Elmisaurus* and *Oviraptor*. Elmisauridae is probably a junior synonym of Caenagnathidae. Its habit may have been an egg or mollusc-eating wader.

297. Czerkas, S.A. 1989. A reevaluation of the plate arrangement on *Stegosaurus stenops*. In *Dinosaurs Past and Present*, Volume II, ed. S.J. Czerkas and E.C. Olson, 82–99. Los Angeles: Natural History Museum of Los Angeles County.

    Reviews the history of *Stegosaurus* reconstructions, focusing on plate arrangements. The plates are properly placed in a single row, as O.C. Marsh once suggested, not in a double row as traditionally restored by several authorities and perpetuated in popular illustrations. (*See* also de Buffrénil et al. 1984 [422]; de Buffrénil et al. 1986 [423].)

298. DeCourten, F.L., and D.A. Russell. 1985. A specimen of *Ornithomimus velox* (Theropoda, Ornithomimidae) from the terminal Cretaceous Kaiparowits Formation of Southern Utah. *Journal of Paleontology* 59:1091–1099.

    A specimen of *Ornithomimus velox* is reported from the Kaiparowitz Formation, supporting the Late Cretaceous age assigned to this Formation. The fauna and biogeography of the area is discussed in relation to this discovery.

299. Dodson, P. 1980. Comparative osteology of the American ornithopods *Camptosaurus* and *Tenontosaurus*. *Mémoires de la Société Géologique de France* 139:81–85.

Contrasts the graviportal ornithopods *Camptosaurus* and *Tenontosaurus*, and discusses their evolutionary relationship. Dodson takes issue with Galton's emphasis on representation of Iguanodontidae as a grade (Galton 1972 [846]). *Camptosaurus* shares many traits with *Iguanodon* and *Ouranosaurus*, and these three genera form the monophyletic taxon Iguanodontidae. *Tenontosaurus*, on the other hand, resembles a primitive hypsilophodont.

300. Dodson, P. 1984. Small Judithian ceratopsids, Montana and Alberta. In *Third Symposium on Mesozoic Terrestrial Ecosystems, Short Papers*, ed. W.E. Reif and F. Westphal, 73–77. Tübingen: ATTEMPTO-Verlag.

Reports the discovery of juvenile ceratopsids from the Judith River Formation, as well as several juvenile hadrosaurs. The finds were made at a new Judith River Formation site at Careless Creek.

301. Dodson, P., and P.J. Currie. 1988. The smallest ceratopsid skull—Judith River Formation of Alberta. *Canadian Journal of Earth Sciences* 25:926–930.

A more complete description of the juvenile ceratopsian reported in Dodson (1984 [300]), the smallest known ceratopsian specimen.

302. Dodson, P., and J.H. Madsen jr. 1981. On the sternum of *Camptosaurus*. *Journal of Paleontology* 55:109–112.

The sternal plate of *Camptosaurus* is described and compared with *Tenontosaurus*. This plate, which languished in a drawer for nearly 100 years, does not add significantly to our knowledge of ornithopod phylogeny but reflects a serious taphonomic problem. Western North American Cretaceous dinosaurs are frequently found as solitary and highly articulated fossils, whereas Jurassic Morrison Formation specimens are usually found as disarticulated piles of bones.

303. Evans, S.E., and A.R. Milner. 1989. *Fulengia*, a supposed early lizard reinterpreted as a prosauropod dinosaur. *Palaeontology* 32:223–230.

Fulengia youngi, originally identified as an Upper Triassic lizard from China, is redescribed as a juvenile prosauropod dinosaur. *Fulengia youngi* is a junior synonym of *Lufengosaurus huenei*. Reviews the dinosaur fauna from the Lufeng Formation in Yunnan.

304. Forster, C.A. 1990. The postcranial skeleton of the ornithopod dinosaur *Tenontosaurus tilletti*. *Journal of Vertebrate Paleontology* 10:273–294.

Discusses *Tenontosaurus tilletti*, an ornithopod from the Cloverly Formation, using material collected from the Bighorn Basin. It was an abundant species, with over 80 known specimens. It was a robust bipedal herbivore, with limited quadrupedal locomotion, using its stiffened tail as a counterbalance. Reviews the systematics of *Tenontosaurus*, and presents a cladogram showing it to be a sister taxon to the higher iguanodonts and the Hadrosauridae. This contradicts earlier classification of *Tenontosaurus tilletti* as a hypsilophodontid.

305. Gallup, M.R. 1989. Functional morphology of the hindfoot of the Texas sauropod *Pleurocoelus* sp. indet. In *Paleobiology of the Dinosaurs*, ed. J.O. Farlow, 71–74. *Geological Society of America Special Paper* no. 238.

Examination of a complete left hind foot of the Lower Cretaceous sauropod *Pleurocoelus* shows possible adaptations for "scratch-digging". The specimen appears to have been trapped in quicksand, then set upon by small predators (*Deinonychus*). The claws on the sauropod's hind foot may have helped the animal find traction on a slippery mud substrate.

306. Galton, P.M. 1969. The pelvic musculature of the dinosaur *Hypsilophodon* (Reptilia: Ornithischia). *Postilla* 131:1–64.

Reviews the pelvic musculature, pubis, and femur of *Hypsilophodon*. The abdomen was fairly large, similar to that of modern ratite birds. The prepubic process did not provide the primary abdominal support.

307. Galton, P.M. 1970. The posture of hadrosaurian dinosaurs. *Journal of Paleontology* 44:464–473.

Hadrosaurs were bipedal. Thoracic and caudal vertebrae were held horizontally, as in many modern birds. Articulated skeletons show that the back was very straight, with a series of ossified tendons which would have inhibited arching or lateral flexing of the back and tail.

308. Galton, P.M. 1973. A femur of a small theropod dinosaur from the Lower Cretaceous of England. *Journal of Paleontology* 47:996–1001.

A short note on a rare find of a small Cretaceous theropod from the Wealden Beds. (*See also* Charig and Milner 1986 [287].)

309. Galton, P.M. 1974a. *Iliosuchus*, a Jurassic dinosaur from Oxfordshire and Utah. *Palaeontology* 19:587–589.

The ilia of *Iliosuchus incognitus*, a small theropod from the Middle Jurassic of Oxfordshire, shows similarities with the ilia of *Stokesosaurus clevelandi* from the Morrison Formation. This supports the hypothesized land bridge that connected North America and Europe during the Jurassic. *Stokesosaurus clevelandi* is renamed *Iliosuchus clevelandii*. (*See* Madsen 1974 [346]. *See also* Galton 1977 [221]; Galton 1980 [222]; Galton and Jensen 1975 [317]; Galton and Powell 1980 [318].)

310. Galton, P.M. 1974b. Notes on *Thescelosaurus*, a conservative ornithopod dinosaur from the Upper Cretaceous of North America, with comments on ornithopod classification. *Journal of Paleontology* 48:1048–1067.

Reviews material of *Thescelosaurus*, and reassigns it from Hypsilophodontidae to Iguanodontidae. *Thescelosaurus* was a graviportal ornithopod. *T. edmontonensis* is probably a junior synonym for *T. neglectus*.

311. Galton, P.M. 1975. English hypsilophodont dinosaurs. *Palaeontology* 18:741–752.

Reviews older material and new discoveries of hypsilophodonts from the British Jurassic and Cretaceous. Describes a new species of *Dryosaurus*, and reassigns some older material is to other taxa.

312. Galton, P.M. 1976a. Prosauropod dinosaurs (Reptilia: Saurischia) of North America. *Postilla* 169:1–98.

Reviews known specimens of North American prosauropods and their classification. *Anchisaurus* is a valid type genus. *Ammosaurus* is not a primitive coelurosaur, but a prosauropod. The quadrupedal prosauropods used small stones in a gastric mill to grind food. They were replaced by ornithischians possessing a more advanced and efficient feeding apparatus.

313. Galton, P.M. 1976b. The dinosaur *Vectisaurus valdensis* (Ornithischia: Iguanodontidae) from the Lower Cretaceous of England. *Journal of Paleontology* 50:976–984.

Reexamines a holotype and three specimens of *Vectisaurus valdensis* (Iguanodontidae) from the Wealden Beds of the Isle of Wight. There were at least six sympatric species of ornithopods in the Isle of Wight Wealden Beds, the most diverse non-hadrosaurian ornithopod fauna known.

314. Galton, P.M. 1985a. Notes on the Melanosauridae, a family of large prosauropod dinosaurs (Saurischia: Sauropodomorpha). *Geobios* 18:671–676.

Refutes earlier claims that various species of prosauropods from the lower Elliot Formation (Upper Triassic) are junior synonyms for *Euskelosaurus brownii*. Reviews material assigned to the family Melanosauridae, and retains the holotype *Melanosaurus readi*. Describes the new genus and species *Camelotia borealis*.

315. Galton, P.M. 1985b. British plated dinosaurs (Ornithischia; Stegosauridae). *Journal of Vertebrate Paleontology* 5:211–254.

Reviews all known species of British Stegosauridae. Reevaluates several species.

316. Galton, P.M., and Coombs, W.P. jr. 1981. *Paranthodon africanus* (Broom) a stegosaurian dinosaur from the Lower Cretaceous of South Africa. *Geobios* 14:299–309.

Because stegosaur cranial material is very rare, the Lower Cretaceous holotype *Paranthodon africanus* is particularly important. The new combination includes the previously designated *Palaeoscincus africanus* and *Paranthodon oweni*. Both names are based on material removed from *Anthodon serrarius*.

317. Galton, P.M., and J.A. Jensen. 1975. *Hypsilophodon* and *Iguanodon* from the Lower Cretaceous of North America. *Nature* 257:668–669.

Discovery of the European genera *Hypsilophodon* and *Iguanodon* in the North American western interior indicates that a land bridge joined the two continents at the end of the Jurassic. (*See also* Galton 1977 [221]; Galton 1980 [222]; Galton 1974a [309]; Galton and Powell 1980 [318].)

318. Galton, P.M., and H.P. Powell. 1980. The ornithischian dinosaur *Camptosaurus prestwichii* from the Upper Jurassic of England. *Palaeontology* 23:411–443.

Redescibes the holotype of *Iguanodon prestwichii* as *Camptosaurus prestwichii*, the only *Camptosaurus* known outside of North America. This supports a land bridge between North America and Europe during the Late Jurassic. (*See also* Galton 1977 [221]; Galton 1980 [222]; Galton 1974a [309]; Galton and Jensen 1975 [317].)

319. Galton, P.M., and H.D. Sues. 1983. New data on pachycephalosaurid dinosaurs (Reptilia: ornithischia) from North America. *Canadian Journal of Earth Sciences* 20:462–472.

Describes several pachycephalosaurid specimens from the Upper Cretaceous of North America, including two new genera, *Stygimoloch spinifer* (Hell Creek Formation), a fierce-looking species with spine-like projections on the squamosal, and *Ornatotholus browni* (Judith River Formation), with a "tuberculate ornamentation" on the skull roof. Discusses the possible function of the domed head in intraspecific combat.

320. Giffin, E.B. 1989. Notes on pachycephalosaurs (Ornithischia). *Journal of Paleontology* 63:525–529.

Several species of pachycephalosaurs have been synonymized under *Pachycephalosaurus wyomingensis*. Describes new specimens, with special reference to the braincase and to changes in dome shape with age. Dome allometry was well established by the time the dome had reached half its final adult length. Two basic dome morphologies probably represent male and female forms. *Stegoceras edmontonense* seems to have been sympatric with *P. wyomingensis* in the Hell Creek Formation.

321. Giffin, E.B. 1989. Pachycephalosaur paleoneurology (Archosauria; Ornithischia). *Journal of Vertebrate Paleontology* 9:67–77.

Pachycephalosaur endocranial casts show a reduction of pontine flexure angle, probably an adaptation to minimize damage from head butting in intraspecific male combat. Other cranial traits include large divergent olfactory bulbs, large olfactory nerves, and a somewhat expanded cerebrum.

322. Giffin, E.B., D.L. Gabriel, and R.E. Johnson. 1987. A new pachycephalosaurid skull (Ornithischia) from the Cretaceous Hell Creek Formation of Montana. *Journal of Vertebrate Paleontology* 7:398–407.

A new species of pachycephalosaur, *Stenotholus kohleri*, is described from the Maastrichtian beds of the Hell Creek Formation. It is apparently related to the genera *Prenocephale* and *Pachycephalosaurus*.

323. Gow, C.E. 1981. Taxonomy of the Fabrosauridae (Reptilia, Ornithischia) and the *Lesothosaurus* myth. *South African Journal of Science* 77:43.

A brief note discussing variation in dental morphology and tooth replacement in the Fabrosauridae, and cautioning researchers against basing taxonomic arguments on dental characters in this family until more information is available. *Lesothosaurus diagnosticus* is probably not a valid species.

324. Hallett, M. 1987. The scientific approach to the art of bringing dinosaurs to life. In *Dinosaurs Past and Present*, Volume I, ed. S.J. Czerkas and E.C. Olson, 97–113. Los Angeles: Natural History Museum of Los Angeles County.

    Restoration of dinosaurs calls for both scientific precision and artistic skill. Discusses basic problems in restoration, such as the coloration of dinosaur integument and hypotheses of dinosaur musculature, and reviews possible uses of computer models in reconstruction. (*See also* Knight 1947 [336]; Osborn 1898 [367]; Paul 1987 [379]; Russell 1987 [390].)

325. Hass, G. 1969. On the jaw musculature of ankylosaurs. *American Museum Novitates* 2399:1–11.

    Describes two skulls and mandibles of *Euoplocephalus* in the American Museum's collection. The skull musculature was relatively weak. This indicates, along with dental evidence, that this species fed on soft plant matter.

326. Heaton, M.J. 1972. The palatal structure of some Canadian Hadrosauridae (Reptilia: Ornithischia). *Canadian Journal of Earth Sciences* 9:185–205.

    Reviews the palatal structure of the Hadrosauridae and Lambeosauridae. Lambeosaurine crests may have functioned in vocalization as trumpeting devices. The position of the internal nares at the rear of the buccal cavity would have allowed hadrosaurs to breathe while chewing, an important consideration if the animals were truly endothermic. (*See* Norford 1973 [366] for a critique, including a sharp rebuttal from Heaton. *See* Hopson 1975 [726] for additional cross references on the structure and function of hadrosaur crests.)

327. Horner, J.R. 1979. Upper Cretaceous dinosaurs from the Bearpaw Shale (marine) of South-Central Montana with a

checklist of Upper Cretaceous dinosaur remains from marine sediments in North America. *Journal of Paleontology* 53:566–577.

Four specimens from the Bearpaw Shale are described and assigned to the genera *Hadrosaurus*, *Lambeosaurus*, and *Panoplosaurus*. A checklist of Upper Cretaceous dinosaurs from North American marine sediments shows that several hadrosaurs and nodosaurs were probably residents of marginal marine habitats. Half of the hadrosaurs in the checklist are juveniles.

328. Horner, J.R. 1983. Cranial osteology and morphology of the type specimen of *Maiasaura peeblesorum* (Ornithischia: Hadrosauridae), with discussion of its phylogenetic position. *Journal of Vertebrate Paleontology* 3:29–38.

Provides a detailed description *Maiasaura peeblesorum* (Horner and Makela 1979 [768]). The species is assigned to the subfamily Hadrosaurinae. Discusses the confusing phylogeny of the hadrosaurs. Although *M. peeblesorum* shares many primitive characteristics with the iguanodontids, it shows an advanced posterior nasal crest. During oceanic regressions, new lowland habitat resulted in a radiation of new hadrosaur species, with subsequent transgressions forcing many species into extinction or migration. Upland species, like *M. peeblesorum*, represent a more conservative evolutionary line than their lowland counterparts. (*See also* Cooper 1977 [192]; Hallam 1978 [196]; Weishampel and Horner 1987 [803].)

329. Horner, J.R. 1984. A "segmented" epidermal tail frill in a species of hadrosaurian dinosaur. *Journal of Paleontology* 58:270–271.

A short note describing a segmented hadrosaur frill impression, evidence that a segmented frill ran from near the base of the tail possibly up to the cervical region. The frill may have been used for visual displays.

330. Horner, J.R. 1988. A new hadrosaur (Reptilia, Ornithischia) from the Upper Cretaceous Judith River Formation of Montana. *Journal of Vertebrate Paleontology* 8:314–321.

A cladistic analysis of Hadrosauridae shows the family to be diphyletic. The two subfamilies should be elevated to family status (Hadrosauridae, Lambeosauridae). Describes a new species, *Brachylophosaurus goodwini*, based on a partial skull and skeleton from the Judith River Formation. This new species shows that the Judith River Formation fauna from Montana are distinctly different from the Judith River Formation fauna from Alberta.

331. Jain, S.L., P.L. Robinson, and T.K. Roy-Chowdhury. 1962. A new vertebrate fauna from the early Jurassic of the Deccan, India. *Nature* 194:755–757.

Most Lower Jurassic outcrops are marine sediments. The fauna described in this preliminary report represent a rare find of Lower Jurassic terrestrial vertebrates from the Kota Formation.

332. Jain, S.L., T.S. Kutty, T. Roy-Chowdhury, and S. Chatterjee. 1975. Sauropod dinosaur from the Lower Jurassic Kota Formation of India. *Proceedings of the Royal Society of London B* 188:221–228.

One of the earliest known sauropods, *Barapasaurus tagorei*, is described from India's Lower Jurassic Kota Formation.

333. Kennedy, W.J., H.C. Klinger, and N.J. Mateer. 1987. First record of an Upper Cretaceous sauropod dinosaur from Zululand, South Africa. *South African Journal of Science* 83:173–174.

Describes fragmentary remains of two sauropods, tentatively assigned to the family Titanosauridae. Sauropod fossils have only been reported once before from the Late Cretaceous of Africa.

334. Kermack, D. 1984. New prosauropod material from South Wales. *Zoological Journal of the Linnean Society* 82:101–117.

New prosauropod material is assigned to the genus *Thecodontosaurus*. The unknown species, probably juveniles of *T. antiquus*, was agile and probably bipedal, using its long tail for balance. The juveniles were probably drowned in a severe storm and washed into the cave where they were discovered.

335. Kielan-Jaworowska, Z. 1968. Results of the Polish-Mongolian palaeontological expeditions—Part I. *Palaeontologia Polonica* 19:1–191.

Three years of Polish-Mongolian exploration in western Mongolia and the Gobi Desert unearthed a wealth of new and significant fossils. No one had braved the rigors of the desert since the four famous expeditions of Roy Chapman Andrews in the 1920's, and three expeditions to many of the same sites in the late 1940's under the Russian J.A. Efremov. This inaugural volume of the first (1963–1965) Polish-Mongolian expedition's discoveries includes a fascinating narrative account of the expedition, the geology of several of the fossil sites, and six paleontological papers. Subsequent expedition reports cover several return visits to various sites. While many of the papers deal with Cenozoic mammals, there are also many significant dinosaur finds, including several carnosaurs. Later reports of the expedition appear in issues of *Palaeontologia Polonica*, and include: Part II, *Pal. Polon.* 21 (1970, 229 pp.); Part III, *Pal. Polon.* 25 (1971, 158 pp.); Part IV, *Pal. Polon.* 27 (1972, 143 pp); Part V, *Pal. Polon.* 30 (1974, 178 pp.); Part VI, *Pal. Polon.* 33 (1975, 200 pp.); Part VII, *Pal. Polon.* 37 (1977, 165 pp.); Part VIII, *Pal. Polon.* 38 (1978, 121 pp.); Part IX, *Pal. Polon.* 42 (1981, 179 pp.).

336. Knight, C.R. 1947. *Animal Anatomy and Psychology for the Artist and Layman*. New York: McGraw-Hill.

Instructions from the master, for would-be restoration artists. Knight's work was ahead of its time in many respects, and this short monograph remains a useful introduction to this marriage of art and science. (*See also* Osborn 1898 [367]; Hallett 1987 [324]; Russell 1987 [390]; Paul 1987 [379].)

337. Kues, B., T. Lehman, and J.K. Rigby jr. 1980. The teeth of *Alamosaurus sanjuanensis*, a Late Cretaceous sauropod. *Journal of Paleontology* 54:864–869.

Describes several sauropod teeth from *Alamosaurus sanjuanensis*, collected from the Late Cretaceous Fruitland and Kirtland Formations in the San Juan Basin. Briefly discusses the taxonomy of the species, which is closely allied to *Titanosaurus*.

338. Kurzanov, S.M., and A.F. Bannikov. 1983. A new sauropod from the Upper Cretaceous of Mongolia. *Paleontological Journal* 17:91–97.

Describes a new genus and species of Mongolian sauropod, *Quaesitosaurus orientalis*, based on a nearly complete skull. The very large middle ear cavity suggests sensitive hearing and a terrestrial habit. The weak jaw, however, implies that it fed on soft aquatic vegetation.

339. Langston, W. jr. 1967. The thick-headed ceratopsian dinosaur *Pachyrhinosaurus* (Reptilia: Ornithischia) from the Edmonton Formation near Drumheller, Canada. *Canadian Journal of Earth Sciences* 4:171–186.

The discovery of a *Pachyrhinosaurus* skull in the Red Deer River Valley extends the range of *P. canadensis*, previously known only from a restricted region in southern Alberta. The skull is well preserved, and bears a resemblance to *Centrosaurus*. *P. canadensis* should not be placed in the monotypic subfamily Pachyrhinosaurinae, as suggested by Huene. The species is characterized by a massive thickened nasal boss. The article is followed by two plates [*See* 340].

340. Langston, W. jr. 1968. A further note on *Pachyrhinosaurus* (Reptilia: Ceratopsia) from the Edmonton Formation near Drumheller, Canada. *Journal of Paleontology* 42:1303–1304.

Reexamination of the skull described in Langston (1967 [339]) removes a major taxonomic problem. The skull supports assigning the specimen to *Pachyrhinosaurus canadensis*, and allying the species with *Centrosaurus* and *Styracosaurus*.

341. Langston, W. 1975. The ceratopsian dinosaurs and associated lower vertebrates from St. Mary River Formation (Maestrichtian) at Scabby Butte, Southern Alberta. *Canadian Journal of Earth Sciences* 12:1576–1608.

Many specimens of *Pachyrhinosaurus* have been found at Scabby Butte. Summarizes the non-mammalian fauna and *Pachyrhinosaurus* specimens from the St. Mary River Formation. *Pachyrhinosaurus* is confirmed as a short-faced ceratopsian, with a spiked frill similar to *Styracosaurus*.

342. Lawson, D.A. 1976. *Tyrannosaurus* and *Torosaurus*, Maestrichtian dinosaurs from Trans-Pecos, Texas. *Journal of Paleontology* 50:158–164.

A maxilla of *Tyrannosaurus rex* and a fragment of frill from *Torosaurus utahensis* dates the Tornillo Group as Late Maastrichtian. Reports a revised diagnosis of *T. utahensis*.

343. Lehman, T.M. 1989. *Chasmosaurus mariscalensis*, sp. nov., a new ceratopsian dinosaur from Texas. *Journal of Vertebrate Paleontology* 9:137–162.

Describes *Chasmosaurus mariscalensis*, a new species of ceratopsian from the upper Aguja Formation (Late Campanian) in Big Bend National Park. The bone bed contains the disarticulated remains of ten to fifteen individuals, juvenile through adult. Sexual dimorphism is evident in browhorncore orientation. This large-horned species is similar to *C. canadensis* and to *Pentaceratops sternbergii*.

344. Lucas, S.G., and A.P. Hunt. 1989. *Alamosaurus* and the sauropod hiatus in the Cretaceous of the North American western interior. In *Paleobiology of the Dinosaurs*, ed. J.O. Farlow, 75–86. Geological Society of America Special Paper no. 238.

Although sauropods are present in Aptian/Albian sediments, they disappear from the western interior fossil record until the Maastrichtian, when *Alamosaurus sanjuanensis* reappears in inland basin deposits. The most likely scenario to explain this "sauropod hiatus" is that sauropods became extinct at the time of the late Albian marine regression, and later reinvaded from South America. Their disappearance may be part of a previously unrecognized terrestrial extinction event.

345. McIntosh, J.S. 1981. Annotated catalogue of the dinosaurs (Reptilia, Archosauria) in the collections of Carnegie Museum of Natural History. *Carnegie Museum of Natural History Bulletin* 18:1–67.

    A systematic catalog of an extremely important dinosaur collection, with detailed annotations and an appendix listing specimens by Carnegie Museum number.

346. Madsen, J.H. 1974. A new theropod dinosaur from the Upper Jurassic of Utah. *Journal of Paleontology* 48:27–31.

    A new genus of dinosaur, *Stokesosaurus clevelandi*, is described from two ilia and a premaxilla collected from the Upper Jurassic Morrison Formation. The species is tentatively placed in the family Tyrannosauridae. (*See also* Galton 1974a [309].)

347. Madsen, J.H. 1976. *Allosaurus fragilis*: a revised osteology. *Utah Geological and Mining Survey Bulletin* 109:1–51.

    Over ten thousand bones, representing at least sixty individuals of *Allosaurus fragilis*, have been recovered from the Late Jurassic Cleveland-Lloyd Dinosaur Quarry in Utah. Based on this extensive material, Madsen presents a revised osteology of this species, originally described by Marsh.

348. Maryańska, T. 1977. Ankylosauridae (Dinosauria) from Mongolia. *Palaeontologia Polonica* 37:85–151.

    Presents a revised diagnosis of the Mongolian Ankylosauridae. Describes two new genera and species, *Saichania chulsanensis* and *Tarchia kielanae*, from the Campanian Barun Goyot Formation. Discusses the distribution and habits of the Asiatic ankylosaurs, and the possibility of their independent evolutionary origin from the Pseudosuchia. A keen olfactory sense probably compensated for their sluggish and inefficient locomotion. Includes a chart of known

Mongolian ankylosaurs and their associated vertebrate fauna, with thirty-six plates.

349. Maryańska, T., and H. Osmólska. 1974. Pachycephalosauria, a new suborder of ornithischian dinosaurs. *Palaeontologia Polonica* 30:45–102.

   Describes new pachycephalosaurid material from the Upper Cretaceous of Mongolia, including three new genera and species, *Tylocephale gilmorei*, *Prenocephale prenes*, and *Homalocephale calathoceros*. On the basis of this material, a new suborder Pachycephalosauria is proposed. Discusses sexual dimorphism and life style of the pachycephalosaurids. Includes nine plates.

350. Maryańska, T., and H. Osmólska. 1975. *Protoceratops*idae (Dinosauria) of Asia. *Palaeontologia Polonica* 33:135–181.

   Discusses several specimens of Asian protoceratopsians uncovered by the various Mongolian expeditions, and reviews their phylogeny. Includes fifty plates.

351. Maryańska, T., and H. Osmólska. 1979. Aspects of hadrosaurian cranial anatomy. *Lethaia* 12:265–273.

   Reviews the cranial anatomy of hadrosaurs from specimens collected in the Upper Cretaceous Nemegt Formation, and specimens from the Paleontological Museum of the USSR Academy of Sciences. Focuses on the supraorbital bones, the possible function of fontanellae in the skull, and the function of circumnarial structures. Cranial crests probably evolved to serve some physiological function, and were secondarily adapted as display organs. (*See* Hopson 1975 [726] for additional cross references on the structure and function of hadrosaur crests.)

352. Maryańska, T., and H. Osmólska. 1981. Cranial anatomy of *Saurolophus angustirostris* with comments on the Asian Hadrosauridae (Dinosauria). *Palaeontologia Polonica* 42:5–24.

   Reviews and reevaluates all Asian hadrosaurs, and provides a supplemental description of *Saurolophus angusti-*

rostris based on new Mongolian material. The crest of this species probably served a thermoregulatory function. (*See* Hopson 1975 [726] for additional cross references on the structure and function of hadrosaur crests.)

353. Mateer, N.J. 1987. A new report of a theropod dinosaur from South Africa. *Palaeontology* 30:141–145.

    Describes a claw and two teeth from an unknown Late Jurassic or Early Cretaceous theropod, collected from two different formations in South Africa.

354. Molnar, R.E. 1974. A distinctive theropod dinosaur from the Upper Cretaceous of Baja California (Mexico). *Journal of Paleontology* 48:1009–1017.

    A new species of large theropod, *Labocania anomala*, is described from fragmentary remains from the Upper Cretaceous of Mexico. As its name implies, it is a somewhat aberrant form, about two-thirds the size of *Tyrannosaurus rex* and similar to certain Asiatic theropods.

355. Molnar, R.E. 1978. A new theropod dinosaur from the Upper Cretaceous of Central Montana. *Journal of Paleontology* 52:73–82.

    A fragmentary skull from the Hell Creek Formation is tentatively identified as a large dromaeosaurid.

356. Molnar, R.E. 1980. An *Albertosaurus* from the Hell Creek Formation of Montana. *Journal of Paleontology* 54:102–108.

    Tentatively identifies a small tyrannosaurid as *Albertosaurus lancensis*. The genus *Albertosaurus* was formerly named *Gorgosaurus*. *Albertosaurus* was faster than most tyrannosaurids, and smaller than the sympatric *Tyrannosaurus rex*.

357. Molnar, R.E. 1984. Ornithischian dinosaurs in Australia. In *Third Symposium on Mesozoic Terrestrial Ecosystems, Short Papers*, ed. W. Reif and F. Westphal, 151–156. Tübingen, Germany: Tübingen University Press.

Briefly surveys the Australian ornithischia, which includes only ankylosaurs and ornithopods. Both groups are restricted to Aptian or Albian strata. While the hypsilophodontids are similar to forms outside Australia, the iguanodontid and ankylosaur fauna show some distinctive differences.

358. Molnar, R.E., T.F. Flannery, and T.H.V. Rich. 1981. An allosaurid theropod dinosaur from the early Cretaceous of Victoria, Australia. *Alcheringa* 5:141–146.

    An astragalus from an unknown species of allosaurid extends the geographic range of the family Allosauridae to the Australian continent, and extends the family's evolutionary span into the Early Cretaceous. It is now unknown only in India and Antarctica.

359. Molnar, R.E., and P.M. Galton. 1986. Hypsilophodontid dinosaurs from Lightning Ridge, New South Wales, Australia. *Geobios* 19:231–239.

    Discusses seven partial femora of an Australian hypsilophodontid, probably *Fulgurotherium australe*. This is the first report of hypsilophodonts from Australia.

360. Molnar, R.E., and N.S. Pledge. 1980. A new theropod dinosaur from South Australia. *Alcheringa* 4:281–287.

    Describes a new genus and species of theropod, *Kakuru kujani*, based on fragmentary remains from South Australia.

361. Morris, W.J. 1973. A review of Pacific Coast hadrosaurs. *Journal of Paleontology* 47:551–561.

    Many fragmentary specimens of hadrosaurs have been collected from marine and near-marine sediments on the Pacific coast. Most are not identifiable below the subfamily level. Discusses the biogeography of North American hadrosaurs, and concludes that the Pacific coast species are similar to the western Canadian and eastern Montana forms. The observed distribution pattern may be partly due to competition, and partly to the regional distribution of habitats.

362. Morris, W.J. 1981. A new species of hadrosaurian dinosaur from the Upper Cretaceous of Baja California-? *Lambeosaurus laticaudas. Journal of Paleontology* 55:453–462.

As the question mark in the title indicates, this new species description is somewhat tentative. *Lambeosaurus laticaudas* is similar to *Hypacrosaurus* and *Corythosaurus*. The animal lived in a marine flood plain environment, and was primarily aquatic.

363. Newman, B.H. 1968. The Jurassic dinosaur *Scelidosaurus harrisoni*, Owen. *Palaeontology* 11:40–43.

Reconsiders the type species *Scelidosaurus harrisoni*, Owen. Owen used the bones of more than one genus in his original description; the new description is based solely on material that is obviously ornithischian.

364. Nicholls, E.L., and A.P. Russell. 1981. A new specimen of *Struthiomimus altus* from Alberta, with comments on the classificatory characters of Upper Cretaceous ornithomimids. *Canadian Journal of Earth Sciences* 18:518–526.

Describes a new specimen of *Struthiomimus altus* from the Oldman Formation. Reviews ornithomimid taxonomy, and concludes that the structure of the manus is the best characteristic separating the four recognized genera of Upper Cretaceous ornithomimids (*Struthiomimus, Ornithomimus, Dromiceiomimus* and *Gallimimus*).

365. Nicholls, E.L., and A.P. Russell. 1985. Structure and function of the pectoral girdle and forelimb of *Struthiomimus altus* (Theropoda: Ornithomimidae). *Palaeontology* 28:643–677.

The first description of the forelimb and pectoral girdle of the ornithomimid *Struthiomimus altus*. The structure of the pectoral girdle gave *Struthiomimus* an extensive reach. The manus probably functioned as a "hooking or clamping structure rather than a grasping or raking one," although what was being hooked or clamped is a mystery. Perhaps the forelimbs were used to grasp small branches or plant fronds to pull them within reach of the mouth. (*Note:* I believe that the forelimb structure of *Struthiomimus*, together with its lack of teeth, argues for a frugivorous habit along the lines suggested by H.F. Osborn (1916 [606]). Low angiosperm shrubs were contemporaneous, and fleshy fruits evolved at about this same period in the Late Cretaceous. (*See* the brief but interesting discussion in Norman 1985 [14].)

366. Norford, B.S. 1973. The palatal structure of some Canadian Hadrosauridae (Reptilia: Ornithischia): discussion. *Canadian Journal of Earth Sciences* 10:109–111.

 A brief note criticizing Heaton (1972 [326]) for omitting data on the locality, stratigraphic context, and age of the hadrosaur specimens cited. Followed by an acidic rebuttal from Heaton which supplies the missing information, along with some pointed remarks about the real purposes of a research paper. (*See* Hopson 1975 [726] for additional cross references on the structure and function of hadrosaur crests.)

367. Osborn, H.F. 1898. Models of extinct vertebrates. *Science* n.s. 7:841–84.

 An interesting early analysis of the problems of museum artwork, restoration, and model construction of dinosaurs, focused on the collection of the American Museum of Natural History. (*See also* Hallett 1987 [324]; Knight 1947 [336]; Paul 1987 [379]; Russell 1987 [390].)

368. Osmólska, H. 1974. New light on the skull anatomy and systematic position of *Oviraptor*. *Nature* 262:683–684.

 New specimens of *Oviraptor* discovered by the Polish-Mongolian expedition cast considerable doubt on *Oviraptor*'s classification as a dinosaur. It is more likely a primitive bird, and is assigned to the family Caenagnathidae. There is also some doubt as to whether this family as a whole are birds. Both *Oviraptor* and *Caenagnathus* may be a continuation of the line of theropods that gave rise to modern birds.

369. Osmólska, H. 1980. The Late Cretaceous vertebrate assemblages of the Gobi Desert, Mongolia. *Mémoires de la Société Géologique de France* 139:145–150.

Presents a preliminary description of three vertebrate assemblages from the Gobi Desert Late Cretaceous (Djadokhta Formation, Barun Goyot Formation, and Nemegt Formation). The Late Cretaceous Mongolian environment was drier and harsher than contemporary North American environments.

370. Osmólska, H., and E. Roniewicz. 1969. Deinocheiridae, a new family of theropod dinosaurs. *Palaeontologia Polonica* 21:5–19.

    Describes a new genus and species of carnosaur, *Deinocheirus mirificus*, from the Mongolian Upper Cretaceous. The unusually long and large forelimbs justify placing the species in a new family Deinocheiridae (superfamily Megalosauroidea).

371. Osmólska, H., E. Roniewicz, and R. Barsbold. 1972. A new dinosaur, *Gallimimus bullatus* n.gen. n.sp. (Ornithomimidae) from the Upper Cretaceous of Mongolia. *Palaeontologia Polonica* 27:103–143.

    Describes a new genus and species, *Gallimimus bullatus*, an ornithomimid from the Gobi Desert Upper Cretaceous. The short manus suggests that the forelimbs were used for finding food by "raking or dragging light material on the ground."

372. Ostrom, J.H. 1961. Cranial morphology of the hadrosaurian dinosaurs of North America. *Bulletin of the American Museum of Natural History* 122:35–186.

    This monograph examines the morphology and functional anatomy of the hadrosaur head and crest. Speculates that the crest functioned to improve olfaction. Hadrosaur vision and equilibrium were highly developed, and the dental batteries and general masticatory apparatus were remarkably sophisticated. Defines three subfamilies based on cranial anatomy: Hadrosaurinae (non-crested), Lambeosaurinae (true narial crests), and Saurolophinae (pseudo-narial crests). (*See* Hopson 1975 [726] for additional cross references on the structure and function of hadrosaur crests.)

373. Ostrom, J.H. 1962. The cranial crests of hadrosaurian dinosaurs. *Postilla* 62:1-29.

Despite long-standing interest in the impressive variety of hadrosaur crests, their function is still unknown. Previous hypotheses centered around their role as a snorkel or air reservoir for a presumed aquatic life style. Ostrom concludes that the crests acted to increase olfactory sensitivity by enlarging the surface area of the olfactory epithelium. (*See* Hopson 1975 [726] for additional cross references on the structure and function of hadrosaur crests.)

374. Ostrom, J.H. 1964. A functional analysis of jaw mechanics in the dinosaur *Triceratops*. *Postilla* 88:1-35.

The dominant theme in ceratopsian evolution has been the structural development of the feeding apparatus. Analyzes seven *Triceratops* skulls to determine dentition, dental occlusion, mandibular mechanics and musculature, and the functional anatomy of cranial structures such as the neck shield. The highly developed shearing dentition and powerful jaws of *Triceratops* imply that it fed upon very tough vegetable matter, such as palm fronds and cycads.

375. Ostrom, J.H. 1969. Osteology of *Deinonychus antirrhopus*, an unusual theropod dinosaur from the Lower Cretaceous of Montana. *Bulletin of the Peabody Museum of Natural History* 30:1-165.

This monograph thoroughly reviews the deadly predator *Deinonychus antirrhopus* ("terrible claw"), one of the most important discoveries in the renaissance of dinosaur studies. This agile and efficient theropod used its huge leg claws to rend its prey, leaping into the air to savage hapless herbivores, or balancing on one leg while attacking with the other. The animal may have hunted in packs, as it is often depicted in popular illustrations. Concurs with Colbert and Russell (1969 [291]) in elevating the subfamily Dromaeosaurinae to the family Dromaeosauridae. Places *Deinonychus* in this family. (*See* Bakker 1986 [417] for an interesting account of how this specimen influenced Ostrom's later work on the relationship between theropods and birds. *See also* [376].)

376. Ostrom, J.H. 1974. The pectoral girdle and forelimb function of *Deinonychus* (Reptilia: Saurischia): a correction. *Postilla* 165:1–11.

Revises the initial description of the pelvic girdle of *Deinonychus antirrhopus* (Ostrom 1969 [375]). A bone tentatively identified as a right pubis is actually a very large right coracoid. The unusual size of the bone is probably related to the use of the arms and hands in catching prey.

377. Ostrom, J.H. 1980. *Coelurus* and *Ornitholestes*: Are they the same? In *Aspects of Vertebrate History: Essays in Honor of Edwin Harris Colbert*, ed. L.L. Jacobs, 245–256. Flagstaff: Museum of Northern Arizona Press.

Coelurus and *Ornitholestes*, discovered by Marsh and Osborn respectively, have often been equated, though the specimens have never been compared. Concludes that they are not the same.

378. Padian, K. 1986. on the type material of *Coelophysis* Cope (Saurischia: Theropoda), and a new specimen from the Petrified Forest of Arizona (Late Triassic: Chinle Formation). In *The Beginning of The Age of Dinosaurs: Faunal Changes Across the Triassic-Jurassic Boundary*, ed. K. Padian, 45–60. Cambridge: Cambridge University Press.

A new specimen of *Coelophysis*, consisting of the pelvis and hindlimbs, prompts a review of the "relatively scrappy" type material for this small theropod dinosaur. Contrasts the traits of primitive theropods with more derived character states in this taxon.

379. Paul, G.S. 1987. The science and art of restoring the life appearance of dinosaurs and their relatives: a rigorous how-to guide. In *Dinosaurs Past and Present*, Volume II, ed. S.J. Czerkas and E.C. Olson, 4–49. Los Angeles: Natural History Museum of Los Angeles County.

Restoration is both a rigorous scientific discipline and an art form. Reviews aspects of skeletal anatomy, stance and gait, integument, and color, all of which must be considered in restoration. Discusses the use of living organisms as models. A thorough look behind the scenes of museum and illustrative restorations, with a comprehensive bibliography. *(See also* Hallett 1987 [324]; Knight 1947 [336]; Osborn 1898 [367]; Russell 1987 [390].)

380. Perle, A. 1985. Comparative myology of the pelvic-femoral region in the bipedal dinosaurs. *Paleontological Journal* 19:105–109.

Delineates three basic types of saurischian pelvic structure based on a review of bipedal dinosaurs: paleopods (brachyiliac structure); prepubic theropods (advanced erect gaits); and opisthopubic theropods (backwardly turned pubis). The latter type bears a strong resemblance to the pelvic structure of *Archaeopteryx*.

381. Rich, T.H.V., and P.V. Rich. 1989. Polar dinosaurs and biotas of the Early Cretaceous of southeastern Australia. *National Geographic Research* 5:15–53.

About one-hundred fifty taxa comprised the flora and fauna of south-central Victoria during the Early Cretaceous. The climate was generally cool and humid, with some seasonality. Juvenile dinosaurs were present, but not necessarily year round. The area was subject to polar nights of up to three months; temperatures may have dropped below freezing. Describes the new hypsilophodonts *Leaellynasaura amicagraphica*, *Atlascopcosaurus loadsi*, and *Fulgurotherium australe*. *(See also* Paul 1988 [439]; Hotton 1980 [727]; Davies 1987 [1018]; Brouwers et al. 1987 [1049]; Rich et al. 1988 [1083], for additional information concerning polar dinosaurs.)

382. Rothschild, B.M. 1988. Stress fracture in a ceratopsian phalanx. *Journal of Paleontology* 62:302–303.

A short note discussing traumatic fractures in Cretaceous dinosaurs. Describes a stress fracture in a ceratopsian phalanx, and the etiology of such fractures in modern animals.

383. Rothschild, B.M. 1990a. Absence of decompression syndrome in recent and fossil Mammalia and Reptilia. *Annals of the Carnegie Museum* 59:287–294.

Many fossil aquatic reptiles and mammals lack the characteristic necrosis that accompanies decompression syndrome. Apparently they had some physiological means of avoiding it. Although this study includes only non-dinosaurian reptiles, it provides a good starting point for research into Rothschild's increasingly important work in paleopathology [*See* 382, 384].

384. Rothschild, B.M. 1990b. Radiologic assessment of osteoarthritis in dinosaurs. *Annals of the Carnegie Museum* 59:295–302.

In the same issues as Rothschild 1990a [383], this short but intriguing article notes the lack of evidence for osteoarthritis in the one-hundred twenty one dinosaur species examined. Weight alone, with its resulting stress on bone structure, does not appear to induce arthritic symptoms.

385. Rowe, T. 1989. A new species of the theropod dinosaur *Syntarsus* from the Early Jurassic Kayenta Formation of Arizona. *Journal of Vertebrate Paleontology* 9:125–136.

This new species, *Syntarsus kayentakatae*, is the first specimen of this southern African genus found in North America. A member of the recently described theropod taxon *Ceratosauria* (Weishampel et al. 1990 [16]), this bird-like species joins several other species in establishing a similarity between African and North American Early Jurassic vertebrates.

386. Rowe, T., E.H. Colbert, and J.D. Nations. 1980. The occurrence of *Pentaceratops* (Ornithischia: Ceratopsia) with a description of its frill. In *Advances in San Juan Basin Paleontology*, ed. S.G. Lucas, J.K. Rigby, and B.S. Kues, 29–48. Albuquerque: University of New Mexico Press.

Pentaceratops is known from the Fruitland Formation (Late Cretaceous). The authors review the five substantial specimens and a handful of fragmentary remains, focusing on the structure and function of the frill.

387. Russell, D.A. 1969. A new specimen of *Stenonychosaurus* from the Oldman Formation (Cretaceous) of Alberta. *Canadian Journal of Earth Sciences* 6:595–612.

Discusses a disarticulated skeleton of *Stenonychosaurus inequalis* from the Oldman Formation. The skull indicates excellent vision and an avian grade of intelligence; the forelimbs show good manual dexterity. The species is closely related to *Saurornithoides*. The rarity of such finds in the Oldman Formation is probably related to the terrestrial habits of small theropods. Most of the Oldman Formation sediments are formed from freshwater deposition.

388. Russell, D.A. 1970. A skeletal reconstruction of *Leptosaurus gracilis* from the Upper Edmonton Formation (Cretaceous) of Alberta. *Canadian Journal of Earth Sciences* 7:181–184.

Reconstructs the small Late Cretaceous ceratopsian *Leptoceratops gracilis*, previously described by Brown and Sternberg. The species belongs to the family Protoceratosidae.

389. Russell, D.A. 1972. Ostrich dinosaurs from the Late Cretaceous of Western Canada. *Canadian Journal of Earth Sciences* 9:375–402.

Three Alberta genera, *Ornithomimus*, *Struthiomimus*, and *Dromiceiomimus*, make up the family Ornithomimidae. *Struthiomimus* is redefined. The ostrich dinosaurs were agile cursorial bipeds, similar in many respects to large modern cursorial birds like the ostrich or cassowary. Reviews known taxa and their distribution, and discusses their morphology, diagnosis, and habits. Their vision was very sharp, probably comparable to modern ratites. Russell suggests that they were carnivorous, perhaps insectivorous, on the basis of their association with the theropods. (*Note:* A conclusion with which I strongly disagree. *See* Nicholls and Russell 1985 [365].)

390. Russell, D.A. 1987. Models, paintings, and the dinosaurs of North America. In *Dinosaurs Past and Present*, Volume I, ed. S.J. Czerkas and E.C. Olson, 114–131. Los Angeles: Natural History Museum of Los Angeles County.

As a paleontologist who neither paints nor builds models, Russell must communicate his scientific ideas to those who can translate them into accurate artistic works. Discusses the controversial model of the hypothetical "dinosauroid", the logical evolutionary end-product of an intelligent reptilian biped. The dinosauroid is what dinosaurs might have evolved into in another 70 million years, if they had not suddenly gone extinct. (*See* [391]. *See also* Hallett 1987 [324]; Knight 1947 [336]; Osborn 1898 [367]; Paul 1987 [379].)

391. Russell, D.A., and R. Séguin. 1982. Reconstructions of the small Cretaceous theropod *Stenonychosaurus inequalis* and a hypothetical dinosauroid. *Syllogeus* 37:1–43.

Stenonychosaurus inequalis is an agile theropod with many bird-like qualities. The authors conjecture that if dinosaurs had not gone extinct, this type of small theropod might have given rise to a race of intelligent dinosaurs. Describes this hypothetical "dinosauroid". (*See also* Russell 1987 [390].)

392. Sahni, A. 1969. The vertebrate fauna of the Judith River Formation, Montana. *Bulletin of the American Museum of Natural History* 147:321–412.

A complete review of the (then known) Judith River Formation fauna, much of which consists of fish and amphibians.

393. Santa Luca, A.P., A.W. Crompton, and A.J. Charig. 1976. A complete skeleton of the Late Triassic ornithischian *Heterodontosaurus tucki*. *Nature* 264:324–328.

Describes the postcranial skeleton of *Heterodontosaurus tucki*, a primitive South African Late Triassic ornithischian, and contrasts it with *Fabrosaurus*. The species was a bipedal cursorial herbivore, with forelimbs adapted for grasping and tearing. It was too specialized to be an ancestral ornithopod.

Discusses the phylogeny of Triassic dinosaurs, and disagrees with Bakker and Galton's conclusion that dinosaurs are monophyletic (Bakker and Galton 1974 [824]).

394. Sanz, J.L., and A.D. Buscalioni. 1987. New evidence of armoured titanosaurs in the Upper Cretaceous of Spain. In *Fourth Symposium on Mesozoic Terrestrial Ecosystems, Short Papers*, ed. P.J. Currie and E. Koster, 197–202. Drumheller, Alta.: Tyrell Museum of Paleontology.

Describes a caudal vertebra and two osteoderms from the Upper Cretaceous of Spain that are assigned to *Titanosaurus*. The osteoderms suggest that this species of sauropod was at least partially armored.

395. Sereno, P.C. 1989. Pachycephalosaurs and ceratopsians (Ornithischia: Marginocephalia). In *The Age of Dinosaurs*, ed. K. Padian and D.J. Chure, 71–79. *Geological Society of America Short Courses in Paleontology* no. 2. Knoxville: The Paleontological Society.

Briefly describes the anatomy of the Marginocephalia, with notes on primary fossil finds and evolutionary relationships.

396. Sereno, P.C., and S. Chao. 1988. *Psittacosaurus xinjiangensis* (Ornithischia: Ceratopsia), a new psittacosaur from the Lower Cretaceous of northwestern China. *Journal of Vertebrate Paleontology* 8:353–365.

Describes a new species of psittacosaur, *Psittacosaurus xinjiangensis*, from one articulated skeleton and scattered remains of several other individuals. Psittacosaurs represent a small early radiation of ceratopsians, and have a relatively homogenous morphology.

397. Sereno, P.C., S. Chao, Z. Cheng, and C. Rao. 1988. *Psittacosaurus meileyingensis* (Ornithischia: Ceratopsia) a new psittacosaur from the Lower Cretaceous of Northeastern China. *Journal of Vertebrate Paleontology* 8:366–377.

Describes *Psittacosaurus meileyingensis*, a new species of psittacosaur. The skull is unusually tall relative to its length, and very broad across the postorbital region. The species was probably sympatric with *P. mongoliensis*.

398. Sues, H.D. 1978. New small theropod dinosaur from the Judith River Formation (Campanian) of Alberta, Canada. *Zoological Journal of the Linnean Society* 62:381–400.

    Describes a new genus and species of small theropod, *Saurornitholestes langstoni*, from the Upper Cretaceous of North America. The species is tentatively placed in the family Dromaeosauridae.

399. Sun, A.L., and K.H. Cui. 1986. A brief introduction to the Lower Lufeng saurischian fauna (Lower Jurassic; Lufeng, Yunnan, People's Republic of China). In *The Beginning of The Age of Dinosaurs; Faunal Changes Across the Triassic-Jurassic Boundary*, ed. K. Padian, 275–278. Cambridge: Cambridge University Press.

    A short but intriguing look at Lower Jurassic vertebrates from the Lower Lufeng Formation. Much important work is being done in China, although most of it is published in Chinese or in relatively obscure journals not indexed in this bibliography.

400. Thulborn, R.A. 1970a. The skull of *Fabrosaurus australis*, a Triassic ornithischian dinosaur. *Palaeontology* 13:414–432.

    Describes a skull of *Fabrosaurus australis* from the late Triassic Red Beds of Lesotho. The predentary bone confirms the species as an ornithischian, and other cranial features suggest it belongs in the Hypsilophodontidae, supporting a monophyletic origin for the ornithischians. Reviews ornithopod origins and phylogeny in light of this new specimen. Only a few characteristics of the skull are truly primitive, though *Fabrosaurus* can still be considered an archetypal ornithischian. There is a substantial gap between the ancestral thecodont and the earliest known ornithischians.

401. Thulborn, R.A. 1970b. The systematic position of the Triassic ornithischian dinosaur *Lycorhinus angustidens*. *Zoological Journal of the Linnean Society* 49:235–245.

Lycorhinus angustidens is reexamined using a new specimen. Formerly classified as a therapsid, it is redescribed as an ornithischian dinosaur, a member of the Hypsilophodontidae closely related to *Heterodontosaurus*. *Heterodontosaurus tucki* is an invalid junior synonym for *Lycorhinus tucki*.

402. Thulborn, R.A. 1972. The post-cranial skeleton of the Triassic ornithischian dinosaur *Fabrosaurus australis*. *Palaeontology* 15:29–60.

    Describes the post-cranial skeleton of the small cursorial biped *Fabrosaurus australis*, from the Upper Triassic Red Beds of Lesotho. Although *Fabrosaurus* is allied with primitive ornithischians, it has relatively few primitive characters. Briefly reviews the origins of the ornithischians from pseudosuchian thecodonts.

403. Thulborn, R.A. 1974. A new heterodontosaurid dinosaur (Reptilia: Ornithischia) from the Upper Triassic Red Beds of Lesotho. *Zoological Journal of the Linnean Society* 55:151–175.

    Describes a new species of ornithischian, *Lycorhinus consors*, from the Upper Triassic of South Africa. It is assigned to the family Heterodontosauridae. Briefly reviews the other family members, *L. angustidens*, *L. tucki*, and *Geranosaurus atavus*. *L. consors* lacks canine teeth. Reviews cheek teeth replacement in the heterodontosaurids. Tooth replacement probably occurred all at once, not gradually as in other ornithischians. Suggests that this family underwent seasonal aestivation, during which the teeth were completely replaced. Reviews ornithopod systematics. (*See* Hopson 1980 [627] for an opposing view. *See* Gow 1975 [625] for a critique.)

404. Thulborn, R.A. 1977. Relationships of the Lower Jurassic dinosaur *Scelidosaurus harrisonii*. *Journal of Paleontology* 51:725–739.

    Reviews the Lower Jurassic ornithischians of England. A reexamination of the type specimen of *Scelidosaurus harrisonii* reveals that it is not a stegosaur but a primitive graviportal ornithopod, tentatively assigned to the family Scelidosauridae. A specimen previously described as a juvenile *Scelidosaurus* is actually an ornithopod similar to *Fabrosaurus australis*, and probably directly descended from *Fabrosaurus*.

405. Tyson, H. 1981. The structure and relationships of the horned dinosaur *Arrhinoceratops* Parks (Ornithischia: Ceratopsidae). *Canadian Journal of Earth Sciences* 18:1241–1247.

    Revises the description of the type specimen of *Arrhinoceratops brachyops* Parks. Only *A. brachyops* can be assigned to this genus; its closest relative is *Torosaurus*. Criticizes the use of the stratigraphic position of isolated frill fragments in assigning species to these two genera.

406. Waldman, M. 1974. Megalosaurids from the Bajocian (Middle Jurassic) of Dorset. *Palaeontology* 17:325–339.

    Redescribes a specimen of *Megalosaurus bucklandi* (possibly a juvenile) as *Megalosaurus hesperis*. Describes *M. nethercombensis*, a new species. Discusses the taxonomy of the Megalosauridae.

407. Wall, W.P., and P.M. Galton. 1979. Notes on pachycephalosaurid dinosaurs (Reptilia: Ornithischia) from North America, with comments on their status as ornithopods. *Canadian Journal of Earth Sciences* 16:1176–1186.

    Although pachycephalosaurids are an aberrant type of ornithopod, a review of the domes of several specimens confirms that they truly are ornithopods. Describes a new species, *Stegoceras browni*, and a new genus, *Gravitholus albertae*, and discusses the endocranial casts and phylogeny of the Pachycephalosauridae. They share many characteristics with primitive ceratopsians, and may form a separate infraorder within the ornithopods.

408. Weishampel, D.B. 1981. The nasal cavity of lambeosaurine hadrosaurids (Reptilia: Ornithischia): comparative anatomy and homologies. *Journal of Paleontology* 55:1046–1057.

Reviews the structure of lambeosaurine nasal cavities, noting several homologies with living reptiles. *Parasaurolophus* shows significant differences in nasal cavity anatomy from the other lambeosaurine hadrosaurs. Discusses the ontogeny of the nasal cavity.

409. Weishampel, D.B., and P.R. Bjork. 1989. The first indisputable remains of *Iguanodon* (Ornithischia; Ornithopoda) from North America; *Iguanodon lakotaensis*, sp. nov. *Journal of Vertebrate Paleontology* 9:56–66.

    Iguanodon lakotaensis, described from the Lakota Formation of South Dakota, represents the first substantial find of this genus in North America. The specimen supports a close connection between Europe and North America during the Early Cretaceous (Barremian).

410. Weishampel, D.B., and J.A. Jensen. 1979. *Parasaurolophus* (Reptilia: Hadrosauridae) from Utah. *Journal of Paleontology* 53:1422–1427.

    Reports an indeterminate species of the genus *Parasaurolophus* from the Kaiparowits Formation. Briefly reviews the fauna from this formation; this is the first specimen that can be determined at the generic level.

411. Wilson, M.C., and P.J. Currie. 1985. *Stenonychosaurus inequalis* (Saurischia: Theropoda) from the Judith River Formation of Alberta: new findings on metatarsal structure. *Canadian Journal of Earth Sciences* 22:1813–1817.

    A partial foot of *Stenonychosaurus inequalis* from the Judith River Formation shows previously unrecognized features of the metatarsus. Similarities between bird and theropod metatarsal structure could be explained by evolutionary convergence.

412. Wyckoff, R.W.G., and F.D. Davidson. 1976. Pleistocene and dinosaur gelatins. *Comparative Biochemistry and Physiology B* 55:95–97.

    Describes techniques for extracting fossil proteins from dinosaur bones and other fossil material.

Iguanodon may have used its spiked thumbs to defend itself against predators. From *Archosauria: A New Look at the Old Dinosaur* by John C. McLoughlin. Copyright © 1979 by John C. McLoughlin. Used by permission of Viking Penguin, a division of Penguin Books USA Inc.

Chapter Five

Warm-Blooded Dinosaurs

Were dinosaurs sluggish, lumbering, cold-blooded brutes? Or were they agile and active, capable of breaking into a trot or even a full gallop? Were they cold-blooded reptilian beasts, or the warm-blooded "dancing dinosaurs" reconstructed by R.T. Bakker (Bakker 1987 [464])?

The controversy dates back to a series of articles by Bakker in which he developed the theory that dinosaurs had endothermic metabolisms more like modern mammals than modern reptiles. He presented several lines of evidence to support this heretical notion (Bakker 1971a [413]; 1972 [414]; 1975 [447]; 1980 [416]).

Bakker argued that, if dinosaurs were endothermic, the ratio of predators to prey in the fossil record should be similar to that calculated for a modern community of endothermic carnivores and herbivores, like that of the Serengeti plain. He also cited several lines of anatomical evidence for endothermy, including the fully erect gait of dinosaurs (an evolutionarily advanced condition), the histology of dinosaur bone, and the possible presence of a network of air sacs with a thermoregulatory function.

The ensuing lively debate reached a crescendo in 1980 with the symposium *A Cold Look at the Warm-blooded Dinosaurs* sponsored by AAAS (Thomas and Olson 1980 [445]). Several of the papers from this fruitful conference are annotated in this chapter.

Part of the argument revolves around the definition of thermoregulatory terminology. What exactly do we mean by warm-blooded? The student is confronted by a bewildering array of terms such as endotherm, homeotherm, ectotherm, poikilotherm, and so forth, which are often used as if they were identical in meaning. Bakker disdains this game of "thermal semantics" (Bakker 1974 [415]; Feduccia 1973 [428]).

Terminology, however, forms the basis of every discipline; arguments over terms are arguments over basic theoretical ideas. The reader will find that Ostrom 1980 [438] provides a glossary nicely summarizing the language of thermoregulation.

For our present purpose, endothermy means that the animal is capable of maintaining a constant body temperature in the face of environmental fluctuations, by means of physiological (i.e. hormonal and neural) control of metabolic heat.

Ectothermic animals, on the other hand, can often keep their internal temperatures fairly stable, but only by means of complex behavioral thermoregulation, including such behaviors as basking at a particular angle to the sun, seeking shade or entering the water at a particular time of day and so forth (Colbert et al. 1946 [553]; Greenberg 1980 [556]; Huey and Pianka 1977 [558]; Loveridge 1984 [561]; Smith 1979 [572]). Ectotherms rely on external radiant heat sources rather than on internal metabolic heat, and lack the physiological mechanisms to compensate for changes in ambient temperature.

Very large ectotherms, however, may have had most of the benefits of endothermy, while retaining the ability to exploit an adaptive zone that true endotherms could not invade (Pough 1980 [568]; Paladino et al. 1990 [564]). For example, ectotherms can reduce food intake and lower body temperatures for extended periods of time until environmental conditions improve.

For ectotherms the size of dinosaurs, large size would, by itself, have conferred a fairly stable high body temperature. Small animals have a large surface area/volume ratio, while large animals have relatively less surface area in proportion to their larger volume (Baur and Freidl 1980 [418]). Such allometric relationships are explored further in Chapter Six. As experiments with alligators and other animals have shown, large ectotherms heat more slowly, but retain heat better due to their larger size (Bell 1980 [550]; Colbert et al. 1946 [553]).

Large ectothermic dinosaurs could have remained active for extended periods of time before needing to "recharge" by basking (Benton 1979 [420]; McGowan 1979 [434]; Spotila 1980 [443]; Spotila et al. 1973 [444]; McNab and Auffenberg 1976 [563]). This inertial homeothermy may have characterized the giant sauropods like *Apatosaurus* and *Diplodocus*. Immense fermentation chambers might have contributed to the sauropod internal furnace (Farlow 1987a [618]; Hungate 1975 [630]; McBee 1971 [634]).

Endothermic carnivores, like lions, tigers, and bears, need more food to sustain their higher metabolic rates and complex nervous systems. Ectothermic carnivores, on the other hand, can get by with much less. We would expect, therefore, that the predator-to-prey ratios in fossil communities would differ significantly for endothermic or ectothermic communities.

Bakker claims that predator/prey ratios based on a census of fossil communities definitely indicates endothermic dinosaurs (Bakker 1975 [447]; 1980 [416]). But Russell, Béland, Tracy, and Farlow have poked gaping holes into what seems at first to be a sublime example of sound paleoecological thought. Calculating predator/prey ratios has many pitfalls (Farlow 1980 [450]; 1983 [451]).

Suppose that tyrannosaurs ate the young of other carnivores, or even devoured their own young (Tracy 1976 [453]; Delaney and Abercrombie 1986 [555]; Pough 1973 [567]). This secondary carnivory would greatly influence the model Bakker uses to calculate predator/prey ratios. It is also difficult to quantify (even today) the amount of wastage that predators leave behind. We can reason only by analogy with modern reptiles or mammals, as is often the case in dinosaur biology.

Another possibility is that dinosaur hunters may have selectively collected the more spectacular large carnivores, ignoring the tawdry disarticulated remains of herds of herbivores (Bakker 1972 [414], Farlow 1976a [593]). Preservation itself may favor either carnivores or herbivores in certain situations. Béland and Russell discuss these problems in detail, along with a multitude of other methodological difficulties in determining fossil predator/prey ratios (Béland and Russell 1979 [448]; 1980 [449]).

Erect stance and rapid gait have also been cited by Bakker and others as evidence of endothermy. This argument usually begins with data from footprints or entire trackways of prints, which provide us with the only evidence we will ever have of dinosaurs in motion. (*See* Trackways [492–516]; Lockley and Conrad 1987 [602]; Lockley et al. 1986 [603].) Bakker's arguments about posture and gait are more convincing than his hypothesis concerning predator/prey ratios.

A fully-erect stance is a significant evolutionary advance, and is associated today with active endothermic animals like mammals and birds. Reptiles generally have low stamina. Their sprawling gait makes it mechanically difficult to run and breathe at the same time. Bursts of speed are energetically very costly for modern reptiles. They have circumvented this constraint by increased reliance on anaerobic metabolism for muscular energy, or by adopting passive defensive strategies. Dinosaurs circumvented this same mechanical constraint by evolving a fully-erect stance, a posture which enabled them to move efficiently and rapidly (Carrier 1987 [465]).

In a curious interdisciplinary twist, R. McNeill Alexander has applied formulas derived for building wooden ships to the mechanics of dinosaur locomotion (Alexander 1976 [454]; 1977 [455]; 1983 [456]; 1985 [457]; 1989 [459]). The dimensionless Froude number relates the behavior of scale model ships to real ships travelling at real speeds.

Alexander extended this nautical dynamic similarity hypothesis to animals in motion. The model predicts that geometrically similar animals of different sizes will use dynamically similar gaits whenever their relative speed makes their Froude numbers equal, a prediction that turns out to be true for animals larger than a cat.

Froude numbers and stride lengths from trackways can be used to estimate dinosaur speeds. *Apatosaurus* turns out to be quite agile for its size, roughly equivalent to an elephant in its locomotory abilities. *Diplodocus* is a bit more of a plodder. *Triceratops*, however, could probably keep pace with a charging rhinoceros. Alexander 1991 [460] is recommended for a general introduction to the fascinating study of paleo-biomechanics. There is, of course, much disagreement over just how fast dinosaurs could move (Kool 1981 [476]; Thulborn 1981 [487]; 1982 [488]; 1984 [489]; 1989 [490]; 1990 [515]). Farlow 1981 [498]; Coombs 1978 [588]).

Another argument for warm-blooded dinosaurs is the brain/body size ratio of dinosaurs. The pre-1970 popular image of dinosaurs as lumbering pinheads does have a certain degree of truth. Their brains were small in relation to their body size. However Hopson and Jerison argue that dinosaur brains were of normal size for their body size when compared to modern reptiles (Hopson 1977 [521]; 1980 [522]; Jerison 1969 [524]). Dinosaur intelligence ranged from the large-brained coelurosaurs to the ponderous, dull, cud-chewing stegosaurs and ankylosaurs (Gould 1978 [520]).

Finally, the presence of Haversian canals in dinosaur bones may imply an endothermic metabolism (Bakker 1972 [414]). Haversian canals in modern mammalian bone carry large blood vessels. Highly vascularized bone may be an indication of an endothermic metabolism.

On the other hand, bone histology may simply reflect rapid growth to a large size (Reid 1978 [440]; 1981 [539]; 1983 [540]; 1984a [541]; 1984b [542]; 1985 [543]; 1987 [544]; de Ricqlès 1974 [545]; de Ricqlès 1980 [546]; de Ricqlès 1983 [547]). Some researchers also point to the smoothness of dinosaur teeth, which lack the seasonal growth rings that form in the teeth of ectotherms. Others have claimed that these growth rings do exist, and that they support ectothermic dinosaurs (Bolt and DeMar 1980 [531]; Johnston 1979 [534]; 1980 [535]; Meinke et al. 1980 [536]; de Ricqlès 1980 [546]; 1983 [547]).

In one sense, at least, the debate over dinosaur thermoregulation shows the best face of modern science. The hot-blooded dinosaur debate has been a powerful goad to productive research in several fields. Despite our inability to ultimately resolve the question, an enormous amount of thought and research has been generated by both sides in this controversy.

Given the complexity of dinosaur biology, it may be wishful thinking to maintain that dinosaurs were all endothermic or all ectothermic. The truth, as truths often do, lies somewhere in between. Certainly the coelurosaurs, ornithomimids and advanced theropod dinosaurs were endothermic, whereas the large sauropods were probably inertial homeotherms. Other dinosaurs would probably have had a level of endothermy intermediate between modern reptiles and mammals.

Some of the most exciting research on dinosaur biology starts with an examination of extant mammals, birds or reptiles. The importance of such studies is emphasized in this chapter by a section devoted to thermoregulation in modern reptiles [*See* 548–576]. Chapter Six surveys research comparing dinosaurs with modern mammals. Chapter Eight covers similarities between dinosaurs and birds.

Comparisons with modern animals, however, must be made cautiously. Dinosaurs were unique animals. They were neither mammals nor reptiles nor birds. They were a form of life never seen before on Earth, and witnessed now only as ghosts and bones.

ENDOTHERM OR ECTOTHERM

413. Bakker, R.T. 1971a. Dinosaur physiology and the origin of mammals. *Evolution* 25:636-658.

    A seminal paper, challenging the prevalent view that dinosaurs were ectotherms. Reviews the evolution of limb length and gait, from the primitive sprawling condition, through the semi-erect gait, to the fully-erect gait of dinosaurs and modern mammals. Fully-erect gaits are associated with the high activity levels characteristic of endotherms. (*See* Carrier 1987 [465].) High activity levels, in turn, create high levels of internal heat, and there is evidence to suggest that dinosaurs were adapted to shed this high heat load. Endothermy in the absence of external insulation like hair or feathers could also explain why there are no very small dinosaurs (under about 3 meters). The only niche available to mammals was precisely the one they occupied, small-bodied nocturnal foragers. Nocturnal habits provided selective pressure for endothermy and insulation. (*See* Crompton et al. 1978 [424]; Bakker 1974 [415].)

414. Bakker, R.T. 1972. Anatomical and ecological evidence of endothermy in dinosaurs. *Nature* 238:81-85.

    An early marshalling of arguments in the endothermy debate. Bakker summarizes his evidence concerning gait, metabolism, bone structure, and predator/prey ratios in the fossil record. Dinosaurs, like modern birds, possessed a network of air sacs to aid in thermoregulation. (*See* Thulborn 1973 [452] for a critique. *See also* Bouvier 1977 [532] for a critique of Bakker's argument for an endothermic bone histology.)

415. Bakker, R.T. 1974. Dinosaur energetics: a reply to Bennet and Dalzell, and Feduccia. *Evolution* 28:497-503.

    Replies to strong criticism of his earlier paper (Bakker 1971a [413]) by Bennet and Dalzell (1973 [419]) and Feduccia (1973 [428]). In a passage somewhat reminiscent of Cope and Marsh, he states that his opponents "consistently distort and misrepresent my arguments." Restates his evidence in light of the two critiques cited.

416. Bakker, R.T. 1980. Dinosaur heresy—dinosaur renaissance: why we need endothermic archosaurs for a comprehensive theory of bioenergetic evolution. In *A Cold Look at the Warm-blooded Dinosaurs*, ed. R.D.K. Thomas and E.C. Olson, 351–462. Washington: AAAS.

A lengthy defense of endothermic dinosaurs, and an excellent introduction to the arguments. Bakker dismisses the idea that mammals were serious competitors of dinosaurs. The opposite was true. He admires (but refutes) Spotila's "Good Reptile" model (Spotila 1980 [443]), and thoroughly reviews the evolutionary advantages of endothermy, even in tropical climates. Limb anatomy restricted most dinosaurs to walking or running over flat surfaces, a niche occupied today by terrestrial carnivores and ungulates.

417. Bakker, R.T. 1986. *The Dinosaur Heresies: New Theories Unlocking the Mystery of the Dinosaurs and Their Extinction.* New York: William Morrow.

A semi-popular account of his "heretical" views on dinosaur metabolism, featuring the author's own illustrations. Includes interesting speculations about sexual selection in dinosaurs and the coevolution of herbivorous dinosaurs and flowering plants.

418. Baur, M.E., and R.R. Freidl. 1980. Application of size-metabolism allometry to therapsids and dinosaurs. In *A Cold Look at the Warm-blooded Dinosaurs*, ed. R.D.K. Thomas and E.C. Olson, 253–286. Washington: AAAS.

Dinosaur evolution must have been constrained by simple physical laws, such as allometric scaling. Dinosaurs were probably not endothermic, based on an analysis of size/metabolism allometry in therapsids and dinosaurs. Endothermy is suitable for the mammalian size range, but not for dinosaurs, who showed an opposite evolutionary trend toward larger and larger sizes.

419. Bennett, A.F., and B. Dalzell. 1973. Dinosaur physiology: a critique. *Evolution* 27:170–174.

Refutes Bakker (1971a [413]), which "contains numerous factual errors, contradictions, and logical faults." Heliothermic homeothermy (e.g. sun basking) is sufficient to maintain a high activity level. Accuses Bakker of an "inadequate analysis of the biomechanics of fossil and contemporary vertebrates" and of failing to establish "a physiological connection between homeothermy, metabolism, and posture." Anticipates Alexander's later work by calling for further research into the dynamics of locomotion to help settle the issue. (*See* Alexander 1976 [454].)

420. Benton, M.J. 1979. Ectothermy and the success of dinosaurs. *Evolution* 33:983–997.

Larger dinosaurs were probably not endotherms, but inertial homeotherms. The generally warm Mesozoic climate was suitable for large ectotherms. Endothermy is not evolutionarily superior to ectothermy in all environments. Ectothermy might help explain why dinosaurs became extinct as the Mesozoic climate cooled.

421. Brink, A.S. 1980. The road to endothermy—a review. *Mémoires de la Société Géologique de France* 139:29–38.

Summarizes the thermal evolution of mammals based on the author's study of *Diademodon*, a possibly endothermic cynodont. Mammalian endothermy is a means to an end, crossing the "thermal barrier" to achieve independence from environmental fluctuations. Avian endothermy, on the other hand, is a consequence of the avian way of life. Reviews the classification of the Synapsida, and proposes raising Reptilia to a Superclass, elevating several reptilian subclasses to class status.

422. de Buffrénil, V., J.O. Farlow, and A. de Ricqlès. 1984. Histological data on structure, growth and possible functions of *Stegosaurus* plates. In *Third Symposium on Mesozoic Terrestrial Ecosystems, Short Papers*, ed. W. Reif and F. Westphal, 31–36. Tübingen: ATTEMPTO-Verlag.

Detailed examination of a plate from *Stegosaurus stenops* indicates that growth was primarily limited to the basal portion of the plate. Plates were covered in life by soft tissue, and were vertical, not horizontal as recently reconstructed. The best hypothesis for their function is Farlow's previous suggestion that they acted to dissipate heat through forced convection. (*See* Farlow et al. 1976 [427]. *See also* [423].)

423. de Buffrénil, V., J.O. Farlow, and A. de Ricqlès. 1986. Growth and function of *Stegosaurus* plates: evidence from bone histology. *Paleobiology* 12:459–473.

    Histological examination of *Stegosaurus* plates suggests that they served primarily in thermoregulation, not defense. Plates were held erect, and were probably covered by soft tissues. Discusses several alternate functional hypotheses, of which the thermoregulatory hypothesis is the most robust. *Stegosaurus* was probably an ectotherm [*See* 422].

424. Crompton, A.W., C.R. Taylor, and J.A. Jagger. 1978. Evolution of homeothermy in mammals. *Nature* 272:333–336.

    Mammalian endothermy evolved in two steps. The first step was the exploitation of the vacant nocturnal insectivorous niche. The first primitive mammals could thrive in this niche at lower body temperatures. Several taxa later independently evolved higher body temperatures and more efficient thermoregulation. Modern nocturnal insectivores (tenrecs, setifers, and hedgehogs) have retained "reptilian-type energetics." Discusses the possibility of endothermy in therapsids. (*Note:* This is particularly interesting in light of possible competition between mammals and dinosaurs. Mammals may have been forced into this nocturnal niche by their inability to compete effectively with diurnal dinosaurs. *See also* Bakker 1971a [413].)

425. Desmond, A.J. 1976. *The Hot-Blooded Dinosaurs: A Revolution in Palaeontology*. New York: Dial Press.

    An entertaining popularization of the endothermy controversy, with an emphasis on the intellectual history of the idea. Contains an excellent chapter on the Victorian dinosaur and extensive material on *Archaeopteryx, Pterodactylus,* and *Pteranodon.* Includes a glossary and references. (*See also* Silverberg 1981 [442].)

426. Dodson, P. 1974. Dinosaurs as dinosaurs. *Evolution* 28:494–497.

Accompanies Bakker 1974 [415] and joins the attack on Feduccia's rebuttal of Bakker's endothermic dinosaurs (Bakker 1971a [413]; Feduccia 1973 [428]). Dinosaurs were not mammals, but this does not make their adaptations automatically inferior, a view Dodson label a "therian-chauvinist attitude". Dinosaurs represent an alternative but effective evolutionary solution to many of the same problems faced by primitive mammals. (*See also* Greenberg 1980 [556].)

427. Farlow, J.O., C.V. Thompson, and D.E. Rosner. 1976. Plates of the dinosaur *Stegosaurus*: forced convection heat loss fins? *Science* 192:1123–1125.

Wind tunnel experiments suggest that *Stegosaurus* plates functioned as forced convection heat exchanger fins. (*See also* de Buffrénil et al. 1984 [422]; 1986 [423]; Greenberg 1980 [556].)

428. Feduccia, A. 1973. Dinosaurs as reptiles. *Evolution* 27:166–169.

Attacks Bakker's "extreme views" on endothermy, as well as those of Ostrom (Bakker 1971a). Distinguishes between ectotherm and poikilotherm, and between homeotherm and endotherm. Accuses Bakker of not defining his terms, and confusing them with one another, a charge that Bakker will later disparage as "thermal semantics" (Bakker 1974 [415]). There was no selective pressure for dinosaurian endothermy, because the Mesozoic climate was warm and stable.

429. Feduccia, A. 1974. Endothermy, dinosaurs, and *Archaeopteryx. Evolution* 28:503–504.

A refutation (in the same issue) of Bakker and Dodson's rebuttal of Feduccia's critique of Bakker's hypothesis (Bakker

1971a [413]; 1974 [415]; Dodson 1974 [426]; Feduccia 1973 [428]). In academia, a good argument is worth its weight in reprints.

430. Folinsbee, R.E., P. Fritz, H.R. Krouse, and A.R. Robblee. 1970. Carbon-13 and Oxygen-18 in dinosaur, crocodile, and bird eggshells indicate environmental conditions. *Science* 168:1353–1356.

Compares C^{13} and O^{18} in dinosaur eggs with the same isotopes in the eggs of living and fossil birds and living crocodiles. Similar environments produce similar isotopic composition of the eggshells.

431. Heinrich, B. 1977. Why have some animals evolved to regulate a high body temperature? *American Naturalist* 111:623–640.

Explores the relation between body temperature, thermoregulation, metabolic rates, and activity patterns. Questions why body temperatures in endotherms evolved set points higher than ambient temperatures. Set points allow for greater enzyme efficiency. They may have evolved from the need to maintain optimal physiological performance under sustained high temperatures due to increased activity levels.

432. Hohnke, L.A. 1973. Haemodynamics in the Sauropoda. *Nature* 244:309–310.

Giraffes have a vertical profile similar to that of sauropod dinosaurs, and have a high blood pressure equal to 125/75 cardiac arterial pressure in a standing giraffe. Measurements of a mounted *Apatosaurus* and *Brachiosaurus* yields crude estimates of their blood pressures, which turn out to be extremely high (216 mm Hg and 568 mm Hg mean arterial pressure respectively). (*See also* Seymour 1976 [441].)

433. Karasov, W.H., and J.M. Diamond. 1985. Digestive adaptations for fueling the cost of endothermy. *Science* 228:202–204.

Mammals process the same diet ten times faster than lizards of the same size eating the same diet (alfalfa pellets), and process it with the same or greater extraction efficiency.

Mammals absorb nutrients faster because of their greater intestinal surface area. The increase in intestinal area for greater nutrient intake is analogous to the increase in surface area in the respiratory system for higher oxygen uptake. Both are vital stages in the evolution of mammalian endothermy.

434. McGowan, C. 1979. Selection pressure for high body temperatures: implications for dinosaurs. *Paleobiology* 5: 285–295.

Most dinosaurs were probably not endothermic. Despite skeletal evidence of rapid locomotion and muscular movement, inertial homeothermy probably sufficed to sustain high activity levels. Large slow-moving sauropods were probably ectothermic.

435. Marx, J.L. 1978. Warm-blooded dinosaurs: evidence pro and con. *Science* 199:1424–1426.

A non-technical summary of the arguments on both sides.

436. Millet, J.S. 1983. Dinosaurs, mammals, and Mesozoic taphonomy. In *Second International Symposium on Mesozoic Terrestrial Ecosystems*, ed. Z. Kielan-Jaworska and H. Osmólska, 209–213, *Acta Palaeontologica Polonica* 28 (1/2).

The slow passage of prey through the reptilian gut decalcifies bone material. Endothermic mammals, on the other hand, pass prey through the gut relatively quickly. Coprocoenoses with undecalcified small vertebral bones should appear in the fossil record at the point at which dinosaurs became endothermic, developing a mammalian grade of digestion. Perhaps the scarceness of mammalian remains results from their digestion by large ectothermic reptiles (i.e. dinosaurs).

437. Ostrom, J.H. 1974. Reply to "dinosaurs as reptiles." *Evolution* 28:491–493.

Part of the series of letters in this issue attacking or defending Bakker and Ostrom (Bakker 1971a [413]). Claims that Feduccia misunderstood Ostrom's intent "in his zeal to restore dinosaurs to their traditional image of sluggish, inactive, ectothermic reptiles." Ostrom cautioned against using vertebrate fossil fauna as indicators of paleoclimate. The interpretation of paleoclimates differs greatly if the animals used as indicator species are endotherms or ectotherms. Dinosaurs should not be used as climatic indicator species if any reasonable doubt exists as to dinosaurian endothermy. (*See also* Bakker 1974 [415]; Dodson 1974 [426].)

438. Ostrom, J.H. 1980. The evidence for endothermy in dinosaurs. In *A Cold Look at the Warm-blooded Dinosaurs*, ed. R.D.K. Thomas and E.C. Olson, 15–54. Washington: AAAS.

    Ostrom offers cautious support for Bakker's hypothesis. Reviews the standard arguments, but goes into more detail on the cardiovascular and zoogeographic evidence. Contains a good synopsis of dinosaur taxonomy and a useful glossary of terms related to thermoregulation.

439. Paul, G.S. 1988. Physiological, migratorial, climatological, geophysical, survival, and evolutionary implications of Cretaceous polar dinosaurs. *Journal of Paleontology* 62:640–652.

    The presence of dinosaurs at the North and South poles during the Cretaceous argues strongly for endothermic dinosaurs. They may have had feathers or fur-like insulation during cooler seasons. Cretaceous polar climates, although perhaps warmer than present, may still have been severely cold. Nor is it likely that the Earth's axial tilt varied significantly from its present value. Although seasonal migrations may have occurred (Hotton 1980 [727]), migratory energetics still argues for warm-blooded dinosaurs. Polar dinosaurs may have been an active center of dinosaur evolution because they existed at the extreme end of their range. Given their ability to cope with seasonal cold and darkness, polar dinosaurs might have survived the impact scenarios presented for the Cretaceous-Tertiary boundary event. Polar dinosaurs also argue against gradual extinction from climatic changes. (*See also* Rich and Rich 1989 [381]; Davies 1987 [1018]; Brouwers et al. 1987 [1049]; Rich et al. 1988 [1083] for additional references on polar dinosaurs.)

440. Reid, R.E.H. 1978. Discrepancies in claims for endothermy in therapsids and dinosaurs. *Nature* 276:757–758.

Takes issue with several of Bakker's arguments, including bone histology, gait, and predator/prey ratios. Haversian bone, for example, may simply be a better mechanical adaptation for large animals. Concludes that "doubtful claims tend to discredit real evidence," but remains unconvinced that any of the evidence is real.

441. Seymour, R.S. 1976. Dinosaurs, endothermy and blood pressure. *Nature* 262:207–208.

A short but intriguing article. Efficient cardiovascular performance is critical for endothermy. High metabolic rates require high blood pressure. Upright stance creates a high blood column, which also requires high blood pressure. Modern endotherms are the only modern terrestrial vertebrates with heads more than 50 cm above the heart. This may be the physiological link between gait and endothermy that Bakker has been challenged to show.

442. Silverberg, R. 1981. Beastly debates. *Harpers*, October, 68–78.

An informative and entertaining general account of the warm/cold blooded debate. The author relates this current controversy to the Victorian debate over the nature and appearance of dinosaurs. A good look at the humanity that lies behind and often shapes cold theory. Highly recommended as a reading for class discussion. (*See also* Desmond 1976 [425].)

443. Spotila, J.R. 1980. Constraints on body size and temperature regulation of dinosaurs. In *A Cold Look at the Warm-blooded Dinosaurs*, ed. R.D.K. Thomas and E.C. Olson, 233–252. Washington: AAAS.

Large dinosaurs were inertial homeotherms. A mathematical model for ectotherm heat production with increased size, body temperature, and climate shows that large ectotherms realize reduced heat requirements in a variety of climates. Reports on experimental heat exchange studies with alligators. (*See* [444]; Bakker 1980 [416]. *See also* [548–576] on thermoregulation in modern reptiles.)

444. Spotila, J.R., P.W. Lommen, G.S. Bakken, and D.M. Gates. 1973. A mathematical model for body temperatures of large reptiles: implications for dinosaur ecology. *American Naturalist* 107:391–404.

Large dinosaurs would have had a constant body temperature because of their large size alone. Develops a mathematical model relating body size, heat capacity, heat storage, and body temperature for hypothetical animals. Reviews possible behavioral thermoregulation in dinosaurs, which might have required different adult and juvenile strategies. Ectothermic dinosaurs would have been subject to extinction through climate change. (*See* [443]. *See also* McNab and Auffenberg 1976 [563].)

445. Thomas, R.D.K., and E.C. Olson, eds. 1980. *A Cold Look at the Warm-blooded Dinosaurs. AAAS Selected Symposium* no. 28. Washington: AAAS.

An invaluable source for the debate over endothermic dinosaurs. All the principal hypotheses are presented, and the result is a lively interchange. Several of the contributions are annotated in this chapter. The lengthy bibliography is especially useful for anyone wishing to pursue this topic.

446. Weaver, J.C. 1983. The improbable endotherm: the energetics of the sauropod dinosaur *Brachiosaurus*. *Paleobiology* 9:173–182.

Sauropods were probably not endothermic, although other dinosaurs probably were. Large sauropods would have starved as endotherms, given their extremely large size, their diet of tough vegetable matter, and the small size of the head through which large quantities of food would have had to pass. Determines food values by a caloric analysis of those extant plant genera which are represented as fossils in the Late Jurassic Morrison Formation. Weaver rejects the elephant as an appropriate model herbivore for comparison with sauropods, and claims that the giraffe is a better choice for a contemporary sauropod grazing model; its head is about the size of that of the *Brachiosaurus*.

PREDATOR/PREY RATIOS

447. Bakker, R.T. 1975. Dinosaur renaissance. *Scientific American* 232 (April):58–79.

    A popular account of Bakker's theories, which drew much public attention to what had hitherto been a purely academic debate. Focuses on the evidence for endothermic predator/prey ratios in the fossil record, and traces the evolution of vertebrates in relation to their distribution.

448. Béland, P., and D.A. Russell. 1979. Ectothermy in dinosaurs—paleoecological evidence from Dinosaur Provincial Park, Alberta. *Canadian Journal of Earth Sciences* 16:250–255.

    Compares predator/prey ratios at three Tertiary sites to the dinosaur community in the Oldman Formation. the Oldman Formation carnivore to herbivore ratio is six times greater than that observed in the Tertiary communities. Bakker's SCA ratio (standing crop to assimilation) for tyrannosaurs is based on the African elephant, which is an unfortunate choice. The elephant is notorious for the amount of unprocessed vegetable matter it excretes (Bakker 1972 [414]). Both Bakker and Farlow 1976a [593] based their census estimates on the existence of a supposed collecting bias against common herbivores, which the authors dismiss as unrealistic. Using their own census estimates, and Bakker's formulas, they estimate a carnivore population three to four times larger than the herbivore population, "clearly not fully endothermic" [*See* 449].

449. Béland, P., and D.A. Russell. 1980. Dinosaur metabolism and predator/prey ratios in the fossil record. In *A Cold Look at the Warm-blooded Dinosaurs*, ed. R.D.K. Thomas and E.C. Olson, 85–102. Washington: AAAS.

    An extension of Béland and Russell (1979 [448]). Reviews the multitude of problems and assumptions associated with the calculation of predator/prey ratios, such as assimilation efficiencies, the relationship between body size and food intake, and the amount of predator wastage. Food intake converges at larger sizes for both endotherms and ectotherms. The fossil record is rarely a reliable index of absolute community structure, and the authors discuss some examples of preservation bias. Existing models predict that Oligocene mammals were ectotherms; clearly the models are inadequate.

450. Farlow, J.O. 1980. Predator/prey biomass ratios, community food webs and dinosaur physiology. In *A Cold Look at the Warm-blooded Dinosaurs*, ed. R.D.K. Thomas and E.C. Olson, 55–84. Washington: AAAS.

Farlow uses a somewhat different approach from Bakker (Bakker 1972 [414]; 1975 [447]; 1980 [416]). He starts with a mathematical model of size versus food consumption for living endotherms and ectotherms, and extrapolates these equations to estimate grazing and predation pressures. His endothermic model yields a dinosaur community comparable in size to modern African communities. Secondary productivity is likewise estimated from extant vertebrates, and compared with carnivore and herbivore density estimates from the Oldman Formation dinosaur community. Farlow stresses that Mesozoic communities may have had structural and functional differences from modern communities. Secondary carnivory and parental care could also have affected predator/prey ratios. (*See also* Tracy 1976 [453]; Delaney and Abercrombie 1986 [555].) Discusses the problem of intake convergence at large size for endotherms and ectotherms, and the difficulty of calculating accurate weights for fossil animals. Cautions that predator/prey ratios alone are not adequate evidence for endothermic dinosaurs.

451. Farlow, J.O. 1983. Dragons and dinosaurs. *Paleobiology* 9:207–210.

Examines recent work on the Komodo dragon in light of problems in interpreting predator/prey ratios. The predator/prey ratio in monitors, slightly higher than in modern mammals, reflects the fact that they are not limited strictly by food. A similar situation might have occurred with extinct ectothermic carnivores, casting doubt on the use of predator/prey ratios as proof of endothermy.

452. Thulborn, R.A. 1973. Thermoregulation in dinosaurs. *Nature* 245:51–52.

   A short but pointed critique of Bakker 1972 [414]. Bakker's estimate of ectothermic prey consumption is based on a dubious assumption for a single species. Points out that small, naked, endothermic hatchlings would have quickly died in the absence of parental care. Small dinosaurs obviously did survive; dinosaurs, therefore, must have been ectothermic. (*Note:* See Chapter Six for a discussion of dinosaur parental care.)

453. Tracy, C.R. 1976. Tyrannosaurs: evidence for endothermy. *American Naturalist* 110:1105–1106.

   Tyrannosaurs could easily have preyed on immature carnivores of other species, or could even have been cannibalistic. Either case would invalidate Bakker's calculation of predator/prey ratios. The apparent rarity of juveniles in the late Mesozoic could be readily explained by hungry tyrannosaurs. (*See also* Farlow 1980 [450]; Delaney and Abercrombie 1986 [555].)

STANCE, GAIT, AND SPEED

454. Alexander, R.McN. 1976. Estimates of speeds of dinosaurs. *Nature* 261:129–130.

   Using Froude numbers, Alexander calculates dinosaur speeds on the basis of stride lengths. Speeds obtained by this method are low, on the order of 1 to 3.6 m s^{-1}. Similar speeds of juvenile and adult sauropods indicates possible herd behavior. (*See also* Kool 1981 [476].)

455. Alexander, R.McN. 1977. Fast locomotion of some African ungulates. *Journal of Zoology* 183:291–300.

   The author chased large animals in Kenya to see how fast they could run. Measures maximum running speed, stride frequency, step length and duty factors, and plots these variables against body mass. Plots Froude numbers against stride and step length. Stride frequencies correlated well with limb length, but less so with body mass. Mean and maximum stride frequency were proportional to hip height.

456. Alexander, R.McN. 1983. A dynamic similarity hypothesis for the gaits of quadrupedal mammals. *Journal of Zoology* 201:135–152.

   Calculation of the dimensionless Froude number makes it possible to predict size, gait and other parameters of locomotion. Different cursorial mammals with equal Froude numbers move in a dynamically similar fashion. Knowing how one animal performs enables us to accurately predict the performance of another animal with an equivalent Froude number. The hypothesis even works fairly well when extended to non-cursorial animals or bipeds.

457. Alexander, R.McN. 1985. Mechanics of posture and gait of some large dinosaurs. *Zoological Journal of the Linnean Society* 83:1–25.

   Alexander brings playing with dinosaurs to new creative heights. Accurate plastic scale models of *Triceratops*, *Tyrannosaurus*, *Stegosaurus*, *Diplodocus* and *Iguanodon* from the British Museum dinosaur series are used to determine volume (by water displacement), bending moments, and center of mass. In the process it is necessary to "amputate" the *Triceratops* model at the elbows and knees to determine its bending moment and saw the tail off the *Diplodocus* to determine the tail's weight and center of mass. *Tyrannosaurus* could easily have walked with tail erect, and *Diplodocus* and *Stegosaurus* supported most of their weight with their hind legs. Sauropods may have held their necks higher than usually depicted, and *Diplodocus* could possibly have reared up on its hind legs to feed, as Bakker and others have restored it.

Describes the use of Froude numbers and duty factors to calculate gait, the allometric relationship between bone length and body mass, and the calculation of bone strength. Concludes that *Triceratops* could have galloped like a rhinoceros, while *Diplodocus* was only capable of a walking gait. Large bipedal dinosaurs would have exerted as much pressure on soft ground as cattle, but sauropods exerted much higher pressure. This would have made one heck of a science fair project. It is also a good example for students, showing what can be done with a little material and a lot of thought.

458. Alexander, R.McN. 1988. *Elastic Mechanisms in Animal Movement*. Cambridge: Cambridge University Press.

    Reviews the role of elasticity in movement, covering everything from click beetles to whales. Of interest chiefly for the last chapter, which compares the elastic similarity hypothesis with the author's own dynamic similarity hypothesis. At any given Froude number, mammals of different size will use the same gait.

459. Alexander, R.McN. 1989. *Dynamics of Dinosaurs and Other Extinct Giants*. New York: Columbia University Press.

    A well-written review of the author's extensive and influential studies of vertebrate locomotion. Considers the dynamics of extinct animals, including dinosaurs, pterosaurs, plesiosaurs, and others, and reviews methods of calculation of dinosaur weight, measurement of speed and gait from trackways, and estimation of dinosaur strength. The speculative chapter on the bioenergetics of social behavior is of particular interest, providing a good summary of current hypotheses on sexual selection in dinosaurs.

460. Alexander, R.McN. 1991. How dinosaurs ran. *Scientific American* 264 (April):130–136.

    A good introduction to the highly technical literature on dinosaurian and mammalian locomotion. Alexander concludes that "I think I am probably fast enough to outrun a pursuing tyrannosaur, but, perhaps fortunately, I am unlikely to have a try."

461. Alexander, R.McN., G.M.O. Maloiy, B. Hunter, A.S. Jayes, and J. Nturibi. 1979. Mechanical stresses in fast locomotion of buffalo (*Syncerus caffer*) and elephant (*Loxodonta africana*). *Journal of Zoology* 189:135–144.

   Analysis of filmed locomotion and dissection of buffalos and African elephants shows that despite their large size there is no indication of unusual stresses in their bones, tendons, or muscles when in rapid motion. Such stresses appear to be independent of body size in large mammals.

462. Anderson, J.F., A. Hall-Martin, and D.A. Russell. 1985. Long bone circumference and weight in mammals, birds, and dinosaurs. *Journal of Zoology* 207:53–61.

   Giant sauropods may have been lighter than previously believed. In modern quadrupedal mammals and bipedal birds, the circumference of the humerus and femur at mid-shaft is closely correlated with body weight. Calculates estimated weights for dinosaurs, based on fossil bone circumference. Weights are generally lighter than those reported by Bakker, Béland and Russell, and others, who have assumed that the cross-sectional area of fossil bones, rather than their circumference, was proportional to body weight. Alexander's calculations, which are based on bone diameter, give intermediate values.

463. Anderson, J.F., H. Rahn, and H.D. Prange. 1979. Scaling of supportive tissue mass. *Quarterly Review of Biology* 54:139–148.

   A ten-fold change in body mass corresponds to a thirteen-fold change in supportive tissue mass across a wide range of vertebrates and invertebrates. This relationship may be independent of the organization of the support elements in vertebrates.

464. Bakker, R.T. 1987. The return of the dancing dinosaurs. In *Dinosaurs Past and Present*, Volume I, ed. S.J. Czerkas and E.C. Olson, 38–69. Los Angeles: Natural History Museum of Los Angeles County.

An exceptionally well-illustrated description of the philosophies and methodologies behind Bakker's lively reconstructions of dinosaurs. Presents a strong case for rapid and agile dinosaurs, capable of speeds up to a full gallop. Concludes that *Stegosaurus* and the diplodocid sauropods could maintain an upright stance.

465. Carrier, D.R. 1987. The evolution of locomotor stamina in tetrapods: circumventing a mechanical constraint. *Paleobiology* 13:326–341.

There is a fundamental evolutionary constraint in the evolution of tetrapod locomotion. The sprawling gait of early tetrapods would have made it difficult to breathe and move at the same time. The resulting low stamina is still seen to a lesser degree in modern lizards. This mechanical constraint was bypassed by running in short bursts powered by anaerobic metabolic pathways (lepidosaurs), or by adopting a passive defense against predation. Reviews the coevolution of respiration and locomotion. Dinosaur ancestors show evidence of circumventing this mechanical constraint, and the upright posture of dinosaurs would have aided in respiration during locomotion. Bakker's assumption that upright stance indicates endothermy may be correct, but not for the reasons he assumes (Bakker 1971a [413]).

466. Day, M.H., ed. 1981. Vertebrate Locomotion. *Symposia of the Zoological Society of London* no. 48. New York: Academic Press.

Includes several useful papers on stance, gait, muscles, bone loading, and adaptations for flight in a variety of vertebrate taxa.

467. Fedak, M.A., N.C. Heglund, and C.R. Taylor. 1982. Energetics and mechanics of terrestrial locomotion. II. Kinetic energy changes of the limbs and body as a function of speed and body size in birds and mammals. *Journal of Experimental Biology* 97:23–40.

One of a series of four papers in this issue, this contribution studies changes in bodily kinetic energy relative to the center of mass, as a function of speed and body size. The equations relating kinetic energy to speed are similar for all bipeds and quadrupeds regardless of size. Proposes a general equation to calculate the rate at which muscles must supply energy for acceleration for a wide range of animals. Elastic recoil may provide a significant portion of kinetic energy in larger animals moving at high speeds.

468. Fedak, M.A., B. Pinshow, and K. Schmidt-Nielsen. 1974. Energy costs of bipedal running. *American Journal of Physiology* 227:1038–1044.

Calculates energy costs for seven species of birds running on a treadmill. Oxygen consumption is linearly related to speed. The slope of this relationship increases more slowly with increasing body size in bipeds than in quadrupeds. Despite gross differences in morphology and gait, there seems to be an underlying similarity in energetic requirements among all bipeds and among all quadrupeds. For larger animals the cost of running on two legs is greater than running on four legs [*See* 469].

469. Fedak, M.A., and H.J. Seeherman. 1979. Reappraisal of energetics of locomotion shows identical cost in bipeds and quadrupeds including ostrich and horse. *Nature* 282:713–716.

Bipeds and quadrupeds of any size show no consistent differences in the energetic cost of locomotion. Though there is no difference in the scaling of energetic costs between bipedal and quadrupedal locomotion, there are differences in locomotory styles which affect energetic cost. Repudiates Fedak's earlier conclusion (Fedak et al. 1974 [468]) that large bipedal dinosaurs must have been slow moving. Previous studies were performed on small animals, up to canine size. Later studies on larger animals render the previous theoretical position untenable.

470. Frey, E. 1984. Aspects of the biomechanics of crocodilian terrestrial locomotion. In *Third Symposium on Mesozoic Terrestrial Ecosystems, Short Papers*, ed. W.E. Reif and F. Westphal, 93–97. Tübingen: ATTEMPTO-Verlag.

Reviews features of crocodile anatomy and crocodilian gaits, and contrasts crocodiles with dinosaurs.

471. Garland, T. jr. 1983. The relation between maximal running speed and body mass in terrestrial mammals. *Journal of Zoology* 199:157–170.

Data on maximum running speeds do not support the elastic similarity hypothesis. Maximum speed is generally correlated with body mass. Although maximum speed in mammals agrees closely with the predictions of the dynamic similarity hypothesis, limb bone proportions seem to correspond best with the geometric similarity hypothesis.

472. Garland, T. jr. 1984. Physiological correlates of locomotory performance in a lizard. *American Journal of Physiology* 247:R806–R815.

Studies locomotion in a population of the iguanid lizard *Ctenosaurus similis*, to see how much variation occurs between individuals. Uses "prodding and pinching" as motivators for experimental locomotion. Considerable variation can be observed within a single population, much of which can be explained by predictor variables such as age, size, and other morphological and physiological factors.

473. Gatesy, S.M., and A.A. Biewener. 1991. Bipedal locomotion: effects of speed, size and limb posture in birds and humans. *Journal of Zoology* 224:127–147.

Seven species of flightless or ground-dwelling birds were filmed while walking or running on a treadmill. Smaller bipeds showed higher stride frequencies, shorter stride lengths, and speed range limitations within a particular gait. Size differences between species lead to consistent differences in stride length, stride frequency, step length, duty factor, and limb excursion. Froude numbers can be used to normalize data for size. Most remaining variation is due to postural differences and variation in limb segment lengths between species. Discusses observed differences between bipedal human and avian locomotion.

474. Heglund, N.C., G.A. Cavagna, and C.R. Taylor. 1982. Energetics and mechanics of terrestrial locomotion. III. Energy changes of the centre of mass as a function of speed and body size in birds and mammals. *Journal of Experimental Biology* 97:41–56.

Calculates the energy required to lift and reaccelerate an animal with each step. Energy requirements increase linearly with speed for all animals, independently of body size (as predicted by Alexander). Small and large quadrupeds show differences in galloping. Small animals use their front legs for braking and hind legs for reacceleration; large animals use both sets of limbs for both purposes [*See* 467, 475, 485].

475. Heglund, N.C., M.A. Fedak, C.R. Taylor, and G.A. Cavagna. 1982. Energetics and mechanics of terrestrial locomotion. IV. Total mechanical energy changes as a function of speed and body size in birds and mammals. *Journal of Experimental Biology* 97:57–66.

Last in this series of articles, this study combines data from the previous three articles. Compares the kinetic energy of the limbs and body relative to the center of mass with the potential and kinetic energy of the center of mass itself. Energy consumed during locomotion is not simply a function of mechanical work done by the muscles. Metabolic energy use increases linearly with speed, and smaller animals use much more energy than larger animals at the same speed. Larger animals may store and recover significant amounts of elastic energy during locomotion [*See* 467, 474, 485].

476. Kool, R. 1981. The walking speed of dinosaurs from the Peace River Canyon, British-Columbia, Canada. *Canadian Journal of Earth Sciences* 18:823–825.

Based on data in Currie and Sarjeant (1979 [496]), the author calculates speeds for seven species from the Peace River Canyon trackways. Reexamines Alexander's methodology (Alexander 1976 [454]) and concludes that, rather than moving slowly, the Peace River dinosaurs were moving at a normal speed for extant bipedal vertebrates.

477. McMahon, T.A. 1975. Using body size to understand the structural design of animals: quadrupedal locomotion. *Journal of Applied Physiology* 39:619–627.

Gait, stride, and other factors of locomotory performance follow simple power laws with respect to quadruped body weight. Three models have been formulated to study locomotion: geometric similarity, elastic similarity, and static stress similarity. Comparison of animals at the transition between trot and gallop supports the elastic similarity model. Running speed is also a function of body size, and is higher in larger animals. Greater speed for greater size may act as an evolutionary pressure for acquiring larger size.

478. McMahon, T.A. 1984. *Muscles, Reflexes and Locomotion.* Princeton: Princeton University Press.

A comprehensive review of muscle mechanics, the relation of musculature to metabolism, and the molecular nature of muscular contraction. Discusses motor control, the mechanics of locomotion, and the effects of body size on locomotion. The author favors the elastic similarity hypothesis, but concludes that "no single principle unites all observations on animal scaling."

479. Newman, B.H. 1970. Stance and gait in the flesh-eating dinosaur *Tyrannosaurus*. *Biological Journal of the Linnean Society* 2:119–123.

A new reconstruction of *Tyrannosaurus* for the British Museum has a more birdlike stance than its predecessors. An ungainly sinuous "bird-like waddling" is proposed for the animal's gait, based on trackways and on skeletal considerations. When at rest, *Tyrannosaurus* folded its front limbs beneath itself like a chicken.

480. Padian, K., and P.E. Olsen. 1989. Ratite footprints and the stance and gait of Mesozoic theropods. In *Dinosaur Tracks and Traces*, ed. D.D. Gillette and M.G. Lockley, 231–241. New York: Cambridge University Press.

Compares dinosaur trackways with footprints of rheas. Theropod footprints are strikingly similar to those made by modern rheas, supporting the phylogenetic hypothesis that birds are descendants of theropods. Modern ratites resemble theropod dinosaurs in bone morphology, joint structure, and articulation. These similarities represent true homologies.

481. Russell, D.A., and P. Béland. 1976. Running dinosaurs. *Nature* 264:486.

    A brief letter concerning an old record of a track of a giant bipedal ornithischian dinosaur from the Colorado Cretaceous. Using Alexander's formulas, the animal's speed is estimated at 27.1 kmh. A similar calculation for tracks of *Dromiceiomimus brevitertius*, an ornithomimid dinosaur, gives a speed of 6.4 kmh, a walk by Alexander's definitions. (*See* Thulborn 1981 [487] for a critique.)

482. Tarsitano, S. 1983. Stance and gait in theropod dinosaurs. In *Second International Symposium on Mesozoic Terrestrial Ecosystems*, ed. Z. Kielan-Jaworska and H. Osmólska, 251–264, *Acta Palaeontologica Polonica* 28 (1/2).

    Reviews the biomechanics of both thecodont and theropod locomotion. Theropods held their vertebral columns at an angle of 20° above the horizontal, as shown by a comparison of muscle scars and anatomical data in crocodiles and theropods. Functional analysis of morphological characters suggests that reconstructions based on avian postures ignore basic differences in osteology and musculature between theropods and birds. (*See also* Padian and Olson 1989 [480].)

483. Taylor, C.R., and V.J. Rowntree. 1973. Running on two or four legs: which consumes more energy? *Science* 179:186–187.

    Chimpanzees and capuchin monkeys expended the same amount of energy during treadmill running on two legs as they did when running all fours.

484. Taylor, C.R., R. Dmi'el, M. Fedak, and K. Schmidt-Nielsen. 1971. Energetic cost of running and heat balance in a large bird, the rhea. *American Journal of Physiology* 221:597–601.

Rhea running costs increased linearly with speed. The cost was twice that calculated for a running quadrupedal mammal of the same size. The same relationship applies to bipedal humans. At high speed, rheas store very large amounts of heat.

485. Taylor, C.R., N.C. Heglund, and G.M.O Maloiy. 1982. Energetics and mechanics of terrestrial locomotion. I. Metabolic energy consumption as a function of speed and body size in birds and mammals. *Journal of Experimental Biology* 97:1–21.

    First of a series of four papers in this issue [*See* 467, 474, 475]. This paper examines metabolic costs of terrestrial locomotion. Formulates a general allometric equation relating oxygen consumption in locomotion at a constant speed to size and body mass. The equation applies equally well to bipeds and quadrupeds.

486. Taylor, C.R., K. Schmidt-Nielsen, and J.L. Raab. 1970. Scaling of energetic cost of running to body size in mammals. *American Journal of Physiology* 219:1104–1107.

    Oxygen consumption increases linearly with speed for seven species of mammal.

487. Thulborn, R.A. 1981. Estimated speed of a giant bipedal dinosaur. *Nature* 292:273–274.

    Refutes Russell and Béland (1976 [481]), and claims that the published data on which they based their study was in error. Based on the author's own examination of photographs of the trackway, the giant dinosaur was moving at a speed of 8.5 kmh, rather than 27.1 kmh.

488. Thulborn, R.A. 1982. Speeds and gaits of dinosaurs. *Palaeogeography, Palaeoclimatology, Palaeoecology* 38:227–256.

    Provides speed estimates for sixty-two dinosaur species, calculated on the basis of equations developed for mammalian locomotion. Smaller bipedal dinosaurs could run up to 35–40 kmh, with ostrich dinosaurs perhaps reaching speeds of 60 kmh. Larger bipeds ran at 15–20 kmh. Quadrupeds were generally restricted to a walk, as low as 6–8 kmh for ankylosaurs and stegosaurs. Ceratopsians may have reached 25 kmh, while sauropods cruised at about 12–17 kmh.

489. Thulborn, R.A. 1984. Preferred gaits of bipedal dinosaurs. *Alcheringa* 8:243–252.

Reports on the application of principles developed by Alexander. Knowing hip height, it is easy to calculate relative stride length from dinosaur trackways. This in turn roughly determines gait. The author calculated gait and speed for 267 bipedal dinosaurs. Most tracks show either a walking or running gait, indicating that the intermediate trot might have been energetically or otherwise unfavorable. This gait preference corresponds to behavioral preferences in modern reptiles (slow or fast) rather than mammals (trot). Trotting is often associated with mammalian herd behavior, perhaps arguing against dinosaur herds. Giant dinosaurs did not run. Perhaps they did not need to run to successfully catch their smaller prey.

490. Thulborn, R.A. The gaits of dinosaurs. 1989. In *Dinosaur Tracks and Traces*, ed. D.D. Gillette and M.G. Lockley, 39–50. New York: Cambridge University Press.

Reviews the three basic dinosaur gaits: walking, trotting and running. Discusses the calculation of relative stride lengths. Large bipedal dinosaurs (1–2 tons and higher) could only walk or trot, while smaller ones could trot or run. Regards the evidence for hopping dinosaurs as dubious. Reviews gait differences between theropods and ornithopods. Quadrupedal dinosaurs were restricted to a slow walk; perhaps large size was a defensive solution.

491. Wade, M. 1989. The stance of dinosaurs and the Cossack dancer syndrome. In *Dinosaur Tracks and Traces*, ed. D.D. Gillette and M.G. Lockley, 73–82. New York: Cambridge University Press.

The "tripod stance" of traditional dinosaur mounting is in error. It ignores the lack of tail drag marks in trackways, and doesn't fit the axially overlapping footprints observed in bipedal trackways. The author labels this careless attitude in restoration as the "Cossack dancer syndrome", because unarmed herbivores would have to have had the agility of a Russian folk dancer to escape predators from the awkward tripodal stance. Discusses stance and gait of a variety of dinosaurs, and concludes that ratite birds are an appropriate locomotory model. Dinosaurs were functional animals. Like modern animals, efficient movement was necessary for survival. Speculates on the behavioral implications of osteological and trackway evidence for attack and escape.

TRACKWAYS

492. Avnimelech, M. 1962. Dinosaur tracks in the Lower Cenomanian of Jerusalem. *Nature* 196:264.

    A short note describing tracks of an unknown theropod found near Jerusalem, perhaps *Elaphrosaurus bambergii*.

493. Baird, D. 1980. A prosauropod trackway from the Navajo Sandstone (Lower Jurassic) of Arizona. In *Aspects of Vertebrate History: Essays in Honor of Edwin Harris Colbert*, ed. L.L. Jacobs, 219–230. Flagstaff: Museum of Northern Arizona Press.

    Reports on the first prosauropod trackway discovered, a trackway made by *Navahopus falcipollex*. Comparison with the Arizonan prosauropod *Ammosaurus* shows *Navahopus* to be a plateosaurid prosauropod.

494. Currie, P.J. 1983. Hadrosaur trackways from the Lower Cretaceous of Canada. In *Second International Symposium on Mesozoic Terrestrial Ecosystems*, ed. Z. Kielan-Jaworska and H. Osmólska, 63–73. *Acta Palaeontologica Polonica* 28 (1/2).

    Hadrosaur trackways are abundant in British Columbia's Peace River Canyon. *Amblydactylus* tracks indicate that the animal was a facultative (not obligatory) biped, and held its tail off the ground as a counterbalance. There is ample evidence of herding. Hadrosaurs could reach a top speed of 8.5 km/hr. Carnivore footprints (*Irenesauripus*) mixed with hadrosaur tracks in deep-water environments suggest that these herbivores found no refuge from attack in the water.

495. Currie, P.J., G.C. Nadon, and M.G. Lockley. 1991. Dinosaur footprints with skin impressions from the Cretaceous of Alberta and Colorado. *Canadian Journal of Earth Sciences* 28:102–115.

Foot pad skin impressions are visible in large ornithopod tracks from the South Platte Formation and St. Mary River Formation. Discusses the depositional conditions necessary for the preservation of such impressions.

496. Currie, P.J., and W.A.S. Sarjeant. 1979. Lower Cretaceous dinosaur footprints from the Peace River Canyon, British Columbia, Canada. *Palaeogeography, Palaeoclimatology, Palaeoecology* 28:103–115.

A new trackway is reported containing prints of the new hadrosaur species *Amblydactylus kortmeyeri*. Prints of two juveniles suggest gregarious juvenile behavior in this species. (*See also* Kool 1981 [476].)

497. Edwards, M.B., R. Edwards, and E.H. Colbert. 1978. Carnosaurian footprints in the Late Cretaceous of eastern Spitzbergen. *Journal of Paleontology* 52:940–941.

A short note on an unknown carnosaur whose presence indicates a much more diverse fauna in the Svalbard area than previously believed.

498. Farlow, J.O. 1981. Estimates of dinosaur speeds from a new trackway site in Texas USA. *Nature* 294:747–748.

Briefly reviews earlier estimates of speeds based on Alexander's formulas; most estimates have been quite low. Farlow reports speeds of up to 39.9 kmh from a Late Cretaceous trackway.

499. Gierliński, G. 1991. New dinosaur ichnotaxa from the Early Jurassic of the Holy Cross Mountains, Poland. *Palaeogeography, Palaeoclimatology, Palaeoecology* 85:137–148.

Describes two new ornithopod ichnospecies, *Anomoepus pienkovskii* and *Moyenisauropus karaszevskii*, and describes two new theropod ichnospecies, *Grallator (Grallator) zvierzi* and *Grallator (Eubrontes) soltykovensis*, based on tracks from Poland's Holy Cross Mountains.

500. Gillette, D.D., and M.G. Lockley, eds. 1989. *Dinosaur Tracks and Traces*. New York: Cambridge University Press.

    The most important single work in modern dinosaur ichnology. Ichnologists study fossil tracks and traces, including such fossil evidence as footprints, nests, and eggshells. The fifty papers comprising the proceedings of the First International Symposium on Dinosaur Tracks and Traces, held in 1986, represent a watershed in the field of vertebrate ichnology. Several of these papers are included in this bibliography. Includes a section on preservation, with methodologies for making casts of tracks. (*See* Lockley 1987a [502].)

501. Ishigaki, S. 1989. Footprints of swimming sauropods from Morocco. In *Dinosaur Tracks and Traces*, ed. D.D. Gillette and M.G. Lockley, 83–86. New York: Cambridge University Press.

    Reports four trackways with unusual prints of swimming sauropods. Because the marks are indistinct, they might have gone unnoticed at other track sites.

502. Lockley, M.G. 1987a. Dinosaur tracks symposium signals a renaissance in vertebrate ichnology. *Paleobiology* 13:246–252.

    A short literature review of the renewed interest in the long moribund field of vertebrate ichnology. The study of dinosaur ichnology has implications for almost every area of paleobiology. (*See* Gillette and Lockley 1989 [500].)

503. Lockley, M.G. 1987b. Dinosaur trackways and their importance in paleontological reconstruction. In *Dinosaurs Past and Present*, Volume I, ed. S.J. Czerkas and E.C. Olson, 80–95. Los Angeles: Natural History Museum of Los Angeles County.

Describes a sauropod trackway made by at least twenty-three sauropods moving slowly as a herd. Larger individuals seem to have led the way. Sauropod tracks show no evidence of tail dragging. Reviews research on other trackways, and discusses the possible herd behavior that several of these sites indicate. (*See also* Lockley and Conrad 1987 [602]; Lockley et al. 1986 [603].)

504. Lockley, M.G. 1989. Tracks and traces: new perspectives on dinosaurian behavior, ecology, and biogeography. In *The Age of Dinosaurs*, ed. K. Padian and D.J. Chure, 134–145. *Geological Society of America Short Courses in Paleontology* no. 2. Knoxville: The Paleontological Society.

Vertebrate ichnology (the study of trace fossils) is a rapidly developing area of dinosaur research. The authors survey the processes by which tracks are preserved, and their paleobiological interpretation, with an emphasis on dinosaur footprints.

505. Lockley, M.G., and C. Jennings. 1987. Dinosaur tracksites of western Colorado and eastern Utah. In *Paleontology and Geology of the Dinosaur Triangle*, ed. W.R. Averett, 86–91. Museum of Western Colorado.

Numerous dinosaur trackways are known in the Triangle, but few are well documented. The authors report on several trackways.

506. Lockley, M.G., and K. Conrad. 1989. The paleoenvironmental context, preservation and paleoecological significance of dinosaur tracksites in the western USA. In *Dinosaur Tracks and Traces*, ed. D.D. Gillette and M.G. Lockley, 121–134. New York: Cambridge University Press.

Trackways, which occur in a wide variety of depositional environments, are an essential clue to the nature of the paleoenvironment. Discusses alluvial, desert, lacustrine, and coastal systems, with examples of ichnofauna and their interpretation in each depositional environment.

507. Moratalla, J.J., J.L. Sanz, and S. Jimenez. 1988. Multivariate-analysis on Lower Cretaceous dinosaur footprints-discrimination between ornithopods and theropods. *Geobios* 21:395–408.

A computer analysis of tridactyl dinosaur footprints of sixty-six Lower Cretaceous species shows that digital width and whole footprint dimensions explain a significant portion of sample variability. Interdigital angulation, often used as a diagnostic character, is highly variable and thus unsuitable for taxonomic purposes. Bivariate analysis of the sixty-six sample footprints can discriminate between theropod and ornithopod footprints with a high degree of accuracy.

508. Mossman, D.J., and W.A.S. Sarjeant. 1983. The footprints of extinct animals. *Scientific American* 248 (January):74–85.

Relates the historic development of ichnology, and explains some of its basic methodologies. Summarizes the significance of tracks for studying the behavior of extinct animals, based in part on the author's work in the Peace River Canyon in British Columbia.

509. Pittman, J.G. 1989. Stratigraphy, lithology, depositional environment, and track type of dinosaur track-bearing beds of the Gulf coastal plain. In *Dinosaur Tracks and Traces*, ed. D.D. Gillette and M.G. Lockley, 135–153. New York: Cambridge University Press.

Reviews Late Cretaceous theropod, ornithopod and sauropod track sites in the coastal plain, and discusses their depositional environment. Most are from the Glen Rose Formation (Trinity Group). Briefly discusses evidence for predation and herding.

510. Platt, N.H., and C.A. Meyer. 1991. Dinosaur footprints from the Lower Cretaceous of northern Spain: their sedimentological and palaeoecological context. *Palaeogeography, Palaeoclimatology, Palaeoecology* 86:321–333.

Describes eighteen footprints of a bipedal ornithopod from the a shallow Lower Cretaceous lake in Northern Spain (western Cameros Basin). Seven tridactyl footprints are also described from this area, and were probably made in a flood plain habitat by an unknown theropod.

511. Sarjeant, W.A.S. 1974. A history and bibliography of the study of fossil vertebrate footprints in the British Isles. *Palaeogeography, Palaeoclimatology, Palaeoecology* 16:265–378.

In addition to an exhaustive bibliography, the work includes valuable illustrations gleaned from obscure journals. Provides an extensive narrative history of the search for fossil vertebrate footprints in the British Isles.

512. Sarjeant, W.A.S. 1989. Ten paleoichnological commandments: a standardized procedure for the description of fossil vertebrate footprints. In *Dinosaur Tracks and Traces*, ed. D.D. Gillette and M.G. Lockley, 369–370. New York: Cambridge University Press.

A short methodological paper outlining a recommended method for recording information on tracks and trackways.

513. Shounan, Z., L. Jianjun, R. Chenggang, N.J. Mateer, and M.G. Lockley. 1989. A review of dinosaur footprints in China. In *Dinosaur Tracks and Traces*, ed. D.D. Gillette and M.G. Lockley, 187–197. New York: Cambridge University Press.

A complete review of all footprints known from China, mainly ornithopods and theropods. Discusses their stratigraphic implications. Most prints come from the Lower Jurassic.

514. Storer, J.E. 1975. Dinosaur tracks, *Columbosauripus ungulatus* (Saurischia, Coelurosauria), from the Dunvegan Formation (Cenomanian) of northeastern British Columbia. *Canadian Journal of Earth Sciences* 12:1805–1807.

Tracks are probably those of *Columbosauripus ungulatus*.

515. Thulborn, T. 1990. *Dinosaur Tracks*. New York: Routledge, Chapman and Hall.

Reviews the extensive literature on dinosaur footprints and trackways. An excellent introduction to the problems of identifying and interpreting trackways, with a discussion of the methodologies used to calculate height, speed, and gait.

516. Tucker, M.E., and T.P. Burchette. 1977. Triassic dinosaur footprints from South Wales; their context and preservation. *Palaeogeography, Palaeoclimatology, Palaeoecology* 22:195–208.

Anchisauripus tracks are described from the Triassic of South Glamorgan in South Wales. The animals (of two species) were bipedal and "strolling". Discusses the nature of the sediments and the implications of sedimentology for the preservation of tracks and the reconstruction of the paleoenvironment.

BRAIN SIZE AND INTELLIGENCE

517. Armstrong, E. 1983. Relative brain size and metabolism in mammals. *Science* 220:1302–1304.

Brain size in mammals has not increased as much as body size. The ratio of brain weight to body weight is strongly correlated to basal metabolic rate. Primates must devote substantially more body metabolism to their large brains than do other mammals. Intelligence does not come without an energetic cost.

518. Berman, D.S., and S.L. Jain. 1982. The braincase of a small sauropod dinosaur (Reptilia: Saurischia) from the Upper Cretaceous Lameta Group, Central India, with review of Lameta Group localities. *Annals of the Carnegie Museum* 51:405–422.

Cretaceous dinosaurs are rarely found in India, and are known mainly from the Lameta Group. Describes the braincase of an unknown sauropod dinosaur. Reviews the Lameta Group fauna, which is dominated by titanosaurid sauropods.

519. Edinger, T. 1975. Paleoneurology 1804–1966, an annotated bibliography. *Advances in Anatomy, Embryology, and Cell Biology* 49 (1/6):1–258.

    A comprehensive annotated bibliography of early research in paleoneurology, including extensive material on dinosaurs.

520. Gould, S.J. 1978. Were dinosaurs dumb? *New Scientist*, 27 July, 266–267.

    A popular account of the ideas in Hopson (1977 [521]) and Jerison (1969 [524]), that dinosaur brains were of normal size for large reptiles. Given the size of dinosaur brains, it is not surprising that we have also found evidence of parental care.

521. Hopson, J.A. 1977. Relative brain size and behavior in archosaurian reptiles. *Annual Review of Ecology and Systematics* 8:429–448.

    A comprehensive review of brain size and possible behaviors of dinosaurs, pterosaurs, and *Archaeopteryx*. Discusses the social behavior of dinosaurs and living reptiles in light of their presumed endothermy. Endocasts of dinosaur brains show that their brains were well within the normal range of reptilian brain/body size. Sauropods, on the other hand, had unusually small brains. Ankylosaurs and stegosaurs were also relatively small brained. The largest brains belonged to the coelurosaurs, carnosaurs, ornithopods, and ceratopsians, in descending order. Discusses the possibility of sexual selection in dinosaurs, and concludes that they probably behaved like modern reptiles, particularly lizards. Parental behavior was like that of the crocodile. Dinosaurs were not physiologically uniform, and only the coelurosaurs were truly endothermic. The rest were intermediate between modern endotherms and ectotherms.

522. Hopson J.A. 1980. Relative brain size in dinosaurs: implications for dinosaur endothermy. In *A Cold Look at the Warm-blooded Dinosaurs*, ed. R.D.K. Thomas and E.C. Olson, 287–310. Washington: AAAS.

The encephalization quotient provides a way to compare dinosaur brains with those of living reptiles. EQ is calculated as the ratio of the measured brain size to the expected brain size for a "standard archosaur" of the same body size. By this standard, dinosaur brains are within normal limits for reptiles of their size. Reviews earlier work by Hopson (1977 [521]) and Jerison (1969 [524]) in support of Feduccia (1973 [428]). Endotherms have proportionately larger brains than ectotherms, consistent with their adaptation for "more intense activity." With the exception of the coelurosaurs, dinosaurs did not possess true mammalian endothermy.

523. Hopson, J.A. 1979. Paleoneurology. In *Biology of the Reptilia, Vol. 9A*, ed. C. Gans, 39–146. New York: Academic Press.

An extensive review of paleoneurology, relating fossil endocasts to modern reptilian brains. Discusses methodologies for comparing brain size and body size, and reviews archosaur brains.

524. Jerison, H.J. 1969. Brain evolution and dinosaur brains. *American Naturalist* 103:575–588.

Dinosaur brains were of normal reptilian size. Brain volume can be roughly determined from endocasts. Reviews the evolution of the brain/body size relationship. Major changes in brain size do not appear before the mammalian/avian grade of evolution. (*See* Hopson 1980 [522].)

525. Martin, R.D. 1981. Relative brain size and basal metabolic rate in terrestrial vertebrates. *Nature* 293:57–60.

It has been widely held that brain size is scaled to changes in body surface area, not body volume. Reexamination of allometric brain/body size relationships in mammals and birds shows no empirical basis for this assumption.

526. Radinsky, L.B. 1978. Evolution of brain size in carnivores and ungulates. *American Naturalist* 112:815–831.

Refutes Jerison's hypothesis that coevolution between carnivores and ungulates has greatly increased the brain size of both. Smart prey requires smarter predators, putting selective pressure on the prey for further increases in brain size to evade smarter predators. No such evolutionary feedback loop exists. Calculation of encephalization quotients (EQ) from fossil data shows no significant differences in brain/body size (EQ's) between carnivores and ungulates.

527. Rich, T.H., and P.V. Rich. 1988. A juvenile dinosaur brain from Australia. *National Geographic Research* 4:148.

    A short letter describing a finely preserved brain of a juvenile ornithopod dinosaur. The brain and eye socket are relatively large for this taxa.

528. Roth, J.J., and E.C. Roth. 1980. The parietal pineal complex among paleovertebrates: evidence for temperature regulation. In *A Cold Look at the Warm-blooded Dinosaurs*, ed. R.D.K. Thomas and E.C. Olson, 189–231. Washington: AAAS.

    The epiphyseal complex functions like an "environmental sensor". The presence of a pineal body in fossils is indicated by a parietal foramen and the shape of the intracranial roof. A pineal body would be a good indication of dinosaur endothermy. Discusses the role of the pineal system in thermoregulation. Dinosaurs show no trace of a parietal eye, and the authors dismiss earlier claims of such discoveries. Perhaps dinosaurs were metabolically similar to the modern dugong or to the edentates, which lack a pineal body and have relatively low body temperatures and metabolic rates.

529. Satinoff, E. 1978. Neural organization and evolution of thermal regulation in mammals. *Science* 201:16–22.

    Instead of just one "integrator" for all thermoregulatory inputs, there may be a separate integrator for each thermoregulatory input. These levels of regulation act together in a hierarchical fashion. Speculates on the evolution of thermoregulation in endothermy in light of this hierarchical control of parallel integrative systems.

530. Wheeler, P.E. 1978. Elaborate CNS cooling structures in large dinosaurs. *Nature* 275:441–442.

The function of the air passages in the crests of the lambeosine hadrosaurs was probably thermoregulatory, protecting the CNS from overheating. Dinosaurs also show evidence of a gular flap and of extensive air sacs (like modern birds); both are thermoregulatory structures. The elaborate central nervous system cooling apparatus may indicate endothermy. (*See* Hopson 1975 [726] for additional cross references on the structure and function of hadrosaur crests.)

BONE TISSUE

531. Bolt, J.R., and R.E. DeMar. 1980. Growth rings in dinosaur teeth. *Nature* 288:194–195.

    Argues against the use of growth rings as evidence of dinosaur ectothermy. (*See* Johnston 1979 [534] for additional cross references on growth rings.)

532. Bouvier, M. 1977. Dinosaur haversian bone and endothermy. *Evolution* 31:449–450.

    Response to Bakker's claim that Haversian bone is evidence of endothermy (Bakker 1972 [414]). Not all mammalian bone is highly vascularized, nor do the original data on which Bakker's claims are based fully support his hypothesis.

533. Enlow, D.H. 1969. The bone of reptiles. *In The Biology of the Reptilia, Vol.1, Morphology A*, ed. C. Gans, A. d'A. Bellairs, and T.S. Parsons, 45–80. New York: Academic Press.

    There is no single pattern for reptilian bony tissue. Discusses structure of bone with respect to growth and remodeling, and describes the range of bony tissues found in reptiles. Dinosaur primary bone is similar to that of other reptiles, but extensive Haversian secondary remodeling sets dinosaur bone apart from that of any known fossil or extant amphibian or reptile.

534. Johnston, P.A. 1979. Growth rings in dinosaur teeth. *Nature* 278:635–636.

Reports finding growth rings in the teeth of several Late Cretaceous dinosaurs. Seasonal growth rings are an indication of ectothermy in modern animals. (*See also* Bolt and DeMar 1980 [531]; Johnston 1980 [535]; Meinke et al. 1980 [536]; de Ricqlès 1980 [546]; 1983 [547].)

535. Johnston, P.A. 1980. Growth rings in dinosaur teeth. *Nature* 278:195.

A detailed reply to Bolt and De Mar (1980 [531]) and Meinke et al.'s (1980 [536]) critique of Johnston's claim for ectothermic dinosaurs on the basis of seasonal growth rings in teeth (*See* Johnston 1979 [534] for additional cross references on growth rings.)

536. Meinke, D.K., K. Padian, and J. Kappelman. 1980. Growth rings in dinosaur teeth. *Nature* 288:193–194.

A short rebuttal to Johnston (1979 [534]). Argues that growth rings, also found in the teeth of Cretaceous birds, are not necessarily an indication of ectothermy. (*See* Johnston 1979 [534] for additional cross references on growth rings.)

537. Pawlicki, R. 1978. Morphological differentiation of fossil dinosaur bone cells-light, transmission electron microscopy, and scanning electron microscopic studies. *Acta Anatomica* 100:411–418.

Two types of osteocytes can be distinguished in dinosaur bone, one having a more elongate shape. Two types of processes can also be identified, one polar and the other extrapolar. Speculates that the two processes served different functions in intercellular communication.

538. Pawlicki, R. 1983. Metabolic pathways of the fossil dinosaur bones. Part 1. Vascular communication system. *Folia Histochemica et Cytochemica* 21:253–262.

Reports on light and electron microscopy of dinosaur bones of several species from Mongolia. Vascular tracts in dinosaur bone have the same origin and serve the same function as those in modern animals.

539. Reid, R.E.H. 1981. Lamellar-zonal bone with zones and annuli in the pelvis of a sauropod dinosaur. *Nature* 292:49–51.

Reports on a specimen of sauropod bone with an ectothermic histology that contradicts de Ricqlès' claims for endothermy in dinosaurs based on fibro-lamellar bone tissue structure. (*See* de Ricqlès 1974 [545]; 1980 [546]; 1983 [547].)

540. Reid, R.E.H. 1983. High vascularity in bones of dinosaurs, mammals, and birds. *Geological Magazine* 120:191–194.

Disputes Ostrom's claim that high vascularity in bone is a product of Haversian remodeling. Dinosaur fibro-lamellar bone vascularity may also be characteristic of primary bone. Includes one plate (follows p.194).

541. Reid, R.E.H. 1984a. Primary bone and dinosaurian physiology. *Geological Magazine* 121:589–598.

Takes issue with claims for dinosaur endothermy based on bone histology. Primary fibro-lamellar bone is widely distributed in dinosaurs, and implies rapid growth to large size, but not necessarily endothermy. Small endotherms like rodents often lack Haversian bone, despite their very high metabolic rate. The real question is whether the evolution of sustained rapid growth corresponds with achieving endothermy.

542. Reid, R.E.H. 1984b. The histology of dinosaurian bone, and its possible bearing on dinosaurian physiology. In *The Structure, Development and Evolution of Reptiles*, ed. M.W.J. Ferguson, 629–663. *Symposium of the Zoological Society of London* no. 52.

Dinosaur metabolism was neither reptilian nor mammalian. Sustained rapid growth does not mean that dinosaurs were endotherms. Even very early therapsids show bone tissue of the type found in dinosaurs, and it is highly unlikely that these therapsids were endotherms. Reviews the various types of bone tissue found in dinosaur bone, and summarizes arguments for and against endothermy based on bone histology. Therapsids evolved external insulation, which allowed them to evolve towards smaller size. This in turn led to the evolution of true endothermy. Dinosaurs, on the other hand, lacked external insulation, and took a different evolutionary path, towards ever larger body sizes. This led to inertial homeothermy rather than endothermy. (*See* Bakker 1971a [413] and Crompton et al. 1978 [424] for a discussion of endothermy and the nocturnal niche occupied by mammals.)

543. Reid, R.E.H. 1985. On supposed haversian bone from the hadrosaur *Anatosaurus*, and the nature of compact bone in dinosaurs. *Journal of Paleontology* 59:140–148.

The specimen, previously identified as dense Haversian bone, is actually primary fibro-lamellar bone. This bone type indicates that dinosaurs achieved a sustained high growth rate, but does not support endothermy.

544. Reid, R.E.H. 1987. Bone and dinosaurian "endothermy". *Modern Geology* 11:133–154.

Haversian systems and fibro-lamellar bone do not prove that dinosaurs were endothermic. Both bone types are found in some ectotherms, and not all endotherms have these traits. Fibro-lamellar bone, for example, is found in ectothermic therapsids. High body temperatures from inertial homeothermy might explain the level of Haversian canals seen in dinosaur bone. Dinosaurs may have no modern thermoregulatory counterparts. Discusses the evolution of true endothermy, and concludes that dinosaurs may have been "failed endotherms".

545. de Ricqlès, A.J. 1974. Evolution of endothermy: histological evidence. *Evolutionary Theory* 1:51–80.

Suggests that endothermy in tetrapods dates back to the Permian, and that dinosaurs were endothermic. Analyzes bone tissue in several fossil groups. Fibro-lamellar bone tissue is associated with active sustained growth. Reviews the developmental histology and seasonal growth patterns of bone, and discusses gait and relative brain sizes in relation to possible dinosaur endothermy. Bakker and Galton's call for a Class Dinosauria is invalid for several reasons (Bakker and Galton 1974 [825]). Endothermy is not a desirable character to use in systematics. Bakker confuses clade with grade. (*See* Charig 1976 [833] for additional cross references critical of Bakker and Galton's proposal.)

546. de Ricqlès, A.J. 1980. Tissue structures of dinosaur bone: functional significance and possible relation to dinosaur physiology. In *A Cold Look at the Warm-blooded Dinosaurs*, ed. R.D.K. Thomas and E.C. Olson, 103–138. Washington: AAAS.

Although it does not definitely establish endothermy in dinosaurs, dinosaur bone histology agrees best with the endothermic hypothesis. Summarizes his research into bone histology and concludes that dinosaur physiology was unique, and that dinosaurs displayed a range of thermoregulatory strategies, from incipient endothermy to full endothermy. Discusses the possible presence of seasonal growth rings in dinosaur bone, and the problem of Haversian structure. Dinosaur bones show evidence of rapid growth and longevity. (*See* Johnston 1979 [534] for additional cross references on growth rings.)

547. de Ricqlès, A.J. 1983. Cyclical growth in the long limb bones of a sauropod dinosaur. In *Second International Symposium on Mesozoic Terrestrial Ecosystems*, ed. Z. Kielan-Jaworska and H. Osmólska, 225–232. *Acta Palaeontologica Polonica* 28 (1/2).

Are there cyclical growth rings in dinosaur bone? Such rings are found in ectothermic bone, but not in the bones of fast-growing endotherms. Despite some indications of cyclical rings, existing data on dinosaur bones is not convincing. (*See* Johnston 1979 [534] for additional cross references on growth rings.) The author examined an incomplete growth series of the Mid-Jurassic sauropod *Bothriospondylus*. The animal took eighteen to twenty-six years to reach just under half its maximum adult size. This pattern of bone growth suggests that the large sauropods were "passive" homeotherms, reaching a state of warm-bloodedness due to large body mass and large amounts of metabolic heat.

THERMOREGULATION OF MODERN REPTILES

548. Anderson, R.A., and W.H. Karasov. 1988. Energetics of the lizard *Cnemidophorus tigris* and life history consequences of food acquisition mode. *Ecological Monographs* 58:79–110.

    Relates the life history characteristics of lizards to differences in food acquisition and foraging habits by examining the energy budget of the lizard *Cnemidophorus tigris*. Wide foragers, compared with ambush foragers, had larger and fewer young per clutch, and a younger age and larger size at first reproduction. Discusses lizard ecology in relation to thermal environments and food intake levels.

549. Auffenburg, W. 1981. *The Behavioral Ecology of the Komodo Monitor*. Gainesville: University of Florida Press.

    An important treatise on lizard ecology and energetics. Reports on the author's thirteen months of field work on the ecology, behavior, and life history of the Komodo dragon.

550. Bell, C.J. 1980. The scaling of the thermal inertia of lizards. *Journal of Experimental Biology* 86:79–85.

    Describes the calculation and interpretation of the thermal time constant, a useful method for determining the thermal behavior of ectotherms. Speculates that, by extension from modern reptiles, dinosaurs would have had great thermal stability. A 2,000 kg lizard could go almost 48 hours without having to bask or otherwise raise its body temperature because of its surface area/volume ratio.

551. Bennett, A.F., and W.R. Dawson. 1976. Metabolism. In *Biology of the Reptilia, Vol. 5A*, ed. C. Gans and W.R. Dawson, 127–223. New York: Academic Press.

An extensive review of reptilian metabolism, including factors affecting resting metabolic rate, the enzymatic mechanisms of metabolism, and aerobic and anaerobic metabolic pathways during activity.

552. Burggren, W.W. 1987. Form and function in reptilian circulations. *American Zoologist* 27:5–19.

The leading article in a symposium on reptilian cardiovascular adaptations. The author reviews the morphology of the reptilian circulatory system and discusses its evolution. This volume contains several useful papers on heat exchange and thermoregulation in reptiles.

553. Colbert, E.H., R.B. Cowles, and C.M. Bogert. 1946. Temperature tolerances in the American Alligator and their bearing on the habits, evolution, and extinction of the dinosaurs. *Bulletin of the American Museum of Natural History* 86:327–373.

Describes a series of experiments on heat load and thermoregulation in the American alligator. Alligators arranged in a bipedal position (a prodigious feat, modestly described in their methodology) increase their body temperature at a slower rate in direct sunlight than alligators raised on all fours. Alligators resting belly to the ground show the most rapid body temperature increase. Like modern alligators, dinosaurs could have controlled their body temperature through various types of behaviors, such as different basking positions relative to the sun. Like large alligators, large dinosaurs would have experienced a relatively slow increase in body temperature due to their size.

554. Crawford, E.C. 1972. Brain and body temperatures in a panting lizard. *Science* 177:431–433.

Describes the role of panting in lizard thermoregulation.

555. Delaney, M.F., and C.L. Abercrombie. 1986. American alligator food habits in north-central Florida. *Journal of Wildlife Management* 50:348–353.

Analyzes the contents of three hundred and fifty alligator stomachs collected from three Florida lakes. Juveniles fed on water bugs, apple snails, crayfish, muskrat and marsh rabbits. Adults fed mainly on turtles and fish. Females preferred mammalian prey, while males preferred to devour other reptiles. Some juveniles were cannibalized. (*See also* Tracy 1976 [453]; Farlow 1980 [450] for a discussion of secondary carnivory in dinosaurs.)

556. Greenberg, N. 1980. Physiological and behavioral thermoregulation in living reptiles. In *A Cold Look at the Warm-blooded Dinosaurs*, ed. R.D.K. Thomas and E.C. Olson, 141–166. Washington: AAAS.

Living reptiles are a useful model for dinosaur thermoregulation. Thermoregulatory strategies form a continuum, based on life history traits and bioenergetics. Reviews strategies of behavioral thermoregulation including aggregation, fossorial behavior (burrowing), and heliothermy (basking), and discusses thermoregulatory behavior in modern lizards. Behavioral thermoregulation is size dependent, and less effective at larger sizes. *Stegosaurus* plates and ceratopsian shields may have functioned in heat exchange to compensate for the surface area/body volume ratio in larger dinosaurs. Posits an "endothermocentric fallacy" akin to Dodson's "therian chauvinism" (Dodson 1974 [426]). (*See also* Farlow et al. 1976 [427]; de Buffrénil et al. 1984 [422]; 1986 [423].)

557. Harlow, H.J., S.S. Hillman, and M. Hoffman. 1976. The effect of temperature on digestive efficiency in the herbivorous lizard, *Dipsosaurus dorsalis*. *Journal of Comparative Physiology* 111:1–6.

The Apparent Digestibility Coefficient (ADC) is a measure of digestive efficiency. Dipsosaurus lizards showed higher ADC's at higher body temperatures, in a linear relationship. The energetic advantage of this adaptation is unknown.

558. Huey, R.B., and E.R. Pianka. 1977. Seasonal variation in thermoregulatory behavior and body temperature of diurnal Kalahari lizards. *Ecology* 58:1066–1075.

Surveys the behavior of desert lizards in relation to sunlight and activity patterns. Basking, shade seeking, and other thermoregulatory behaviors, help lizards control body temperature with respect to variation in the ambient environment.

559. Huey, R.B., E.R. Pianka, and T.W. Schoener, eds. 1983. *Lizard Ecology: Studies of a Model Organism*. Cambridge: Harvard University Press.

Synthesizes the burgeoning literature on lizard ecology, with sixteen contributions covering the physiological, behavioral, and population ecology of lizards. Includes material on sexual selection, life history traits, and the evolution of lizards.

560. Huey, R.B., and M. Slatkin. 1976. Cost and benefits of lizard thermoregulation. *Quarterly Review of Biology* 51:363–384.

Formulates a mathematical model for lizard thermoregulation. Behavioral and physiological thermoregulation are both energetically costly. The model predicts that if costs are high, thermoregulation may not be a beneficial strategy. Optimum physiological temperatures may not be ecologically optimal. More energy can be put into thermoregulation when food is abundant. Predation and competition can also influence thermoregulatory behavior.

561. Loveridge, J.P. 1984. Thermoregulation in the Nile Crocodile, *Crocodylus niloticus*. In *The Structure, Development and Evolution of Reptiles*, ed. M.W.J. Ferguson, 443–467. *Symposium of the Zoological Society of London* no. 52.

Studies thermoregulatory behavior in Nile Crocodiles. Behaviors include basking, entering or leaving the water, cooling through the tongue and the roof of the mouth, and using aquatic weeds on the back as insulation. All size classes were examined; larger crocodiles showed slower heating rates during basking. Crocodiles basked during the day, but reached peak activity in early evening.

562. Lutcavage, M., and P.L. Lutz. 1986. Metabolic rate and food energy requirements of the leatherback sea turtle, *Dermochelys coriacea*. *Copeia* 1986:796–798.

A short note reporting metabolic rates for hatchling leatherback turtles. Their metabolic rate is three times that of green turtle hatchlings, perhaps due to their higher activity levels.

563. McNab, B.K., and W. Auffenberg. 1976. The effect of large body size on the temperature regulation of the Komodo dragon, *Varanus komodoensis*. *Comparative Biochemistry and Physiology* 55A:345–350.

The thermal physiology of large reptiles may be considerably different in the field than in the laboratory. Wild lizards may not be thermally helpless when the sun sets. Behavioral thermoregulation permits Komodo monitors to maintain body temperatures significantly higher than ambient temperatures. Compares thermal conductance of mammals and reptiles over a wide range of body sizes. Large reptiles (above 100 kg) are more like large mammals than previously believed. Confirms Spotila's conclusion that dinosaurs achieved thermal constancy through large size (Spotila et al. 1973 [444]).

564. Paladino, F.V., M.P. O'Connor, and J.R. Spotila. 1990. Metabolism of leatherback turtles, gigantothermy and thermoregulation of dinosaurs. *Nature* 344:858–860.

Leatherback turtles are one of the largest living reptiles. Resting and nesting adults showed body temperatures intermediate between allometric predictions for mammals and reptiles. Proposes the term "gigantothermy" for the convergence in thermoregulation between large endotherms and large ectotherms. Large dinosaurs would have been able to survive in a wide range of thermal environments due to gigantothermy. Gigantothermy is defined as "the maintenance of constant, high body temperatures by means of large body size, low metabolic rate, and use of peripheral tissues as insulation."

565. Pianka, E.R. 1986. *Ecology and Natural History of Desert Lizards: Analyses of the Ecological Niche and Community Structure.* Princeton: Princeton University Press.

   A comprehensive survey of desert lizard ecology by the leading authority. Pianka's study of life history traits in lizards has helped revolutionize the study of lizard biology. Includes foraging methods, reproductive tactics, and activity patterns with respect to thermoregulation.

566. Porter, W.P., and D.M. Gates. 1969. Thermodynamic equilibria of animals with environment. *Ecological Monographs* 39:227–244.

   Reviews heat transfer, energy budgets, and climatic niche for reptiles (desert iguanas), mammals and birds. "Climate space" is defined as the three-dimensional space formed by the axes of absorbed radiation, wind speed, and air temperature. Considers hypothetical thermal outcomes based on body size, metabolism, and insulation (fur or feathers). (*See also* Spotila et al. 1972 [573].)

567. Pough, F.H. 1973. Lizard energetics and diet. *Ecology* 54:837–844.

   In some families of lizards, size is directly related to diet. In these families, lizards weighing less than 50–100 grams are carnivorous, while those over 300 grams are herbivorous (though their juveniles are initially carnivorous). In other families, however, large lizards are carnivorous. The retention of carnivorous habits with maturity may be a result of morphological specializations, for example, the long tongue of the chameleon, or the loss of legs in the carnivorous snakes. Carnivory is a suitable strategy for large lizards if they can easily capture sizeable prey. (*See* Wilson and Lee 1974 [576].)

568. Pough, F.H. 1980. Advantages of ectothermy for tetrapods. *American Naturalist* 115:92–112.

   Reptilian thermoregulation is no less advanced than mammalian and avian patterns, just different in nature. Discusses the nature of endothermy and ectothermy, and reviews reptilian circulatory system adaptations. Low energy demand is the secret of reptilian and amphibian success. Ecological and morphological adaptations in ectothermic reptiles let them exploit adaptive zones that are unavailable to mammals and birds.

569. Ralph, C.L., B.T. Firth, and J.S. Turner. 1979. The role of the pineal body in ectotherm regulation. *American Zoologist* 19:273–293.

The pineal body plays an important role in behavioral thermoregulation and physiological control of thermoregulatory systems in modern reptiles. The authors discuss its functions and neural connections.

570. Shine, R. 1986. Food habits, habitats, and reproductive biology of four sympatric species of varanid lizards in tropical Australia. *Herpetologica* 42:346–360.

Varanid lizards are usually considered to be unspecialized carnivores. There are, however, major differences between sympatric species in terms of diet, habitat use, and reproduction. Each species exploits local conditions opportunistically. The differences between species are the result of these local adaptations, not of competition between the species.

571. Smith, E.N. 1976. Heating and cooling rates of the American alligator, *Alligator mississippiensis*. *Physiological Zoology* 49:37–48.

Alligators were heated and cooled in air and water. Heating rates were greater than cooling rates, and the difference between rates of heating and cooling increased with increasing size. Recommends the use of the thermal time constant instead of the rate term (°C/min) to describe heating and cooling rates. The data suggests an increasing degree of physiological thermoregulation with increasing size. Alligators may accomplish this by means of cardiovascular adjustments. (*See* Bell 1980 [550] for the methodology of calculating the thermal time constant.)

572. Smith, E.N. 1979. Behavioral and physiological thermoregulation of crocodilians. *American Zoologist* 19:239–247.

Crocodiles use a combination of behavioral and physiological thermoregulation strategies. Behavioral strategies include basking or seeking water. Physiological strategies include changing the blood flow to the skin and surface musculature. Larger crocodiles are better able to alter their heat exchange rates than smaller ones.

573. Spotila, J.R., O.H. Soule, and D.M. Gates. 1972. Biophysical ecology of the alligator: heat energy budgets and climate spaces. *Ecology* 53:1094–1102.

Plots climate space diagrams for large and small alligators. Alligators rely on the thermal properties of water for their survival, and also use water as a place to hunt. Large alligators can survive beyond the limits of their optimal climate space because of their large size and consequent greater capacity to store heat. Small alligators cannot survive beyond the limits of their climate space. (*See* Porter and Gates 1969 [566] for a discussion of climate space.)

574. Stevenson, R.D. 1985. Body size and limits to the daily range of body temperature in terrestrial ectotherms. *American Naturalist* 125:102–117.

Mathematical modeling of heat transfer in ectotherms predicts that large ectotherms might be restricted to areas with small seasonal temperature changes. Discusses implications of the model for behavior and activity patterns. Large inertial homeotherms can be active over longer periods of time.

575. Wieser, W. 1985. A new look at energy conversion in ectothermic and endothermic animals. *Oecologia* 66:506–510.

Energetic models cannot explain why endotherms are less efficient in converting food into biomass than are ectotherms. Ecological and evolutionary factors must also be considered. By increasing total metabolic power ten-fold, but holding reproductive costs constant, endotherms have achieved "emancipation from the burden of reproduction."

576. Wilson, K.J., and A.K. Lee. 1974. Energy expenditure of a large herbivorous lizard. *Copeia* 1974:338–348.

Partitions the energy budget of the large herbivorous lizard *Egernia cunninghami* between maintenance, foraging, and thermoregulation. Large size leads to the selection of larger prey in order to minimize the higher foraging rates that are a consequence of larger body size. Large lizards must be omnivorous. The high cost of catching vertebrate prey may explain the relative scarcity of large carnivorous lizards. (*See also* Pough 1973 [567].)

THE FAR SIDE   By GARY LARSON

"It's roughage, and that's about it."

The Far Side, copyright 1988 & 1991 Universal Press Syndicate. Reprinted with permission. All rights reserved.

Chapter Six

Dinosaur Ecology

In order to reconstruct the ecology of the ancient world, we must first understand the ecology of the modern world. How do animals seek their prey? How do they select habitats in which their reproductive success will be highest? How do the physical and biological constraints of their evolutionary heritage and their environment interact to shape their life history characteristics? (Dunham et al. 1989 [592]; Begon and Mortimer 1986 [671]; Case 1978 [674]; Fowler 1981 [680]; Pianka 1970 [700]; Pianka 1983 [701]).

We cannot hope for ultimate answers to these questions about dinosaurs, when all we have are a handful of bones and a motley collection of tracks and traces. But we can make reasonable assumptions about what their lives must have been like, based on the lives of the modern animals they most resemble, either physically or ecologically.

We can reconstruct at least the broad outlines of ancient environments from the abundant geological and biological clues in the fossil record. A knowledge of the depositional characteristics of sedimentary environments tells us whether the area we are examining was once a shallow freshwater lake, a cool upland meadow, or a vast deltaic plain, braided by stream channels.

From the countless grains of pollen and leaf impressions scattered throughout the layers of sedimentary rock, we can reconstruct the flora through which the dinosaurs moved, the plants they must have eaten, even the temperature and precipitation they experienced (Behrensmeyer and Kidwell 1988 [578]; Béland and Russell 1978 [579]; Dodson et al. 1980 [591]; Jerzykiewicz and Sweet 1987 [600]; Lehman 1987 [601]; Lucas and Niall 1983 [605]; Russell et al. 1980 [608]).

A wealth of microfossils further fills in dark corners of the forgotten past (Brinkman 1990 [583]; Dodson 1987 [589]; Eberth 1990 [1020]). Knowing the species of fish, crocodiles, turtles, molluscs, and plankton, we can add yet more detail to our growing picture of the lost world of the dinosaurs (Fraser and Walkden 1983 [595]; Padian 1989 [607]).

One of the most important breakthroughs in the past two decades has been the growing awareness of how much the present can teach us about the past. Body size, for example, is a life-history variable of great ecological significance for dinosaurs. Recent work in this area on modern birds and mammals should have enormous significance for the interpretation of dinosaur ecology (Calder 1983 [672]; Calder 1984 [673]; Damuth 1981 [677]; Harestad and Bunnell 1979 [682]; Peters 1983 [697]; Peters and Raelson 1984 [698]; Peters and Wassenberg 1983 [699]; Schmidt-Nielsen 1984 [703]; Reiss 1985 [736]). Implications of body size for stance and gait are discussed in Chapter Five.

Another fruitful line of current research is the study of herbivory. No one has ever found a dinosaur with the remains of a flowering plant clasped in its stilled jaws, but we can surmise with reasonable certainty that many, if not most, dinosaurs fed on gymnosperms and on the tender angiosperms that spread rapidly throughout the Cretaceous globe.

From our knowledge of herbivory in modern reptiles, birds, and mammals, we can make reasonable inferences about herbivory in dinosaurs. General articles on herbivore coevolution, plant defense systems, and herbivore gut flora are integrated in this chapter with material on dinosaur herbivory. Studies of specific modern herbivores (elephants, cassowaries, hippos, giraffes etc.) are treated in the section covering the ecology of modern animals.

Knowing the type of dentition and jaw mechanisms revealed by detailed studies of fossilized hadrosaurs, ceratopsians, and others, we can deduce the vegetation types they fed on, and compare their browse profiles with those of contemporary herbivores (Farlow 1976a [593]).

Large herbivorous dinosaurs would have had an immense effect on vegetation simply by passing through it, as shown by studies of modern elephants (Laws 1970 [687]; Laws et al. 1975 [688]). In one such study, a small bull herd pushed over 29% of the mature trees, destroying an average of 7% of the trees per year (Wing and Buss 1970 [708]). Average-size elephant herds, with a biomass of about 10,000 kg, require 6% of their live weight in foliage per day, or about 600 kg of forage. Brush fires typically follow elephant damage, completing the cycle of forest conversion to grassland.

Dinosaurs, like elephants, would have also excreted large amounts of seeds, dispersing them in a rich growth medium (Janzen 1984 [631]). The paths of elephants through the forest can be followed long after they have departed, by noting the circular patches of tall vegetation that arise from their excrement. Dinosaurs would have similarly enriched the soil by adding colossal amounts of manure.

Early angiosperms are thought to have been "weedy generalists", colonizing species adapted to spread quickly through the type of disturbed habitat that herbivorous dinosaurs would have left in their wake (Doyle and Hickey 1976 [244]; Hickey and Doyle 1977 [247]; Retallack and Dilcher 1981 [258]; Retallack and Dilcher 1986 [259]). The disturbance of large herds of herbivorous dinosaurs would have cleared vast patches of cycads and other gymnosperms, opening up new habitat for the invading angiosperms (Coe et al. 1987 [614]; Weishampel and Norman 1989 [655]; Wing and Tiffney 1987 [656]).

Bakker (1978 [611]) goes so far as to credit dinosaurs with "inventing" flowering plants. Whether you find Bakker's coevolution hypothesis credible depends to a large extent on which timetable you accept for the origin and radiation of angiosperms. Did the plants radiate as a direct result of dinosaur herbivory, or did the Cretaceous dinosaurian herbivores radiate to adapt to the new tender angiosperm vegetation? Flowers may have affected dinosaurs as much as dinosaurs affected flowers.

Whichever hypothesis prevails, there is no doubt that a significant change occurred in browse height and feeding niches, somewhere between the large sauropods of the Jurassic and the low-browsing herbivores of the Cretaceous. The Cretaceous browse-height pattern compares favorably with that of modern mammalian herbivores (Coe et al. 1987 [614]; Weishampel and Norman 1989 [655]).

Dinosaurs consumed enormous amounts of vegetation every day. *Apatosaurus* ate over 92 kg of plant matter per day, and the towering *Brachiosaurus* shoveled in over 122 kg per day (Coe et al. 1987 [614]). Dinosaurs on the Morrison plain may have sustained an incredible 93,000 kg of dinosaur biomass per square kilometer!

In addition to disturbance, grazing itself may affect the growth rate and growth characteristics of vegetation. Studies by McNaughton on the effects of Serengeti grazers suggest that these modern herbivores create a "grazing lawn", facilitating energy flow through the ecosystem (McNaughton 1976 [691]; 1984 [635]; 1985 [636]). Belsky (1986

[613]), however, reviews the evidence for the coevolution of grasses and grazers and questions McNaughton's conclusions.

How did ancient plants defend themselves against herbivory? Modern gymnosperms have relatively unspecialized chemical defenses, relying on the gradual buildup of compounds in long-lasting evergreen leaves. Angiosperms, on the other hand, are noted for an array of sophisticated chemical defenses (Coley 1983 [615]; Coley et al. 1985 [616]; Freeland and Janzen 1974 [619]; Kubitzki and Gottlieb 1984 [633]).

While gymnosperms had millions of years to coevolve defenses against dinosaur herbivory, the newly evolved angiosperms were probably not as well defended, and offered a rich and easily digested food source for herbivorous dinosaurs. As the angiosperms radiated, they began to evolve the more efficient chemical defenses that characterize most species in the modern flora (Rhoades 1985 [642]; Rosenthal and Janzen 1979 [645]).

Finally, the evolution of larger fruits at the end of the Cretaceous suggests that frugivory was becoming an important component of Mesozoic ecology. In modern tropical forests from 50% to 75% of trees with fleshy fruits are adapted to attract herbivores for seed dispersal (Howe and Smallwood 1982 [629]). While some Cretaceous birds were probably frugivorous, small to medium sized bipedal dinosaurs were probably also important frugivores and seed dispersal agents.

Tiffney calculated diaspore size from seven Cretaceous floras, and found that most diaspores were relatively small (Tiffney 1984 [652]). In the Late Cretaceous, however, diaspore size increases abruptly. Berries and thick-walled drupes and seeds enter the fossil record.

Angiosperms with large seeds and fruits could now invade the closed gymnosperm forest canopy, because their embryos had sufficient nutrition to establish themselves on the forest floor. They could persist as shaded seedlings, drawing on stored reserves until gaps opened up in the gymnosperm canopy. Gaps from severe weather, natural treefall, and dinosaur disturbance must have been common events in Cretaceous forests.

This increase in diaspore size probably marks the advent of coevolved animal-seed dispersal systems. One obvious candidate for a frugivorous dinosaur is *Struthiomimus*. Its diet has long been a source of speculation. Barnum Brown claimed that it ate small crabs and other seafood. William Beebe thought it ate insects and ants, though its limbs

Dinosaur Ecology

are poorly adapted for digging in the dirt (Norman 1985 [14]). Henry Fairfield Osborn suggested in the early 1900's that *Struthiomimus* was adapted for foraging on small trees and shrubs (Osborn 1916 [606]). Its limbs are well suited for grasping such vegetation and pulling it to the animal's mouth (Nicholls and Russell 1985 [365]). Russell (1972 [389]) dismissed this idea, and made *Struthiomimus* into a predator on small animals, but Osborn's hypothesis is the only one that explains many aspects of the anatomy of this highly evolved bipedal dinosaur.

Perhaps a good modern analog for *Struthiomimus* and similar Cretaceous frugivores is the modern cassowary, a large ratite that consumes the fruit of at least seventy-five plant species in the Australian rain forest (Stocker and Irvine 1983 [706]; Crome 1975 [716]).

Dinosaurs were relatively sophisticated herbivores, with jaw mechanisms generally superior to those of modern herbivorous reptiles. While the iguana is restricted to simple cropping (Throckmorton 1976 [648]), ornithopod dinosaurs developed specialized hinge mechanisms to permit grinding of food (Norman and Weishampel 1985 [639]; Norman 1984 [796]). Similar adaptations for jaw rotation are found in other groups.

Some dinosaurs with weak teeth, like the sauropods, probably relied on swallowing stones to grind plants in a gastric mill (Bakker 1971b [577]; Galton 1986 [623]; Stokes 1987 [647]). Many dinosaur species had advanced dental batteries with rows of replacement teeth similar to modern reptiles and sharks. Teeth worn by continuous consumption of tough vegetation were readily replaced (Gow 1975 [625]; Hopson 1980 [627]).

Even when plant matter is thoroughly chewed, it is difficult to digest. Fermentation of plant matter by gut microbes helps modern herbivores break down the thick cell walls of plants (Hungate 1975 [630]; McBee 1971 [634]). It is not a great leap of faith to assume that some, or even most, herbivorous dinosaurs shared the same microbial fermentation system so widespread among modern herbivores (Farlow 1987 [618]).

Microbial fermentation also has interesting implications for parental care. Hatchling iguanas, for example, must eat the feces of the adult to acquire an inoculation of gut microbes. Other animals accomplish this generational transfer by regurgitating food into the nest (Rogers 1985 [644]; Troyer 1982 [786]).

Parental care in dinosaurs has been an active area of speculation and research, with several intriguing lines of evidence emerging in recent years (Coombs 1982 [751]; Coombs 1989 [753]; Winkler and Murry 1989 [790]; Fiorillo 1987 [757]; Forster 1990 [758]). The work of John Horner in unearthing the Egg Island and Egg Mountain sites in Montana has been especially important in this regard. Horner established that hypsilophodonts and hadrosaurs were nesting in colonies, much like modern seabirds (Horner and Gorman 1988 [41]; Horner 1982 [765]; 1984 [766]; 1989 [767]; Horner and Makela 1979 [768]; Horner and Weishampel 1989 [770]).

Careful study of the nests revealed further insights into juvenile and parental behavior. The lower halves of the hypsilophodont eggs, for example, were still intact in the nest, indicating that the precocial animals left the nest right after hatching. The hadrosaur nests, on the other hand, contained only fragmented shells; the young must have remained in the nest for some time after hatching. Clutches found at several horizons throughout Horner's dig show that the nesting dinosaurs displayed a site fidelity analogous to many modern colonial birds, returning to the same site year after year to breed.

At least some species of dinosaurs probably used underground or buried nests, in the manner of crocodilians and modern megapode birds (Seymour 1979 [782]; Seymour and Ackerman 1980 [783]). The maternal behavior of alligators might be a useful model for dinosaur parental behavior (Garrick and Lang 1977 [722]; Garrick et al. 1978 [723]; Hunt and Watanabe 1982 [771]; Kushlan 1973 [774]; Kushlan and Kushlan 1980 [775]; Woodward et al. 1984 [791]).

Coombs gives a thorough review of modern analogs for dinosaur nesting behavior (Coombs 1989 [753]). Nest temperatures may have determined sex ratios, as they do in modern sea turtles, crocodilians, and other reptiles (Bull 1980 [743]; Chabreck 1973 [748]; Deeming and Ferguson 1989 [754]; Paladino et al. 1989 [778]; Standora and Spotila 1985 [784]; Vogt and Bull 1984 [788]).

Several authors have commented on the supposed rarity of juveniles in the fossil record. Callison and Quimby demonstrate that many specimens thought to be juveniles are actually small adults, and they provide an ontogenetic model to distinguish juveniles from adults (Callison and Quimby 1984 [745]). Callison suggests that juveniles may be more abundant than we think (Callison 1987 [584]). Richmond proposes that the combination of large size and slow growth rate would

Dinosaur Ecology

naturally lead to a slow rate of population replacement, and therefore few juveniles (Richmond 1965 [780]). Tracy suggests that secondary carnivory might be the cause of the scarcity of juveniles. The juvenile fossil record imay be biased by hungry Tyrannosaurs (Tracy 1976 [453]).

Courtship behavior and sexual selection in dinosaurs has also received much attention, with several studies focusing on the role of horns, frills, and crests in intraspecific competition and the attraction of mates. We must use caution in selecting living models for dinosaur behavior. The ideal organisms would be animals that are closely related, morphologically similar, or ecologically equivalent (Coombs 1989 [753]). Trivers (1985 [740]) is highly recommended for an introduction to modern behavioral ecology.

This chapter includes several articles on modern animals, both herbivores and carnivores, that might serve as good models for dinosaur behavior and ecology (*See* for example Coe et al. 1976 [676]; Lock 1972 [689]; McNaughton and Georgiadis 1986 [692]; Owen-Smith 1988 [693]; Pellew 1984 [696];Sinclair and Norton-Griffiths 1979 [705]; Laurie 1982 [729]).

Deinonychus and other small predatory dinosaurs, for instance, may have hunted in packs. Modern studies of lions and other pack hunters might explain how and why this behavior evolved (Caraco and Wolf 1975 [659]; Farlow 1976b [663]; MacDonald 1983 [666]; Paul 1987 [667]). Carnivores that hunt in packs gain a "flexible body mass", an aggregate predator weight that can be readily adjusted to the size and nature of a particular prey species (Earle 1987 [662]).

By analogy with modern horned mammals (Geist 1966 [724]; Geist 1974 [725]), the ceratopsians probably used their elaborate frilled shields and horns in intraspecific combat and display, presumably to establish dominance hierarchies, defend territories, and attract females (Farlow and Dodson 1975 [720]; Molnar 1977 [732]).

The pachycephalosaurs used their domed heads in a similar fashion, engaging in intraspecific head-butting contests (Galton 1971 [721]; Sues 1978 [738]). The fact that these dinosaurs are sexually dimorphic with respect to dome morphology offers strong support for this hypothesis (Chapman et al. 1981 [714]).

The crests of hadrosaurs may have been used in visual displays for competition and courtship. They may have also been used in vocalization for species recognition, group cohesion, courtship and other types of social behavior (Hopson 1975 [726]; Weishampel 1981 [741]).

There is good evidence for herding and other types of gregarious behavior (Lockley et al. 1983 [730]; Ostrom 1972 [733]). Careful analysis of trackways reveals that many species traveled in herds. Thulborn presents evidence of a stampede, probably caused by the approach of a carnosaur (Thulborn and Wade 1979 [739]). Currie and Dodson (1984 [717]) describe a case of mass death of a herd of ceratopsians. Additional material on trackways will be found in Chapter Five [492–516].

It is difficult to convey the depth and breadth of the growing field of modern ecology, and the rapidly expanding field of paleoecology in a single chapter. Much has been included, but of necessity much has been left to the imagination and curiosity of the reader. I have tried to single out those areas which I feel show the greatest promise for future research, drawing on the work of paleontologists and adding much material from modern terrestrial ecology.

Following a section on general dinosaur ecology are sections examining dinosaurs as herbivores, including several general articles on herbivory and plant defenses, and dinosaurs as carnivores, including papers on modern social carnivores and scavengers.

These are followed by a section on the ecology of those modern animals, like the elephants, small ungulates, and large flightless birds, which are most often selected as models for dinosaur ecology. This section also includes several theoretical papers on general animal ecology, including life history theory and the effects of body size on ecological requirements. The chapter concludes with a section on dinosaur behavior, including relevant material on the social behavior of ecologically similar birds, mammals, and reptiles, and a section surveying the growing literature on dinosaur and reptilian nesting habits, eggs, and juveniles.

ECOLOGY OF DINOSAURS

577. Bakker, R.T. 1971b. Ecology of *Brontosaurus. Nature* 229:172–174.

Brontosaurus (=*Apatosaurus*) was long thought to be an aquatic animal, and is often depicted in older illustrations as immersed in a steamy swamp. The weak teeth that supposedly implied a diet of soft swampy vegetation may not have been critical in digestion; the animal may have had a gastric mill to grind tough vegetation. The high external nares, purported to function in snorkel-type breathing, are also found in fully terrestrial lizards. *Brontosaurus* limbs were elephantine, not unlike the less robust limbs of the hippopotamus. Sauropods would not have been able to escape from theropods by entering the water. (*See also* Coombs 1975 [587].)

578. Behrensmeyer, A.K., and S.M. Kidwell, eds. 1988. Ecological and evolutionary implications of taphonomic processes. *Palaeogeography, Palaeoclimatology, Palaeoecology* 63:1–291.

Fossil preservation depends on a combination of paleoenvironmental conditions and the habits of the animals themselves. This special issue features fourteen articles examining the ecological implications of taphonomic processes in a variety of ancient habitats.

579. Béland, P., and D.A. Russell. 1978. Paleoecology of Dinosaur Provincial Park (Cretaceous), Alberta, interpreted from the distribution of articulated vertebrate remains. *Canadian Journal of Earth Sciences* 15:1012–1024.

Articulated remains are not uniformly distributed in the Oldman Formation at Dinosaur Provincial Park. The distribution may be related to paleoenvironmental gradients, particularly a decline in primary productivity from west to east within the Park. Discusses the trophic relationships of an ectothermic dinosaur community, and dinosaur habitat preferences. Woody plants supported the large herbivore biomass in the Park, and the herbaceous layer was relatively unimportant.

580. Benton, M.J. 1979. Ecological succession among Late Palaeozoic and Mesozoic tetrapods. *Palaeogeography, Palaeoclimatology, Palaeoecology* 26:127–150.

Reviews the available niches of the Upper Paleozoic and Mesozoic, and the animals that filled them. "Ecological replacement", where one species comes to occupy a niche previously occupied by another species, occurs frequently in major taxa during this period. Available niches are plotted against time for major taxa. The ecological advantages of ectothermy (water conservation, tolerance of a wide temperature range, and decreased food requirements) helped archosaurs replace therapsids. The ornithischian radiation was fueled by the radiation of the gymnosperms upon which they fed. An appendix lists early tetrapods and their ecological niches [*See* 581].

581. Benton, M.J. 1983. Dinosaur success in the Triassic: a non-competitive ecological model. *Quarterly Review of Biology* 58:29–51.

Thecodonts did not become dominant until the therapsids had all but disappeared, nor did dinosaurs become dominant until the thecodonts had died out. These faunal replacements were not the result of competition. Changes in climate and vegetation led to the extinctions of several groups at the end of the Triassic, opening many niches to the opportunistically radiating dinosaurs. (For additional references on faunal replacement and competition, *See* Bonaparte 1982 [209]; Benton 1979 [580]; Charig 1984 [586]; Crompton and Attridge 1986 [617]; Galton 1986 [623]; Charig 1980 [794]; Tucker and Benton 1982 [801]; Bonaparte 1969 [805].)

582. Benton, M.J. 1984. Small companions of early dinosaurs. *Nature* 307:111–112.

A short news note reviewing recent work on the reptilian fauna of the Bristol fissures, a cave system containing the remains of small reptiles that coexisted with dinosaurs. (*See also* Fraser 1988 [594]; Fraser and Waldken 1983 [595].)

583. Brinkman, D.B. 1990. Paleoecology of the Judith River Formation (Campanian) of Dinosaur Provincial Park, Alberta, Canada: evidence from vertebrate microfossil localities. *Palaeogeography, Palaeoclimatology, Palaeoecology* 78:37–54.

Thirty-four vertebrate taxa examined from screenwashed samples from the Judith River Formation show a non-random distribution which reflects ecological zonation of the coastal plain. Two ecological assemblages can be identified, an inland assemblage appearing in the lower beds, and a coastal assemblage in the upper beds. Ceratopsians are members of the coastal assemblage, while *Troödon* and *Thescelosaurus* are members of the inland community. This study supports Eberth (1990 [1020]) in demonstrating that vertebrate microfossils are "sensitive to local environmental conditions." (*See also* Dodson 1987 [589].)

584. Callison, G. 1987. Small problems: biological implications of tiny dinosaurs. In *Dinosaurs Past and Present*, Volume I, ed. S.J. Czerkas and E.C. Olson, 70–79. Los Angeles: Natural History Museum of Los Angeles County.

Small saurischians and ornithischians, about the size of a chicken (1 kg), are rare finds. Their presence in the fossil record, often as fragmentary remains, suggests the probability that they, and the remains of juveniles of larger species, may have been more abundant than we think. Reviews some of the ecological advantages of small size, and its implications for metabolic rates and surface/volume allometric relationships. Such "r-selected" organisms can thrive in unpredictable environments.

585. Carpenter, K. 1987. Paleoecological significance of droughts during the Late Cretaceous of the western interior. In *Fourth Symposium on Mesozoic Terrestrial Ecosystems, Short Papers*, ed. P.J. Currie and E. Koster, 42–47. Drumheller, Alta.: Tyrell Museum of Paleontology.

Droughts are not limited to arid environments, but can occur wherever climates are seasonal. Reviews the effects of drought on vegetation and vertebrates. Vertebrates usually die from lack of food in droughts, not from lack of drinking water. Predators benefit from the increased number of weakened herbivores. Droughts may have been common in upland environments. Cites circumstantial evidence from museum specimens of possible drought-related pathologies.

586. Charig, A. 1984. Competition between therapsids and archosaurs during the Triassic period: a review and synthesis of current theories. In *The Structure, Development and Evolution of Reptiles*, ed. M.W.J. Ferguson, 597–628. *Symposia of the Zoological Society of London* no. 52.

Archosaurs replaced therapsids during the Triassic as the dominant terrestrial vertebrates. This faunal replacement was the result of competition between the two sympatric groups, which occupied the same broad adaptive niche. This is contrary to the opinions expressed by Tucker and Benton (Benton 1983 [581]; Tucker and Benton 1982 [801]). There are several possible explanations for the archosaurs' success, such as their improved stance and locomotion, or physiological improvements such as endothermy or a better system of nitrogen excretion. None of the physiological scenarios are "sufficiently well founded," whereas locomotory improvements are obvious from the fossil record. (*See* Benton 1983 [581] for additional cross references on faunal replacement and competition.)

587. Coombs, W.P. jr. 1975. Sauropod habits and habitats. *Palaeogeography, Palaeoclimatology, Palaeoecology* 17:1–33.

The usual picture of sauropods immersed up to their necks in water is incorrect. This image was probably created by Owen, and copied by later authorities. We cannot infer habitat preference solely from dentition; not all aquatic vegetation is soft. Interpretation of narial structure is also ambiguous. The long neck could have functioned as a snorkel, but would have worked equally well as a means of reaching tall vegetation on land. Sauropod body shape is similar to that of modern large terrestrial tetrapods. Sauropods were probably capable of rearing up on their hind legs to reach high branches. They entered the water at least on occasion, and their trackways suggest gregarious behavior. (*See also* Bakker 1971b [577].)

588. Coombs, W.P. jr 1978. Theoretical aspects of cursorial adaptations in dinosaurs. *Quarterly Review of Biology* 53:393–418.

A review of physical constraints on cursorial animals finds several traits invariably associated with the cursorial habit over a wide range of taxa. These include long limbs, small forelimbs (bipeds), hinge-like joints, and the reduction of the tibia-fibula and radius-ulna to single structures. Reviews the potential speeds of dinosaurs, and classifies them as graviportal, mediportal, subcursorial or cursorial. Small ornithischian bipeds and small theropods were the fastest, but they were slower than the fastest modern runners. Quadrupedal species could move at about the speed of a hippopotamus. 50 kg is the optimum mass for top running speed.

589. Dodson, P. 1987. Microfaunal studies of dinosaur paleoecology, Judith River Formation of southern Alberta. In *Fourth Symposium on Mesozoic Terrestrial Ecosystems, Short Papers*, ed. P.J. Currie and E. Koster, 70–75. Drumheller, Alta.: Tyrell Museum of Paleontology.

Sixteen-thousand microfossils were collected from twenty-four sites in the Judith River Formation (Campanian) to test the utility of microfossil evidence in paleoecological research. Microfossils reflect the known relative abundance of dinosaurs, and are thus a potentially important source of ecological information. (*See also* Eberth 1990 [1020] and Brinkman 1990 [583].)

590. Dodson, P. 1990. Counting dinosaurs: how many kinds were there? *Proceedings of the National Academy of Sciences* 87:7608–7612.

Our understanding of dinosaur diversity is hampered by poor taxonomy, problems in stratigraphic interpretation, and bias in preservation and collection. Since 1824, 540 genera and about 800 species of dinosaurs have been proposed; only 285 genera and 336 species are valid. About 2,100 articulated dinosaur specimens exist in the world's museum collections. Almost half of these species are only represented by a single specimen, and 74% are represented by five or fewer specimens. Discusses continental and chronological distribution of dinosaurs. About 40% of known species are from the last 10 million years of the Mesozoic; many periods are poorly documented. Estimates longevity of genera in the fossil record, and discusses three models of dinosaur diversity. Estimates range from 645 up to 3,285 genera, with 900 to 1,200 genera the most likely conservative estimate. A maximum of 100 genera existed at any one time, which compares reasonably well with modern large mammals. (*See also* Russell 1984 [1031] for additional cross references on estimating species diversity.)

591. Dodson, P., A.K. Behrensmeyer, R.T. Bakker, and J.S. McIntosh. 1980. Taphonomy and palaeoecology of the dinosaur beds of the Jurassic Morrison Formation. *Paleobiology* 6:208–232.

The distribution of species in the Morrison Formation parallels the broad distribution across varied habitats seen in modern communities of large mammals. Describes the lacustrine, riverine, and flood plain environments existing on a vast alluvial plain. *Camarasaurus*, *Apatosaurus*, *Diplodocus*, *Allosaurus* and *Stegosaurus* were the most abundant species, and formed a true community. Their remains are most common in channel deposits. Discusses gregarious behavior, displayed by *Camarasaurus* and *Diplodocus*, and the relatively solitary behavior of *Apatosaurus*. Large herbivores frequented shorelines and swamps, but were neither aquatic nor semi-aquatic. Precipitation was seasonal, and water was probably a limiting factor during part of the year. This may have prompted large-scale annual migrations. Taphonomic characteristics result in mass beds of poorly articulated bones.

(*See* Brouwers et al. 1987 [1049] for additional cross references on polar dinosaurs and migration.)

592. Dunham, A.E., K.L. Overall, W.P. Porter, and C.A. Forster. 1989. Implications of ecological energetics and biophysical and developmental constraints for life-history variation in dinosaurs. In *Paleobiology of the Dinosaurs*, ed. J.O. Farlow, 1–19. *Geological Society of America Special Paper* no. 238.

It is difficult to discuss the life history of extinct animals, but the authors offer a good review of the basic problems and possibilities in extending this active area of modern ecological research to the study of dinosaur ecology. A computer simulation of dinosaur demographics shows that, within the assumptions of the model, life histories with a first age of reproduction of twenty years are most unlikely to evolve. Estimates made by Case (1978 [674]) based on the assumption of an ectothermic metabolism, are much too high. Mathematical models of energy constraints suggest that large dinosaurs required a minimum of five years or more (around ten to twelve years) to mature. This model does not assume either an endothermic or ectothermic metabolism. Incorporates microclimate assumptions, based on modern southern Louisiana climates, into an improved heat-exchange model. The model predicts that an annual migration would have been necessary for dinosaurs to maintain thermal balance year round. Nutritional models suggest that large herbivorous dinosaurs relied on bacterial fermentation. (*See* Brouwers et al. 1987 [1049] for additional cross references on polar dinosaurs and migration. *See* Farlow 1987a [618] for additional cross references on fermentation in herbivores.)

593. Farlow, J.O. 1976a. A consideration of the trophic dynamics of a Late Cretaceous large-dinosaur community. *Ecology* 57:841–857.

The large size of the dinosaur population in the Oldman Formation (Late Cretaceous) argues against endothermic metabolism. Estimates of annual secondary productivity of endothermic herbivores indicate that such large herbivore populations would outstrip estimated available primary productivity. The collection bias for large carnivores, however, prevents this methodology from conclusively establishing dinosaurian metabolism. Presents a mathematical model of the trophic dynamics of the Oldman Formation community, and compares it with similar estimates for comparable communities of large mammals. Discusses probable dinosaur diets and community ecology. (*See also* Béland and Russell 1979 [448].)

594. Fraser, N. 1988. At the feet of the dinosaurs. *New Scientist*, 8 October, 39–42.

Karst habitat in Britain at the Triassic/Jurassic boundary has yielded the remains of sphenodontids and other small reptiles, thecodonts, early mammals and other animals that lived at the feet of early dinosaurs. The remains are found in caves and fissures. Many of these animals were probably insectivorous. (*See* [595]; Benton 1984 [582].)

595. Fraser, N.C., and G.M. Walkden. 1983. The ecology of a Late Triassic reptile assemblage from Gloucestershire, England. *Palaeogeography, Palaeoclimatology, Palaeoecology* 42:341–365.

Describes a Late Triassic reptilian assemblage gleaned from British caves and fissures. This is a technical paper covering the same ground as Fraser's subsequent popular account. (*See* [594]; Benton 1984 [582].)

596. Galton, P.M. 1971a. *Hypsilophodon*, the cursorial non-arboreal dinosaur. *Nature* 231:159–161.

Contrary to previous suggestions by Swinton and others, the primitive bipedal ornithischian *Hypsilophodon* was not arboreal. A reconsideration of its functional anatomy shows it to be cursorial, adapted for fast terrestrial running [*See* 597].

597. Galton, P.M. 1971b. The mode of life of *Hypsilophodon*, the supposedly arboreal ornithopod dinosaur. *Lethaia* 4:453–465.

A more detailed analysis of the argument presented in Galton 1971a [596]. *Hypsilophodon* was well adapted for a fully cursorial, not arboreal, lifestyle.

598. Gould, S.J. 1981. Palaeontology plus ecology as palaeobiology. In *Theoretical Ecology: Principles and Applications*. 2d ed., ed. R.M. May, 295–317. Oxford: Blackwell.

A seminal paper on a controversial issue. Gould decries the common picture of paleontology as "the dullest variety of empirical cataloguing practiced by the narrowest of specialists." The modern development of theoretical ecology has breathed new life into paleontology. Gould discusses diversity, adaptive strategies, and mass extinctions as examples of how ecology has illuminated paleontological theory.

599. Hotton, N. III, P.D. MacLean, J.J. Roth, and E.C. Roth, eds. 1986. *The Ecology and Biology of Mammal-like Reptiles*. Washington: Smithsonian Institution Press.

A comprehensive collection of papers surveying the ecology and evolution of this critical tetrapod group. Therapsids gave rise to mammals, and may have competed with early archosaurs. (*See* Benton 1983 [581] for additional cross references on faunal replacement and competition between therapsids, thecodonts, and dinosaurs.)

600. Jerzykiewicz, T., and A.R. Sweet. 1987. Semiarid flood plain as a paleo-environmental setting of the Upper Cretaceous dinosaurs: sedimentological evidence from Mongolia and Alberta. In *Fourth Symposium on Mesozoic Terrestrial Ecosystems, Short Papers*, ed. P.J. Currie and E. Koster, 120–124. Drumheller, Alta.: Tyrell Museum of Paleontology.

Both Mongolian and southern Albertan paleosols show evidence of arid and semiarid conditions in the Late Cretaceous, and both are rich in dinosaur remains. The semiarid flood plain environment contrasts with the subtropical and tropical swamps usually depicted as typical dinosaur environments.

601. Lehman, T.M. 1987. Late Maastrichtian paleoenvironments and dinosaur biogeography in the western interior of North America. *Palaeogeography, Palaeoclimatology, Palaeoecology* 60:189–217.

Three depositional environments, piedmont, alluvial plain, and coastal lowlands, can be identified in the late Maastrichtian North American western interior. Several major physiographic changes, such as the retreat of the inland sea, greatly altered the stable environments that had persisted through much of the Late Cretaceous. Three faunas arose which were adapted to these new depositional environments. An *Alamosaurus* fauna inhabited seasonal, semiarid, southern intermontane basins. A *Triceratops* fauna dwelled in the humid coastal flood plains and swamps that bordered the northern edge of the retreating sea. A *Leptoceratops* fauna lived in cooler piedmont habitats along the Cordilleran Overthrust Belt. This adaptability argues against dinosaur extinction from an inability to cope with altered climatic conditions.

602. Lockley, M.G., and K. Conrad. 1987. Mesozoic tetrapod tracksites and their application in paleoecological census studies. In *Fourth Symposium on Mesozoic Terrestrial Ecosystems, Short Papers*, ed. P.J. Currie and E. Koster, 148–153. Drumheller, Alta.: Tyrell Museum of Paleontology.

    Paleoecological reconstruction based on body fossils is consistent with interpretations based on tracks. Briefly reviews data for two major southwestern American sites, Popo Agie and Sloan Canyon (Late Triassic), and discusses Jurassic and Cretaceous track sites. (*See* [603]. *See also* Lockley 1987b [503].)

603. Lockley, M.G., K.J. Houck, and N.K. Prince. 1986. North America's largest dinosaur trackway site: implications for Morrison Formation paleoecology. *Geological Society of America Bulletin* 97:1163–1176.

    The world's largest continuously mapped trackway assemblage lies in the Purgatoire Valley of Colorado's Upper Jurassic Morrison Formation. The tracks are found in a lacustrine environment, and comprise over 100 trackways with some 1,300 footprints of bipedal and quadrupedal dinosaurs. A wealth of ecological information can be extracted from this assemblage, including predator/prey ratios (about 1:30), speeds, and behavior. Rare sauropod tracks are found here, mixed with tridactyl ornithopod tracks, indicating gregarious behavior between these taxa. (*See* [602]. *See also* Lockley 1987b [503].)

604. Lucas, S.G. 1980. Dinosaur communities of the San Juan Basin: a case for lateral variations in the composition of Late Cretaceous communities. In *Advances in San Juan Basin Paleontology*, ed. S.G. Lucas, J.K. Rigby, and B.S. Kues, 337–393. Albuquerque: University of New Mexico Press.

Complete skeletal finds are rare in the basin. The revolution in paleoecology has concentrated on other sites with more dramatic fossils. Lucas compares two assemblages from different depositional environments. The Fruitland ecosystem consists of coastal river deposits and their associated poorly-drained flood plains. Lucas describes a *Parasaurolophus* community, with a complex association of lower vertebrates based on euryhaline fishes. Upland terrestrial communities were dominated by hadrosaurs and ceratopsians, with tyrannosaurs as top carnivores. The *Alamosaurus sanjuanensis* community appears less complex, but additional work may uncover the lower trophic levels. The two communities are correlated with differences in the physical environments. Discusses aspects of lateral variation in dinosaur communities.

605. Lucas, S.G., and J.M. Niall. 1983. Vertebrate paleoecology of the Late Campanian (Cretaceous) Fruitland Formation, San Juan Basin, New Mexico (USA). In *Second International Symposium on Mesozoic Terrestrial Ecosystems*, ed. Z. Kielan-Jaworska and H. Osmólska, 195–204. *Acta Palaeontologica Polonica* 28 (1/2).

Analyzes the deltaic depositional environment of the Fruitland formation, and reconstructs a hypothetical food web for a *Parasaurolophus* community. Many r-strategist species (fish, turtles, etc) inhabited a physically stressed fluctuating deltaic environment, characterized by unstable vegetation patterns. Dinosaurs were K-strategists, less subject to physical stress due to their larger size. Cretaceous extinctions were less dramatic for r-strategists, already adapted to highly stressful environments, than for the K-strategist dinosaurs.

606. Osborn, H.F. 1916. Skeletal adaptations of *Ornitholestes, Struthiomimus, Tyrannosaurus*. *Bulletin of the American Museum of Natural History* 35:733–771.

   This classic paper is relevant to recent studies on the ecology of ornithomimids. (*See* Nicholls and Russell 1985 [365].) Reviews earlier work by C.W. Beebe (insectivorous habit), and B. Brown (shoreline crustacean feeding habit). Proposes an ostrich model, in which *Struthiomimus* browses on leaves and buds from shrubs and low trees.

607. Padian, K. 1989. Other Mesozoic vertebrates of the land, sea, and air. In *The Age of Dinosaurs*, ed. K. Padian and D.J. Chure, 146–161. *Geological Society of America Short Courses in Paleontology* no. 2. Knoxville: The Paleontological Society.

   A comprehensive review of several taxa of the reptiles, mammals and amphibians that shared the planet with the dinosaurs, though each group is considered only briefly.

608. Russell, D.A., P. Béland, and J.S. McIntosh. 1980. Paleoecology of the dinosaurs of Tendaguru (Tanzania). *Mémoires de la Société Géologique de France* 139:169–175.

   The famous Late Jurassic Tendaguru beds resulted from sporadic deposition near a warm shallow sea. The fauna is dominated by several species of sauropods, including *Brachiosaurus*, and a diverse assemblage of smaller herbivores and the carnivorous *Allosaurus*. The fauna is less diverse than that reported for Dinosaur Provincial Park.

609. Thulborn, R.A. 1991. Morphology, preservation and palaeobiological significance of dinosaur coprolites. *Palaeogeography, Palaeoclimatology, Palaeoecology* 83:341–366.

   A comprehensive review of dinosaur coprolites. Dinosaur droppings can provide useful information on diet and behavior, despite the uncertainty inherent in their interpretation.

610. Whybrow, P.J. 1981. Evidence for the presence of nasal salt glands in the Hadrosauridae (Ornithischia). *Journal of Arid Environments* 4:43–57.

Anatomical features of the skulls of some hadrosaurs are similar to cranial features of some reptiles and birds. These structures accommodate nasal salt glands, which function in the secretion of excess salts. Hadrosaur crests may have primarily functioned, not as display or vocalization organs, but as organs for the secretion of excess salt acquired in eating large amounts of brackish-water vegetation. (*See* Hopson 1975 [726] for additional cross references on the structure and function of hadrosaur crests.)

HERBIVORES

611. Bakker, R.T. 1978. Dinosaur feeding behavior and the origin of flowering plants. *Nature* 274:661–663.

An important and controversial paper, relating work on early angiosperms by Doyle and Hickey with dinosaur herbivory (*See* Chapter Three). Early angiosperms were weedy plants and small shrubs growing in disturbed habitats. Late Jurassic herbivores were primarily tall sauropods, with long necks capable of browsing high vegetation. By the Late Cretaceous, however, this browse profile had changed dramatically. Hadrosaurs, ankylosaurs, and ceratopsians were low browsers. Intense low browsing introduced new selective pressures on floras, favoring plants like angiosperms that could rapidly recolonize closely cropped areas. Angiosperms appear about five to ten million years after the Cretaceous radiation of ornithischian herbivores, as "an evolutionary response" to the change from high browsing to low browsing. (*Note:* This is the classic chicken/egg problem. While I have no doubt that Bakker is essentially correct in claiming that angiosperms and herbivorous dinosaurs coevolved, the key question is which came first, and this depends on when you date the angiosperm radiation. *See*, for example, Lidgard and Crane 1988 [252]; Weishampel and Norman 1989 [655]; Wing and Tiffney 1987 [656]. It is just as likely that low-browsing dinosaurs were an evolutionary response to the global spread of tender angiosperms, and that flowers "invented" low-browsing dinosaurs. *See* Coe et al. 1987 [614] for additional cross references on the coevolution of dinosaurs and land plants.)

612. Beck, C.B. 1988. *Origin and Evolution of Gymnosperms.* New York: Columbia University Press.

Ten articles discuss the evolution of gymnosperms. These plants, at least prior to the Late Cretaceous, would have formed the chief food of dinosaurian herbivores. *(See also* Beck 1976 [235] for a similar work on angiosperms).

613. Belsky, A.J. 1986. Does herbivory benefit plants? A review of the evidence. *American Naturalist* 127:870–892.

Reviews a decade of growing literature on the possible mutualistic coevolved relationship between grasses and grazers. Do plants benefit from being regularly cropped? Concludes that there is a lack of hard evidence to support the hypothesis. The only hard evidence of compensatory growth (overcompensation) comes from laboratory studies or experiments on crop plants. Criticizes McNaughton's work on methodological grounds (McNaughton 1984 [635]; 1985 [636]; 1976 [691]).

614. Coe, M.J., D.L. Dilcher, J.O. Farlow, D.M. Jarzen, and D.A. Russell. 1987. Dinosaurs and land plants. In *The Origins of Angiosperms and their Biological Consequences,* ed. E.M. Friis et al., 225–258. Cambridge: Cambridge University Press.

"No frond has ever been found with clear impressions of dinosaur teeth preserved on it, nor has any thorn been discovered embedded in what was once the flesh of a dinosaur." Nevertheless, it obvious that dinosaurian herbivores had complex interactions with terrestrial plants. This excellent review covers several aspects of dinosaur/plant coevolution, focusing on the "browse line", and the effect of dinosaurs on early angiosperm evolution. Oldman Formation dinosaurs show a browse profile intermediate between earlier Morrison

Formation dinosaurs and modern Amboseli mammals, suggesting a long-term trend in the reduction of browsing height *(See also* Bakker 1978 [611]). Contrasts increases in dinosaur diversity with changes in relative diversity of angiosperms and other elements of the Mesozoic flora. Dinosaur-mediated dispersal may have been critical in the spread of early angiosperms. It is unlikely that vegetation changes led to dinosaur extinction, although the sudden loss of dinosaurian herbivores would have greatly affected subsequent vegetation types. (For additional cross references on the coevolution of dinosaurs and land plants, *See* Bakker 1978 [611]; Friis et al. 1987 [620]; Howe 1985 [628]; Janzen and Martin 1982 [632]; Weishampel and Norman 1987 [654]; Weishampel and Norman 1989 [655]; Wing and Tiffney 1987 [656].)

615. Coley, P.D. 1983. Herbivory and defensive characteristics of tree species in a lowland tropical forest. *Ecological Monographs* 53:209–233.

Pioneer species have lower levels of quantitative defenses (chemical and mechanical) against herbivory. Persistent species have higher levels of leaf fiber (tougher leaves), and phenols. Pioneers experienced six times the herbivory level experienced by persistent species. Pioneers species can tolerate higher levels of herbivory because they have "cheaper" leaves and faster growth rates. Discusses the evolution of plant defensive systems and the model of plant apparency. Low defensive levels can only be successful if the herbivore populations themselves are limited by predation or other factors. (*See* Coley et al. 1985 [616] for additional cross references on plant defenses against herbivores.)

616. Coley, P.D., J.P. Bryant, and F.S. Chapin III. 1985. Resource availability and plant antiherbivore defense. *Science* 230:895–899.

Herbivory exerts a very strong selective pressure on plant evolution, as evidenced by the "extraordinary array" of secondary compounds that defend plants against herbivores. In environments with low resource availability (light, water, nutrients) selection favors plants with slow growth rates and high levels of chemical defenses. Where resources are more abundant, selection favors plants with lower levels of defensive compounds and faster growth rates. (For additional references on plant defenses against herbivores, *See* Coley 1983 [615]; Freeland and Janzen 1974 [619]; Kubitzki and Gottlieb 1884 [633]; Rhoades 1985 [642]; Rosenthal and Janzen 1979 [645].)

617. Crompton, A.W., and J. Attridge. 1986. Masticatory apparatus of the larger herbivores during Late Triassic and Early Jurassic times. In *The Beginning of The Age of Dinosaurs*; *Faunal Changes Across the Triassic-Jurassic Boundary*, ed. K. Padian, 223–236. Cambridge: Cambridge University Press.

Reviews the evidence for competitive replacement of therapsids and rhynchosaurs by archosaurs, and concludes that the question of competition remains unresolved. The transition may not have been as abrupt as usually claimed. The replacement of herbivores with a relatively strong masticatory apparatus by herbivores (early dinosaurs) with a relatively weak and inefficient masticatory apparatus poses a serious problem for the hypothesis of competitive displacement. There are some indications of a mass extinction at the end of the Carnian, which might explain the faunal transition. (*See* Benton 1983 [581] for additional cross references on faunal replacement and competition.)

618. Farlow, J.O. 1987. Speculations about the diet and digestive physiology of herbivorous dinosaurs. *Paleobiology* 13:60–72.

Dinosaurs, like many modern herbivorous lizards, turtles, birds and mammals, probably relied on a symbiotic hindgut flora to ferment vegetation. Large body size and slow metabolic rates in dinosaurs would have resulted in slow passage time of food through the gut, with a long exposure time for microflora to break down the tough cell walls of plant material. Given the enormous size of many dinosaur herbivores, the immense fermentation chambers would have generated a significant source of internal heat, perhaps making sauropods "fermentative endotherms". Discusses dinosaur diets and metabolic rates. (For additional cross references on fermentation in herbivores, *See* Dunham et al. 1989 [592]; Hungate 1975 [630]; McBee 1971 [634]; Rogers 1985 [644]; Clemens and Maloiy 1982 [675]; Demment and Van Soest 1985 [678]; Troyer 1982 [786].)

619. Freeland, W.J., and D.H. Janzen. 1974. Strategies in herbivory by mammals: the role of plant secondary compounds. *American Naturalist* 108:269–289.

Discusses dosage effects and detoxification of plant secondary compounds in mammalian herbivory. The ubiquitous nature of such defensive compounds is reflected in herbivore preferences for plants with low levels of secondary metabolites, their caution in sampling new plants, and their consumption of a wide variety of food plants. (*See* Coley et al. 1985 [616] for additional cross references on plant defenses against herbivores.)

620. Friis, E.M., W.G. Chaloner, and P.R.Crane, eds. 1987. *The Origins of Angiosperms and Their Biological Consequences.* Cambridge: Cambridge University Press.

A landmark work in understanding the interrelationship between dinosaurian herbivores and the emerging angiosperm flora. Most of the essays in this collection are analyzed in this bibliography. (*See* Coe et al. 1987 [614] for additional cross references on the coevolution of dinosaurs and land plants.)

621. Galton, P.M. 1973. The cheeks of ornithischian dinosaurs. *Lethaia* 6:67–89.

The success of the ornithischian herbivores in replacing the formerly dominant prosauropods is partly due to their evolution of cheeks. Cheeks prevent loss of food from the sides of the jaw while chewing. Cheeks and self-sharpening cheek teeth enabled ornithischians to thrive on a diet of tougher plant material. Reviews cranial anatomy and dentition in ornithischians.

622. Galton, P.M. 1985. Diet of prosauropod dinosaurs from the late Triassic and early Jurassic. *Lethaia* 18:105–123.

Prosauropods like *Anchisaurus*, *Yunnanosaurus* and *Massospondylus* were the first dinosaurs adapted for a herbivorous diet. Reviews prosauropod herbivorous adaptations in the teeth and jaws, and the function of longer necks in high browsing. Refutes earlier suggestions that prosauropods were predators or scavengers.

623. Galton, P.M. 1986. Herbivorous adaptations of Late Triassic and Early Jurassic dinosaurs. In *The Beginning of The Age of Dinosaurs; Faunal Changes Across the Triassic-Jurassic Boundary*, ed. K. Padian, 203–221. Cambridge: Cambridge University Press.

    Reviews the skull structure, dentition, and possible gastric mills of early herbivorous dinosaurs. The success of the prosauropods, with their relatively poor herbivorous adaptations, may have been due to the presence of a gastric mill or to their improved gait. Compares herbivorous adaptations in the ornithischians. (*See* Benton 1983 [581] for additional cross references on faunal replacement and competition.)

624. Golley, F.B. 1969. Caloric value of wet tropical forest vegetation. *Ecology* 50:517–519.

    Presents mean caloric values for four types of tropical forest vegetation and several types of food within each forest type (canopy leaves, stems, fruits, roots, etc.). Tropical vegetation has a lower caloric value than alpine or temperate vegetation, suggesting a latitudinal and altitudinal gradient in plant energy content.

625. Gow, C.E. 1975. A new heterodontosaurid dinosaur from the Redbeds of South Africa showing clear evidence of tooth replacement. *Zoological Journal of the Linnean Society* 57:335–339.

    Describes a new species of heterodontosaurid, *Lanasaurus scalpridens*, based on a partial lower jaw. The jaw shows evidence of regular waves of tooth replacement. Suggests that Thulborn's description of *Lycorhinus consors*

(Thulborn 1974 [403]), is dubious, and that this species may actually be *Lanasaurus*.

626. Herrera, C.M. 1985. Determinants of plant-animal coevolution: the case of mutualistic dispersal of seeds by vertebrates. *Oikos* 44: 132–141.

   There is a general lack of specificity in coevolved systems of seed dispersal by vertebrates. Reviews selective pressures on seeds and their dispersers, and concludes that plant adaptations for seed dispersal by animals is "of a very coarse nature."

627. Hopson, J.A. 1980. Tooth function and replacement in Early Mesozoic ornithischian dinosaurs: implications for aestivation. *Lethaia* 13: 93–105.

   Reviews the evidence for Thulborn's hypothesis that ornithischians aestivated during the annual dry season in southern Africa (Thulborn 1978 [651]). Aestivation is seasonal dormancy during the summer, and is milder than true hibernation. Reviews heterodontosaurid dentition, particularly cheek teeth, tooth wear patterns, and tooth replacement, focusing on *Lanasaurus scalpridens*, *Lycorhinus angustidens*, and *Heterodontosaurus tucki*. Disagrees with Thulborn's hypothesis that cheek dentition was replaced rapidly during aestivation, citing evidence for multiple waves of continuous tooth replacement.

628. Howe, H.F. 1985. Gomphothere fruits: a critique. *American Naturalist* 125:853–865.

   Refutes Janzen and Martin (1982 [632]). Large herbivorous mammals can be poor dispersal agents. Criticizes their "vague historical hypothesis" and "ambiguous adaptive syndrome." Living dispersal agents could adequately explain their observations, without resorting to the (easier to observe) domestic stock. The megafaunal hypothesis, however, might have some merit; it might explain other botanical anomalies such as thorns high atop canopy trees. (*See* Coe et al. 1987 [614] for additional cross references on the coevolution of dinosaurs and land plants.)

629. Howe, H.F., and J. Smallwood. 1982. Ecology of seed dispersal. *Annual Review of Ecology and Systematics* 13:201–228.

A comprehensive review of the evolutionary ecology of seed dispersal. Discusses three hypotheses to explain dispersal ecology: the escape hypothesis, colonization hypothesis, and directed dispersal hypothesis. Over half the plants in a given community are dispersed by animals. Coevolved disperser and dispersal syndromes are relatively coarse, operating mainly at higher taxonomic levels.

630. Hungate, R.E. 1975. The rumen microbial system. *Annual Review of Ecology and Systematics* 6:39–66.

Reviews the microbial populations of the ruminant gut (protozoa and bacteria) and develops a mathematical model for their role in fermentation. A variety of microbial niches exist within and between ruminant species. (*See* Farlow 1987a [618] for additional cross references on fermentation in herbivores.)

631. Janzen, D.H. 1984. Dispersal of small seeds by big herbivores: foliage is the fruit. *American Naturalist* 123:338–353.

The small seeds of many herbaceous dicots are adapted for dispersal by large herbivores who devour the entire plant, and excrete the seeds at another location. This syndrome would select for nutritious foliage with low chemical defenses. Such seeds are small, tough, and hard, designed to survive passage through the herbivore's gut. (*Note:* Although Janzen doesn't make the connection, this hypothesis has powerful implications for large herbivorous dinosaurs, who most likely devoured entire herbaceous primitive angiosperms, rather than delicately cropping their foliage. This could help explain the rapid spread of angiosperms through a variety of disturbed habitats. *See also* the works on elephants, such as Wing and Buss 1970 [708].)

632. Janzen, D.H., and P.S. Martin. 1982. Neotropical anachronisms: the fruits the Gomphotheres ate. *Science* 215:19–27.

The extinction of Pleistocene megafaunal herbivores greatly altered the seed dispersal, and consequent distribution, of many Central American plants. The reintroduction of large seed-dispersing herbivores such as horses and cows has restored some of this lost range. See Howe 1985 [628] for a refutation. (*Note:* A similar pattern might have existed for plants that relied on dinosaurs for dispersal. See Coe et al. 1987 [614] for additional cross references on the coevolution of dinosaurs and land plants.)

633. Kubitzki, K., and O.R. Gottlieb. 1984. Phytochemical aspects of Angiosperm origin and evolution. *Acta Botanica Neerlandica* 33:457–468.

Part of the success of early angiosperms can be attributed to their formidable chemical defenses against herbivores. Angiosperms improved the use of shikimate-derived precursors for secondary compounds, and developed compounds with a much higher reduction-oxidation potential than more primitive plant groups, opening up a broader range of available variation in secondary compounds. Discusses the coevolution of herbivores and angiosperm defensive compounds. (*See* Coley et al. 1985 [616] for additional cross references on plant defenses against herbivores.)

634. McBee, R.H. 1971. Significance of intestinal microflora in herbivory. *Annual Review of Ecology and Systematics* 2:165–176.

The most successful large herbivores rely on symbiotic microbial fermentation in a foregut or rumen. Discusses the role of the cecum in microbial fermentation, and the role of coprophagy in nutrition. (*See* Farlow 1987a [618] for additional cross references on fermentation in herbivores.)

635. McNaughton, S.J. 1984. Grazing lawns: animals in herds, plant form, and coevolution. *American Naturalist* 124:863–886.

A good review of the author's work on coevolution between grasses and grazers. Hypothesizes that the maintenance of "grazing lawns" by herbivores, such as the ungulate herds of the Serengeti, increases the quality of the available food supply. Demonstrates this hypothesis by the use of fenced plots amidst grazing lawns. Concentrated herbivore populations "have a drastic effect on vegetation geometry, as well as its standing crop and productivity." (*See also* McNaughton 1976 [691]; 1985 [636]. *See* Belsky 1986 [613] for an opposing view.

636. McNaughton, S.J. 1985. Ecology of a grazing ecosystem: the Serengeti. *Ecological Monographs* 55:259–294.

Fenced plots were used to compare Serengeti aboveground vegetative biomass and primary productivity in grazed and ungrazed sections. Herbivores adjusted population densities to grassland productivity. Grazing stimulated net primary productivity, especially at intermediate grazer population densities. Energy and nutrient flows are accelerated by intense herbivory, suggesting coevolution between grasses and grazers [*See* 635].

637. Martin, J. 1987. Mobility and feeding of *Cetiosaurus* (Saurischia, Sauropoda): why the long neck? In *Fourth Symposium on Mesozoic Terrestrial Ecosystems, Short Papers*, ed. P.J. Currie and E. Koster, 154–159. Drumheller, Alta.: Tyrell Museum of Paleontology.

Cetiosaurus could not have reached the tops of tall Jurassic trees simply by stretching its long neck, but its available foraging radius with each step was still quite large. Perhaps it was an opportunistic biped, rearing up on hind legs to reach the tallest vegetation. Briefly describes a new mounting technique which avoids drilling holes in the skeletal elements of the sauropod neck.

638. Maryańska, T., and H. Osmólska. 1983. Some implications of hadrosaurian postcranial anatomy. In *Second International Symposium on Mesozoic Terrestrial Ecosystems*, ed. Z. Kielan-Jaworska and H. Osmólska, 205–207. *Acta Palaeontologica Polonica* 28 (1/2).

A reconsideration of the anterior thoracal vertebral column and neck, and the peculiar pelvicosacral articulation found in *Saurolophus* and other hadrosaurs, indicates that the animals walked with spines horizontal to the ground and with the neck held vertically. They could probably raise the spine 50° above the horizontal for high browsing of vegetation.

639. Norman, D.B., and D.B. Weishampel. 1985. Ornithopod feeding mechanisms: their bearing on the evolution of herbivory. *American Naturalist* 126:151–164.

    Why didn't mammals radiate as large herbivores during the Mesozoic? Models of the ornithopod skull permit an analysis of the kinematics of dinosaurian herbivory. Reviews the evolution of ornithopod jaw mechanisms. Most living reptilian herbivores rely on cropping (*See* Throckmorton 1976 [648]), but ornithopod dinosaurs developed a transverse power stroke. Its mechanism was very different from the anisognathous system used by modern mammals. This efficient power stroke, based on an isognathic jaw frame, contributed to the rise and radiation of ornithopods [*See* 640].

640. Norman, D.B., and D.B. Weishampel. 1987. Vegetarian dinosaurs chew it differently. *New Scientist*, 7 May, 42–45.

    A good popular treatment of the authors' extensive research into ornithopod jaw mechanics and the evolution of dinosaur herbivory. Covers the same ground as Norman and Weishampel 1985 [639].

641. Ostrom, J.H. 1964. A reconsideration of the paleoecology of hadrosaurian dinosaurs. *American Journal of Science* 262:975–997.

    Hadrosaurs lived in lowland coastal plains, in warm-temperate to subtropical climates, dominated by mixed conifer-angiosperm forests. Few predators shared this environment with ceratopsians and hadrosaurs. Hadrosaurs were not aquatic, contrary to the way they are often depicted, although they may have retreated to the water to avoid predation. They did not eat aquatic plants as their primary diet, but fed on tougher terrestrial vegetable matter, such as conifer needles and deciduous fruits and twigs. Their duck-like bills may have been used to strip leaves and shoots from branches.

Two useful tables summarize the major Late Cretaceous dinosaur flora and fauna of western North America. *(See also* Bakker 1971b [577] for a similar reevaluation of *Apatosaurus* habits.)

642. Rhoades, D.F. 1985. Offensive-defensive interactions between herbivores and plants: their relevance in herbivore population dynamics and ecological theory. *American Naturalist* 125:205–238.

    Plants are often well defended against herbivory, and are not simply passive victims of herbivore attack. Reviews plant chemical defenses against herbivory, and herbivore adaptations to cope with such defenses. Proposes several characteristics separating "stealthy" and "opportunistic" herbivores, representing two very different approaches to coping with plant defensive compounds. Stealthy herbivores minimize damage to the plant and minimize its chemical response. Opportunistic herbivores take advantage of plant stress and other factors that reduce the ability of the plant to defend itself. Discusses locusts and moths as model herbivores in this system. (*See* Coley et al. 1985 [616] for additional cross references on plant defenses against herbivores.)

643. Rockwood, L.L. 1973. The effect of defoliation on seed production of six Costa Rican tree species. *Ecology* 54:1363–1369.

    Experimental defoliation of six tree species reduced fruit numbers and weights in defoliated trees. Over 80% of the defoliated trees produced no fruit at all. Both growth and reproduction are a function of total leaf area, and heavy defoliation has a profound impact on plant fitness.

644. Rogers, K.L. 1985. Possible physiological and behavioral adaptations of herbivorous dinosaurs. *Journal of Vertebrate Paleontology* 5:371–372.

    Draws parallels between colonial nesting in hadrosaurs at the Late Cretaceous Two Medicine Formation nesting site and the nesting habits of modern herbivorous iguanas (*Iguana iguana*). Colonial nesting would have aided transmission of the gut microflora necessary for fermentation. Such transmission was probably accomplished by coprophagy, or the eating of fecal matter by the young. (*See* Farlow 1987a [618] for additional cross references on fermentation in herbivores.)

645. Rosenthal, G.A., and D.H. Janzen, eds. 1979. *Herbivores: Their Interaction With Secondary Plant Metabolites.* New York: Academic Press.

Twenty contributions examine the effects of plant secondary compounds on herbivores. Part one deals with how plants construct their chemical defenses, and how herbivores have evolved to handle them, while part two examines individual groups of defensive compounds. (*See* Coley et al. 1985 [616] for additional cross references on plant defenses against herbivores.)

646. Stokes, W.L. 1964. Fossilized stomach contents of a sauropod dinosaur. *Science* 143:576–577.

Fossilized stomach contents are very rare. This sauropod stomach contained sections of twigs or branches 2.5 cm long and 1 cm in diameter. No leaves were found, but fragments of broken or digested bone suggest that sauropods may have been omnivorous.

647. Stokes, W.L. 1987. Dinosaur gastroliths revisited. *Journal of Paleontology* 61:1242–1246.

Reviews the evidence that exotic polished stones associated with dinosaur remains are stomach stones, or gastroliths. Reverses the author's previous opinion; the stones are, in fact, gastroliths.

648. Throckmorton, G.S. 1976. Oral food processing in two herbivorous lizards, *Iguana iguana* (Iguanidae) and *Uromastix aegyptius* (Agamidae). *Journal of Morphology* 148:363–390.

Uses dissection and films to study the feeding mechanism of these two herbivorous lizards. Both *Iguana iguana* and *Uromastix aegyptius* feed by cropping, separating a piece of vegetation from the whole plant. Tongue and head movements are used to manipulate the food, which is not chewed but passed directly to the gut. Teeth are adapted for shearing plant material [See 649]. Reviews jaw structure and muscular function in food processing.

649. Thulborn, R.A. 1971. Tooth wear and jaw action in the Triassic ornithischian dinosaur *Fabrosaurus*. *Journal of Zoology* 164:165–179.

   Patterns of wear in tooth crowns of *Fabrosaurus* indicate a normal modern reptilian pattern of tooth wear and replacement for this genus. The pattern of tooth wear results from vertical jaw action [See 648]. This pattern is different from that of other ornithopods, which have a grinding or milling motion in food processing. Reviews jaw mechanics of early ornithischians. The primitive jaw mechanism of *Fabrosaurus* confirms the "archetypal ornithopod" status previously suggested for this dinosaur.

650. Thulborn, R.A. 1974. Thegosis in herbivorous dinosaurs. *Nature* 250:729–731.

   Thegosis is the process by which teeth are sharpened by being ground together. Tooth wear patterns in ornithischians parallel patterns associated with thegosis in modern mammals.

651. Thulborn, R.A. 1978. Aestivation among ornithopod dinosaurs of the African Trias. *Lethaia* 11:185–198.

   Ornithopod dinosaurs of the Upper Triassic in southern Africa underwent dry-season dormancy (aestivation) to cope with seasonal changes. This hypothesis is suggested by a series of "stacked inferences" based on an examination of tooth wear and tooth replacement patterns in fabrosaurids (*Fabrosaurus australis*) and heterodontosaurids (*Lanasaurus scalpridens*). During aestivation, ornithopods underwent wholesale replacement of worn teeth. (*See* Hopson 1980 [627] for a critical response.)

652. Tiffney, B.H. 1984. Seed size, dispersal syndromes, and the rise of the angiosperms: evidence and hypothesis. *Annals of the Missouri Botanical Gardens* 71:551–576.

Reviews the evolution of propagule size and dispersal in Cretaceous and early Tertiary angiosperms. Although most Cretaceous diaspores (the reproductive unit that is dispersed) were fairly small, seed and fruit size was increasing towards the end of the Cretaceous. This change probably paralleled the increasing importance of animals as dispersal agents, and also reflected the increasing penetration of angiosperms into closed-canopy gymnosperm forests. (*See also* Nicholls and Russell 1985 [365]; Wing and Tiffney 1987 [656].)

653. Weishampel, D.B. 1983. Hadrosaurid jaw mechanics. In *Second International Symposium on Mesozoic Terrestrial Ecosystems*, ed. Z. Kielan-Jaworska and H. Osmólska, 271–280. *Acta Palaeontologica Polonica* 28 (1/2).

    Hadrosaur jaw systems present an interesting solution to jaw limitations in reptilian herbivores. Mammalian herbivores, with anisognathous jaws, developed an efficient transverse power stroke. Modern reptiles chew up and down, not side to side, because their isognathous jaws restrict lateral movement. Three-dimensional computer simulations were used to model various kinematic linkage systems. The streptostylic jaw mechanism best accounts for observed tooth wear in hadrosaurs.

654. Weishampel, D.B., and D.B. Norman. 1987. Dinosaur-plant interactions in the Mesozoic. In *Fourth Symposium on Mesozoic Terrestrial Ecosystems, Short Papers*, ed. P.J. Currie and E. Koster, 228–233. Drumheller, Alta.: Tyrell Museum of Paleontology.

    Summarizes recent progress made in the study of the interaction of dinosaurs and plants. (*See* Coe et al. 1987 [614] for additional cross references on the coevolution of dinosaurs and land plants.)

655. Weishampel, D.B., and D.B. Norman. 1989. Vertebrate history in the Mesozoic; jaws, plants, and evolutionary metrics. In *Paleobiology of the Dinosaurs*, ed. J.O. Farlow, 87–100. *Geological Society of America Special Paper* no. 238.

Reviews coevolution of Mesozoic animals (including mammals, therapsids, and dinosaurs) and vegetation. Discusses rates of evolution in the various groups, and compares this data with evolutionary metrics of angiosperms, gymnosperms and pteridophytes. Reviews food processing in the different Mesozoic groups. Large terrestrial herbivores aided the shift from K-selected gymnosperms to r-selected angiosperms, which in turn favored the shift from high-browsing sauropods to the low-browsing herbivores of the Late Cretaceous. (*See* Coe et al. 1987 [614] for additional cross references on the coevolution of dinosaurs and land plants.)

656. Wing, S.L., and B.H. Tiffney. 1987. The reciprocal interaction of angiosperm evolution and tetrapod herbivory. *Review of Paleobotany and Palynology* 50:179–210.

A comprehensive review of the coevolution between dinosaurs and plants. Describes three broad stages: generalized herbivory, with mostly large herbivores and r-selected colonizing angiosperms; generalized herbivory with the increasing importance of larger angiosperm diaspores and their dispersal by smaller herbivores (dinosaurs and birds); diverse large diaspores, with a reduced importance of large herbivores and generalized herbivory. Extinction of herbivores at the K/T boundary radically changed selective pressures on angiosperms. (*See* Coe et al. 1987 [614] for additional cross references on the coevolution of dinosaurs and land plants.)

CARNIVORES

657. Bartram, B.C.R. 1979. Serengeti predators and their social systems. In *Serengeti: Dynamics of an Ecosystem*, ed. A.R.E. Sinclair and M. Norton-Griffiths, 221–248. Chicago: University of Chicago Press.

Discusses the social systems, prey, and hunting methods of lions, leopards, cheetahs, wild dogs, and spotted hyenas.

Predation has little effect on ungulate population size, which is limited primarily by food supply.

658. Buffetaut, E., and V. Suteethorn. 1989. A sauropod skeleton associated with theropod teeth in the Upper Jurassic of Thailand: remarks on the taphonomic and palaeoecological significance of such associations. *Palaeogeography, Palaeoclimatology, Palaeoecology* 73:77–83.

   Describes a partial skeleton of an unknown sauropod, associated with several teeth of an unknown carnosaur. Briefly reviews similar earlier discoveries.

659. Caraco, T., and L.L. Wolf. 1975. Ecological determinants of group sizes of foraging lions. *American Naturalist* 109:343–352.

   Relates group size of foraging lions to environmental conditions. Optimum group size determinants include prey biomass and capture efficiency. Large foraging groups (six to eight females) enhance reproductive success. When lions are feeding on abundant large herbivores, they form larger groups than the group size predicted by maximum foraging efficiency. Concludes that "the benefits of sociality may far outweigh maximizing achieved foraging efficiency."

660. Coombs, W.P. jr. 1980. Swimming ability of carnivorous dinosaurs. *Science* 207:1198–1200.

   Describes Lower Jurassic tracks of a large theropod from Connecticut State Dinosaur Park. The tracks suggest that the animal was floating or half submerged, pushing off on the bottom sediments with the tips of its toes. The animal is tentatively identified as a species of *Eubrontes*. The tracks cast doubt on the ability of herbivores to escape predation by entering the water.

661. Currie, P.J. 1987. Theropods of the Judith River Formation of Dinosaur Provincial Park, Alberta, Canada. In *Fourth Symposium on Mesozoic Terrestrial Ecosystems, Short Papers*, ed. P.J. Currie and E. Koster, 52–59. Drumheller, Alta.: Tyrell Museum of Paleontology.

Fourteen theropod species are known from the Judith River Formation. Compares cranial material (frontals) from several species.

662. Earle, M. 1987. A flexible body mass in social carnivores. *American Naturalist* 129:755–760.

Uses an allometric model to study the relation between pack size and prey size in a wide range of modern mammalian social carnivores. There are two ways for predators to hunt larger prey: becoming large themselves, or hunting in packs. Pack hunting allows predators to adopt a "flexible body mass", adjusting their combined weight to the weight of their intended prey. (*See* Damuth 1981 [677] for additional cross references on the relationship between body size, home range, and population density.)

663. Farlow, J.O. 1976b. Speculations about the diet and foraging behavior of large carnivorous dinosaurs. *American Midland Naturalist* 95:186–191.

Speculates on diet and pack behavior in carnivorous dinosaurs. Juvenile diets were probably different from adult diets. Juveniles probably ate invertebrates and small vertebrates, as do modern juvenile crocodiles and monitor lizards. Pack hunting was probably necessary to bring down large herbivores like sauropods. Draws a number of analogies between possible carnosaur behavior and the behavior of modern carnivorous reptiles and mammals.

664. Gittleman, J.L. 1985. Carnivore body size: ecological and taxonomic correlates. *Oecologia* 67:540–554.

Carnivore body size does not correlate with habitat, latitudinal gradients, activity cycles, or ecological zone. While predator size is broadly correlated with prey size, predators can get around this constraint to some extent by adopting flexible hunting strategies. Larger predators prey on a wider range of prey.

665. Houstan, D.C. 1979. The adaptations of scavengers. In *Serengeti; Dynamics of an Ecosystem*, ed. by A.R.E. Sinclair

and M. Norton-Griffiths, 263–286. Chicago: University of Chicago Press.

The distinction between mammalian predators and scavengers is unjustified. All mammalian carnivores are primarily predators, and will scavenge opportunistically. Many species of birds, on the other hand, are exclusively scavengers. Scavenger and predator populations are controlled by the migratory cycles of their prey. Avian scavengers are better able to take advantage of the inevitable deaths in migrating herds.

666. MacDonald, D.W. 1983. The ecology of carnivore social behavior. *Nature* 301:379–384.

Discusses the selective pressures on carnivore social behavior, and variations in cost/benefit tradeoffs. Benefits of social groups can vary from species to species or from one population to the next. Many mammalian carnivores, like red foxes and European badgers, live in groups but hunt alone; others, like lions, live and hunt in packs. Group sizes and territory sizes are constrained by the dispersion of resources. Variation in ecological circumstances has produced highly flexible social systems in social carnivores.

667. Paul, G.S. 1987. Predation in the meat-eating dinosaurs. In *Fourth Symposium on Mesozoic Terrestrial Ecosystems, Short Papers*, ed. P.J. Currie and E. Koster, 173–178. Drumheller, Alta.: Tyrell Museum of Paleontology.

Preliminary notes based on research for Paul 1988 [668]. Dinosaur predators probably used "hit and run" tactics, opting for a swift strike and patiently awaiting a lingering death. This contrasts with the "protracted wrestling matches" depicted in the popular media. Predatory dinosaurs behaved more like sharks than lions in this respect. Briefly discusses pack hunting in predators.

668. Paul, G.S. 1988. *Predatory Dinosaurs of the World*. New York: Simon and Schuster.

An interesting compendium of predatory dinosaurs. The reader is cautioned, however, that several authorities have dismissed Paul's classification scheme as idiosyncratic and unacceptable. Gauthier's proposed phylogeny is considered more reliable for overall theropod classification (Gauthier 1986 [907]). With this caveat, there is much useful information here on the general ecology of carnivorous dinosaurs, and basic data (usually with skeletal illustration) for each individual taxon.

669. Schaller, G.B. 1972. *The Serengeti Lion: A Study of Predator-Prey Relations*. Chicago: University of Chicago Press.

This classic study of the African lion is based on over three years of intensive field work in the Serengeti. Surveys all aspects of lion life history, including pride structure, reproduction, diet, social behavior, and hunting methods. Includes chapters on the leopard, cheetah, wild dog, and miscellaneous other predators, including hyenas, jackals and man. Concludes with a chapter on the dynamics of predation.

670. Vézina, A.F. 1985. Empirical relationships between predator and prey size among terrestrial vertebrate predators. *Oecologia* 67:555–565.

Examination of 117 predator species, including every class of terrestrial vertebrate predators, resulted in three models for three types of prey specialists: carnivores, piscivores, and insectivores. Insectivores prey on a wider range of body sizes than do carnivores, and take prey that is proportionately smaller. Larger carnivores show an increased ratio of prey/predator weight. Piscivores are intermediate in every respect to carnivores and insectivores. Develops a mathematical model to predict daily kill rates and the upper limit to predator biomass.

ECOLOGY OF MODERN ANIMALS

671. Begon, M., and M. Mortimer. 1986. *Population Ecology: A Unified Study of Plants and Animals*. 2d ed. Oxford: Blackwell Scientific.

The extension of life history theory to the study of dinosaur ecology is an exciting and promising endeavor. This introduction to population ecology surveys demographics and life history traits, discussing intraspecific and interspecific competition models, predation, and community structure.

672. Calder, W.A. III. 1983. Ecological scaling: mammals and birds. *Annual Review of Ecology and Systematics* 14:213–230.

   Body size is a critical element in determining life history characteristics. The allometric equation $Y = aM^b$, where M is equal to body mass, has many ecological implications. Reviews predictions made by this equation for crop turnover time, foraging efficiency, and population density. Relates r and K-selection traits to the allometry of body size.

673. Calder, W.A. III. 1984. *Size, Function, and Life History.* Cambridge, MA: Harvard University Press.

   A thorough treatise on the allometric relationships of body size in modern mammals and birds, and the effects of allometric relationships on life history. Includes over 750 allometric equations. Size is a critical determinant of an animal's basic biology and ecological adaptations.

674. Case, T.J. 1978. Endothermy and parental care in the terrestrial vertebrates. *American Naturalist* 112:861–874.

   Suggests a different course of evolution for the altricial habit. Discusses life history characteristics, such as age, size of young, and juvenile mortality, in relation to endothermy and parental care. Food acquisition and predation are more important factors than body size in shaping reproductive traits, except at extremely small and large body sizes. The critical step in the evolution of the altricial habit occurred in very small mammals; smaller altricial young were less energetically costly for evolving endotherms to produce. Larger therapsids were more likely to develop parental care. Reptiles paradoxically hatch precocial young from smaller eggs, perhaps due to their less complex neural development. (*See* Hopson 1973 [686]; Dunham et al. 1989 [592].)

675. Clemens, E.T., and G.M.O. Maloiy. 1982. The digestive physiology of three East African herbivores: the elephant, rhinoceros, and hippopotamus. *Journal of Zoology* 198:141–156.

Compares three large African ungulates, the elephant, hippopotamus, and rhinoceros. The digestive tracts and gut contents were dissected and analyzed. While the hippo feeds on grasses, the elephant also eats stems, bark, and leaves. The Black Rhinoceros is a strict browser, feeding primarily on leaves and very rarely eating grasses. All three rely to some degree on microbial fermentation.

676. Coe, M.J., D.H. Cummings, and J. Phillipson. 1976. Biomass and production of large African herbivores in relation to rainfall and primary production. *Oecologia* 22:341–354.

Biomass and secondary productivity of large African savanna herbivores is highly correlated with average annual rainfall. Carrying capacity is directly related to climate, particularly precipitation.

677. Damuth, J. 1981. Population density and body size in mammals. *Nature* 290:699–700.

Mammalian herbivores show an inverse correlation between body size and population density. The linear relationship has a slope of -0.75. The amount of energy used by a population of a species in a community is independent of the species body size. Secondary productivity of local herbivore populations is also independent of their body size. Body size explains 74% of the global variation in mammalian population density. (For additional references on the relationship between body size, home range, and population density, *See* Earle 1987 [662]; Fowler 1981 [680]; Harestad and Bunnell 1979 [682]; Henneman 1983 [683]; Owen-Smith 1988 [693]; Peters 1983 [697]; Peters and Raelson 1984 [698]; Peters and Wassenberg 1983 [699].)

678. Demment, M.W., and P.J. Van Soest. 1985. A nutritional explanation for body-size patterns of ruminant and nonruminant herbivores. *American Naturalist* 125:641–672.

Reviews the relationship between body size and digestive capacity. Gut volume is a constant proportion of body weight. Extends this relationship to a study of the relative efficiencies of ruminant and nonruminant herbivores. Reviews the nutritional quality of various types of plant matter, and the relative proportions of quality food in various habitats. As plant standing crop increases, the proportion of low-quality fibrous vegetation increases. High-quality foliage for herbivores is generally rare. Only smaller animals, with lower metabolic requirements, can survive by seeking only high-quality foods. Vegetation factors constitute an evolutionary constraint for the digestive systems of herbivores of various sizes. Retention times increase with body size, and digestibility is a function of retention time. Large herbivores are constrained to a high-fiber diet which is hard to ruminate. Longer retention times due to large size renders selective retention unnecessary. Thus there are upper limits for ruminant body size, and most modern large herbivores are nonruminants. (*See* Farlow 1987a [618] for additional cross references on fermentation in herbivores.)

679. Elder, W.H., and D.H. Rodgers. 1975. Body temperature in the African elephant as related to ambient temperature. *Mammalia* 39:395–399.

Data on elephant body temperature has been restricted to trained Asian elephants. The technique involves inserting a rectal thermometer at arm's length for one minute. Needless to say, little equivalent data has been available for wild African elephants. Data gathered from dart-drugged African elephants suggests that their internal temperature is directly related to ambient temperature. Ambient temperature may be an important factor in their thermoregulatory behavior.

680. Fowler, C.W. 1981. Density dependence as related to life history strategy. *Ecology* 62:602–610.

Examines mathematical models relating life history traits and population density dependence in light of published data. Large mammalian species experience density-dependent changes at high population levels, close to their carrying capacity. (*See* Damuth 1981 [677] for additional cross references on the relationship between body size, home range, and population density.)

681. Hanks, J., and J.E.A. McIntosh. 1972. Population dynamics of the African elephant (*Loxodonta africana*). *Journal of Zoology* 169:29–38.

As elephant population density increases, the mean age at puberty and the mean calving interval also increases. Calving interval is more important in the density-dependent control of elephant populations. Demographic models show that juvenile mortality rate in the first year is critical in population regulation.

682. Harestad, A.S., and F.L. Bunnell. 1979. Home range and body size-a reevaluation. *Ecology* 60:389–402.

For mammals, birds, and lizards, body size is related to home range by the equation $H=aW^k$. The exponent of this relationship, however, may differ significantly from $k=0.75$, a value claimed in previous studies. The expected value is $k=0.75$ only if home range is a function of metabolic rate. A review of numerous mammalian species shows that k has a higher value for both herbivores (0.80–1.24) and carnivores (1.04–1.68). With increasing size, a large mammal must extend its home range beyond the size predicted from its metabolic rate. The reduction in useable food supply for larger herbivores may be related to increasing patchiness of resources with expanded home range. The larger k value for carnivores demonstrates that more energy per unit area is available in primary production than in secondary production. Larger predators must overlook smaller prey items, and thus experience a steep decline in habitat productivity with increasing body size. (*See* Damuth 1981 [677] for additional cross references on the relationship between body size, home range, and population density.)

683. Henneman, W.W. III. 1983. Relationship among body mass, metabolic rate, and the intrinsic rate of natural increase in mammals. *Oecologia* 56:104–108.

Estimates the intrinsic rate of natural increase (r) for forty-four species of mammals, in order to examine the possible trade off between maintenance costs (metabolism) and reproductive costs in life history characteristics. The growth rate r is linearly correlated with body size, and to some extent with metabolic rate; knowing body size, we can predict r (Cole method). (*See* Damuth 1981 [677] for additional cross references on the relationship between body size, home range, and population density.)

684. Hirst, S.M. 1975. Ungulate-habitat relationships in South African woodland/savanna communities. *Wildlife Monographs* 44:1–60.

Reviews habitat characteristics and associated ungulate habits, population dynamics, habitat selection, and community ecology in a savanna environment outside Kruger National Park, South Africa. Calculates primary and secondary (herbivore) productivity over the annual wet/dry season.

685. Hoffman, M.A. 1983. Energy metabolism, brain size, and longevity in mammals. *Quarterly Review of Biology* 58:495–512.

Encephalization is a function of brain weight and body weight. Oxygen consumption in the brain is proportional to both these variables. Explores allometric relationships between brain size and body size, and relates these variables to life span. Mammalian life span is directly proportional to the degree of encephalization, and inversely proportional to the basal metabolic rate per unit weight.

686. Hopson, J.A. 1973. Endothermy, small size, and the origin of mammalian reproduction. *American Naturalist* 107:446–452.

Many of the reproductive adaptations of modern mammals, such as small eggs, altricial young, and elaborate parental care, are a result of selection for efficient endothermy and smaller adult size. Discusses the evolution of viviparity, and of egg-laying mammals. Small endothermic young would have extremely high metabolic rates. As a result, small birds and mammals have essentially ectothermic hatchlings, with low metabolic rates, which become fully endothermic only when they reach maturity. This necessitates complex and continuing parental care. (*See also* Case 1978 [674].)

687. Laws, R.M. 1970. Elephants as agents of habitat and landscape changes in East Africa. *Oikos* 21:1–15.

African bush elephants (*Loxodonta africana*) profoundly affect their habitat. The typical cycle begins with the destruction of the understory, followed by the destruction of forest trees. Damage radiates outward from an initial focal point, such as a water hole or river bank. Discusses food and habitat requirements, and social organization into families and clans. Very large herds, with consequently high food requirements, can have a catastrophic effect on vegetation.

688. Laws, R.M., I.S.C. Parker, and R.C.B. Johnstone. 1975. *Elephants and their Habitats*. Oxford: Clarendon Press.

A comprehensive ecological survey of the elephants of North Bunyoro, Uganda, and their effect on their habitat. Includes population dynamics, nutrition, growth, reproduction and social behavior.

689. Lock, J.M. 1972. The effects of hippopotamus grazing on grasslands. *Journal of Ecology* 60:445–467.

Several enclosures were used to compare grazed and ungrazed tracts to determine the effects of hippo grazing. Changes in protected vegetation over a two-year period demonstrate that trampling and grazing by hippos has a profound effect on maintaining natural vegetation and mosaic patterns of vegetation growth.

690. McNab, B.K. 1978. The evolution of endothermy in the phylogeny of mammals. *American Naturalist* 112:1–22.

Discusses the transition from ectothermy to endothermy in mammalian evolution. Reviews the interrelationship of body size and thermoregulation. Large inertial homeotherms gave rise to smaller nocturnal endotherms. Small endotherms can't be directly derived from small ectotherms. The evolution of endothermic mammals from advanced therapsids can be explained in part by a shift by carnivorous therapsids to smaller prey. This shift may have been an adaptation to avoid competition.

691. McNaughton, S.J. 1976. Serengeti migratory wildebeest: facilitation of energy flow by grazing. *Science* 191:92–94.

The passage of a million wildebeest over the Serengeti plain in four days in 1974 converted senescent grassland into a productive grazing lawn. Although the immediate effect appeared to be devastating, within three weeks the area was highly productive. Gazelle followed the wildebeest, and showed a preference for the areas cropped by the wildebeest. Wildebeest grazing stimulates energy flow through the ecosystem, increasing forage quality for the gazelle. (*See* McNaughton 1984 [635]; 1985 [636]. *See* Belsky 1986 [613] for an opposing view.)

692. McNaughton, S.J., and N.J. Georgiadis. 1986. Ecology of African grazing and browsing mammals. *Annual Review of Ecology and Systematics* 17:39–65.

A comprehensive review of African herbivores, and the complex manner in which they partition available resources. Discusses body size, feeding preferences, distribution, life history, and population ecology. Heterogeneity of local habitat is an important factor in maintaining species diversity. Our information on species interactions is very fragmentary. (*See also* McNaughton 1984 [635].)

693. Owen-Smith, R.N. 1988. *Megaherbivores: the Influence of Very Large Body Size on Ecology.* Cambridge: Cambridge University Press.

Reviews the ecology of large mammalian herbivores, including elephants, hippos, giraffes and rhinos, discussing their phylogeny, distribution, habitat, nutrition, life history and social behavior. Focuses on the relationship between body size and ecological characteristics. The comprehensive bibliography makes this an excellent starting point for research into large modern herbivores. (*See* Damuth 1981 [677] for additional cross references on the relationship between body size, home range, and population density.)

694. Owen-Smith, R.N., and P. Novellie. 1982. What should a clever ungulate eat? *American Naturalist* 119:151–178.

Develops an optimal foraging model for large herbivores. "Clever ungulates" should select a diet that optimizes intake rate for the most limiting nutrients. Crude protein intake does not seem to be the limiting nutrient for African ungulates. Compares model prediction with the actual foraging strategies of living ungulates. Energy content, rather than protein content, seems to be the "target nutrient" of ungulate foraging.

695. Pedley, T.J. 1987. How giraffes prevent oedema. *Nature* 329:13–14.

Offers a physiological explanation for why giraffes don't suffer massive oedema in their feet, or suffer massive blood flow to the head when they bend over to drink. (*Note:* Sauropods must have had to solve the same physiological problem.)

696. Pellew, R.A. 1984. The feeding ecology of a selective browser, the giraffe (*Giraffa Camelopardalis tippelskirchi*). *Journal of Zoology* 202:57–81.

Large herbivores can manipulate feeding behavior to maximize their reproductive success. Giraffes alter their feeding behavior to optimize metabolic needs in relation to habitat. Their choice of feeding habitat varies with seasonal production of new shoots. They select new shoots with high protein content, and show strong selection for minor species in their habitat. Breeding females select a high-energy diet. During the dry season, when food quality and biomass decline, giraffes devote more time to foraging and minimize non-essential activities.

697. Peters, R.H. 1983. *The Ecological Implications of Body Size.* Cambridge: Cambridge University Press.

Reviews allometric relationships in living ungulates with an emphasis on their importance in such ecological processes as life history, materials flow, population density, community structure, and behavior. Contains extensive appendices listing known allometric relationships for a wide variety of organisms, complete with literature references, range of W, intercepts and slopes. (*See* Damuth 1981 [677] for additional cross references on the relationship between body size, home range, and population density.)

698. Peters, R.H., and J.V. Raelson. 1984. Relations between individual size and mammalian population density. *American Naturalist* 124:498–517.

Using previously published data, the authors examine Damuth's relationship between body size and population density. When examined within geographic regions, Damuth's relationship does not explain the variance in the data as well as the global figure does. The large variance limits the equation's usefulness in predicting values for individual species, although the general relationship remains useful. Other factors must also be taken into account when calculating population density and home range. (*See* Damuth 1981 [677] for additional cross references on the relationship between body size, home range, and population density.)

699. Peters, R.H., and K. Wassenberg. 1983. The effect of body size on animal abundance. *Oecologia* 60:89–96.

Tests Damuth's hypothesis on the allometric relationship between body size and population density by reviewing studies published from 1961 and 1978. Damuth's analysis seems correct; density declines roughly as $W^{-0.75}$. Residual variation is high, however, and there are major differences between various groups of animals. The analysis predicts that large carnivores will face a decreasing resource base of large prey, because production per unit biomass declines with increasing prey size. (*See* Farlow 1976a. *See also* Damuth 1981 [677] for cross references on the relationship between body size, home range, and population density.)

700. Pianka, E.R. 1970. On r- and K-selection, *American Naturalist* 104:592–597.

A classic paper expanding McArthur and Wilson's concepts of r- and K-selection. K represents the carrying capacity of an ecosystem, while r represents the intrinsic rate of reproduction. "K-selected" organisms exist in a fairly stable climate, with constant population size and density-dependent mortality, and are characterized by high levels of competition, high longevity, large body size, and iteroparity (repeated reproductive events). "r-selected" organisms exist under variable climates, with density-independent mortality, and are characterized by small body size, short life, a high rate of reproduction, and semelparity (a single reproductive event). (*Note:* Dinosaurs under this scheme would be K-selected).

701. Pianka, E.R. 1983. *Evolutionary Ecology*. 3d ed. New York: Harper and Row.

    A classic text in modern ecology from one of its most influential practitioners. Includes physiological ecology, population and community ecology, and biogeography.

702. Pickett, S.T.A., and P.S. White, eds. 1985. *The Ecology of Natural Disturbance and Patch Dynamics*. New York: Academic Press.

    Twenty-one contributors survey the effects of such disturbance phenomena as fires, hurricanes, tree-canopy gaps, freeze damage, landslides, and biotic disturbance. These natural disturbances create a heterogeneous or "patchy" environment, with consequent dynamic ecological responses by plant and animal populations.

703. Schmidt-Nielsen, K. 1984. *Scaling: Why is Animal Size So Important?* Cambridge: Cambridge University Press.

    A good introduction to allometric scaling, and the critical importance of body size in skeletal structure, metabolism, respiration, cardiovascular systems, activity levels and body temperatures. Includes a few references to dinosaur biology, but focuses on living vertebrates.

704. Sikes, S.F. 1971. *The Natural History of the African Elephant*. New York: American Elsevier.

A classic monograph on the natural history of the African elephant, including its taxonomy, anatomy, physiology, life history, and social behavior.

705. Sinclair, A.R.E., and M. Norton-Griffiths, eds. 1979. *Serengeti, Dynamics of an Ecosystem.* Chicago: University of Chicago Press.

Includes thirteen papers describing the ecological dynamics of a contemporary ecosystem that may in many respects parallel the herbivore-carnivore systems of the Mesozoic. Includes articles on grassland/herbivore dynamics, predator/prey systems, and foraging systems of carnivores and herbivores. (*See* Houstan 1979 [665]; Bartram 1979 [657].)

706. Stocker, G.C., and A.K. Irvine. 1983. Seed dispersal by cassowaries (*Casuarius casuarius*) in North Queensland's rain forests. *Biotropica* 15:170–176.

Seeds are not greatly affected by passage through the gut of the cassowary. Of the seventy-eight species of plants which cassowaries ate, some germination from dung was observed for seventy species. Cassowaries are important dispersal agents for many Australian rain forest plants. The distribution of their food supply may shape their social behavior. (*See also* Crome 1975 [716]; Bertram 1980 [711]. *Note:* Cassowaries, like the emu and ostrich, are interesting analogs for the behavior and ecology of medium sized bipedal dinosaurs.)

707. Sukumar, R. 1990. *The Asian Elephant: Ecology and Management.* Cambridge: Cambridge University Press.

A definitive current review of the Asian elephant. Discusses habitat utilization, nutrition, life history traits, herd movements, and the effects of elephants on vegetation.

708. Wing, L.D., and I.O. Buss. 1970. Elephants and forests. *Wildlife Monographs* 19:1–92.

A comprehensive monograph on the African elephant, and its effect on its habitat. Covers social behavior, migration and other movements, and diet. Includes a thorough analysis of the interaction between elephants and plants. (*Note:* Much of this work is relevant to consideration of the effects of large herbivorous dinosaurs on vegetation, particularly the discussions of disturbance effects and seed dispersal.)

SOCIAL BEHAVIOR

←709. Avery, R.A. 1976. Thermoregulation, metabolism and social behavior in Lacertidae. In *Morphology and Biology of Reptiles*, ed. A. d'A. Bellairs and C.B. Cox, 245–259. *Linnean Society Symposium Series* no. 3. London: Academic Press.

Lizards have relatively precise control of internal temperature through behavioral thermoregulation. As latitude increases, lizards in the Northern Hemisphere have correspondingly less time to spend on social behavior, and show decreasing behavioral plasticity and intelligent behavior. Complex social behavior is only possible in favorable thermoregulatory environments.

710. Berger, J. 1981. The role of risks in mammalian combat: zebra and onager fights. *Zeitschrift fuer Tierpsychologie* 56:297–304.

Equids have no horns or other special structures for fighting, and must rely on unbalancing and biting their opponents. Zebra (*Equus burchelli*) and onager (*E. hemionus*) fighting is constrained by the danger of injury due to loss of balance. Rearing and similar tactics increase the probability of successful bites, but also increase the risk of injury. The more evenly matched the opponents, the greater the risk of injury.

←711. Bertram, B.C.R. 1980. Vigilance and group size in ostriches. *Animal Behaviour* 28:278–286.

As group size increased, individual vigilance decreased. Males were more vigilant than females. Reviews the advantages of group behavior for reducing predation. Group behavior in ostriches decreased the vulnerability of the individual ostrich, and increased the time individuals could spend feeding. The vulnerability of the group to predator attack, however, was only slightly reduced. (*See* Stocker and Irvine 1983 [706]; Crome 1975 [716].)

712. Boucot, A. J. 1990. *Evolutionary Paleobiology of Behavior and Coevolution*. Amsterdam: Elsevier.

An encyclopedic review of behavior inferred from the fossil record. Although the dinosaur content is minimal, the volume conveys the vast scope of paleobehavioral studies, and the methodologies used in extracting behavioral information from fossilized vertebrates and invertebrates.

713. Brattstrom, B.H. 1974. The evolution of reptilian social behavior. *American Zoologist* 14:35–49.

Reptile behavior is complex and plastic. Lizards that show territorial behavior in the wild, for example, switch to dominance hierarchies when confined in the laboratory. Discusses territorial and sexual display behavior, and the role of color in social behavior. Briefly speculates on dinosaur behavior. Odor and color were probably critical cues for dinosaur social behavior.

714. Chapman, R.E., P.M. Galton, J.J. Sepkoski jr., and W.P. Wall. 1981. A morphometric study of the cranium of the pachycephalosaurid dinosaur *Stegoceras*. *Journal of Paleontology* 55:603–618.

Uses principal component analysis for fifteen cranial measurements of twenty-nine specimens of *Stegoceras*. Cranial morphology is surprisingly uniform in most species, and these characters may not be taxonomically useful. Two categories of domes are revealed through bivariate analysis of *S. validus*. This variation probably represents sexual dimorphism. The larger and thicker domes are probably males. The thicker dome is most likely the result of sexual selection for thicker domes in ritual male head-butting contests. (*See* Molnar 1977 [732] for additional cross references on the use of horns and domes in intraspecific combat.)

715. Cox, B. 1976. Fossilized fury. *Nature* 260:748–749.

A brief review of the application of sexual selection theory to dinosaurs, citing several early works in behavioral ecology that were influential in shaping key paleontological papers.

716. Crome, F.H.J. 1975. Some observations on the biology of the cassowary in Northern Queensland. *Emu* 76:8–14.

Examines the diet and social behavior of the cassowary (*Casuarius casuarius*). Their diet consists of fruit from low branches and fallen fruit. The breeding seasons coincides with the maximum availability of fruit in the rain forest. The solitary behavior of cassowaries during most of the year contrasts with the gregarious behavior observed in other ratites, and may be related to the cassowary's more constant food supply. (*See* Bertram 1980 [711]; Stocker and Irvine 1983 [706])

717. Currie, P.J., and P. Dodson. 1984. Mass death of a herd of ceratopsian dinosaurs. In *Third Symposium on Mesozoic Terrestrial Ecosystems, Short Papers*, ed. W. Reif and F. Westphal, 61–66. Tübingen: ATTEMPTO-Verlag.

Presents evidence that a herd of *Centrosaurus* met with a tragic mass death, similar to that sometimes observed in large herds of modern mammals.

718. Dodson, P.T. 1976. Quantitative aspects of relative growth and sexual dimorphism in *Protoceratops*. *Journal of Paleontology* 59:929–940.

Uses biometric analysis on an ontogenetic series of skulls and skeletons of *Protoceratops andrewsi*. Sexual dimorphism is established for this species, and is an important source of variability.

719. Emlen, S.T., and L.W. Oring. 1977. Ecology, sexual selection, and the evolution of mating systems. *Science* 197:215–223.

An important theoretical paper which examines the ecological conditions under which various types of mating systems will evolve. The higher the potential for monopolizing mates or resources, the more intense sexual selection will be, and the greater the probability of a polygamous mating system.

720. Farlow, J.O., and P. Dodson. 1975. The behavioral significance of frill and horn morphology in ceratopsian dinosaurs. *Evolution* 29:353–361.

Although enlarged frills may have served to increase the power of the jaws, they also served a sexual display function. Sexual dimorphism is evident in frill morphology. Horns also functioned in courtship displays and in intraspecific combat for mates or territory. Both frills and horns also served as a signal for species recognition. (*See* Molnar 1977 [732] for additional cross references on the use of horns and domes in intraspecific combat.)

721. Galton, P.M. 1971. A primitive dome-headed dinosaur (Ornithischia: Pachycephalosauridae) from the Lower Cretaceous of England and the function of the dome in pachycephalosaurids. *Journal of Paleontology* 45:40–47.

Describes a new species of primitive pachycephalosaurid, *Yaverlandia bitholus*, from the Wealden (Lower Cretaceous). The species is described from a skull cap, which is compared with the skull cap of *Stegoceras*. *Y. bitholus* is intermediate between *Stegoceras* and *Hypsilophodon* in many respects, though closer to the latter. The thick dome characteristic of the pachycephalosaurids probably functioned as a battering ram in intraspecific head-butting contests. (*See* Molnar 1977 [732] for additional cross references on the use of horns and domes in intraspecific combat.)

722. Garrick, L.D., and J.W. Lang. 1977. Social signals and behaviors of adult alligators and crocodiles. *American Zoologist* 17:225–239.

Compares the reproductive behavior of *Alligator mississippiensis*, *Crocodylus acutus*, *and C. niloticus*, including territorial defense and courtship, nesting and incubation behavior, and hatching and post-hatching signal behavior. The increased importance of vocal signals in the alligator seems to be related to its dimly lit and heavily vegetated habitat. Crocodilian communication shows adaptations for a more open visual environment, and also for its higher population densities in which visual signals might be more ambiguous.

➡723. Garrick, L.D., J.W. Lang, and H.A. Herzog jr. 1978. Social signals of adult American alligators. *Bulletin of the American Museum of Natural History* 160:153–192.

Adult alligators exhibit a complex array of communicative behaviors. Eighteen signaling behaviors were observed, roughly classified as eight visual, six vocal and four nonvocal signals. Many behaviors contained a combination of vocalization and postural elements. The complex behavioral patterns suggest a sophisticated social organization.

724. Geist, V. 1966. The evolution of horn-like organs. *Behaviour* 27:175–214.

An influential article describing the role of sexual selection in mammalian horns. The independent evolution of horns in several mammalian families is related to their function in intraspecific wrestling and ramming contests in the defense of territory and the establishment of dominance hierarchies. Horns also function as display organs for attracting mates. Geist's work is frequently cited in studies speculating on the analogous function of dinosaur horns and those of modern mammals. (*See* Molnar 1977 [732] for additional cross references on the use of horns and domes in intraspecific combat.)

➡725. Geist, V. 1974. On the relationship of social evolution and ecology in ungulates. *American Zoologist* 14:205–220.

A complex theoretical paper discussing sixteen ecological hypotheses that shape the social behavior of ungulate populations. Relevant ecological variables include forage quality, biomass and productivity of forage plants, habitat structure and stability, and predator density and diversity. (*See* Molnar 1977 [732] for additional cross references on the use of horns and domes in intraspecific combat.)

726. Hopson, J.A. 1975. The evolution of cranial display structures in hadrosaurian dinosaurs. *Paleobiology* 1:21–43.

Hadrosaur crests served as visual display organs in sexual selection. The crests of lambeosine hadrosaurs also served as vocal resonators in acoustical displays. Crests were sexually dimorphic and species-specific. Kritosaurs (primitive hadrosaurs) also engaged in ritual head-butting contests, using their small nasal horn. (For additional references on the structure and function of hadrosaur crests, See Heaton 1972 [326]; Maryańska and Osmólska 1979 [351]; Maryańska and Osmólska 1981 [352]; Norford 1973 [366]; Ostrom 1961 [372]; Ostrom 1962 [373]; Wheeler 1978 [530]; Molnar 1977 [732]; Weishampel 1981 [741]. *See also* Molnar 1977 [732] for additional cross references on the use of horns and domes in intraspecific combat.)

727. Hotton, N. III. 1980. An alternative to dinosaur endothermy: the happy wanderers. In *A Cold Look at the Warm-blooded Dinosaurs*, ed. R.D.K. Thomas and E.C. Olson, 311–350. Washington: AAAS.

Dinosaurs were inertial homeotherms, and probably adopted annual migration patterns to maintain thermal stability in the seasonal Mesozoic climate. (For additional references on polar dinosaurs and migration, *See* Rich and Rich 1989 [381]; Paul 1988 [439]; Davies 1987 [1018]; Brouwers et al. 1987 [1049]; Rich et al. 1988 [1083].)

728. Krebs, J.R., and N.B. Davies. 1991. *Behavioural Ecology: An Evolutionary Approach*. 3d ed. Oxford: Blackwell Scientific.

A current and comprehensive review of behavioral ecology, a field with much promise for application to the study of dinosaur behavior. Topics include life history theory, competition, predator/prey interactions, sexual selection, parental investment, mating systems and cooperative behavior.

729. Laurie, A. 1982. Behavioural ecology of the Greater one-horned rhinoceros (*Rhinoceros unicornis*). *Journal of Zoology* 196:307–341.

Rhinoceros population densities were highest in habitats with highly diverse early successional vegetation. They consumed 183 species (57 families), but fed mainly on grasses, which formed 70–89% of the diet. Rhinos did not show true territorial behavior, perhaps because their preferred habitat offered poor visibility and an unpredictable distribution of resources. Rhinos rarely formed social groups, and most groups observed consisted of cow-calf pairs or sub-adult males. Sub-adult male groups perhaps formed to guard against predators or attacks by aggressive adult males. Describes a wide range of auditory, visual and olfactory behaviors, and reviews similar behaviors in other rhino species.

730. Lockley, M.G., B.H. Young, and K. Carpenter. 1983. Hadrosaur locomotion and herding behavior: evidence from footprints from the Mesaverde Formation, Grand Mesa Coalfield, Colorado. *Mountain Geology* 20:5–14.

Hadrosaur footprints from Gunnison, Colorado are unusually large, and include a few prints of a carnosaur, probably *Albertosaurus*. Step and stride length estimates suggest a slow rate of movement. Alexander's equations for stride length are questionable for hadrosaur tracks (*See* Chapter Five). The hadrosaurs were abundant and gregarious, and their tracks indicate definite herding behavior, presumably as a defense against predation.

731. MacLean, P.D. 1989. *The Triune Brain in Evolution: Role in Paleocerebral Functions*. New York: Plenum.

A good review, with an extensive bibliography, of a fascinating approach to the evolution of the brain. The brains of advanced mammals are wrapped around an older reptilian brain, which influences our thoughts, emotions and behavior. The triune brain consists of a Protoreptilian Formation, a Paleomammalian Formation (limbic system), and a Neomammalian Formation. (*Note:* This is an advanced treatise covering the same ground as Carl Sagan's popular *Dragons of Eden* [New York: Random House, 1977]).

732. Molnar, R.E. 1977. Analogies in the evolution of combat and display structures in ornithopods and ungulates. *Evolutionary Theory* 3:165–190.

The wide range of horns, frills and crests observed in ceratopsians, pachycephalosaurids, and hadrosaurs is analogous to the elaborate cranial structures of modern ungulates. The evolution of such structures in dinosaurs corresponds to the evolutionary scheme suggested for modern ungulates: use of the teeth, lateral displays, striking blows with the head, frontal visual display and ritual combat. Hadrosaur crests may have functioned as either display structures or as weapons in head-butting contests. (*See* Hopson 1975 [726] for additional cross references on the structure and function of hadrosaur crests. For additional references on the use of horns and domes in intraspecific combat, *See* Chapman et al. 1981 [714]; Farlow and Dodson 1975 [720]; Galton 1971 [721]; Geist 1966 [724]; Geist 1974 [725]; Hopson 1975 [726]; Sues 1978 [738].)

733. Ostrom, J.H. 1972. Were some dinosaurs gregarious? *Palaeogeography, Palaeoclimatology, Palaeoecology* 11:287–301.

Plots and analyzes the tracks of *Eubrontes*, *Anchisauripus*, and *Grallator* at the Mt. Tom site. 70% of the tracks are nearly parallel, particularly those of *Eubrontes*. Reviews several other track sites with similar evidence of gregarious behavior. It is highly unlikely that physical barriers would have channeled the animals' movements at every site. The most likely explanation for the non-random patterns observed is that many dinosaur species travelled in herds.

734. Ostrom, J.H. 1984. Social and unsocial behavior in dinosaurs. *Bulletin of the Field Museum of Natural History* 55:10–21.

An excellent introduction to the study of dinosaur behavior. Highly recommended for classroom use. Discusses feeding behavior, courtship behavior, defense against predators, and social behavior [*See* 735].

735. Ostrom, J.H. 1986. Social and unsocial behavior in dinosaurs. In *Evolution of Animal Behavior: Paleontological and Field Approaches*, ed. M.H. Nitecki and J.A Kitchell, 41–61. London: Oxford University Press.

Essentially the same article as Ostrom 1984 [734], with very slight revision.

736. Reiss, M.J. 1985. The allometry of reproduction: why larger species invest relatively less in offspring. *Journal of Theoretical Biology* 113:529–544.

The amount of energy that females can invest in offspring depends on the amount of non-reproductive energy required by that female, which is in turn related to female body size. Develops an allometric mathematical model to demonstrate that larger species invest less energy in offspring per unit time, relative to their body size.

737. Rothschild, B.M., and D.S. Berman. 1991. Fusion of caudal vertebrae in Late Jurassic sauropods. *Journal of Vertebrate Paleontology* 11:29–36.

Fusion of sauropod caudal vertebrae is not a pathological condition. It probably helped hold the tail erect, as well as serving some unknown behavioral function. The trait might be sexually dimorphic, suggesting that the rigid tail functioned as a whip in male intraspecific combat, or perhaps helped the female arch her tail in reproduction.

738. Sues, H.D. 1978. Functional morphology of the dome in pachycephalosaurid dinosaurs. *Neues Jahrbuch für Geologie und Paläontologie Monatshefte* 8:459–472.

Photoelastic analysis of the skull of Stegoceras validus supports the hypothesis that the thickened dome of pachycephalosaurs could have functioned as a battering ram in intraspecific head-butting contests. The force of the blows would have been transmitted back through the highly ossified skull to the occipital condyle and down the vertebral column. (*See* Molnar 1977 [732] for additional cross references on the use of horns and domes in intraspecific combat.)

739. Thulborn, R.A., and M. Wade. 1979. Dinosaur stampede in the Cretaceous of Queensland. *Lethaia* 12:275–279.

Numerous tracks in West Central Queensland are evidence of a stampede by several species of small to medium-size bipedal dinosaurs. Ornithopods and coelurosaurs were apparently gathered at the muddy shore of a shrunken lake when a large carnosaur approached. The carnosaur triggered a mass stampede, with the animals running at maximum speed.

740. Trivers, R. 1985. *Social Evolution*. Menlo Park: Benjamin-Cummings.

A classic text on behavioral ecology, from a key figure in the development of the field. Covers the genetic and evolutionary aspects of behavior, kinship theory, parent-offspring interaction, parental investment, sex ratios, female choice, cooperative behavior and deceptive behavior.

741. Weishampel, D.B. 1981. Acoustic analysis of potential vocalization in lambeosaurine dinosaurs (Reptilia: Ornithischia). *Paleobiology* 7:252–261.

Analysis of the structure of lambeosaurine crests shows that they could have acted as vocal resonators. Adults would have produced low-frequency vocalizations. Juveniles, lacking lateral diverticula, would have vocalized at higher frequencies. The structure of the inner ear confirms that hadrosaurs could have heard a wide range of frequencies. (*See* Hopson 1975 [726] for additional cross references on the structure and function of hadrosaur crests.)

NESTS, EGGS, AND JUVENILES

742. Ackerman, R.A., R.C. Seagrave, R. Dmi'el, and A. Ar. 1985. Water and heat exchange between parchment-shelled reptile eggs and their surroundings. *Copeia* 1985:703–711.

Presents a mathematical model for water and heat exchange in incubating reptilian eggs. Water is exchanged as water vapor, and the rate of water exchange depends in part on the nature of the solid and gas phases of the substrate in which the eggs are incubated. Larger eggs are better buffered against excessive water exchange than smaller eggs. Egg clutches behave in some respects as if they were a single large egg.

743. Bull, J.J. 1980. Sex determination in reptiles. *Quarterly Review of Biology* 55:3–21.

Reviews temperature-dependent sex determination in reptiles (turtles, lizards, and alligators). Incubation temperature can determine sex ratios in the nests of many reptiles. This type of sex determination is basically incompatible with genetic sex determination (X and Y chromosomes). Discusses the relative selective advantages of genetic and environmental sex determination, and their relation to life history and parental incubation. (*See* Paladino et al. 1989 [778] for additional cross references on temperature-dependent sex ratios and underground nesting.)

744. Burghardt, G.M. 1977. Of iguanas and dinosaurs: social behavior and communication in neonate reptiles. *American Zoologist* 17:177–190.

Examines social behavior in juvenile snakes, turtles, crocodiles and iguanas. Neonate reptilian behavior is more complex than previously believed, and we should not casually dismiss extant reptile behavior as a model for the "advanced" social behavior of juvenile dinosaurs.

745. Callison, G., and H.M. Quimby. 1984. Tiny dinosaurs: are they fully grown? *Journal of Vertebrate Paleontology* 3:200–209.

Uses ontogenetic patterns in precocial cursorial birds to examine the developmental stages of small dinosaur specimens of several species (mainly coelurosaurs and fabrosaurs). The degree of bone ossification and the growth pattern observed in these specimens, about the size of chickens, indicates that they are sub-adult to adult, not juvenile. The model permits prediction of ontogenetic stage and adult size based on measurements of the tibia and femur. (*See also* Galton 1982 [759]; Callison and Quimby 1984 [745].)

746. Campbell, H.W. 1972. Ecological or phylogenetic interpretations of crocodilian nesting habits. *Nature* 238:404–405.

Crocodiles are flexible in the type of nest they build, adapting the nest type to local ecological conditions. The same species may construct either a simple hole or a covered mound nest in different parts of its range.

747. Case, T.J. 1978. Speculations on the growth rate and reproduction of some dinosaurs. *Paleobiology* 4:320–328.

Calculates an age at first reproduction of 20 to 62 years for ectothermic dinosaurs. This delayed reproductive maturity would have put strong selective pressure on high juvenile survivorship. The relatively large size of dinosaur eggs, and their moderate clutch size compared to modern reptiles, supports this hypothesis. Estimates first reproductive age for *Protoceratops grangeri* (8–23 years) and *Hypselosaurus* (25–72 years). (*See* Dunham et al. (1989) for a contrasting view.)

748. Chabreck, R.H. 1973. Temperature variation in nests of the American alligator. *Herpetologica* 29:48–51.

The temperatures of three alligator nests were continuously monitored. Although mean daily air temperatures varied 9.3°C, daily nest temperatures varied only 1.2°C. Heat from the decomposition of the vegetation used to construct the nest kept nest temperatures an average of 1.4°C warmer than air temperatures.

749. Chabreck, R.H. 1975. Moisture variation in nests of the American alligator (*Alligator mississippiensis*). *Herpetologica* 31:385–389.

The moisture inside three alligator nests ranged from 45.4% to 79.0% during the nesting season. Half of this variation is accounted for by variation in water depth and rainfall. Compares natural nest moisture with moisture content in artificial nests.

750. Coombs, W.P. jr. 1980. Juvenile ceratopsians from Mongolia-the smallest known dinosaur specimens. *Nature* 283:380–381.

Describes two very small hatchlings, probably *Psittacosaurus mongoliensis*, from Mongolia. The tiny hatchlings, smaller than a domestic pigeon, were too small to be endothermic. Their small size also argues against parental care, and tooth wear and bone ossification patterns suggest that the hatchlings were precocial.

751. Coombs, W.P. jr. 1982. Juvenile specimens of the ornithischian dinosaur *Psittacosaurus*. *Palaeontology* 25:89–107.

    Describes two juveniles of *Psittacosaurus mongoliensis*. Speculates that juveniles may have formed sibling cohorts, and discusses the evidence for parental care in dinosaurs. Rostral bone morphology shows that Psittacosauridae is a sister group to Ceratopsia. (*See also* Forster 1990 [758].)

752. Coombs, W.P. jr. 1986. A juvenile ankylosaur referable to the genus *Euplocephalus* (Reptilia, Ornithischia). *Journal of Vertebrate Paleontology* 6:162–173.

    Describes a juvenile ankylosaur of the genus *Euoplocephalus*. Discusses ontogenetic differences between juvenile and adult ankylosaurs, contrasting them with differences reported by Galton 1982 [759] for the juvenile and adult *Stegosaurus*. (*See also* Callison and Quimby 1984 [745].)

753. Coombs, W.P. jr. 1989. Modern analogs for dinosaur nesting and parental behavior. In *Paleobiology of the Dinosaurs*, ed. J.O. Farlow, 21–53. *Geological Society of America Special Paper* no. 238.

    A comprehensive review of modern animals that can serve as models for nesting and parental care in dinosaurs. These include crocodiles, ratite birds (ostrich etc.) and megapode (mound nesting) birds. Discusses pre-nesting behavior, site selection, nest construction, site fidelity, egg laying, egg properties, colonial nesting, nest failure, nest guarding, and parental care of hatchlings. Speculates on dinosaur behavior based on this review of contemporary analogs. Endothermy does not require parental care, but ectothermy would not exclude it.

754. Deeming, C., and M. Ferguson. 1989. In the heat of the nest. *New Scientist*, 25 March 25, 33–38.

Crocodiles and alligators can adjust nest temperature, and thereby change the sex ratio of the offspring. At 30°C the embryos all develop into females; at 33°C the embryos all develop into males. Intermediate temperatures produce intermediate sex ratios. The rapid comeback of the American alligator, following severe hunting pressure, is due to the ability of the alligator to hatch nests consisting of mostly female offspring. Similarly, turtles and crocodilians survived the Cretaceous-Tertiary boundary event by adjusting their sex ratios. Dinosaurs probably relied on genetic sex determination, due to the interrelationship of their large size, rapid growth, and hypothalamic "set point". They could not adjust to rapid environmental change, as could crocodilians, and this contributed to their extinction. (*See* Paladino et al. 1989 [778] for additional cross references on temperature-dependent sex ratios and underground nesting.)

755. Dugan, B.A., A.S. Rand, G.M. Burghardt, and B.C. Bock. 1981. Interactions between nesting crocodiles and iguanas. *Journal of Herpetology* 15:409–414.

Similarity of nesting requirements and overlap in breeding seasons causes American crocodiles (*Crocodylus acutus*) and Green Iguanas (*Iguana iguana*) to nest in close proximity at several sites in Panama. Crocodiles attack the nesting iguanas, and sometimes eat them. Iguanas in turn dig up the crocodile's eggs.

756. Erben, H.K., J. Hoefs, and K.H. Wedepohl. 1979. Paleobiological and isotopic studies of eggshells from a declining dinosaur species. *Paleobiology* 5:380–414.

Eggshells of the Late Cretaceous species *Hypselosaurus priseus* show evidence of excessive thickening and thinning of eggshells. Their extinction is attributed to eggshell thinning. These pathological changes are associated with hormonal response to changing environmental conditions, analogous to the thinning seen in the shells of modern fish-eating birds in response to pesticide pollution.

757. Fiorillo, A.R. 1987. Significance of juvenile dinosaurs from Careless Creek Quarry (Judith River Formation), Wheatland County, Montana. In *Fourth Symposium on Mesozoic Terrestrial Ecosystems, Short Papers*, ed. P.J. Currie and E. Koster, 88–95. Drumheller, Alta.: Tyrell Museum of Paleontology.

The remains of several species of juveniles at the Careless Creek Quarry contradicts the hypothesis that dinosaurs nested solely in upland areas. The animals found in this coastal lowland environment are too small to have migrated there from an upland nesting site. Caution is urged in making oversimplified general statements about dinosaur nesting habits, given the diverse nature of dinosaurs.

758. Forster, C.A. 1990. Evidence for juvenile groups in the ornithopod dinosaur *Tenontosaurus tilletti* Ostrom. *Journal of Paleontology* 64:164–165.

A brief article describing two previously collected juvenile groups of *Tenontosaurus tilletti*. The two groups suggest that this species remained together for some time after hatching. Reviews previous juvenile studies. (*See also* Coombs 1982 [751].)

759. Galton, P.M. 1982. Juveniles of the stegosaurian dinosaur *Stegosaurus* from the Upper Jurassic of North America. *Journal of Vertebrate Paleontolgy* 2:47–62.

Describes two partial juvenile skeletons of *Stegosaurus* from the Morrison Formation, and contrasts them with juveniles of the stegosasaurid *Kentrosaurus*. Lists several differences between juvenile and adult stegosaurs. (*See also* Callison and Quimby 1984 [745]; Coombs 1986 [752].)

760. Galton, P.M. 1983. A juvenile stegosaurian dinosaur, *Omosaurus phillipsi* Seeley from the Oxfordian (Upper Jurassic) of England. *Geobios* 16:95–101.

Describes the femur of *Omosaurus phillipsi*, claimed to be the only stegosaur known from the lower Upper Jurassic. While the specimen is definitely a stegosaur, it is a juvenile. It is also not diagnostic, and the species described from it is not valid.

761. Grine, F.E., and J.W. Kitching. 1987. Scanning electron microscopy of early dinosaur egg shell structure: a comparison with other rigid Sauropsid eggs. *Scanning Microscopy* 1:615–630.

Early Jurassic sauropod eggs have a shell structure similar to that of bird and crocodile eggs. It is very unlike the structure of turtle and squamate reptile eggs.

762. Hirsch, K.F. 1989. Interpretations of Cretaceous and pre-Cretaceous eggs and shell fragments. In *Dinosaur Tracks and Traces*, ed. D.D. Gillette and M.G. Lockley, 89–97. New York: Cambridge University Press.

The fossil record is biased in favor of species with hard-shelled eggs. Discusses problems of classification and description in fossil eggshells, and cautions against speculation on the evolution of eggshell structure until more information is available.

763. Hirsch, K.F., K.L. Stadtman, W.E. Miller, and J.H. Madsen jr. 1989. Upper Jurassic dinosaur egg from Utah USA. *Science* 243:1711–1713.

A rare egg from the Upper Jurassic is described. Containing unidentified embryonic remains, the egg shows a pathological multilayered shell.

764. Hirsch, K.F., R.G. Young, and H.J. Armstrong. 1987. Eggshell fragments from the Jurassic Morrison Formation of Colorado. In *Paleontology and Geology of the Dinosaur Triangle*, ed. W.R. Averett, 79–84. Museum of Western Colorado.

Eggshells from the Jurassic are relatively rare, but they have been found at three localities in the Triangle: the Callison Quarry, Garden Park, and the Young Locality. Briefly surveys each site. Turtle-like and bird-like shell fragments have been found, though the latter may actually be dinosaur eggs.

765. Horner, J.R. 1982. Evidence of colonial nesting and 'site fidelity' among ornithischian dinosaurs. *Nature* 297:675–676.

Colonial nesting sites of ornithopods are found along three separate horizons. The animals returned repeatedly to the same nesting site.

766. Horner, J.R. 1984. The nesting behavior of dinosaurs. *Scientific American* 214 (April):130–137.

A good summary of Horner's important work in exhuming and interpreting dinosaur nesting sites. Recommended for classroom reading.

767. Horner, J.R. 1989. Ecologic and behavioral implications derived from a dinosaur nesting site. In *Dinosaurs Past and Present*, Volume II, ed. S.J. Czerkas and E.C. Olson, 50–63. Los Angeles: Natural History Museum of Los Angeles County.

The Egg Mountain and Egg Island nesting sites in the Two Medicine Formation were small islands near the shore of an intermittent alkaline lake. The two species that shared these islands, a small hypsilophodontid and a second unidentified species, show a pattern of colonial nesting. Discusses the paleoenvironmental setting of the nesting ground, and describes its excavation. The unbroken lower halves of the hypsilophodont eggs indicates that the precocial young left the nest shortly after hatching. The regular patterns of eggs observed indicates that the parent manipulated the eggs after they were laid. Nests are located about the same distance apart as the reach of the adult (*Note:* Similar to the pattern observed in many modern colonial nesting birds). Young dinosaurs probably remained on the islands until the end of summer, when the receding lake waters would have opened a pathway to the mainland for the now well developed juveniles.

768. Horner, J.R., and R. Makela. 1979. Nest of juveniles provides evidence of family structure among dinosaurs. *Nature* 282:296–298.

Fifteen juvenile hadrosaurs (about 1 m long) were discovered, together with eggshells, in and around a concave nest. The presence of the same-sized young in the nest suggests that they were receiving parental care. Describes the new hadrosaurine species *Maiasaura peeblesorum*. (*See* Horner 1983 [328].)

769. Horner, J.R., and D.B. Weishampel. 1988. A comparative embryological study of two ornithischian dinosaurs. *Nature* 332:256–257.

Describes the new species *Orodromeus makelai*, the first known hypsilophodont from the North American Campanian. Adults, juveniles, and eggs of this species and of *Maiasaura peeblesorum* represent a rare find. Even rarer is the discovery of embryonic dinosaurs of both species.

770. Horner, J.R., and D.B. Weishampel. 1989. Dinosaur eggs: the inside story. *Natural History*, December, 61–67.

A well-written summary of Horner's work at the Egg Mountain and Egg Island nesting sites. Discusses the nesting habits and parental care of *Orodromeus makelai* and *Maiasaura peeblesorum*. *Maiasaura* covered its large mud nest with a layer of vegetation; the altricial young grew quickly. *Orodromeus* hatchlings, on the other hand, were precocial; they were able to fend for themselves as hatchlings.

771. Hunt, R.H., and M.E. Watanabe. 1982. Observations on the maternal behavior of the American alligator, *Alligator mississippiensis*. *Journal of Herpetology* 16:236–239.

Four female alligators in Okefenokee Swamp were observed for six years. Vocalizations were very important in maternal-juvenile interactions. One alligator was completely blind, but was still able to protect her brood through vocalizations. Describes nest guarding and juvenile dispersal.

772. Jain, S.L. 1989. Recent dinosaur discoveries in India, including eggshells, nests and coprolites. In *Dinosaur Tracks and Traces*, ed. D.D. Gillette and M.G. Lockley, 99–108. New York: Cambridge University Press.

Trace fossils are rare in the Indian fossil record. Reviews known egg sites, including an "extensive hatchery" filled with spherical eggs, many of them unhatched. Coprolites have also been reported, but not definitely linked to dinosaurs. Includes a table listing known species of Indian dinosaurs.

773. Kurzanov, S.M., and K.E. Mikhailov. 1989. Dinosaur eggshells from the Lower Cretaceous of Mongolia. In *Dinosaur Tracks and Traces*, ed. D.D. Gillette and M.G. Lockley, 109–113. New York: Cambridge University Press.

   Describes a Lower Cretaceous nest, inferred from the distribution of eggshell fragments. The nest is believed to have been a shallow open cup, and the condition of the fragments indicates that the young probably remained in the nest after hatching.

774. Kushlan, J.A. 1973. Observations on maternal behavior in the American alligator *Alligator mississippiensis*. *Herpetologica* 29:256–257.

   Alligators in the Everglades were observed guarding nests and attacking intruders. Alligators also opened the nest for hatchlings, and responded to juvenile distress calls by attacking the researcher. The enraged mother retrieved the youngster in her mouth.

775. Kushlan, J.A., and M.S. Kushlan. 1980. Function of nest attendance in the American alligator. *Herpetologica* 36:27–32.

   Alligators use a graded series of aggressive responses to nest disturbance, culminating in an attack. The response depends partly on the intensity of the threat, and is more complex than reported by Garrick et al. (1978 [723]).

776. Magnusson, W.E., A.P. Lima, and R.A. Sampaio. 1987. Sources of heat for nests of *Paleosuchus trigonatus* and a review of crocodilian nest temperatures. *Journal of Herpetology* 19:199–207.

   Nests of *Paleosuchus trigonatus* are placed next to termite mounds in order to keep them above ambient temperatures. Reviews control of nest temperatures in other crocodilians.

777. Norman, D.B. 1988. Embryos in dinosaur nests. *Nature* 332:202–203.

A brief review of three discoveries of embryonic dinosaurs.

778. Paladino, F.V., P. Dodson, J.K. Hammond, and J.R. Spotila. 1989. Temperature-dependent sex determination in dinosaurs? Implications for population dynamics and extinction. In *Paleobiology of the Dinosaurs*, ed. J.O. Farlow, 63–70. *Geological Society of America Special Paper* no. 238.

Modern reptiles are able to modify sex ratios in hatchlings by varying nest temperatures. If dinosaurs followed this same model, cooling climates at the end of the Cretaceous could have resulted in broods of predominantly one sex, contributing to dinosaur extinction. (For additional references on temperature-dependent sex ratios and underground nesting, *See* Seymour 1979 [782]; Bull 1980 [743]; Deeming and Ferguson 1989 [754]; Seymour and Ackerman 1980 [783]; Vogt and Bull 1984 [788]; Williams et al. 1984 [789].)

779. Pond, C.M. 1983. Parental feeding as a determinant of ecological relationships in Mesozoic terrestrial ecosystems. In *Second International Symposium on Mesozoic Terrestrial Ecosystems*, ed. Z. Kielan-Jaworska and H. Osmólska, 215–224. *Acta Palaeontologica Polonica* 28 (1/2).

Lactation allows mammals to feed young in the absence of other suitable food supplies. Thus mammals were suitable r-strategist colonists, able to exploit unstable environments. Dinosaurs were better adapted to stable K-type environments where diverse flora and fauna would provide food for juveniles of all sizes. Parental feeding in birds is most developed among the more advanced groups, suggesting that it is a derived behavior not shared by the ancestral dinosaur. Lactation and parental feeding may be as important as viviparity and endothermy in understanding Mesozoic community ecology.

780. Richmond, N.D. 1965. Perhaps juvenile dinosaurs were always scarce. *Journal of Paleontology* 39:503–505.

Reviews speculation on the scarcity of juvenile dinosaurs in the fossil record. Large size and longevity should lead to a slow rate of population replacement (K-selection). Dinosaur life history may have been similar to some modern turtles that maintain populations close to their carrying capacity and have replacement rates on the order of 1% per year. (*See also* Case 1978.)

781. Sahni, A. 1989. Paleoecology and paleoenvironments of the Late Cretaceous dinosaur eggshell sites from peninsular India. In *Dinosaur Tracks and Traces*, ed. D.D. Gillette and M.G. Lockley, 179–185. New York: Cambridge University Press.

    Describes the Late Cretaceous Lameta Formation dinosaur ichnofauna, and the utility of egg sites in reconstructing the paleoenvironment. The fauna is dominated by titanosaurid sauropods, and most eggs are assigned to this taxon.

782. Seymour, R.S. 1979. Dinosaur eggs: gas conductance through the shell, water loss during incubation and clutch size. *Paleobiology* 5:1–11.

    Shell measurements and pore geometry allow estimates of gas diffusion through dinosaur eggshells. Mathematical analysis yields shell thickness estimates larger than those observed. Eggshell thinning may not be pathological, but rather an adaptation to underground nesting. Dinosaurs probably buried their eggs in holes or nest mounds, with or without added vegetable matter, as do many large modern reptiles. Such subterranean nesting would have limited clutch size in large sauropods. Sauropods probably divided their total clutch over several separate nests. (*See* Paladino et al. 1989 [778] for additional cross references on temperature-dependent sex ratios and underground nesting.)

783. Seymour, R.S., and R.A. Ackerman. 1980. Adaptations to underground nesting in birds and reptiles. *American Zoologist* 20:437–447.

    Megapode birds, and several species of turtles and crocodiles, incubate their eggs in mounds or underground nests. This environment differs radically from that experienced by eggs in aerial nests. Buried nests experience high humidity, high carbon dioxide tension and low oxygen tension. The nature of the substrate, parental manipulation of the nest, and the presence of organic matter can also affect the nest environment. Discusses the implications of these findings for dinosaur eggs, which were probably also buried in the ground. (*See* Paladino et al. 1989 [778] for additional cross references on temperature-dependent sex ratios and underground nesting.)

784. Standora, E.A., and J.R. Spotila. 1985. Temperature dependent sex determination in sea turtles. *Copeia* 1985:711–722.

Reviews the literature for the molecular basis of temperature-dependent sex determination, known to occur in several species of sea turtles. Such sex determination was probably common in dinosaurs, and may have contributed to their extinction. Deteriorating climate at the end of the Cretaceous would have led to generations of unisexual offspring.

785. Tracy, C.R., and E.H. Snell. 1985. Interrelations among water and energy relations of reptilian eggs, embryos, and hatchlings. *American Zoologist* 25:999–1008.

Reptilian eggs can be either endohydric, supplied at oviposition with all the water they need to develop, or ectohydric, needing to absorb water to complete their development. Larger eggs behave as though they were endohydric regardless of eggshell properties. The ecology of reptilian eggs is critical in the understanding of their life history.

786. Troyer, K. 1982. Transfer of fermentative microbes between generations in a herbivorous lizard. *Science* 216:540–542.

Captive iguana hatchlings (*Iguana iguana*) do not grow as rapidly as wild hatchlings unless fed fresh fecal material from an adult iguana. Eating fecal matter (coprophagy) transfers gut microflora to the juvenile, which will aid in the fermentation of their vegetable diet. The need for such transfer could have selected for social groups in herbivorous dinosaurs. (*See* Farlow 1987a [618] for additional cross references on fermentation in herbivores.)

787. Vianey-Liaud, M., S.L. Jain, and A. Sahni. 1987. Dinosaur eggshells (Saurischia) from the Late Cretaceous Intertrappean and Lameta Formations (Deccan, India). *Journal of Vertebrate Paleontology* 7:408–424.

Identifies eggshells from the Late Cretaceous Intertrappean and Lameta Formations as sauropod eggs, based on microstructural analysis. This conclusion is consistent with sauropod skeletal remains found nearby.

788. Vogt, R.C., and J.J. Bull. 1984. Ecology of hatchling sex ratio in map turtles. *Ecology* 65:582–587.

Map turtle nests showed a bimodal distribution between all male and all female hatchlings. Male nests were sited in cool temperature areas in vegetation, while female nests were located in high temperature areas in open sand. Sex ratios were heavily influenced by local conditions and seasonal temperature variations. (*See* Paladino et al. 1989 [778] for additional cross references on temperature-dependent sex ratios and underground nesting.)

789. Williams, D.L.G., R.S. Seymour, and P. Kerourio. 1984. Structure of fossil dinosaur eggshell from the Aix Basin, France. *Palaeogeography, Palaeoclimatology, Palaeoecology* 45:23–37.

Four types of dinosaur eggs are described from Late Cretaceous beds in southern France. Estimates of water conductance are much higher than avian values, suggesting that the eggs were incubated under high humidity, probably in underground nests. Thin eggshells were probably an adaptation to underground nesting, not a pathological condition. (*See* Paladino et al. 1989 [778] for additional cross references on temperature-dependent sex ratios and underground nesting.)

790. Winkler, D.A., and P.A. Murry. 1989. Paleoecology and hypsilophodontid behavior at the Proctor Lake dinosaur locality (Early Cretaceous), Texas. In *Paleobiology of the Dinosaurs*, ed. J.O. Farlow, 55–61. *Geological Society of America Special Paper* no. 238.

The Twin Mountains Formation beds yield evidence of a hypsilophodont nesting site. Juvenile remains at the lowland, semiarid Proctor Lake site suggest that larger juveniles formed cohorts. The presence of older juveniles in at least one nest indicates the possibility of parental care.

791. Woodward, A., T. Hines, C. Abercrombie, and C. Hope. 1984. Spacing patterns in alligator nests. *Journal of Herpetology* 18:8–12.

Alligator nests near a Florida lake show distinct clumping. Social aggregation explains the nest distribution.

Variation in ceratopsian horn and frill morphology. Top: *Chasmosaurus*. Middle: *Styracosaurus*. Bottom: *Torosaurus*. From *Archosauria: A New Look at the Old Dinosaur* by John C. McLoughlin. Copyright © 1979 by John C. McLoughlin. Used by permission of Viking Penguin, a division of Penguin Books USA Inc.

Chapter Seven

Dinosaur Evolution

In the waning days of the Triassic, dinosaurs were mostly small and ecologically rather unimportant creatures, dwelling in the shadows of other primitive archosaurs. The carnivorous pseudosuchians were the great predators, filling the niche that would later fall to carnosaurs like *Tyrannosaurus* and *Allosaurus*. The pseudosuchians were so successful that archosaurs completely replaced therapsids as the dominant terrestrial vertebrates (Charig 1980 [794], Bonaparte 1982 [209]; Benton 1979 [580]; Benton 1983 [581]; Charig 1984 [586]; Crompton and Attridge 1986 [617]).

The thecodonts made their evolutionary debut in the Lower Triassic. They were primitive carnivores, with a sprawling stance and plodding gait. By the Middle Triassic, the biomass of archosaurs approached that of the therapsids; by the Late Triassic the archosaurian carnivores ruled the ecological roost (Benton 1984a [792]; Tucker and Benton 1982 [801]; Benton 1984b [804]). Their evolutionary success was largely due to their improved erect stance. This significant evolutionary advance gave them the speed and agility to use their sharp teeth to best advantage.

Therapsids vanished by the Late Triassic, and interspecific competition between archosaurs intensified. Some evolved into larger and fiercer carnivores. Others adapted a different strategy, and switched to a herbivorous diet. Aided by their fully-improved stance, the herbivorous archosaurs rapidly displaced the dominant therapsid herbivores (Charig 1980 [794]).

Where did the dinosaurs come from? Are they a "natural" taxon, stemming from a common ancestor? (A taxon (taxa) is any unit of taxonomic classification, such as a species, genus, or family) Or did dinosaurs evolve from more than one ancestral group? Much of the research on dinosaur evolution has centered on these two questions (Bonaparte 1969 [805]; Padian 1989 [816]).

Kevin Padian's excellent collection of essays *The Beginning of The Age of Dinosaurs* is recommended for a coherent overall view of the world into which the dinosaurs were born. (*See* Welles 1986 [824] for example. Several other papers from this collection are also included.)

Dinosaurs are diapsid reptiles, so called because of the two openings at the rear of their skull, a feature they share with lizards, snakes, birds, and crocodiles. The Diapsida diverged early in the Permian, and gave rise to two major lineages. One led to modern snakes and lizards, while the other terminated in the Rhynchosaurs and Prolacertiformes. These latter taxa disappeared by the Middle Triassic.

Towards the end of the Permian, the Proterosuchids and Erythrosuchids split off; both lines died out before the Mid-Triassic. The crocodile line emerged in the Late Permian and early Triassic, with Rauisuchids, Aetosaurs and Phytosaurs as close allies. All but the crocodiles had vanished by the Jurassic.

Dinosaurs evolved in the early to Mid-Triassic, with ornithosuchids and pterosaurs forming a closely related lineage. Ornithosuchids didn't survive the Triassic, but pterosaurs ruled the Cretaceous skies. Birds evolved from small theropod dinosaurs at some point in the Late Jurassic or Early Cretaceous (a topic covered in Chapter 8).

This outline of diapsid evolution is now generally accepted. Discussions at the Third Symposium on Mesozoic Terrestrial Ecosystems, held at Tübingen in 1984, revealed widespread support for this phylogeny. Several of the papers from this landmark conference are analyzed in this chapter.

Although we know which group of ancestors dinosaurs came from, their precise parentage is still a matter of dispute. The section in this chapter on the origin of dinosaurs illustrates the principal arguments. It is generally agreed that dinosaurs came from thecodont reptiles (Colbert 1964 [808]; Novas 1989 [815]; Thulborn 1971 [818]; Welles 1986 [824]).

The semi-improved stance of thecodonts was a quantum evolutionary jump from the primitive sprawl of the therapsids. Dinosaurs completed this evolutionary trend, developing the fully-improved or erect stance that guaranteed their evolutionary success. But which thecodont group gave rise to dinosaurs? Did different lineages of dinosaurs arise independently from more than one group of thecodonts?

The arguments are often subtle, and address obscure points of anatomy. Ankle joints, for instance, are of primary importance in determining the ancestors of dinosaurs (Chatterjee 1985 [807]; Cooper 1980 [809]; Cruickshank 1975 [810]; Cruickshank 1979 [811]; Cruickshank and Benton 1985 [812]; Thulborn 1982 [822]; Chatterjee 1982 [836]). They are one of the few features of thecodont anatomy sufficiently differentiated to make realistic comparisons possible.

How are the known genera of dinosaurs related to one another? Until recently, the classification of dinosaurs was a relatively moribund area of research; with the advent of cladistic analysis, dinosaur systematics has once again became a hot topic. Much recent work has focused on constructing cladograms of the various dinosaur lineages.

The symposium *Dinosaur Systematics* is a watershed in the renewal of interest in the phylogeny of dinosaurs (Currie and Carpenter 1990 [841]). Several of the papers presented at thus symposium are analyzed in this chapter. Those seeking the most current information on the taxonomy of dinosaurs should also consult *The Dinosauria*, which summarizes current knowledge about each principal dinosaur taxon (Weishampel et al. 1990 [16]).

Readers unfamiliar with the intricacies of cladistic analysis will find much of this literature confusing. Ridley's *Evolution and Classification* is recommended as an introduction to cladistics. Its glossary will help breach the seemingly impenetrable wall of cladistic vocabulary. (Ridley 1986 [862]. *See also* Cracraft and Eldredge, 1979 [839]; Sereno 1990 [867].) Many of the technical terms used in this chapter are also defined in the glossary at the end of this bibliography.

While space precludes a detailed discourse on cladistics, a few terms are essential to understand the importance of several of the papers which follow. Cladistics is based on the identification of shared derived characters. All organisms at a certain grade, or general level of development, have some things in common. Men and salamanders have four limbs. But four limbs isn't a useful character trait to classify animals at or above the level of amphibians. It is a symplesiomorphic character, or shared primitive trait.

Instead, cladists look for shared traits which are secondarily derived from the ancestral state. Certain specialized cranial features, for example, unite the ceratopsians into a single taxon. Suppose that only a few genera in this taxon have a particular arrangement of horns on their shield, indicating a shared ancestry. This shared derived character, or "synapomorphy", might be a useful taxonomic tool to unite these genera in a single phylogenetic line.

This reliance on apomorphic (derived) characters has resulted in some major overhauls of traditional dinosaur classification schemes, which were formerly based on gross morphological similarities (Molnar 1990 [854]). All systems of classification, however, share a common problem. It is very difficult, and sometimes impossible, to distinguish between homologous and analogous traits.

Homologous traits arise because both taxa came from a common ancestor, even though the trait may serve a vastly different function in different organisms. Analogous traits evolved independently, through convergent evolution, to fill the same basic function in otherwise unrelated animals. The wings of a bat and the wings of an insect are analogous structures, while the wings of a bat and the arms of a human are homologous structures. Convergence leads to superficially similar traits (analogous structures). Only true homologies can be used to construct cladograms.

One of the ultimate goals of cladistic analysis is to identify "natural" groupings, those that actually stem from a common ancestor. Such groups are called "monophyletic". The two closest dichotomous branches of such a monophyletic grouping are termed "sister groups". A taxon might be diphyletic, stemming from two separate ancestral groups, or polyphyletic, with multiple independent ancestral lines artificially grouped into a single taxon.

Are dinosaurs a monophyletic group? The latest consensus is that they are a monophyletic taxon, though the arguments are still heated (Bonaparte 1976 [806]; Novas 1989 [815]; Paul 1984a [817]; Thulborn 1980 [821]; Bakker and Galton 1974 [825]; Charig 1976 [833]; Evans 1988 [845]; Paul 1984b [860]; Sereno 1986 [865]]).

Gauthier, Bakker, and others have turned up the heat with radical phylogenetic proposals, at least some of which may be winning acceptance. Birds, for example, now find themselves in the Theropoda, along with *Tyrannosaurus* Rex. (Gauthier 1986 [907]). If birds are really direct descendants of theropod dinosaurs, should Dinosauria be elevated to a Class, perhaps replacing the old Class Aves (Bakker and Galton 1974 [825]; Charig 1976 [833])?

The issues are not wholly resolved, and it remains to be seen how our emerging picture of the true relationship between dinosaurs, birds, and modern reptiles will filter down into the public consciousness.

The division of this chapter into articles on general evolution, dinosaur origins, and taxonomy and phylogeny, is a bit artificial. These three topics are inextricably intertwined. The first section includes articles of general interest, or those examining the evolution of a particular functional or morphological detail. The second section includes studies focused on the question of the ultimate ancestry of dinosaurs, while the third section deals with questions of dinosaur classification.

THE EVOLUTION OF DINOSAURS

792. Benton, M.J. 1984a. The relationships and early evolution of the Diapsida. *Zoological Society of London Symposium* no. 52:575–596.

    The Diapsida (crocodiles, lizards and snakes) diverged during the Permo-Triassic into Ledpidosauria and Archosauria. Benton proposes a new cladistic analysis of these two lineages. Thecodonts replaced mammal-like reptiles in the mid to late Triassic. By the late Triassic, both groups had died out, and the formerly rare dinosaurs radiated opportunistically into the vacant niches. There is no evidence of competition between diapsids and mammal-like reptiles. Climatic change may have driven therapsids into extinction.

793. Charig, A.J. 1972. The evolution of the archosaur pelvis and hindlimb: an explanation in functional terms. In *Studies in Vertebrate Evolution*, ed. K.A. Joysey and T.S. Kemp, 121–155. New York: Winchester Press.

    There is no evidence of a trend towards bipedality in early archosaur evolution. The "fully-improved" vertical stance does not require bipedality; quadrupedality is not necessarily a secondary condition in archosaur evolution. Dinosaurs evolved a vertical posture, separating them from the semi-improved quadrupedal thecodonts. This postural improvement is sometimes, but not always, associated with bipedality. (*See* Cooper 1980 [809] for a contrasting view.)

794. Charig, A.J. 1980. Differentiation of lineages among Mesozoic tetrapods. *Mémoires de la Société Géologique de France* 139:207–210.

    The neotetrapods, (dinosaurs, mammals, and birds) completely replaced the palaeotetrapods in an evolutionary explosion in the Middle to Late Triassic. Charig reviews the faunal replacement of the Triassic, crediting the victory of the archosaurs to their semi-improved and fully-improved stance. Lacks a bibliography. (*See* Benton 1983 [581] for additional cross references on faunal replacement and competition.)

795. Colbert, E.H. 1991. *Evolution of the Vertebrates: a History of the Backboned Animals Through Time*. 4th ed. New York: Wiley.
   The latest edition of a classic text on vertebrate paleontology.

796. Norman, D.B. 1984. On the cranial morphology and evolution of ornithopod dinosaurs. In *The Structure, Development and Evolution of Reptiles*, ed. M.W.J. Ferguson. Zoological Society of London Symposium no. 52:521–547.
   Illustrates and compares the crania of the four basic ornithopod grades: fabrosauroid, hypsilophodontoid, iguanodontoid and hadrosauroid. The various types of cranial kinesis result from functional adaptations for increasingly advanced herbivory. The cranial specialization of the pleurokinetic hinge, developed in the iguanodontoids and probably in hadrosauroids, explains the evolutionary success of the ornithopods. It reduces the stresses caused by transverse shearing of the jaws. Presents a cladogram for the ornithopods. (*See* Weishampel 1984 [802] for additional cross references on the evolution of jaw mechanisms.)

797. Ostrom, J.H. 1966. Functional morphology and evolution of the ceratopsian dinosaurs. *Evolution* 20:290–308.
   Seeks a functional explanation for the short-frilled (*Torosaurus*) and long frilled (*Triceratops*) lines of ceratopsians. Ceratopsians show an increasingly sophisticated set of adaptations for eating tough vegetation (presumably palms and cycads). These adaptations include complex dental batteries, with rows of replacement teeth, and variations in frill morphology. Long-frilled species derived a stronger bite from stronger jaw muscles attached to larger frills. Short-frilled species increased their bite by means of somewhat stronger jaw muscles, and compensated for the greater leverage of the larger frill by improvements in jaw mechanics.

798. Padian, K., and W.A. Clemens. 1985. Terrestrial vertebrate diversity: episodes and insights. In *Phanerozoic Diversity*

Patterns: Profiles in Macroevolution, ed. J.W. Valentine, 41–96. Princeton: Princeton University Press.

An increasing focus on changes in species diversity prompts this general review of diversity patterns in vertebrate evolution. Phylogenetic and biogeographic hypotheses about vertebrate history can be studied through the analysis of cladistic patterns. Discusses "the case of the missing Lower Jurassic," and the problem of the Cretaceous-Tertiary boundary.

799. Radinsky, L.B. 1987. *The Evolution of Vertebrate Design*. Chicago: University of Chicago Press.

An authoritative and readable introduction to the overall pattern of vertebrate evolution. Written as a text for non-biology majors, it is a perfect introduction for paleontologists, geologists, and others with little or no biological background.

800. Stanley, S.M. 1973. An explanation for Cope's rule. *Evolution* 27:1–26.

Cope's Rule states that there is a pronounced tendency of animals to evolve towards larger sizes. This seems odd, because there is no intrinsic selective advantage of large size. A better interpretation of Cope's Rule might be that animals tend to originate at a size smaller than the optimal adaptive size, and gradually increase toward the optimum. "Large-scale adaptive breakthroughs" seem to be limited to smaller size ranges. (*Note:* See Chapter Six for possible adaptive advantages of larger size.)

801. Tucker, M.E., and M.J. Benton. 1982. Triassic environments, climates and reptile evolution. *Palaeogeography, Palaeoclimatology, Palaeoecology* 40:361–379.

Mammal-like reptiles, rhynchosaurs, and aetosaurs disappeared quickly in the Upper Triassic (middle Norian). The rapidity of their disappearance argues against competition as a primary cause. New floras, adapted to more arid conditions, displaced the old lowland bush vegetation that these reptiles depended upon. The dinosaurs radiated only after these groups had gone extinct. (*See also* Benton 1983

[581] for additional cross references on faunal replacement and competition.)

802. Weishampel, D.B. 1984. Evolution of jaw mechanisms in ornithopod dinosaurs. *Advances in Anatomy, Embryology, and Cell Biology* 87:1–116. Berlin: Springer-Verlag.

    This monograph consists of an extensive and detailed review of Weishampel's lengthy study of ornithopod jaw mechanisms, including fifty species covering all five ornithopod families. Fabrosaurids show the most primitive jaw mechanism, consisting of a rigid skull and rigid mandible. From this condition, two additional jaw types have evolved in ornithopods; both types incorporate a transverse jaw motion. One type mobilizes the lower jaw to rotate medially during the power stroke; the second type mobilizes the upper jaw to rotate laterally during the power stroke. These evolutionary changes are probably related to evolutionary changes in Mesozoic flora. (*See also* Norman and Weishampel 1985 [639]; Norman and Weishampel 1987 [640]; Weishampel 1983 [653]; Norman 1984 [796].)

803. Weishampel, D.B., and J.R. Horner. 1987. Dinosaurs, habitat bottlenecks, and the St. Mary River Formation. In *Fourth Symposium on Mesozoic Terrestrial Ecosystems, Short Papers*, ed. P.J. Currie and E. Koster, 222–227. Drumheller, Alta.: Tyrell Museum of Paleontology.

    The Bearpaw marine incursion substantially reduced habitat space, and fragmented dinosaur populations. Following the withdrawal of the Bearpaw Sea, the upland habitat represented in the St. Mary River Formation represents the first colonizable habitat. Examination of these sediments should reveal the workings of an evolutionary bottleneck, with recolonization, radiation of terrestrial faunas, and a gradual faunal succession toward a new equilibrium. (*See also* Cooper 1977 [192]; Hallam 1978 [196]; Horner 1983 [328].)

ORIGIN OF DINOSAURS

804. Benton, M.J. 1984b. Fossil reptiles of the German Late Triassic and the origin of the dinosaurs. In *Third Symposium on Mesozoic Terrestrial Ecosystems, Short Papers*, ed. W. Reif and F. Westphal, 13–18. Tübingen: ATTEMPTO-Verlag.

    Benton (1983 [581]) argues that dinosaur radiation followed a mass extinction of reptiles in the late Triassic. Accounts of dinosaurs prior to the Upper Carnian (late Triassic) are doubtful. Examination of specimens from southwest Germany supports a mass extinction in the middle Norian and a very rapid subsequent radiation of dinosaurs. (*See* [805] and additional cross references in Benton 1983 [581].)

805. Bonaparte, J.F. 1969. Comments on early saurischians. *Zoological Journal of the Linnean Society* 48:471–480.

    Dinosaurs replaced pseudosuchian thecodonts during the Upper Triassic. The two orders of dinosaurs diverged well in advance of this faunal replacement. Relates the origin of the Prosauropoda, Coelurosauria, and Carnosauria. *Ornithosuchus* is probably a thecodont, not a dinosaur. Triassic carnosaurs disappeared in the Triassic, and are an entirely different group from the later Mesozoic carnosaurs. The saurischians radiated early in the Triassic, with carnosaurs, sauropodomorphs, and coelurosaurs evolving independently from a common ancestral stock. (*See* [804] and Benton 1983 [581] for additional cross references on faunal replacement and competition.)

806. Bonaparte, J.F. 1976. *Pisanosaurus mertii* Casamiquela and the origin of the Ornithischia. *Journal of Paleontology* 50:808–820.

    This species is the oldest known ornithischian, and a member of the family Heterodontosauridae. Saurischians and ornithischians share several derived characters and are probably a monophyletic group. (*See* Charig 1976 [833] for additional cross references on dinosaur monophyly.) Reviews skeletal material and contrasts this species with other Triassic ornithischians.

807. Chatterjee, S. 1985. *Postosuchus*, a new thecodontian reptile from the Triassic of Texas and the origin of tyrannosaurs. *Philosophical Transactions of the Royal Society of London B* 309:395–460.

Postosuchus kirkpatricki is a carnivorous thecodont from the late Triassic Dockum Group. Its "crocodile-normal" ankle joint suggests that it was a pseudosuchian thecodont. *Postosuchus* is placed in the family Poposauridae, which probably gave rise to the tyrannosaurs. True carnosaurs did not appear until the late Triassic. Allosaurids and tyrannosaurids represent separate phylogenetic lines.

808. Colbert, E.H. 1964. Relationship of the saurischian dinosaurs. *American Museum Novitates* 2181:1–24.

Triassic saurischians can be divided into an exclusively bipedal group (Coelurosauria and part of Carnosauria) and a more primitive partly quadrupedal group (Prosauropoda and part of Carnosauria). This traditional scheme is unnatural, as is the taxon Carnosauria. The Triassic carnosaurs are unrelated to the later true carnosaurs, which are derived from coelurosaurs. Saurischians arose from thecodont stock, diverging into palaeosaurs, plateosaurs, and coelurosaurs, the latter adapted for rapid bipedal movement. The palaeosaurs died out by the early Jurassic, while the plateosaurs (or prosauropods) gave rise to the giant quadrupedal herbivores. Triassic ornithischians can be divided into three suborders: Theropoda (includes carnosaurs and coelurosaurians), Palaeopoda (includes palaeosaurians and plateosaurians—*See also* Vanheerden 1978 [823]), and Sauropoda (includes Brachiosauridae and Titanosauridae).

809. Cooper, M.R. 1980. The prosauropod ankle and dinosaur phylogeny. *South African Journal of Science* 76:176–178.

Based on ankle morphology, *Vulcanodon* and the other sauropods are descended from the prosauropods. Quadrupedality is secondarily derived in sauropods. (*See* Charig 1972 [793] for an alternate hypothesis.)

810. Cruickshank, A.R.I. 1975. The origin of sauropod dinosaurs. *South African Journal of Science* 71:89–90.

    Criticizes earlier work by Raath on the lowermost Jurassic dinosaur *Vulcanodon karibaensis*. *Vulcanodon* is actually the first sauropod, not a prosauropod as Raath claimed.

811. Cruickshank, A.R.I. 1979. The ankle joint in some early archosaurs. *South African Journal of Science* 75:168–178.

    Describes two major evolutionary trends evident within the archosaur ankle, based on a study of six Triassic archosaurs. The "crocodile-normal" joint is typical of prosauropods, coelurosaurs and ornithischians. The "crocodile-reversed" ankle joint is found in carnosaurs and sauropods.

812. Cruickshank, A.R.I., and M.J. Benton. 1985. Archosaur ankles and the relationships of the thecodontian and dinosaurian reptiles. *Nature* 317:715–717.

    All forms with the AM advanced-mesotarsal ankle (i.e. all dinosaurs) are probably related. Supports the hypothesis that dinosaurs are a monophyletic group. (*See* Charig 1976 [833] for additional cross references on dinosaur monophyly.)

813. Ewer, R.F. 1965. The anatomy of the thecodont reptile *Euparkeria capensis* Broom. *Philosophical Transactions of the Royal Society B* 248:379–435.

    Provides a detailed description of the thecodont *Euparkeria capensis*, first described by R. Broom in 1913. This carnivorous facultative biped could be directly ancestral to prosauropods and sauropods, but not to ornithischians or birds.

814. Galton, P.M. 1989. Prosauropoda: the basal Sauropodomorpha. In *The Age of Dinosaurs*, ed. K. Padian and D.J. Chure, 80–84. *Geological Society of America Short Courses in Paleontology* no. 2. Knoxville: The Paleontological Society.

Prosauropods represent the first radiation of herbivorous dinosaurs. Briefly discusses their origin and systematics.

815. Novas, F.E. 1989. The tibia and tarsus in Herrerasauridae (Dinosauria, Incertae sedis) and the origin and evolution of the dinosaurian tarsus. *Journal of Paleontology* 63:677–690.

The family Herrerasauridae contains the oldest known dinosaurs. The primitive tibia and tarsus are reminiscent of the lagosuchid thecodonts. This tibiotarsal anatomy is good evidence of dinosaur monophyly, with the lagosuchid thecodonts as a sister group. (*See* Charig 1976 [833] for additional cross references on dinosaur monophyly.)

816. Padian, K. 1989. The origin of dinosaurs and the beginning of The Age of Dinosaurs. In *The Age of Dinosaurs*, ed. K. Padian and D.J. Chure, 7–21. *Geological Society of America Short Courses in Paleontology* no. 2. Knoxville: The Paleontological Society.

Reviews the basic characteristics and the classification of dinosaurs, their evolutionary origin and their phylogeny.

817. Paul, G.S. 1984a. The segnosaurian dinosaurs: relics of the prosauropod-ornithischian transition? *Journal of Vertebrate Paleontology* 4:507–515.

Segnosaurus and *Erlikosaurus*, previously described as Late Cretaceous theropods, are actually derived prosauropods. Many of their characteristics, such as beaked jaws with teeth, are early ornithischian traits. Presents a cladogram in which segnosaurs are shown as intermediate between the early prosauropods and later ornithischians. This supports the hypothesis that dinosaurs are a monophyletic group. (*See* Charig 1976 [833] for additional cross references on dinosaur monophyly.)

818. Rowe, T. 1989. The early history of theropods. In *The Age of Dinosaurs*, ed. K. Padian and D.J. Chure, 100–112. *Geological Society of America Short Courses in Paleontology* no. 2. Knoxville: The Paleontological Society.

Surveys the origins and anatomy of the Triassic and Jurassic theropods. Discusses the phylogeny of the two main lineages, the ceratosaurs and tetanurines (carnosaurs and coelurosaurs).

819. Thulborn, R.A. 1971. Origins and evolution of ornithischian dinosaurs. *Nature* 234:75–78.

Ornithischians are a monophyletic group descended from pseudosuchian thecodonts. Ornithischians dispersed well before the Upper Triassic. Iguanodontidae represents a grade, rather than a true clade, of advanced hypsilophodonts. Presents a revised scheme of ornithischian phylogeny.

820. Thulborn, R.A. 1977. Relationships of the Lower Jurassic dinosaur *Scelidosaurus harrisonii*. *Journal of Paleontology* 51:725–739.

The ancestry of stegosaurs and ankylosaurs is unknown. The Lower Jurassic *Scelidosaurus* has been described as a very primitive stegosaur or ankylosaur. *S. harrisonii* does not seem to be related to either group. The species is assigned to the family Scelidosauridae.

821. Thulborn, R.A. 1980. The ankle joints of archosaurs. *Alcheringa* 4:241–261.

Archosaur ankle joints are very important in our understanding of archosaur phylogeny. Reviews the ankle joints of proterosuchid thecodonts and other early archosaurs. Ankle morphology suggests that archosaurs, rhynchosaurs and parathecodontians all stem from a common ancestor, perhaps an eosuchian reptile. Thulborn recognizes two basic types of ankle joints, mesotarsal and crocodiloid; both types evolved independently from a "duplex" ankle joint in the earliest archosaurs. This duplex joint is similar to that of the primitive ornithischian *Pisanosaurus mertii*. While most dinosaurs are probably descended from pseudosuchian thecodonts, the question of dinosaur monophyly remains unresolved (*See* Charig 1976 [833] for additional cross references on dinosaur monophyly.)

822. Thulborn, R.A. 1982. Significance of ankle structures in archosaur phylogeny. *Nature* 299:657.

A letter to Nature in which Thulborn criticizes Chatterjee's (1982 [836]) analysis of archosaur ankle joints. Followed by a short rebuttal from Chatterjee.

823. Vanheerden, J. 1978. *Herrerasaurus* and the origin of the sauropod dinosaurs. *South African Journal of Science* 74:187–189.

Prosauropods are too specialized to have been ancestral to sauropods. The term "Prosauropoda" is a misnomer. Prosauropods should be classified under Palaeopoda, which includes the Staurikosauridae, Plateosauridae and Anchisauridae. (*See also* Colbert 1964 [808].) *Herrerasaurus* and *Ischisaurus* should be placed in the new family Herrerasauridae, while *Staurikosaurus* should be placed in the new family Staurikosauridae.

824. Welles, S.P. 1986. Thoughts on the origin of the Theropoda. In *The Beginning of The Age of Dinosaurs; Faunal Changes Across the Triassic-Jurassic Boundary*, ed. K. Padian, 31–34. Cambridge: Cambridge University Press.

The most likely ancestral stock for the theropods is the Proterosuchia. The Pseudosuchia, considered by many to be the source of the theropods, have a highly developed crocodiloid tarsus. This tarsus is too specialized a structure for pseudosuchians to have given rise to the bipedal theropods.

TAXONOMY AND PHYLOGENY

825. Bakker, R.T., and P.M. Galton. 1974. Dinosaur monophyly and a new class of vertebrates. *Nature* 248:168–172.

Proposes a new Class Dinosauria including birds and dinosaurs, based primarily on the possession of endothermy. Archosauria would be restricted to crocodiles, thecodonts, and pterosaurs. Dinosaurs are monophyletic. (*See* Thulborn 1975

[916] for a critique. *See also* Charig 1976 [833] for additional cross references on dinosaur monophyly.)

826. Benton, M.J. 1985. Classification and phylogeny of the diapsid reptiles. *Zoological Journal of the Linnean Society* 84:97–164.

   Diapsida, comprised of the taxa Lepidosauria and Archosauria, is a monophyletic taxon. Presents a new cladistic classification for the Diapsida which differs in several respects from the traditional scheme. (*See* Tarsitano and Hecht 1984 [870] for an opposing opinion. *See also* Evans 1988 [845].)

827. Benton, M.J, and J.L. Clark. 1988. Archosaur phylogeny and the relationships of the Crocodylia. In *The Phylogeny and Classification of the Tetrapods* Vol.1, ed. M.J. Benton, 295–338. *Systematics Association Special Volume* 35A, Oxford: Clarendon Press.

   Archosaurs form a monophyletic group, comprising living birds and crocodiles, and about one-hundred genera of dinosaurs, pterosaurs, and thecodonts. (*See also* Charig 1976 [833] for additional cross references on dinosaur monophyly.) Reviews early archosaurs and crocodylomorphs in detail, and proposes cladograms for their relationships.

828. Bonaparte, J.F. 1986. The early radiation and phylogenetic relationships of the Jurassic sauropod dinosaurs, based on vertebral anatomy. In *The Beginning of The Age of Dinosaurs; Faunal Changes Across the Triassic-Jurassic Boundary*, ed. K. Padian, 247–258. Cambridge: Cambridge University Press.

   The enormous size of Late Triassic sauropods required extensive skeletal modification. Sauropods evolved from advanced Prosauropoda; *Vulcanodon* represents the first stage of this evolution. Reviews the families of sauropods and their phylogeny.

829. Brett-Surman, M.K. 1979. Phylogeny and palaeobiogeography of hadrosaurian dinosaurs. *Nature* 277:560–562.

   Large vertebrates like hadrosaurs and ceratopsians were probably not spread from continent to continent by waif dispersal or rafting. Their presence in South America indicates the presence of a substantial land bridge at some time in the past. Hadrosaur biogeography should be considered in any reconstruction of Cretaceous geography. Presents a new hadrosaur phylogeny which incorporates specimens outside of North America for the first time.

830. Carpenter, K. 1990. Ankylosaur systematics: example using *Panoplosaurus* and Edmontonia (Ankylosauria: Nodosauridae). In *Dinosaur Systematics: Approaches and Perspectives*, ed. K. Carpenter and P.J. Currie, 281–298. Cambridge: Cambridge University Press.

Discusses the systematics of the Nodosauridae using the genera *Panoplosaurus* and *Edmontonia* as examples. Much of the skeleton is useful in Ankylosaur systematics.

831. Chapman, R.E. 1990. Shape analysis in the study of dinosaur morphology. In *Dinosaur Systematics: Approaches and Perspectives*, ed. K. Carpenter and P.J. Currie, 21–42. Cambridge: Cambridge University Press.

Adapts the morphometric technique of Resistant-Fit Theta-Rho-Analysis for use in dinosaur taxonomy, and explains its use with a series of cranial examples. The technique starts with the digitizing of landmark coordinates and outlines of anatomical structures. Computer analysis of this data yields a geometric polygonal framework, which can then be used in comparative phenetic analysis.

832. Chapman, R.E., and M.K. Brett-Surman. 1990. Morphometric observations on hadrosaurid ornithopods. In *Dinosaur Systematics: Approaches and Perspectives*, ed. K. Carpenter and P.J. Currie, 163–177. Cambridge: Cambridge University Press.

Applies Resistant-Fit Theta-Rho-Analysis to hadrosaurs. The results support hadrosaur monophyly, and suggest that the muzzle and narial region and the shape of pelvic elements are the most taxonomically useful characters.

833. Charig, A.J. 1976. "Dinosaur monophyly and a new class of vertebrates": a critical review. In *Morphology and Biology of Reptiles*, ed. A. Bellairs and C.B. Cox, 65–104. *Linnean Society Symposium Series* no. 3. London: Academic Press.

   A detailed critique of Bakker and Galton's (1974 [825]) controversial proposal for a new Class Dinosauria. (*See also* de Ricqlès 1974 [545]; Thulborn 1975 [916].) Charig maintains that there is no definite proof that dinosaurs are monophyletic, or that dinosaurs were endothermic, or that dinosaurs gave rise to birds. The elevation of dinosaurs to a Class Dinosauria is "totally unwarranted." (*See also* Bonaparte 1976 [806]; Cruickshank and Benton 1985 [812]; Novas 1989 [815]; Paul 1984a [817]; Thulborn 1980 [821]; Bakker and Galton 1974 [825]; Benton and Clark 1988 [827]; Charig 1976 [833]; Evans 1988 [845]; Paul 1984b [860]; and Sereno 1986 [865] for further discussion of dinosaur monophyly.)

834. Charig, A.J., J. Attridge, and A.W. Crompton. 1965. On the origin of the sauropods and the classification of the Saurischia. *Proceedings of the Linnean Society* 176, Pt. 2:197–221.

   Presents a traditional view of saurischian phylogeny, with a detailed review of sauropod phylogeny. Saurischia is divided into Theropoda and Sauropodomorpha, the latter comprising the Prosauropoda and Triassic carnosaurs. Within the suborder Sauropodomorpha are the infra-orders Prosauropoda and Sauropoda; within the suborder Theropoda are the infra-orders Coelurosauria and Carnosauria.

835. Charig, A.J., and A.C. Milner. 1990. The systematic position of *Baryonyx walkeri*, in the light of Gauthier's reclassification of the Theropoda. In *Dinosaur Systematics: Approaches and Perspectives*, ed. K. Carpenter and P.J. Currie, 127–140. Cambridge: Cambridge University Press.

   A new family Baryonychidae is proposed for *Baryonyx walkeri*, which amends Gauthier's classification of the theropods (Gauthier 1986 [907]). Gauthier's scheme is criticized, though acknowledged as the best present outline of theropod classification.

836. Chatterjee, S. 1982. Phylogeny and classification of thecodontian reptiles. *Nature* 295:317-320.

The skull and skeletal morphology of thecodonts is very uniform, but the ankle joints are surprisingly variable. They are thus a useful character for thecodont classification. The ankle joint evolved from a simple hinge, for sprawling gaits, to a complex lever, for semi-improved and fully-improved gaits. Distinguishes four basic types of ankle joints: primitive metotarsal (PM), crocodile-normal (CN), crocodile reverse (CR), and advanced metotarsal (AM).

837. Coombs, W.P. 1978. The families of the ornithischian dinosaur order Ankylosauria. *Palaeontology* 21:143-170.

The two principal families of the Cretaceous suborder Ankylosauria, the Ankylosauridae and the Nodosauridae, differ from one another in several characters. We find very conservative evolutionary patterns, however, within each family. *Scelidosaurus* has been proposed as a possible ancestor of the Ankylosauria. The true ancestry of ankylosaurs, and their connection to other Ornithischia, remains a mystery.

838. Coombs, W.P. jr. 1988. The status of the dinosaurian genus *Diclonius* and the taxonomic utility of hadrosaurian teeth. *Journal of Paleontology* 62:812-817.

Hadrosaur teeth are highly variable, even within a single dental battery, and are therefore taxonomically useless. Reviews *Diclonius* and other hadrosaurs identified solely on the basis of their teeth. Rejects the genus *Diclonius* as well as *Trachodon mirabilis*.

839. Cracraft, J., and N. Eldredge, eds. 1979. *Phylogenetic Analysis and Paleontology*. New York: Columbia University Press.

Seven articles from the proceedings of a symposium discuss the reconstruction of phylogeny for fossil animals. Five papers debate the philosophy and methodology of such analysis, followed by two commentaries.

840. Currie, P.J. 1989. Theropod dinosaurs of the Cretaceous. In *The Age of Dinosaurs*, ed. K. Padian and D.J. Chure, 113-120.

Geological Society of America Short Courses in Paleontology no. 2. Knoxville: The Paleontological Society.

Focuses on the later development of theropods in the Northern Hemisphere, including their basic biology and systematics.

841. Currie, P.J., and K. Carpenter, eds. 1990. *Dinosaur Systematics: Approaches and Perspectives*. New York: Cambridge University Press.

An impressive collection of essays spanning the rapidly advancing field of dinosaur systematics. The wealth of new finds and the advent of cladistic analysis has revolutionized the field. Several of the articles in this collection are analyzed in this chapter.

842. Currie, P.J., J.K. Rigby jr., and R.E. Sloan. 1990. Theropod teeth from the Judith River Formation of southern Alberta. In *Dinosaur Systematics: Approaches and Perspectives*, ed. K. Carpenter and P.J. Currie, 107–125. Cambridge: Cambridge University Press.

Theropod teeth from the Judith River Formation are diagnostic, and in some cases can be identified to the level of species. There is little developmental variation. Theropod teeth can help determine stratigraphic ages and the nature of paleoenvironments.

843. Dodson, P. 1975. Taxonomic implications of relative growth in lambeosaurine hadrosaurs. *Systematic Zoology* 24:37–54.

Allometric analysis reveals that some taxa of lambeosine hadrosaurs are actually juvenile forms of other taxa. Alberta's Oldman Formation has yielded three genera and twelve closely related species. Biometric analysis shows that only five or six of forty-eight proposed cranial characters are taxonomically useful. Several taxa must be abandoned. *Corythosaurus* and *Lambeosaurus* are valid genera, and *L. lambei*, *L. clavinitialis*, and *C. casuarius* are valid species. Perhaps the supposed rarity of juvenile dinosaurs is merely an artifact of their misclassification as other species.

844. Dodson, P. 1990. On the status of the ceratopsids *Monoclonius* and *Centrosaurus*. In *Dinosaur Systematics: Approaches and Perspectives*, ed. K. Carpenter and P.J. Currie, 231–254. Cambridge: Cambridge University Press.

Biometric analysis demonstrates that *Monoclonius* and *Centrosaurus* are distinct genera. *Styracosaurus* is more closely related to the latter. *Brachyceratops*, once thought to be a juvenile form of *Monoclonius*, is a valid genus. Presents a cladogram of the centrosaurine ceratopsians.

845. Evans, S.E. 1988. The early history and relationships of the Diapsida. In T*he Phylogeny and Classification of the Tetrapods; Volume 1, Amphibians, Reptiles, Birds*, ed. M.J. Benton, 221–260. *Systematics Association Special Volume* 35A, Oxford: Clarendon Press.

Presents a new cladistic analysis of the Diapsida, based on fifty-six genera and almost two hundred osteological characters. Diapsiad is a monophyletic taxon, consisting of the primitive Araeoscelidia and the more advanced Neodiapsida. The latter is divided into the monophyletic taxa Archosauromorpha and Lepidosauromorpha. (*See* Benton 1985a [826]; Tarsitano and Hecht 1984 [870] for additional cross references on diapsid monophyly. *See also* Charig 1976 [833] for additional cross references on dinosaur monophyly.)

846. Galton, P.M. 1972. Classification and evolution of ornithopod dinosaurs. *Nature* 239:464–466.

Premaxillary teeth are not a useful taxonomic character for hypsilophodonts; such teeth are widespread among dinosaurs. Proposes a revised classification of the cursorial ornithopods, including the new family Fabrosauridae. Iguanodontidae is really a grade, consisting of all graviportal ornithopods without the cranial specializations of hadrosaurs or pachycephalosaurs. (*See* Dodson 1980 [299] for an alternate hypothesis on Iguanodontidae.)

847. Gardiner, B.G. 1982. Tetrapod classification. *Zoological Journal of the Linnean Society* 74:207–232.

Proposes a new supercohort Haemothermia, along with other radical systematic hypotheses. Anapsids, diapsids and synapsids are all paraphyletic groups. Haemothermia includes the two cohorts Aves and Mammalia. Birds are a sister taxon to mammals, and crocodiles are a sister taxon to these two. Dinosaurs are placed in the supercohort Archosauria, along with the Crocodilia. (*See* Kemp 1988 [849] and Benton 1984c [919] for a critique.)

848. Horner, J.R. 1990. Evidence of diphyletic origination of the hadrosaurian (Reptilia: Ornithischia) dinosaurs. In *Dinosaur Systematics: Approaches and Perspectives*, ed. K. Carpenter and P.J. Currie, 179–187. Cambridge: Cambridge University Press.

    A cladistic analysis of hadrosaurs suggests that the group is diphyletic. Hadrosaurs form two families, the Hadrosauridae, forming a sister taxon with *Iguanodon*, and Lambeosauridae, forming a sister taxon with *Ouranosaurus*.

849. Kemp, T.S. 1988. Haemothermia or Archosauria? The interrelationships of mammals, birds and crocodiles. *Zoological Journal of the Linnean Society* 92:67–104.

    Gardiner (1982 [847]) introduced the term Haemothermia to unite birds and mammals as endothermic sister groups. Only eight of his twenty-eight defining characters are valid. Twenty-four characters, however, unite birds and crocodiles in the conventional (and preferable) taxon Archosauria. Discusses philosophical and empirical problems in cladistic analysis.

850. Kolata, G.B. 1975. Paleobiology: random events over geological time. *Science* 189:625–626+.

    A statistical model of the outcome of random events in evolution might help distinguish deterministic patterns from those generated randomly. Cladistic models incorporating random events can produce computer generated patterns strikingly similar to known phylogenetic relationships of extinct taxa.

851. Lehman, T.M. 1990. The ceratopsian subfamily Chasmosaurinae: sexual dimorphism and systematics. In *Dinosaur Systematics: Approaches and Perspectives*, ed. K. Carpenter and P.J. Currie, 211–229. Cambridge: Cambridge University Press.

Advocates returning to the subfamily names Chasmosaurinae and Centrosaurinae for the long-frilled and short-filled ceratopsians respectively. Proposes a revision of species in the Chasmosaurinae. Discusses sexual dimorphism in ceratopsians.

852. McIntosh, J.S. 1989. The sauropod dinosaurs: a brief survey. In *The Age of Dinosaurs*, ed. K. Padian and D.J. Chure, 85–99. *Geological Society of America Short Courses in Paleontology* no. 2. Knoxville: The Paleontological Society.

Reviews the anatomy, systematics, and evolution of the sauropods.

853. McIntosh, J.S. 1990. Species determination in sauropod dinosaurs with tentative suggestions for their classification. In *Dinosaur Systematics: Approaches and Perspectives*, ed. K. Carpenter and P.J. Currie, 53–69. Cambridge: Cambridge University Press.

Vertebral characters are particularly important in the classification of sauropods. There are six valid sauropod families: Vulcanodontidae, Cetiosauridae, Brachiosauridae, Camarasauridae, Diplodocidae, and Titanosauridae. Sauropod classification is difficult. Skulls are rare, and usually not found with post-cranial material.

854. Molnar, R.E. 1990. Variation in theory and in theropods. In *Dinosaur Systematics: Approaches and Perspectives*, ed. K. Carpenter and P.J. Currie, 71–79. Cambridge: Cambridge University Press.

Dinosaur taxonomists usually cannot apply biological criteria to their specimens, and are forced to rely heavily on gross morphological differences. Small sample sizes often make it difficult to categorize variation within and between species. Variation could be due to sexual dimporphism, individual variation, or developmental changes.

855. Norman, D.B. 1984. A systematic reappraisal of the reptile order ornithischia. In *Third Symposium on Mesozoic Terrestrial Ecosystems, Short Papers*, ed. W. Reif and F. Westphal, 157–162. Tübingen: ATTEMPTO-Verlag.

    Ornithischians are a monophyletic group. The suborder Thyreophora is revived, to include Stegosauridae and Ankylosauridae. Scelidosauridae is a sister group to these two taxa. A cladogram of the ornithischians is presented with these and other controversial revisions.

856. Norman, D.B. 1989. Ornithopod dinosaurs: relationships, structure, and habits. In *The Age of Dinosaurs*, ed. K. Padian and D.J. Chure, 58–70. *Geological Society of America Short Courses in Paleontology* no. 2. Knoxville: The Paleontological Society.

    Studies the relationship between the three main ornithopod lines: the heterodontosaurs, the hypsilophodonts, and the iguanodonts. Discusses their locomotion, feeding, and social behavior.

857. Norman, D.B. 1990. A review of *Vectisaurus valdensis*, with comments on the family Iguanodontidae. In *Dinosaur Systematics: Approaches and Perspectives*, ed. K. Carpenter and P.J. Currie, 147–161. Cambridge: Cambridge University Press.

    Vectisaurus valdensis is actually a juvenile *Iguanodon*. The Iguanodontidae is still a valid taxon, though more restrictive than formerly. Offers a revised cladogram of the advanced ornithopods, based on Sereno's proposed cladogram (Sereno 1984 [864]).

858. Olshevsky, G. 1978. *The Archosaurian Taxa (Excluding Crocodylia)*. Toronto: G&T Enterprises.

    Published as an occasional serial called *Mesozoic Meanderings*, this work includes a list of all taxa known in 1978, with the author and date of each classification.

859. Ostrom, J.H., and P. Wellnhofer. 1990. *Triceratops*: an example of flawed systematics. In *Dinosaur Systematics: Approaches and Perspectives*, ed. K. Carpenter and P.J. Currie, 245–254. Cambridge: Cambridge University Press.

Although sixteen species of *Triceratops* have been named, the genus was not formally described until recently. Many species are systematically unacceptable. The history of *Triceratops* discoveries is an example of the pitfalls of sloppy systematics. Horns, for example, show much developmental and sexual variation because they are involved in sexual selection. Therefore they are not useful taxonomic traits.

860. Paul, G.S. 1984b. The archosaurs: a phylogenetic study. In *Third Symposium on Mesozoic Terrestrial Ecosystems, Short Papers*, ed. W.E. Reif and F. Westphal, 175–180. Tübingen: ATTEMPTO-Verlag.

Disagrees with those who base phylogenetic trees primarily on ankle joint morphology. (*See* Cruickshank and Benton 1985 [812].) Presents a cladogram of the archosaurs, and discusses several problems in archosaurian phylogeny. Dinosaurs are a monophyletic group that includes lagosuchids, staurikosaurs, herrerasaurs, theropods, birds, prosauropods, sauropods, and ornithischians. (*See also* Charig 1976 [833] for additional cross references on monophyly.)

861. Raath, M.A. 1990. Morphological variation in small theropods and its meaning in systematics: evidence from *Syntarsus rhodesiensis*. In *Dinosaur Systematics: Approaches and Perspectives*, ed. K. Carpenter and P.J. Currie, 91–105. Cambridge: Cambridge University Press.

Small theropods are fragile; they are often poorly preserved. A synthesis of small theropod taxonomy would be "a vain and forlorn task." *Syntarsus rhodesiensis* is one of the best preserved theropods. Raath reviews its osteology, examining traits which might be useful in theropod classification. *Syntarsus* shows sexual dimorphism, and indications of social behavior.

862. Ridley, M. 1986. *Evolution and Classification: the Reformation of Cladism.* New York: Longman.

The advent of cladism in dinosaur biology has prompted a comprehensive reevaluation of traditional classification schemes. This text is a useful review of the development, philosophy, and methodology of cladistic analysis. Includes an extensive bibliography and glossary.

863. Russell, D.A. 1984. A check list of the families and genera of North American dinosaurs. *Syllogeus* 53:1–35.

Catalogs one hundred twenty one known North American genera, representing thirty four dinosaur families. Entries include family, geologic age, genus, geologic horizon, and literature reference.

864. Sereno, P.C. 1984. The phylogeny of the Ornithischia; a reappraisal. In *Third Symposium on Mesozoic Terrestrial Ecosystems, Short Papers*, ed. W. Reif and F. Westphal, 219–226. Tübingen: ATTEMPTO-Verlag.

A preliminary revision of the Ornithischia. The short note is accompanied by a proposed cladogram and a lengthy list of the synapomorphies used to construct it. (*See also* Sereno 1986 [865]; Norman 1990 [857].)

865. Sereno, P.C. 1986. Phylogeny of the bird-hipped dinosaurs (Order Ornithischia). *National Geographic Research* 2:234–256.

New finds from Mongolia and China permit a revised cladistic analysis of the Ornithischia, a monophyletic group. The primitive *Lesothosaurus* is separated as a sister taxon to the remaining ornithischians. The new taxon Euornithopoda contains the heterodontosaurs, hypsilophodonts, iguanodonts and hadrosaurs. Thyreophora is restricted to the monophyletic taxon comprising stegosaurs, *Scelidosaurus*, *Scutellosaurus*, and ankylosaurs. Ornithopods, heterodontosaurs, pachycephalosaurs, and ceratopsians also form a monophyletic group, which includes most ornithischian taxa. (*See also* Charig 1976 [833] for additional cross references.)

866. Sereno, P.C. 1989. Evolution of the bird-hipped dinosaurs (Ornithischia). In *The Age of Dinosaurs*, ed. K. Padian and D.J. Chure. *Geological Society of America Short Courses in Paleontology* no. 2. Knoxville: The Paleontological Society.

Reviews the ornithischian dinosaurs. *Lesothosaurus* is a model primitive ornithischian. Discusses the classification of the Thyreophora (armored dinosaurs), the dinosaurian "ungulates" (ornithopods), and the Marginocephalia (ceratopsians and pachycephalosaurs).

867. Sereno, P.C. 1990. Clades and grades in dinosaur systematics. In *Dinosaur Systematics: Approaches and Perspectives*, ed. K. Carpenter and P.J. Currie, 9–20. Cambridge: Cambridge University Press.

A good introduction to the theory and technique of cladistic analysis, using dinosaur cladograms as examples.

868. Sereno, P.C. 1991. *Lesothosaurus*, "Fabrosaurids", and the early evolution of Ornithischia. *Journal of Vertebrate Paleontology* 11:168–197.

An examination of new material of the basal ornithischian *Lesothosaurus diagnosticus* leads to a reevaluation of primitive ornithischians. *Fabrosaurus australis* is a nomen dubium, invalidating the family Fabrosauridae. "Fabrosaurid" is merely a grade of primitive ornithischians which lack the shared derived traits of other clades. Other dubious taxa include *Revueltosaurus callendri*, *Xiaosaurus dashanpensis*, and *Nanosaurus agilis*. *Tawasaurus*, *Fulengia*, and parts of the holotype of *Technosaurus* are actually juvenile prosauropods. *Pisanosaurus mertii* is probably the most primitive ornithischians.

869. Sues, H.D. 1977. Dentaries of small theropods from the Judith River Formation (Campanian) of Alberta, Canada. *Canadian Journal of Earth Sciences* 14:587–592.

The small theropods of the Judith River Formation pose a difficult problem for taxonomists. Describes three dentaries of small theropods. The specimens support the hypothesis of two distinct families of small theropods, Saurornithidae and Dromaeosauridae.

870. Tarsitano, S.F., and M.K. Hecht. 1984. Ancestor worship and the lepidosaur-archosaur dichotomy. In *Third Symposium on Mesozoic Terrestrial Ecosystems, Short Papers*, ed. W.E. Reif and F. Westphal, 237–242. Tübingen: ATTEMPTO-Verlag.

Argues that the relationship between the archosaurs and the lepidosaurs represents an "ancient dichotomy", with the two groups diverging very early. The authors argue against a monophyletic classification of diapsid reptiles. The archosaurs and lepidosaurs probably diverged at an early amniote stage before the fenestration of the skull. (*See also* Benton 1985 [826]; Evans 1988 [845].)

871. White, T.E. 1973. Catalogue of the genera of dinosaurs. *Annals of the Carnegie Museum* 44:117–155.

An alphabetical list of the genera known as of 1973, with location, type specimens, author, locality and year for each entry.

872. Xijn, Z. 1983. Phylogeny and evolutionary stages of Dinosauria. In *Second International Symposium on Mesozoic Terrestrial Ecosystems*, ed. Z. Kielan-Jaworska and H. Osmólska, 295–306, *Acta Palaeontologica Polonica* 28 (1/2).

Proposes a major taxonomic revision of the Dinosauria, based on several new specimens from China. Xijn retains the basic division into Ornithischia and Saurischia, but introduces a new suborder Armatosauria, with superfamilies Scelidosauroidea, Stegosauroidea, Oligosauroidea, and Polysacralosauroidea, and five new superfamilies in the Pachycephalosauroidea: Tianchungosauroidea, Chaoyoungosauroidea, Ceratopsoidea, and Pachycephalosauroidea. The author also discusses general patterns in dinosaur evolution, and delineates four broad stages in this process.

873. Zhiming, D. 1990. Stegosaurs of Asia. In *Dinosaur Systematics: Approaches and Perspectives*, ed. K. Carpenter

and P.J. Currie, 255–268. Cambridge: Cambridge University Press.

Stegosaurs probably arose in eastern Asia. Eight new Asian genera have been discovered in the past twenty years. Discusses the origin of stegosaurs in light of the Asian material, and presents a revised classification of the Stegosaurinae.

Archaeopteryx lithographica pursues its prey. From *Archosauria: A New Look at the Old Dinosaur* by John C. McLoughlin. Copyright © 1979 by John C. McLoughlin. Used by permission of Viking Penguin, a division of Penguin Books USA Inc.

Chapter Eight

Dinosaurs and Birds

The discovery of *Archaeopteryx* sent shock waves through the Victorian scientific community. With Darwin's theory of evolution being universally debated, a well preserved specimen showing clear affinities for both reptiles and birds was a critically important missing link.

Were it not for the distinct imprint of feathers in the finely-grained limestone slab, *Archaeopteryx* would have been classified as a small carnivorous dinosaur. In fact, one such misclassified specimen languished for years until J.H. Ostrom recognized it in a Dutch museum (Ostrom 1970 [886]).

The phylogeny of *Archaeopteryx* is still a matter for considerable debate. The prevailing view is that it represents an evolutionary branch removed from the main line of descent of modern birds (Kessler 1984 [883]; Martin 1985 [884]; Thulborn 1984 [893]; Chatterjee 1991 [901]; Gauthier and Padian 1989 [936]). Some scientists leave open the question of direct descent, or argue that *Archaeopteryx* is in fact ancestral to the Class Aves (Buehler 1986 [874]; Walker 1984 [897]).

Others question the systematic suitability of the Class Aves, proposing a Class Dinosauria to contain both birds and dinosaurs (Bakker and Galton 1974 [825]) or placing birds within the Theropoda, as the only surviving representative of that lineage (Gauthier 1986 [907]; Gauthier and Padian 1985 [936]; Gauthier and Padian 1989 [961]).

Is Aves a monophyletic taxon? At the heart of this argument is the debate over the ultimate evolutionary origin of birds. Did they evolve from thecodonts, crocodiles, or theropod dinosaurs? Even mammals have been proposed as candidates for the proto-bird (Benton 1984c [919]; Gardner 1982 [847]).

T.H. Huxley recognized the dinosaurian affinities of *Archaeopteryx*, comparing it with fossil dinosaurs and with living ratite birds (DiGregorio 1982 [89]; Bibby 1972 [85]; Huxley 1870 [91]).

Heilmann's classic *Origin of the Birds* (Heilmann 1926 [939]) turned the debate in a new direction, making a case for the origin of birds from thecodont reptiles. This hypothesis still receives some support (Hecht and Tarsitano 1982 [881]; Hecht and Tarsitano 1983 [882]; Tarsitano and Hecht 1980 [892]; Brodkorb 1971 [921]; Whetstone and Martin [955]).

Others have proposed a third alternative, claiming that birds are descended from crocodiles (Walker 1972 [952]; 1977 [917]; 1980 [896]; 1984 [897]; McGowan and Baker 1981 [943]; Martin 1983 [944]; Martin 1984 [963]; Martin et al. 1980 [945]; Whetstone and Martin 1979 [955]; Whetstone and Martin 1981 [956]).

The cursorial theropod hypothesis is the best hypothesis that explains the mounting evidence on avian origins (Molnar 1985 [885]; Thulborn 1984 [893]; Currie 1985 [902]; Galton 1970 [906]; Osmólska 1981 [913]; Thulborn 1975 [916]; Gingerich 1973 [938]; Caple et al. 1983 [959]; Thulborn 1987 [975]). Ostrom proposed, in a long series of papers, that birds evolved from a small bipedal theropod dinosaur, probably a coelurosaur (Ostrom 1973 [948]; 1974 [966]; 1975 [949]; 1976b [967]; 1979 [968]; 1985 [888]; 1986 [969]). It was an agile ground predator, and its feathered wings aided in catching insect prey. Gauthier (1986 [907]) provides convincing cladistic evidence to support Ostrom. An interesting extension of this hypothesis is the possibility that *Archaeopteryx* foraged for fish by spreading its feathered wings in a canopy, as do modern birds like the herons (Thulborn and Hamley 1985 [895]).

The idea that birds are descendants of bipedal dinosaurs has a romantic flair that appeals to our sense of evolutionary justice. The "Age of Dinosaurs" is still ongoing. As Gauthier and Padian (1989 [961]) tell us:

> This realization is an especially effective one to bring to students, who delight in knowing that they eat dinosaur at thanksgiving, have dinosaur baths in their backyards, and occasionally go out for dinosaur McNuggets. (p.125)

The most recent chapter in this long-running controversy is Sankar Chatterjee's discovery of *Protoavis*, an ancient bird that considerably predates *Archaeopteryx* (Anderson 1991 [899]; Beardsley 1986 [900]; Chatterjee 1991 [901]). Its age and avian characteristics cast considerable doubt on the formerly unassailable hypothesis of direct descent of birds from theropod dinosaurs. The Late Triassic *Protoavis* occurs so close to the presumed origin of the dinosaurs that Chatterjee suggests both lineages may descend from an even more distant common ancestor.

Feduccia dismisses Chatterjee's analysis as "reading tea leaves in the bottom of a dark cup," and Cracraft protests that Chatterjee ignores hard cladistic evidence in his conclusions (Anderson 1991 [899]). Whatever the outcome, the discovery of *Protoavis* has fanned the flames of inquiry and debate over avian origins.

Chatterjee's claims that *Protoavis* was capable of true flapping flight has also spurred the long-standing debate between proponents of the cursorial and arboreal origins of flight. His forthcoming monograph on the flight capabilities of *Protavis* will no doubt ruffle a few scientific feathers.

Could *Protoavis* or *Archaeopteryx* fly? And if so, did they scramble into the treetops and glide off into space, like a modern hoatzin, or did they rise flapping from the ground in full powered flight? The question of the arboreal or cursorial origin of flight has been a fruitful spur to research. Both the arboreal theory and the cursorial theory have several supporters. (For the arboreal theory, *See* Martin 1983 [944]; Bock 1985 [957]; Bock 1986 [958]; Tarsitano 1985 [974]. For the cursorial theory, *See* Kurzanov 1982 [909]; Kurzanov 1985 [911]; Gauthier and Padian 1985 [936]; Ostrom 1974 [966]; Ostrom 1976b [967]; Ostrom 1979 [968]; Ostrom 1986 [969]; Padian 1985 [970].) The debate has prompted a reexamination of the aerodynamics of a variety of modern and extinct birds, reptiles, and mammals (Caple et al 1983 [959]; Padian 1985 [970]; Rayner 1988 [971]).

The aerodynamic nature of the feather has also been questioned. It is generally believed that the asymmetry of feathers indicates an aerodynamic function, but this hypothesis has recently been challenged. Did feathers evolve specifically for flight, or did they initially serve some other purpose, such as thermoregulatory insulation (Feduccia 1974 [879]; Thulborn 1984 [893]; Feduccia 1985 [904]; Martin 1984 [963]; Ostrom 1974 [966]; Regal 1975 [972]; Tarsitano 1985 [974]; Thulborn 1987 [975])? One researcher has proposed that feathers originated as downy plumage on juvenile theropod dinosaurs, which subsequently gave rise to birds by progenesis (Thulborn 1987 [975]).

The recent flap over *Archaeopteryx* feather imprints is a good example of the tangled web of historical conspiracy theories in science. The astronomer Fred Hoyle created a minor scandal by claiming that

Owen deliberately purchased his *Archaeopteryx* specimen knowing that its feather imprints had been forged. This curious claim has been soundly scuttled (Charig et al. 1986 [876]; Dickson 1987 [878]; Gould 1987 [880]; Rietschel 1985 [890]; Wellnhofer 1988 [898]).

Although *Archaeopteryx* may not be a direct ancestor of modern birds, it is still one of the earliest birds we know, and continues to deserve our attention. Mid-Jurassic sediments are rare; we face a large gap between *Archaeopteryx* and the scattered specimens from the Cretaceous. The recent International *Archaeopteryx* Conference in Eichstätt is a good source of research on every aspect of *Archaeopteryx*; several papers from the conference proceedings are analyzed in this chapter.

If birds are directly descended from dinosaurs, then in reality the dinosaurs have never left us. Whenever we see a heron foraging in a still pool, or hear the beak of a swallow snap shut on an insect, we are witnessing the survival of the evolutionary architecture of the dinosaurs.

ARCHAEOPTERYX

874. Buehler, P. 1986. *Archaeopteryx*: a discussion of present research on the Jurassic birds. *Journal of Ornithology* 127:487–508.

    Reviews the results of the International *Archaeopteryx* Conference held in Eichstätt in 1984. (*See also* Ruben 1991 [891].) *Archaeopteryx* evolved from a primitive theropod dinosaur, and was in the direct line of ancestry of modern birds. It had true powered flight and probably launched from and landed on tree trunks. Avian flight probably evolved from gliding between trees.

875. Charig, A. 1985. Analyses of several problems associated with *Archaeopteryx*. In *The Beginning of Birds, Proceedings of the International Archaeopteryx Conference*, Eichstätt, 1984, ed. M.K. Hecht, J.H. Ostrom, G. Viohl, P. Wellnhofer, 21–30. Willibaldsburg: Jura-Museums Eichstätt.

    Groups and summarizes the many problems facing *Archaeopteryx* scholars. These include problems relating to the specimens, interpretation of structure, phylogeny and paleoecology.

876. Charig, A.J., F. Greenaway, A.C. Milner, C.A. Walker, and P.J. Whybrow. 1986. *Archaeopteryx* is not a forgery. *Science* 232:622–626.

    Careful matching of hairline cracks and dendrites in the slab and counterslab of the holotype specimen leads Charig to conclude that there is no additional cement layer that might have been added by someone forging feather imprints. The feathers are genuine. (*See also* Gould 1987 [880]; Rietschel 1985 [890]; Dickson 1987 [878]; Owen 1863 [889]; Wellnhofer 1988 [898].)

877. Cracraft, J. 1977. John Ostrom's studies on *Archaeopteryx*, the origin of birds, and the evolution of avian flight. *Wilson Bulletin* 89:488–492.

A literature review of Ostrom's work on *Archaeopteryx* (Ostrom 1970 [886]; 1973 [948]; 1974 [966]; 1975 [949]; 1976a [887]; 1976b [967]). Although critical of some of Ostrom's conclusions, Cracraft finds "most of his arguments persuasive." Praises Ostrom's meticulous work, and his emphasis on homologies and shared derived characters in phylogenetic reconstruction. (*See also* Ostrom 1979 [968]; Ostrom 1986 [969]; Caple et al. 1983 [959]. *See* Ostrom 1985 [888] for cross references to Ostrom's critics.)

878. Dickson, D. 1987. Feathers still fly in row over fossil bird. *Science* 238:475–476.

    A news account of claims and counterclaims made in the *Archaeopteryx* forgery dispute. The British Museum responds to Sir Fred Hoyle and N.C. Wickramasinghe's press conference, which was held to refute the Museum's evidence that the specimens are genuine. (*See* Charig et al. 1986 [876] for additional cross references concerning the *Archaeopteryx* forgery claim.)

879. Feduccia, A. 1974. Endothermy, dinosaurs, and *Archaeopteryx. Evolution* 28:503–504.

    Refutes Ostrom's claim that *Archaeopteryx* feathers served as endothermic insulation, and declares the entire issue of whether feathers functioned for flight or insulation a "moot question". (*See* Regal 1975 [972] for additional cross references on the insulatory function of feathers.)

880. Gould, S.J. 1987. The fossil fraud that never was. *New Scientist*, 12 March, 32–36.

    Disparages the theory that a disgruntled Richard Owen deliberately purchased a known forgery to use against T.H. Huxley. Summarizes Charig's research into the forgery claim, with several photographs of the specimen, and accuses the astronomer Hoyle of "ripping off cardboard history for his own purposes." (*See* Charig et al. 1986 [876] for additional cross references concerning the *Archaeopteryx* forgery claim.)

881. Hecht, M.K., and S. Tarsitano, 1982. The paleobiology and phylogenetic position of *Archaeopteryx*. *Geobios (Special Mémoire)* 6:141–149.

Reviews theories of crocodile, theropod, and thecodont ancestry of birds, and concludes that *Archaeopteryx* is most closely related to thecodonts. (*See* Heilmann 1926 [939] for additional cross references on the origin of birds from thecodonts.) It was capable of limited powered flight, and launched from trees or ocean cliffs, to glide and scavenge over open areas such as beaches. (*See* Heilmann 1926 [939] for additional cross references to the thecodont hypothesis. Critical of Ostrom's theropod hypothesis. *See* Cracraft 1977 [877] for a review of Ostrom's work, with cross references. *See also* Ostrom 1985 [888] for additional cross references to Ostrom's critics.)

882. Hecht, M., and S. Tarsitano, 1983. *Archaeopteryx* and its paleoecology. In *Second International Symposium on Mesozoic Terrestrial Ecosystems*, ed. Z. Kielan-Jaworska and H. Osmólska, p.133–136, *Acta Palaeontologica Polonica* 28 (1/2).

A brief review of *Archaeopteryx* yields three hypotheses for its origin: crocodilian, thecodontian, and dinosaurian. The bird has no synapomorphies (shared derived characters) with either theropods or crocodiles that are not also present in thecodonts. It is probably derived from thecodont stock, and used its weak gliding flight to scan shoreline detritus for carrion. (*See* Heilmann 1926 [939] for additional cross references to the thecodont hypothesis. Critical of Ostrom's theropod hypothesis. *See* Cracraft 1977 [877] for a review of Ostrom's work, with cross references. *See also* Ostrom 1985 [888] for additional cross references to Ostrom's critics.)

883. Kessler, E. 1984. Lower Cretaceous birds from Cornet (Roumania). In *Third Symposium on Mesozoic Terrestrial Ecosystems, Short Papers*, ed. W.E. Reif and F. Westphal, 119–121. Tübingen: ATTEMPTO-Verlag.

Describes a new species *Limnornis corneti* (Limnornithidae, Limnornithiformes) from the same stratigraphic layer as

Archaeopteryx. Limnornis is similar to modern birds, and its simultaneity with *Archaeopteryx* indicates that *Archaeopteryx* should not be thought of as the direct ancestor of modern birds.

884. Martin, L.D. 1985. The relationship of *Archaeopteryx* to other birds. In *The Beginning of Birds, Proceedings of the International Archaeopteryx Conference*, Eichstätt, 1984, ed. M.K. Hecht, J.H. Ostrom, G. Viohl, and P. Wellnhofer, 177–184. Willibaldsburg: Jura-Museums Eichstätt.

    Haeckel placed *Archaeopteryx* in the subclass Sauriurae. Martin adds all terrestrial Mesozoic birds to this subclass, retaining Haeckel's subclass Ornithurae for all other Mesozoic birds. Proposes dividing Ornithurae into two infraclasses: Odontoholcae (new rank) for Hesperornithoformes, and Neornithes for *Ichthyornis* and later birds. *Archaeopteryx* is not ancestral to any modern birds; features of the skull and tarsometatarsus place it on an evolutionary side branch. (Critical of Ostrom's theropod hypothesis. *See* Cracraft 1977 [877] for a review of Ostrom's work, with cross references. *See also* Ostrom 1985 [888] for additional cross references to Ostrom's critics.)

885. Molnar, R.E. 1985. Alternatives to *Archaeopteryx*: a survey of proposed ancestral birds. In *The Beginning of Birds, Proceedings of the International Archaeopteryx Conference*, Eichstätt, 1984, ed. M.K. Hecht, J.H. Ostrom, G. Viohl, P. Wellnhofer, 209–217. Willibaldsburg: Jura-Museums Eichstätt.

    Considers several specimens suggested as ancestral to *Archaeopteryx*, and briefly reviews the theropod, thecodont and crocodilian hypotheses for avian origin. Favors a theropod origin; many of the characteristics reputed to link birds and crocodiles also occur in theropods.

886. Ostrom, J.H. 1970. *Archaeopteryx*, notice of a "new" specimen. *Science* 170:537–538.

    Ostrom discovered a fourth *Archaeopteryx* specimen (in the Teyler Museum, Netherlands) which had been misclassified as a pterosaur. The manus and horny claws are unusually well preserved. (*See* Cracraft 1977 [877] for a review of Ostrom's work, with cross references. *See also* Ostrom 1985 [888] for additional cross references to Ostrom's critics.)

887. Ostrom, J.H. 1976a. *Archaeopteryx* and the origin of birds. *Biological Journal of the Linnean Society* 8:91–182.

    This lengthy monographic review questions many previous hypotheses concerning *Archaeopteryx*. There is no ossified sternum. The pubis is not directed backwards at a sharp angle, and the forelimbs are not particularly birdlike. Homologous features indicate a close relationship between *Archaeopteryx* and theropod dinosaurs. The review caps a series of earlier papers by Ostrom on the nature and relationships of *Archaeopteryx* (*See* Cracraft 1977 [877] for a review and critique of Ostrom's earlier work. *See also* Ostrom 1985 [888] for additional cross references of Ostrom's critics.)

888. Ostrom, J.H. 1985. The meaning of *Archaeopteryx*. In *The Beginning of Birds, Proceedings of the International Archaeopteryx Conference*, Eichstätt, 1984, ed. M.K. Hecht, J.H. Ostrom, G. Viohl, and P. Wellnhofer, 161–176. Willibaldsburg: Jura-Museums Eichstätt.

    Summarizes the author's position on the flight capability, classification, and evolutionary significance of *Archaeopteryx*, replying to several critiques by Tarsitano, Hecht, and Martin. (*See* Cracraft 1977 [877] for a critical review of Ostrom's work and additional cross references. For other criticism of Ostrom's work, *See* Hecht and Tarsitano 1982 [881]; Hecht and Tarsitano 1983 [882]; Martin 1985 [884];Tarsitano and Hecht 1980 [892]; Walker 1980 [896]; Walker 1984 [897]; Hecht 1985 [908]; Martin 1983 [944]; Martin et al. 1980 [945]; Walker 1972 [952]; Whetstone and Martin 1979 [955]; Whetstone and Martin 1981 [956]; Bock 1986 [958]; Martin 1984 [963]; Olson and Feduccia 1979 [965].)

889. Owen, R. 1863. On the *Archaeopteryx* of von Meyer. *Philosophical Transactions of the Royal Society of London* 153:33–47.

Dr. Hermann Von Meyer's specimen consists of a single feather. Describes in detail an additional specimen purchased for the British Museum from Dr. Andreas Wagner. Makes comparisons with analogous structures in the pterodactyl. Owen concludes that *Archaeopteryx* was indeed a bird. (*See* Charig et al. 1986 [876] for cross references to the accusation that Owen deliberately purchased a known forgery.)

890. Rietschel, S. False forgery. In *The Beginning of Birds, Proceedings of the International Archaeopteryx Conference*, Eichstätt, 1984, ed. M.K. Hecht, J.H. Ostrom, G. Viohl, P. Wellnhofer, 371–376. Willibaldsburg: Jura-Museums, Eichstätt.

Archaeopteryx is not a forgery, but a genuine fossil bird. Systematically refutes the hoax theory, and concludes that the astronomers didn't give the matter sufficient study before "bursting into print." (*See* Charig et al. 1986 [876] for additional cross references concerning the *Archaeopteryx* forgery claim.)

891. Ruben, J. 1991. Reptilian physiology and the flight capacity of *Archaeopteryx*. *Evolution* 45:1–17.

If *Archaeopteryx* had a reptilian physiology, it could have used its "burst-level" muscle capacity to take off from the ground, or to achieve powered flight when launching from a tree. Reviews the results of the Eichstätt conference (International *Archaeopteryx* Conference), which generally demonstrated that *Archaeopteryx* could not launch into powered flight from the ground. (*See also* Buehler 1986 [874].) Assumptions that *Archaeopteryx* required an avian metabolism for powered flight ignore recent findings on reptilian thermoregulatory abilities. An ectothermic *Archaeopteryx* could have achieved powered flight with less than half the flight muscle volume of modern birds. It would, however, have been limited to flapping flights of short distance and duration.

892. Tarsitano, S., and M.K. Hecht. 1980. A reconsideration of the reptilian relationships of *Archaeopteryx*. *Zoological Journal of the Linnean Society* 69:149–182.

Considers six hypotheses to explain the origin of *Archaeopteryx*, and adds a seventh. *Archaeopteryx* is descended from thecodonts. (*See* Heilmann 1926 [939] for additional cross references to the thecodont hypothesis. See Thulborn and Hamley 1982 [894] for a critique. Critical of Ostrom's theropod hypothesis. See Cracraft 1977 [877] for a review of Ostrom's work, with cross references. *See also* Ostrom 1985 [888] for additional cross references to Ostrom's critics.)

893. Thulborn, R.A. 1984. The avian relationships of *Archaeopteryx*, and the origin of birds. *Zoological Journal of the Linnean Society* 82:119–158.

Archaeopteryx is neither an ancestral bird nor an ideal intermediate between reptiles and birds. It is a theropod dinosaur, and none of its derived characters are shared with modern birds; its feathers are homologous structures probably present in other small theropods. *Archaeopteryx* is not a valid starting point for debating the origin of flight. (*See* Regal 1975 [972] for additional cross references on the insulatory function of feathers.)

894. Thulborn, R.A., and T.L. Hamley. 1982. The reptilian relationships of *Archaeopteryx*. *Australian Journal of Zoology* 30:611–634.

Reexamines seven alternative hypotheses proposed by Tarsitano and Hecht (1980 [892]) to explain the origin of *Archaeopteryx*. Concludes that the only acceptable hypothesis is that *Archaeopteryx* is closely related to the theropod dinosaurs. Theropoda is probably a diphyletic or polyphyletic group, a grade rather than a clade.

895. Thulborn, R.A., and T.L. Hamley. 1985. A new paleoecological role for *Archaeopteryx*. In *The Beginning of Birds, Proceedings of the International Archaeopteryx Conference*, Eichstätt, 1984, ed. M.K. Hecht, J.H. Ostrom, G.

Viohl, and P. Wellnhofer, 81–89. Willibaldsburg: Jura-Museums Eichstätt.

The jaws, teeth, and hindlimb structure of *Archaeopteryx* indicate that it was an active and agile hunter, feeding on fishes, worms, and small tetrapods. It was probably not insectivorous. Feather vane assymetry does not necessarily indicate flight. *Archaeopteryx* probably used its wings as a sunshade or canopy to forage for aquatic prey, in the manner of modern herons and egrets.

896. Walker, A.D. 1980. The pelvis of *Archaeopteryx*. *Geological Magazine* 117:595–600.

Corrects several misinterpretations of the skull and pubis of *Archaeopteryx*. The traditional view of the opisthopubic pelvis is upheld; the pubis is rotated back below the ischium as in modern birds. Rotation must have been nearly complete by the Upper Jurassic, suggesting an early origin of birds. (Critical of Ostrom's theropod hypothesis. *See* Cracraft 1977 [877] for a review of Ostrom's work, with cross references. *See also* Ostrom 1985 [888] for additional cross references to Ostrom's critics.)

897. Walker, A.D. 1984. The braincase of *Archaeopteryx*. In *The Beginning of Birds, Proceedings of the International Archaeopteryx Conference*, Eichstätt, 1984, ed. M.K. Hecht, J.H. Ostrom, G. Viohl, and P. Wellnhofer, 122–134. Willibaldsburg: Jura-Museums Eichstätt.

Reinterprets the otic region of the braincase of the London specimen, and raises the possibility that the specimen may be a juvenile. Favors a direct ancestry of modern birds from *Archaeopteryx*, and casts doubt on the crocodilian origin hypothesis, which the author formerly supported. (*See* Walker 1972 [952] for additional cross references on the origin of birds from crocodiles. Critical of Ostrom's theropod hypothesis. *See* Cracraft 1977 [877] for a review of Ostrom's work, with cross references. *See also* Ostrom 1985 [888] for additional cross references to Ostrom's critics.)

898. Wellnhofer, P. 1988. A new specimen of *Archaeopteryx*. *Science* 240:1790–1792.

Reports on a new specimen from Solnhofen. The left wing has clear feather imprints, which the author considers the final blow to Hoyle's forgery claims. (*See* Charig et al. 1986 [876] for additional cross references concerning the *Archaeopteryx* forgery claim.)

DINOSAURS AND BIRDS

899. Anderson, A. 1991. Early bird threatens *Archaeopteryx*'s perch. *Science* 253:35.

A preliminary response to Chatterjee (1991 [901]) by Feduccia and Cracraft. Without having examined the completed manuscript, both authorities take issue with its hypotheses regarding the avian relationship of *Protoavis*, and its ability to fly. Feduccia concludes that "All you can say about *Protoavis* is that it's a small Triassic reptile of unknown affinity."

900. Beardsley, T. 1986. Fossil bird shakes evolutionary hypothesis. *Nature* 322:677.

A preliminary report on Chaterjee's discovery of *Protoavis*, which predates *Archaeopteryx* by 75 million years. It has several reptilian characteristics. Combined with its extreme age, this suggests that birds are not descended from dinosaurs. (*See* Chatterjee 1991 [901].)

901. Chatterjee, S. 1991. Cranial anatomy and relationships of a new Triassic bird from Texas. *Philosophical Transactions of the Royal Society of London B* 332:277–342.

This long awaited and controversial paper provides a detailed description of a Late Triassic pheasant-sized bird from the Dockum formation. It predates *Archaeopteryx* by about 75 million years. *Protoavis texensis* has many avian and theropod characteristics, though it is closer to birds than to theropods. Its binocular vision suggests an active, visually-oriented predatory life style. Cladistic analysis of cranial characters confirms that Aves is a monophyletic class. *Archaeopteryx*, a "living fossil", is relegated to an evolutionary dead end. Theropods share a common ancestry with birds, but the ancestral form may not itself have been a theropod. The analysis focuses on cranial morphology, and a forthcoming paper will examine the post-cranial skeleton and the flight capabilities of *Protoavis*. (*See* Anderson 1991 [899].)

902. Currie, P.J. 1985. Cranial anatomy of *Stenonychosaurus inequalis* (Saurischia; Theropoda) and its bearing on the origin of birds. *Canadian Journal of Earth Sciences* 22:1643–1658.

  Suggests a shared ancestry between *Stenonychosaurus inequalis* and the Saurornithidae. (*See also* Currie 1987 [903].) Several features of the skull, like the periotic sinuses, suggest that birds evolved from small carnivorous dinosaurs. (*See also* Currie 1987 [903]; Wilson and Currie 1985 [918].)

903. Currie, P.J. 1987. Bird-like characteristics of the jaws and teeth of troödontid theropods. *Journal of Vertebrate Paleontology* 7:72–81.

  Teeth of the family Troödontidae are distinct from those of other theropods; they lack interdental plates. Following a reexamination of all jaws and teeth assigned to *Troödon*, *Stenonychosaurus*, and *Pectinodon*, Currie concludes that the latter two are synonymous with *Troödon*. Troödontidae has precedence over the name Saurornithidae. (*See also* [902].) Troödontid teeth have a constriction between the root and the crown. Such teeth are more like those of birds than of other theropod dinosaurs.

904. Feduccia, A. 1985. On why the dinosaur lacked feathers. In *The Beginning of Birds, Proceedings of the International Archaeopteryx Conference*, Eichstätt, 1984, ed. M.K. Hecht, J.H. Ostrom, G. Viohl, and P. Wellnhofer, 75–79. Willibaldsburg: Jura-Museums Eichstätt.

  Refutes the insulatory hypothesis for the evolution of feathers. Evolution for flight created a preadaptation for avian endothermy. (*See* Regal 1975 [972] for additional cross references on the insulatory function of feathers.)

905. Feduccia, A. 1986. The scapulocoracoid of flightless birds: a primitive avian character similar to that of theropods. *Ibis* 128:128–131.

The flightless ratites have a distinctive scapulocoracoid which represents the primitive condition for birds; this condition is similar to that of the theropod dinosaurs. *Archaeopteryx*, on the other hand, has a scapula and coracoid closer to that of modern carinate birds. *Archaeopteryx* is less useful than the living ratites in determining which characteristics of the scapula and coracoid are primitive.

906. Galton, P.M. 1970. Ornithischian dinosaurs and the origin of birds. *Evolution* 24:448–462.

Frames the hypothesis, based primarily on similarities in the avian and ornithischian pubis, that primitive birds evolved from cursorial bipedal dinosaurs. (*See* Ostrom 1985 [888]; Walker 1977 [917].) Refutes the theory of thecodontian ancestry for birds, which dates back to Heilmann (1926 [939]), anticipating the subsequent work by Ostrom.

907. Gauthier, J. 1986. Saurischian monophyly and the origin of birds. In *The Origin of Birds and the Evolution of Flight*, ed. K. Padian, 1–55, *California Academy of Sciences Memoirs* no. 8.

A thorough review of competing hypotheses for avian origins and a rigorous analysis of the diagnostic features of relevant taxa. Saurischia is deemed a monophyletic taxa, united by ten synapomorphies, and including all birds and dinosaurs that share a more recent common ancestor with birds than do the ornithischians. The problematic taxa Aves is placed within the Theropoda and supplemented by the new taxa Aviales and Ornithurae. (*See* Martin 1983 [944].)

908. Hecht, M.K. 1985. The biological significance of *Archaeopteryx*. In *The Beginning of Birds, Proceedings of the International Archaeopteryx Conference*, Eichstätt, 1984, ed.

M.K. Hecht, J.H. Ostrom, G. Viohl, and P. Wellnhofer, 149–160. Willibaldsburg: Jura-Museums Eichstätt.

Using *Archaeopteryx* as an example, the author reviews the three competing hypotheses for the origin of birds: dinosaurian, thecodontian and crocodilian. (*See* Heilmann 1926 [939] for cross references to the thecodont hypothesis. *See* Walker 1972 [952] for cross references to the crocodilian hypothesis. Critical of Ostrom's theropod hypothesis. *See* Cracraft 1977 [877] for a review of Ostrom's work, with cross references. *See also* Ostrom 1985 [888] for additional cross references to Ostrom's critics.)

909. Kurzanov, S.M. 1982. Structural characteristics of the fore limbs of *Avimimus*. *Paleontological Journal* 16:108–112.

Avimimus portentosus shows many distinctly bird-like characteristics. Examination of the humerus and ulna shows that *Avimimus* had wings and associated flight muscles, and probably feathers. The short and wide "wings" could probably not have been used for full powered flight, permitting only short hops when chasing prey or being chased. The presumed covering of feathers also implies that *Avimimus* was a warm-blooded theropod [*See* 910, 911].

910. Kurzanov, S.M. 1983. New data on the pelvic structure of *Avimimus*. *Paleontological Journal* 17:110–111.

A new pelvic fragment from *Avimimus portentosus* permits a better description of its pelvic structure. Presents a brief revised diagnosis of the avimimid family [*See* 909, 911]).

911. Kurzanov, S.M. 1985. The skull structure of the dinosaur *Avimimus*. *Paleontological Journal* 19:92–99.

Describes the skull structure of *Avimimus*, based on new Mongolian material. Notes several bird-like characteristics, including the dome-like shape of the skull roof, the pattern of impressions of blood vessels on the skull, the lowering of the quadrate bone, and the rearward movement of the nasal apertures from the lateral to the dorsal side of the skull. Blood-vessel impressions suggest that the head may have been insulated by feathers. These traits place the genus well along the pathway towards a true avian skull. Features of the skull are consistent with flight, and *Avimimus* supports a cursorial origin of flight. Discusses the evolutionary relationship between birds and theropods [*See* 909, 910].

912. Lowe, P.E. 1935. On the relationship of the Struthiones to the dinosaurs and the rest of the avian class, with special reference to *Archaeopteryx*. *Ibis* 13:398–432.

   An interesting, and somewhat radical proposal for the classification of birds. "Bird reptiles", or Ornithosuchia, separated from thecodont stock well before the Pseudosuchia gave rise to dinosaurs. Struthiomimes are coelurosaurs, and this group diverged from the Pseudosuchian line prior to its division into the Ornithischia and Saurischia. *Archaeopteryx* is not an ancestral bird. It is much too specialized and "purely reptilian."

913. Osmólska, H. 1981. Coosified tarsometatarsi in theropod dinosaurs and their bearing on the problem of bird origins. *Palaeontologia Polonica* 42:79–95.

   Describes a new theropod genus and species, *Elmisaurus rarus*, from limb remains, and an indeterminate theropod species from a fragment of tarsometatarsus. A new family, Elmisauridae, is proposed to include this species, *Chirostenotes*, and *Macrophalangia*. Fusion of the tarsometatarsus offers additional evidence linking birds and theropod dinosaurs. Such fusion is evident in theropods as early as the Late Triassic.

914. Raath, M.A. 1985. The theropod dinosaur *Syntarsus* and its bearing on the origin of birds. In *The Beginning of Birds, Proceedings of the International Archaeopteryx Conference*, Eichstätt, 1984, ed. M.K. Hecht, J.H. Ostrom, G. Viohl, and P. Wellnhofer, 219–227. Willibaldsburg: Jura-Museums, Eichstätt.

   Skeletal features of the forelimb, hindlimb and otic region of the skull of *Archaeopteryx* show homologous similarity to those of the early Jurassic theropod *Syntarsus*. *Syntarsus*, or one of the other Procompsognathidae species, played a key role in the evolution of *Archaeopteryx* and modern birds.

915. Silyn-Roberts, H., and R.M. Sharp. 1989. The similarity of preferred orientation development in eggshell calcite of the dinosaurs and birds. *Proceedings of the Royal Society of London B* 235:347–363.

    X-Ray diffraction shows that the development of shell deposition of calcite in Upper Cretaceous dinosaur eggs is more like that of ratite birds than of living reptiles. This suggests that dinosaurs and birds had similar physiology of eggshell development.

916. Thulborn, R.A. 1975. Dinosaur polyphyly and the classification of archosaurs and birds. Australian *Journal of Zoology* 23:249–270.

    Critiques Bakker and Galton (1974 [825]) in detail. Saurischia is a diphyletic taxa, evolved from two separate thecodont lines. Ornithischian ancestry is still unclear. Birds are descended from theropod dinosaurs, but the arguments for dinosaurian endothermy are unconvincing.

917. Walker, A.D. 1977. Evolution of the pelvis in birds and dinosaurs. In *Problems in Vertebrate Evolution*, ed. S.M. Andrews, R.S. Miles and A.D. Walker, 319–357. *Linnean Society Symposium Series* no. 4.

    Examines the role of the opisthopubic pelvis in avian evolution. Galton's explanation for the backward rotation of the pubis is inadequate. (*See* Galton 1970 [906].) Walker maintains that the Jurassic crocodilian *Hallopus* shows evidence of an opisthopubic pelvis, supporting a crocodilian origin for birds. (*See* Walker 1984 [897] for a subsequent moderation of this position. *See* Walker 1972 [952] for additional cross references on the origin of birds from crocodiles.)

918. Wilson, M.C., and P.J. Currie. 1985. *Stenonychosaurus inequalis* (Saurischia; Theropoda) from the Judith River

(Oldman) Formation of Alberta; new findings on metatarsal structure. *Canadian Journal of Earth Sciences* 22:1813–1817.

An examination of metatarsal bones from *S. inequalis* shows further similarities with the Saurornithidae. Tendencies toward metatarsal fusion in theropods are reminiscent of the fused tarsometatarsus of birds, but this may be due to simple convergence. (*See also* Currie 1985 [902]; Currie 1987 [903].)

PHYLOGENY AND EVOLUTION OF BIRDS

919. Benton, M.J. 1984c. Is a dog more like a lizard or a chicken? *New Scientist*, 16 August, 18–19.

    A short article summarizing the phylogenetic scheme proposed in Gardiner 1982 [847]. Gardiner puts birds and mammals into a new taxon, the supercohort Haemothermia. Discusses problems of cladistic analysis, such as the difficulty of separating true synapomorphies from convergent characters.

920. Brett-Surman, M.K., and G.S. Paul. 1985. A new family of bird-like dinosaurs linking Laurasia and Gondwanaland. *Journal of Vertebrate Paleontology* 5:133–138.

    Describes *Avisaurus archibaldi* from metatarsi, and assigns the species to the new family Avisauridae (Suborder Theropoda). Metatarsi from Montana and Argentina are both *A. archibaldi*. This is the first time that a Cretaceous dinosaur genus has been reported from Laurasia and Gondwanaland during this period, a time when the two land masses were supposedly separate.

921. Brodkorb, P. 1971. Origin and evolution of birds. In *Avian Biology I*, ed. D.S. Farner, J.R. King, and K.C. Parkes, 19–55. New York: Academic Press.

    A good literature review of the state of knowledge of avian origins in the late 1960's, a time when Ostrom was starting to revolutionize the field. Claims birds are descended from thecodont reptiles such as *Euparkeria*. (*See also*

Heilmann 1926 [939] for additional cross references to the thecodont hypothesis.)

922. Brodkorb, P. 1976. Discovery of a Cretaceous bird, apparently ancestral to the orders Coraciiformes and Piciformes (Aves: Carinatae). *Smithsonian Contributions to Paleobiology* 27:67–73.

Describes *Alexornis antecedens*, an Upper Cretaceous bird from the Bocona Roja Formation in Mexico. Concludes that the species is ancestral to the orders Piciformes and Coraciiformes. Proposes a new order (Alexornithiformes) and a new family (Alexornithidae) for this species, and claims that the specimen was (then) the only known Cretaceous bird [*See* 921]. Several papers on Cenozoic fossil birds also appear in this volume.

923. Bühler, P., L.D. Martin, and L.M. Witmer. 1988. Cranial kinesis in the Late Cretaceous birds *Hesperornis* and *Parahesperornis*. *Auk* 105:111–122.

Prokinesis, in which the upper jaw moves as a unit, is the primitive condition for the Hesperornithoformes. Although prokinesis is associated with pterygoid segmentation in modern birds, the correlation is misleading. Hesperornithiform birds have jaws showing prokinesis and also have primitive unsegmented pterygoids.

924. Cracraft, J. 1971. Caenagnathiformes: Cretaceous birds convergent in jaw mechanisms to dicynodont reptiles. *Journal of Paleontology* 45:805–809.

Sternberg placed *Caenagnathus collinsi* in the Reptilia. Cracraft compares *C. collinsi* with *C. sternbergi* and suggests that both species, as well as the order Caenagnathiformes, belong in the Class Aves. Although *Caenagnathus* is distinctly reptilian in appearance, it is definitely avian in its affinities. The evolution of the jaw structure, modified for shearing herbaceous material, is convergent with the jaws of dicynodont reptiles.

925. Cracraft, J. 1973. Continental drift, paleoclimatology, and the evolution and biogeography of birds. *Journal of Zoology* 169:455–545.

Relates the biogeography of the higher taxa of birds to the patterns of climate and continental drift in the Mesozoic. The distribution of birds in pre-drift Gondwanaland was a major factor in their subsequent dispersal. Reviews patterns of continental drift worldwide.

926. Cracraft, J. 1974. Phylogeny and evolution of the ratite birds. *Ibis* 116:494–521.

Ideas about ratite evolution have been shaped by biogeography more than by morphology. Cladistic analysis of paleognathous birds shows the tinamous to be the closest ratite relatives. Paleognathiformes is probably a monophyletic taxon. Reviews four alternate phylogenetic hypotheses, and dismisses all of them. Ratites are not primitive within the paleognathous birds; they show many advanced characteristics. (*See* McGowan 1984 [942] for an opposing view.) Flightlessness arose only once within the ratites. Presents a revised classification of Paleognathiformes.

927. Cracraft, J. 1986. The origin and early diversification of birds. *Paleobiology* 12:383–399.

Uses non-avian theropods as an out group for the cladistic analysis of primitive birds, based on seventy-three characters. Focuses on the divergence between the Neornithes clades Paleognathae and Neognathae, and concludes that these taxa are monophyletic sister groups. Birds probably originated in the Jurassic; the Neornithes arose in the Early Cretaceous.

928. Cracraft, J. 1988a. Early evolution of birds. *Nature* 331:389–390.

A brief summary (with several references) of a phylogenetic hypothesis for the origin of birds, prompted by Sanz et al. (1988 [950]). Many features of modern birds evolved very early in the fossil record.

929. Cracraft, J. 1988b. The major clades of birds. In The *Phylogeny and Classification of the Tetrapods; Vol. 1, Amphibians, Reptiles, Birds*, ed. M.J. Benton, 339–361. *Systematics Association Special Volume* 35A, Oxford: Clarendon Press.

Reviews the synapomorphies postulated to relate the major avian taxa. Extant birds fall into the monophyletic taxa Neornithes, with the sister clade Hesperornithiformes. *Archaeopteryx* is the sister group of the latter taxa. Within the Neornithes, the Paleognathae (ratites and tinamous) and Neognathae (all other living birds) form two basic lineages.

930. Currie, P.J. 1981. Bird footprints from the Gething Formation (Aptian, Lower Cretaceous) of northeastern British Columbia, Canada. *Journal of Vertebrate Paleontology* 1:257–264.

Reports on a siltstone slab from the Gething Formation in British Columbia's Peace River Canyon. The slab contains over 200 bird footprints. Describes *Aquatilavipes swiboldae* on the basis of these prints. They are the oldest bird tracks known, and were probably made by a marsh bird. The prints show a group of four individuals engaged in feeding in shallow water. The tracks are compared with those of dinosaurs and modern marsh birds.

931. Elźanowski, A. 1976. Palaeognathous bird from the Cretaceous of Central Asia. *Nature* 264:51–53.

Describes two skulls from the Cretaceous of the Gobi desert, and assigns them to the species *Gobipteryx minuta*. This species is the oldest paleognathous bird. The specimens support a northern dispersal pattern in the paleognathous birds [*See* 932].

932. Elźanowski, A. 1981. Embryonic bird skeletons from the Late Cretaceous of Mongolia. *Palaeontologia Polonica* 42:147–177.

Describes seven embryonic skeletons, probably belonging to *Gobipteryx minuta*. The specimens were discovered by the 1971 Polish-Mongolian expedition. The skeletons show several avian characteristics and suggest an advanced capacity for flight [See 931].

933. Elżanowski, A. 1983. Birds in Cretaceous ecosystems. In *Second International Symposium on Mesozoic Terrestrial Ecosystems*, ed. Z. Kielan-Jaworska and H. Osmólska, p.75–92, *Acta Palaeontologica Polonica* 28 (1/2).

Terrestrial bird fossils are relatively rare. Fish eating birds and shore birds are more readily preserved. This may be due to reptilian scavengers focusing on terrestrial animals that were large enough to be detected and small enough to be swallowed whole. The displacement of lower teleost fishes to deeper waters by Perciformes and other modern fishes simultaneously reduced competition for prey and reduced the accessibility of prey species for piscivorous birds (Ichthyornithes and Hesperornithes). Flightless and foot-propelled diving birds were abundant in the warm Cretaceous seas. (*See* [934]. *See also* Kurochkin 1985 [941] on the abundance of birds in the Cretaceous.) Early land birds were probably precocial ground-nesters.

934. Elżanowski, A., and P.M. Galton. 1991. Braincase of *Enaliornis*, an Early Cretaceous bird from England. *Journal of Vertebrate Paleontology* 11:90–117.

Provides a detailed description of the braincase of this primitive genus. The brain suggests that the animal was a diving bird, consistent with the leg bones which are indicative of a foot-propelled diver. Its phylogeny is difficult to determine; most of the characteristics it shares with other birds are plesiomorphic [*See also* 933].

935. Feduccia, A. 1980. *The Age of Birds*. Cambridge: Harvard University Press.

A well-written and comprehensive survey of the origin and evolution of birds. Includes a chapter on *Archaeopteryx* and a chapter on the evolution of flight.

936. Gauthier, J., and K. Padian, 1985. Phylogenetic, functional and aerodynamic analysis of the origin of birds. In *The Beginning*

of Birds, Proceedings of the International Archaeopteryx Conference, Eichstätt, 1984, ed. M.K. Hecht, J.H. Ostrom, G. Viohl, and P. Wellnhofer, 185-198. Willibaldsburg: Jura-Museums Eichstätt.

Birds are descendants of the coelurosaurian dinosaurs. Proposes cladograms which relate thecodonts, birds, dinosaurs and other archosaurs. Reviews the arboreal flight hypothesis and concludes that the cursorial hypothesis is the most parsimonious explanation.

937. Gill, F.B. 1990. *Ornithology*. New York: W.H. Freeman.

An excellent introduction to the biology of birds, emphasizing their evolution. (*See also* Welty 1988 [954].)

938. Gingerich, P.D. 1973. Skull of *Hesperornis regalis* and early evolution of birds. *Nature* 243:70-73.

Provides a new reconstruction of the skull of *Hesperornis*, an early predaceous diving bird discovered by O.C. Marsh. The skull supports the evolution of birds from theropods.

939. Heilmann, G. 1926. *Origin of the Birds*. London: Witherby (also 1927, N.Y.: Appleton).

An influential early work, assigning avian origins to the pseudosuchian thecodonts. Heilmann's thesis shaped the debate over the origin of birds for over 50 years. (*See* Brodkorb 1971 [921]; Hecht and Tarsitano 1982 [881]; Hecht and Tarsitano 1983 [882]; Tarsitano and Hecht 1980 [892]; and Hecht 1985 [908] for recent papers supporting this hypothesis.)

940. Houde, P. 1986. Ostrich ancestors found in the Northern Hemisphere suggest new hypothesis of ratite origins. *Nature* 324:563-565.

Ostrich ancestors may belong to a Northern Hemisphere group called the *Lithornis*-cohort. These hen-sized paleognathous birds were capable of flight. The ostrich may have evolved in the Northern Hemisphere some time after the breakup of Gondwanaland, emigrating from Europe to Africa during the early to middle Tertiary. Kiwis may have also evolved from this group.

941. Kurochkin, E.N. 1985. A true carinate bird from Lower Cretaceous deposits in Mongolia and other evidence of Early Cretaceous birds in Asia. *Cretaceous Research* 6:271–278.

Archaeopteryx may be an atypical Jurassic bird. Describes *Ambiortus dementjevi* (Ambiortiformes, Ambiortidae) from a partial skeleton. This new order and family are true carinate birds. They are also the oldest birds known from Asia. Either *Archaeopteryx* gave rise to advanced carinate forms in only ten to twelve million years, or such birds already existed at the same time as *Archaeopteryx*. Numerous feather fossils from Mongolia and other Russian sites indicates that birds were common in Cretaceous biotas. (*See also* Elzanowski 1983 [933] regarding the abundance of Cretaceous birds.)

942. McGowan, C. 1984. Evolutionary relationships of ratites and carinates: evidence from ontogeny of the tarsus. *Nature* 307:733–735.

Disputes the widespread belief that ratites are a degenerate offshoot of the carinate birds. Identifies two tarsal conditions. Carinate birds have a synapomorphic pretibial bone; ratites have an ascending process fused with the astragalus, as do theropod dinosaurs. Ratites are primitive, not derived as previously claimed. (*See* Cracraft 1974 [926].)

943. McGowan, C., and A.J. Baker. 1981. Common ancestry for birds and crocodiles? *Nature* 289:97–98.

Criticizes the crocodilian origin theory. (*See* the rebuttal from Whetstone and Martin [956] which follows this letter. *See also* Walker 1972 [952] for additional cross references on the origin of birds from crocodiles.)

944. Martin, L.D. 1983. The origin and early radiation of birds. In *Perspectives in Ornithology*, ed. A.H. Brush and G.A. Clark jr., 291–338. Cambridge: Cambridge University Press.

Argues for a crocodilian origin for birds. Subscribes to an arboreal origin of flight, though this hypothesis is not necessarily supported or opposed by crocodilian origins. Reviews the primary taxa of Mesozoic birds and the Early Tertiary radiation of birds. Followed on pages 338–353 by critical commentaries from D.W. Steadman and P.V. Rich. (*See* Walker 1972 [952] for additional cross references on the origin of birds from crocodiles. Critical of Ostrom's theropod hypothesis. *See* Cracraft 1977 [877] for a review of Ostrom's work, with cross references. *See also* Ostrom 1985 [888] for additional cross references to Ostrom's critics.)

945. Martin, L.D., J.D. Stewart, and K.N. Whetstone. 1980. The origin of birds: structure of the tarsus and teeth. *Auk* 97:86–93.

Challenges the dinosaurian origin theory. Reexamines the structure of the tarsus and the dentition of *Archaeopteryx* and other Mesozoic birds and reptiles. The pretibial bone of birds and the astragalus of theropods are not homologous; primitive avian dentition is more crocodilian than dinosaurian. (*See* Walker 1972 [952] for additional cross references on the origin of birds from crocodiles. Critical of Ostrom's theropod hypothesis. *See* Cracraft 1977 [877] for a review of Ostrom's work, with cross references. *See also* Ostrom 1985 [888] for additional cross references to Ostrom's critics.)

946. Olson, S.L. 1982. A critique of Cracraft's classification of birds. *Auk* 99:733–739.

Claims that Cracraft's phylogenetic scheme is "frequently misleading or erroneous." Cracraft ignores critical synapomorphies and misinterprets convergent characters.

947. Olson, S.L. 1985. The fossil record of birds. In *Avian Biology VIII*, ed. D.S. Farner, J.R. King, and K.C. Parkes, 80–238. New York: Academic Press.

A comprehensive review of the literature on fossil birds.

948. Ostrom, J.H. 1973. The ancestry of birds. *Nature* 242:136.

Summarizes the evidence that birds evolved from coelurosaurian dinosaurs. (*See* Cracraft 1977 [877] for a review of Ostrom's work, with cross references. *See also*

Ostrom 1985 [888] for additional cross references to Ostrom's critics.)

949. Ostrom, J.H. 1975. The origin of birds. *Annual Review of Earth and Planetary Science* 1975:55-77.
A comprehensive review of theories on avian origins which concludes that small theropods gave rise to birds. A good summation of several earlier papers by Ostrom on this subject. (*See* Cracraft 1977 [877] for a review of Ostrom's work, with cross references. *See also* Ostrom 1985 [888] for additional cross references to Ostrom's critics.)

950. Sanz, J.L., J.F. Bonaparte, and A. Lacasa. 1988. Unusual Early Cretaceous birds from Spain. *Nature* 331:433-435.
Describes a feather and skeleton (lacking skull) from the Las Hoyas outcrop. The unnamed bird shows an unusual combination of primitive and derived characteristics, making it an intermediate form between *Archaeopteryx* and later birds and a sister taxon to the Ornithurae (*See also* Cracraft 1988a [928].)

951. Swinton, W.E. 1975. *Fossil Birds*. London: British Museum of Natural History.
A brief, authoritative, and well-written introduction to fossil birds, including a chapter on flight and a glossary.

952. Walker, A.D. 1972. New light on the origin of birds and crocodiles. *Nature*: 237:257-263.
A thorough presentation of the hypothesis that birds are descended from crocodiles. A comparison between the skull of the Triassic crocodilian *Sphenosuchus* and that of modern crocodiles shows several points of similarity. *Sphenosuchus* also appears to be cursorial, suggesting that crocodiles became amphibious to avoid competition from coelurosaurs. (*See also* Walker 1984 [897]; Walker 1977 [917]; McGowan and Baker 1981 [943]; Martin 1983 [944]; Martin et al. 1980 [945]; Whetstone and Martin 1979 [955]; Whetstone and Martin 1981 [956]; and Martin 1984 [963] for additional articles on the origin of birds from crocodiles. Critical of Ostrom's

theropod hypothesis. *See* Cracraft 1977 [877] for a review of Ostrom's work, with cross references. *See also* Ostrom 1985 [888] for additional cross references to Ostrom's critics.)

953. Walker, C.A. 1981. A new subclass of birds from the Cretaceous of South America. *Nature* 292:51–53.

New specimens from the Upper Cretaceous of Argentina represent a new subclass of birds, the Enantiornithes. The structure of the sternum indicates that they were weak fliers, or perhaps flightless.

954. Welty, J.C. 1988. *The Life of Birds.* 4th ed. New York: Saunders.

A classic textbook on avian biology, in its fourth edition. (*See also* Gill 1990 [937].)

955. Whetstone, K.N., and L. Martin. 1979. New look at the origin of birds and crocodiles. *Nature* 279:234–23.

Supports a thecodont origin for both birds and crocodiles, on the basis of detailed study of the otic region (middle ear). Birds and crocodiles share a homologous development of the fenestra pseodorotunda and a network of pneumatic spaces in the bones around the middle ear. (*See* Walker 1972 [952] for additional cross references on the origin of birds from crocodiles. Critical of Ostrom's theropod hypothesis. *See* Cracraft 1977 [877] for a review of Ostrom's work, with cross references. *See also* Ostrom 1985 [888] for additional cross references to Ostrom's critics.)

956. Whetstone, K., and L.D. Martin. 1981. Common ancestry for birds and crocodiles? A reply. *Nature* 289:98.

Reply to a letter by McGowan and Baker (1981 [943]) in the same issue, which criticizes the crocodilian origin theory. (*See* Walker 1972 [952] for additional cross references on the origin of birds from crocodiles. Critical of Ostrom's theropod hypothesis. *See* Cracraft 1977 [877] for a review of Ostrom's work, with cross references. *See also* Ostrom 1985 [888] for additional cross references to Ostrom's critics.)

FLIGHT

957. Bock, W.J. 1985. The arboreal theory for the origin of birds. In *The Beginning of Birds, Proceedings of the International Archaeopteryx Conference*, Eichstätt, 1984, ed. M.K. Hecht, J.H. Ostrom, G. Viohl, and P. Wellnhofer, 199–207. Willibaldsburg: Jura-Museums Eichstätt.

    The arboreal theory of flight is preferable. Numerous traits needed to evolve before flight was possible. These include endothermy, bipedality, feathers and small body size.

958. Bock, W.J. 1986. The arboreal origin of avian flight. In *The Origin of Birds and the Evolution of Flight*, ed. K. Padian, 57–72. *California Academy of Sciences Memoirs*. no. 8.

    A companion piece to Ostrom (1986 [969]), arguing against Ostrom's cursorial hypothesis. Contrasts the arboreal and cursorial hypotheses. Much depends on the habitat and life style we assume for the "protobird". Discusses possible arboreal functions of avian body size, bipedalism, homeothermy, feathers, and the structure of the wing and tail. Gravity provided the momentum for flight; jumping or parachuting from trees led to gliding, which in turn led to powered flight. The arboreal habit may have arisen when small animals took to the trees for safe resting and nesting spots.

959. Caple, G., R.P. Balda, and W.R. Willis. 1983. The physics of leaping animals and the evolution of preflight. *American Naturalist* 121:455–467.

    Flight requires lift, thrust and power, and control of pitch, roll and yaw. A simple mathematical analysis of the basic physical requirements of flight supports Ostrom's hypothesis of a bipedal cursorial habit for early birds.

960. Feduccia, A., and H.B. Tordoff. 1979. Feathers of *Archaeopteryx*: asymmetric vanes indicate aerodynamic function. *Science* 203:1021–1022.

    Archaeopteryx feathers display an asymmetric shape similar to the feathers of modern birds. This asymmetry is associated with powered flight. Thus *Archaeopteryx* was capable of gliding, if not full powered flight. Proponents of a flightless *Archaeopteryx* will have to explain the asymmetry to justify their hypothesis. (*See also* Norberg 1985 [964].)

961. Gauthier, J.A., and K. Padian. 1989. The origin of birds and the evolution of flight. In *The Age of Dinosaurs*, ed. K. Padian and D.J. Chure, 121–133. *Geological Society of America Short Courses in Paleontology* no. 2. Knoxville: The Paleontological Society.

Contrasts several hypotheses concerning the origin of birds. Birds might have evolved from the crocodylomorphs, thecodontians, or theropod dinosaurs. The authors favor a theropod origin. Discusses the arboreal and cursorial hypotheses that have been advanced to explain the evolution of flight.

962. Maderson, P.F.A. 1972. On how an archosaurian scale might have given rise to an avian feather. *American Naturalist* 106:424–428.

Biophysical, developmental, and anatomical studies suggest that elongated scales gave rise to protofeathers.

963. Martin, L.D. 1984. The origin of birds and of avian flight. In *Current Ornithology I*, ed. R.F. Johnston, 105–129. London: Plenum Press.

A comprehensive review of Martin's defense of Walker's theory of crocodilian origin for birds, and a critique of Ostrom's theory of dinosaur origins. Discusses arboreal versus cursorial theories of avian bipedality, and concludes that feathers may have evolved initially to function in thermoregulation. (*See also* Feduccia 1985 [904]. *See* Walker 1972 [952] for additional cross references to the origin of birds from crocodiles. Critical of Ostrom's cursorial theropod hypothesis. *See* Cracraft 1977 [877] for a review of Ostrom's work, with cross references. *See also* Ostrom 1985 [888] for additional cross references to Ostrom's critics.)

964. Norberg, R.A. 1985. Function of vane asymmetry and shaft curvature in bird flight feathers; inferences on flight ability of *Archaeopteryx*. In *The Beginning of Birds, Proceedings of the International Archaeopteryx Conference*, Eichstätt, 1984, ed. M.K. Hecht, J.H. Ostrom, G. Viohl, and P. Wellnhofer, 303–318. Willibaldsburg: Jura-Museums Eichstätt.

A detailed and illustrated analysis of the function of feathers in flight in modern birds, with specific reference to the role of feather structure. Although these features in *Archaeopteryx* are consistent with either gliding or powered flight, the author concludes that powered flight is the more likely alternative (*See also* Feduccia and Tordoff 1979 [960].)

965. Olson, S.L., and A. Feduccia. 1979. Flight capability and the pectoral girdle of *Archaeopteryx*. *Nature* 278:247–248.

Contends that the furcula would have provided sufficient attachment for flight muscles in *Archaeopteryx*. The dorsal elevators in modern birds are capable of sustaining a recovery stroke in powered flight, and the acute angle of the *Archaeopteryx* scapula and coracoid indicates that its elevators might have functioned in this capacity. A keeled sternum is an enhancement of flight, not a prerequisite. Ostrom's theory is thus invalidated. (*See* Ostrom 1974 [966].)

966. Ostrom, J.H. 1974. *Archaeopteryx* and the origin of flight. *Quarterly Review of Biology* 49:27–47.

Archaeopteryx specimens seem to support neither the arboreal nor the cursorial hypothesis. It is similar in almost every detail to a coelurosaur, suggesting that *Archaeopteryx* was a ground-dwelling predator. Feathers originated as insulation, and played no initial role in flight (*See* Regal 1975 [972] for additional cross references on the insulatory function of feathers.) Secondary modification of the forelimb feathers for prey capture preadapted the bird limb for flight. (*See* Olson and Feduccia 1979 [965]. *See also* Cracraft 1977 [877] for a review of Ostrom's work, with cross references. *See also* Ostrom 1985 [888] for additional cross references to Ostrom's critics.)

967. Ostrom, J.H. 1976b. Some hypothetical anatomical stages in the evolution of avian flight. *Smithsonian Contributions to Paleobiology* 27:1–21.

Using extant specimens of *Archaeopteryx*, as well as modern birds, Ostrom tries to reconstruct the anatomical changes associated with flight. The coracoid bone is particularly critical in the evolution of flight. Modifications for more efficient prey capture created preadaptations for powered flight. (*See* Cracraft 1977 [877] for a review of Ostrom's work, with cross references. *See also* Ostrom 1985 [888] for additional cross references to Ostrom's critics.)

968. Ostrom, J.H. 1979. Bird flight: how did it begin? *American Scientist* 67:46–56.

A good summary of Ostrom's cursorial flight hypothesis. Birds are the only vertebrate fliers that use only the forelimbs for flight. Avian flight must have evolved by a radically different route. Ostrom summarizes skeletal features of *Archaeopteryx* and concludes that its flight apparatus was extremely primitive, while its hindlimb structures for running on the ground were relatively advanced. Features of the foot are similar to modern ground-dwelling birds. *Archaeopteryx* was probably insectivorous, and used its feathered limbs to help capture prey (*See* Cracraft 1977 [877] for a review of Ostrom's work, with cross references. *See also* Ostrom 1985 [888] for additional cross references to Ostrom's critics.)

969. Ostrom, J.H. 1986. The cursorial origin of avian flight. In *The Origin of Birds and the Evolution of Flight*, ed. K. Padian, 73–81. *California Academy of Sciences Memoirs* no. 8.

Takes issue with his "friendly adversary Walter Bock" (Bock 1986 [958]) who "still firmly believes that birds learned to fly by falling out of trees." Discusses possible flight features of *Archaeopteryx*, and concludes that it was clearly adapted as a ground dweller. (*See* Cracraft 1977 [877] for a review of Ostrom's work, with cross references. *See also* Ostrom 1985 [888] for additional cross references to Ostrom's critics.)

970. Padian, K. 1985. The origins and aerodynamics of flight in extinct vertebrates. *Palaeontology* 28:413–433.

Gliding is not a prerequisite for powered flight. Flight in pterosaurs and birds probably originated from the ground, while bats show evidence of a gliding, arboreal past. A reexamination of the aerodynamics of the pterosaurs shows them to be capable of very active flight, comparable to that of modern birds. (*See* Rayner 1988 [971].)

971. Rayner, J.V.M. 1988. The evolution of vertebrate flight. *Biological Journal of the Linnean Society* 34:269–287.

Gliding is a preadaptation for powered flight. Slow flight in birds and bats is derived, relative to flapping flight. *Archaeopteryx* shows adaptations for gliding, but not for a running cursorial habit. Competing models for the evolution of flight are examined in terms of energetic costs and ecological efficiency. (*See* Padian 1985 [970].)

972. Regal, P.J. 1975. The evolutionary origin of feathers. *Quarterly Review of Biology* 50:35–66.

Feathers arose as adaptations to intense solar radiation. This insulatory function was a preadaptation for endothermy. The function of feathers shifted at some point in time from excluding heat to conserving heat. (*See* Feduccia 1974 [879]; Thulborn 1984 [893]; Feduccia 1985 [904]; Martin 1984 [963]; Ostrom 1974 [966]; Tarsitano 1985 [974]; and Thulborn 1987 [975] for additional cross references on the insulatory function of feathers.)

973. Stapel, S.O., J.A.M. Leunissen, M. Versteeg, J. Wattel, and W.W. De Jong. 1984. Ratites as oldest offshoot of avian stem—evidence from α-crystallin A sequences. *Nature* 311:257–259.

Did flying birds evolve from flightless birds, or is flightlessness a secondary (derived) trait? Compares the amino acid sequence of a protein in the lens of the eye of ratites with the same amino acid sequence in the eyes of reptiles (alligator and tegu), and a group of fourteen avian species. On the basis of this trait, ratites are monophyletic, and form a sister group to other birds. Ratites are primitive birds, which separated very early in avian evolution from the other birds. Reviews other biochemical evidence supporting this phylogeny. The data supports the hypothesis that flight "developed late in avian evolution."

974. Tarsitano, S. 1985. The morphological and aerodynamic constraints on the origin of avian flight. In *The Beginning of Birds, Proceedings of the International Archaeopteryx Conference*, Eichstätt, 1984, ed. M.K. Hecht, J.H. Ostrom, G. Viohl, and P. Wellnhofer, 319–332. Willibaldsburg: Jura-Museums Eichstätt.

Basic aerodynamic principles constrain the evolution of flight. Wing elevators are not essential to flight, only to taking off from the ground. The arboreal hypothesis is correct, and *Archaeopteryx* shows many features associated with gliding. Feathers evolved specifically for flight, not thermoregulation. While not a direct descendent of modern birds, *Archaeopteryx* represents a comparable level of avian organization. (*See* Regal 1975 [972] for additional cross references on the insulatory function of feathers.)

975. Thulborn, R.A. 1987. The origin of feathers. In *Fourth Symposium on Mesozoic Terrestrial Ecosystems, Short Papers*, ed. P.J. Currie and E. Koster, Drumheller, Alta.: Tyrell Museum of Paleontology, 216–221.

It is unlikely that feathers only served a single function. Down feathers may be more primitive than contour feathers, and may have functioned to insulate juvenile theropod dinosaurs. Birds may have evolved from theropods by a process of progenesis, an accelerated development of the reproductive organs of juveniles. (*See* Regal 1975 [972] for additional cross references on the insulatory function of feathers.)

Chapter Nine

Death of the Dinosaurs

The race is not always to the swift, nor victory to the strong. Despite their unprecedented conquest of the biosphere, dinosaurs vanished at the end of the Cretaceous as if a black curtain had been pulled over the Mesozoic stage. The curtain of doom may have been a literal one, a vast Earth-encircling dust cloud thrown up by the impact of a comet or an asteroid.

Modern debates over dinosaur extinction have centered on L.W. Alvarez's asteroid impact theory. His discovery of an unusual iridium anomaly precisely at the Cretaceous-Tertiary boundary was the smoking gun that renewed widespread interest in dinosaur extinction (Alvarez 1983 [1036]; Alvarez et al. 1980 [1037]; 1984 [1038]).

Circumstantial evidence in support of Alvarez continues to mount. Shocked quartz grains at the Cretaceous-Tertiary boundary suggest a momentous collision. Such grains are commonly associated with impact craters; cathodoluminescence studies suggest that their origin is not volcanic (Bohor et al. 1984 [1043]; 1987 [1044]; Owen and Anders 1988 [1078]).

Evidence of huge tidal deposits throughout the Caribbean could be remnants of a gigantic tsunami that emanated from a possible impact site in the Gulf of Mexico. Craters off the coasts of Texas, Colombia, and the Yucatan have all been suggested as the site of the fatal blow (Bourgeois et al. 1988 [1047]; Dietz 1991 [1053]; Florentin et al. 1991 [1054]; Hildebrand and Boynton 1990 [1061]; Hildebrand and Penfield 1990 [1062]; Kunk et al. 1989 [1068]; Sigurdsson et al. 1991 [1087]).

Whatever happened at the Cretaceous-Tertiary boundary had profound repercussions for all animal and plant life, marine and terrestrial. There are tantalizing clues in the fossil record. Why were calcareous planktonic species devastated, while siliceous forms escaped relatively unscathed? Why were broadleaved evergreens destroyed, while deciduous species survived (Wolfe 1987 [1136])?

It is difficult to accurately measure a short interval of geologic time in the fossil record (Baadsgard et al. 1988 [976]). Yet in that thin clay layer found at Gubbio, Italy, and elsewhere are strange and curious anomalies that hold the key to a cosmic puzzle. Did the Cretaceous expire with a bang or a whimper?

Gradualists maintain that dinosaurs were decreasing in species diversity towards the end of the Cretaceous. It wouldn't take a random blow from space to finish them off, merely an unfortunate, but plausible sequence of terrestrial events, such as massive volcanism, sea-level regression and turnover of the carbon-dioxide rich waters of the deep ocean (Clemens 1982 [1015]; Kauffman 1984 [1023]; Sloan et al. 1986 [1033]; Officer and Drake 1983 [1075]).

In fact, dinosaurs might have survived the Cretaceous-Tertiary boundary, at least in some locations. Rigby, Russell and others offer evidence that dinosaurs existed in the Paleocene. The primary fossil evidence, often consisting of teeth, is controversial (Charig 1989 [1014]; Fassett 1982 [1021]; Rigby 1989 [1029]; Rigby et al. 1987 [1030]; Russell 1984 [1031]; Sloan et al. 1986 [1033]). Are the fossils truly Paleocene, or are they reworked Cretaceous fossils lying in Paleocene sediments?

What really occurred was probably far more complex than most students of dinosaur biology imagine. The intricate patterns of extinction and survival, changes in geochemistry, magnetic polarity, sea level, ocean acidity, vegetation structure, global temperature, and a host of other physical and biotic factors must all be explained by any plausible extinction theory.

Consider for a moment the hypothetical incoming asteroid, ten kilometers wide and hurtling into the Gulf of Mexico at cosmic speeds. The impact and explosion would dwarf the energy of the world's entire nuclear arsenal (Alvarez and Asaro 1990 [1039]). From the shallow marine sediments a plume of steam and debris shoots upward, achieving escape velocity before settling into low orbit (Melosh 1982 [1072]; Croft 1982 [1051]). Through the winds of the upper atmosphere the dust shroud spreads, enveloping the Northern Hemisphere completely, and obscuring the southern sun as well.

Many animals are killed outright, pulverized by the explosion or swept away by a monstrous tidal wave over 100 feet tall (Bourgeois et al. 1988 [1047]). Darkness settles over the Earth at high noon. Photosynthesis stops, and plankton and terrestrial plants die of

Death of the Dinosaurs

starvation (Griffis and Chapman 1988 [1059]; Pollack et al. 1983 [1080]; Toon et al. 1982 [1091]; Wolfe 1991 [1096]; Arthur et al. 1987 [1113]). Foraging in the dark for ever fewer scraps of living vegetation, the herbivores gradually succumb as well, followed shortly by the carnivores that preyed on them. For a brief period, detritivores and scavengers rule the world (Sheehan and Hansen 1986 [1005]; Arthur et al. 1987 [1113]).

The force of the impact triggers episodes of intense volcanism and earthquake activity. The Deccan Traps unleash a flood of molten basalt that covers a large portion of India (Courtillot 1990 [1140]; McLean 1985 [1145]; Rampino and Strothers 1988 [1152]). Kinetic energy released as heat from the impacting asteroid sparks a global wildfire that devastates terrestrial floras, and adds even more smoke and dust to the thick blanket of death that girdles the globe. The wildfires leave behind a thin layer of soot that is still visible in boundary layer sediments (Melosh et al. 1990, Venkatesan and Dahl 1989, Wolbach et al. 1985).

In the sea, a major long-term ecological disruption is underway. The increasingly acid ocean waters kill the calcareous plankton, and dissolve calcareous sediments on the ocean floor (Crutzen 1987 [1052]). This releases immense amounts of carbon dioxide into the atmosphere, adding to the outgassing of numerous volcanos and combustion gases from the raging forest fires. A feedback loop between ocean and atmosphere creates a greenhouse effect, further stressing the organisms that have managed to survive the initial blow (Hsü et al. 1982 [1064]; O'Keefe and Ahrens 1989 [1076]).

A massive pulse of organic carbon from burned and starved terrestrial organisms floods into the sea, causing deoxygenation and stagnation, and further upsetting the delicate geochemical balance that persisted for most of the Mesozoic (Hsü 1986 [989]).

Finally, when the dust settles, the planet is transformed. Tropical conditions have given way to a temperate climate. For a while, ferns dominate the land, slowly giving way to pines and finally to the recovering angiosperms. Dormant plants, living roots, and seed banks in the soil gradually restore a semblance of ecological normalcy (Knoll 1984 [1119]; Saito et al. 1986 [1125]; Spicer 1989 [1126]; Van Valen and Sloan 1977 [1135]).

The rules, however, have changed forever. The dinosaurs have vanished, and the wealth of ecological niches they formerly occupied are opened up for the rapidly radiating mammals.

This scenario explains many of the geochemical and biological anomalies that mark the Cretaceous-Tertiary boundary. Was our planet the victim of a random blow from space? Given the probability of such collisions, considered over vast stretches of geologic time, it would be far more unlikely if the Earth had managed to avoid being a target for cosmic debris (Shoemaker 1983 [1086]).

Scores of papers have supported or assailed the asteroid impact theory. Those seeking an introduction to the controversy are referred to the proceedings of two important conferences held at Snowbird, Utah. Snowbird I and Snowbird II provide an excellent survey of the complex geochemical, astrophysical and biological problems presented by the impact theory (Chapman 1989 [983]; Silver and Schultz 1982 [1088]; Sharpton and Ward 1990 [1153]).

Not everyone accepts the impact theory; there are several interesting alternatives. Some scientists believe that volcanism itself can account for extinction and other boundary phenomena, without resorting to extraterrestrial explanations. Perhaps there are as yet undiscovered long-term planetary cycles within the Earth's mantle. (Courtillot 1990 [1140]; Hallam 1987 [1143]; Henbest 1989 [1144]; Moses 1989 [1146]).

Earlier discussions of dinosaur extinction centered on the possibility of a nearby supernova explosion, or perhaps a dramatic solar flare. A supernova might account for the iridium anomaly, while bathing the planet in deadly cosmic rays and severely depleting the ozone layer (Clark et al. 1977 [1107]).

Perhaps, instead of an asteroid, a comet or cometary swarm slammed into the Mesozoic world (Hut et al. 1987 [1065]). One mechanism recently proposed for generating infalling comets is an invisible solar companion, usually called Nemesis. Nemesis, in its highly eccentric orbit, sweeps close enough on each return to perturb the Oort cloud of comets on the fringes of the solar system. The cloud disgorges several comets, some of which fall into the Sun's gravity well and are swept in towards the Earth (Davis et al. 1984 [1100]; Hills 1984 [1101]; Raup 1986 [1104]).

Whatever killed the dinosaurs has led us to examine in detail the nature and causes of mass extinction events, of which the terminal

Cretaceous event is only one of many. Some even question whether such events truly exist, or are just artifacts of the methodologies used to study them (Benton 1985 [978]; Hoffman 1985 [988]; Newell 1982 [1027]).

The same criticism is levelled at proponents of the apparent periodicity of extinctions (Patterson and Smith 1989 [996]; Quinn and Signor 1989 [997]). Raup and Sepkoski and others present evidence for a 20 to 30 million year cycle (Raup and Sepkoski 1986 [999]; 1988 [1000]; Alvarez and Muller 1984 [1041]). Possible explanations for this periodicity include oscillations of the solar system about the galactic plane (Rampino and Strothers 1984 [1082]; Schwartz and James 1984 [1085]), long term convective cycles in the Earth's mantle (Moses 1989 [1146]), and the passage of the Sun through the spiral arms of the galaxy (Napier and Clube 1979 [1074]).

Perhaps we are so fascinated by the death of the dinosaurs because we hear in their expiring sigh the intimation of our own mortality. Will we vanish in a nuclear holocaust analogous to that which killed the previous masters of the planet? Or will we perhaps go quietly extinct, having altered planetary climate and chemistry beyond our ability to adapt?

The literature on dinosaur extinction has expanded as rapidly as the dust plume of the impacting asteroid, and could easily form a book-length bibliography all its own (Fouty 1987 [987]). The choice of what to include or exclude was particularly difficult. Within the parameters of currency, authority, and availability, I have tried to give ample space to each of the major scenarios devised to explain the demise of the dinosaurs, as well as competing theories on Mesozoic climate and vegetation before and after the terminal Cretaceous event.

CATASTROPHIC EXTINCTION

976. Baadsgard, H., J.F. Lerbekmo, and I. McDougall. 1988. A radiometric age for the Cretaceous-Tertiary boundary based upon K-Ar, Rb-Sr, and U-Pb ages of bentonites from Alberta, Saskatchewan, and Montana. *Canadian Journal of Earth Sciences* 25:1088–1097.

    Uses three radiometric methods to age the bentonites in coal seams at three locations. The average measurements yield a mean age of 64.3 million years ago plus or minus 1.2 mya for the Cretaceous-Tertiary boundary. Discusses statistical problems associated with precise determination of the Cretaceous-Tertiary boundary.

977. Béland, P., P. Feldman, J. Foster, D. Jarzen, G. Norris, G. Pirozynski, G. Reid, J.R. Roy, D. Russell, and W. Tucker. 1977. Cretaceous-Tertiary extinctions and possible terrestrial and extraterrestrial causes. *Syllogeus* 12:1–162.

    Features eleven articles on Cretaceous-Tertiary boundary extinction. Topics include the supernova theory, solar flares, angiosperm palynology, and magnetic polarity reversals. Annotated bibliographies accompany each article. A good review of the pre-Alvarez extinction theories.

978. Benton, M.J. 1985. Mass extinction among non-marine tetrapods. *Nature* 316:811–814.

    It is difficult to sort out mass extinction events from normal background levels of extinction. The Cretaceous extinction is really the result of a slightly higher background extinction rate coupled with a depressed origination rate for new taxonomic families. (*See* Quinn and Signor 1989 [997] for additional cross references on distinguishing between mass extinctions and background extinctions.)

979. Benton, M.J. 1986. More than one event in the Late Triassic mass extinction. *Nature* 321:857–861.

    The Late Triassic experienced a mass extinction on the same scale as that which killed the dinosaurs. Marine families declined 23%, with a similar reduction for terrestrial species. The extinction seems to have occurred in two phases, separated by 12–17 million years. This is at odds with predictions of a 26–million year cycle of extinctions.

980. Berggren, W.A., and J.A. Van Couvering, eds. 1984. *Catastrophes and Earth History: The New Uniformitarianism.* Princeton: Princeton University Press.

   Presents eighteen papers from a symposium on problems of the Cretaceous-Tertiary boundary event. A good source for basic review articles on problems of stratigraphy, climate, marine extinctions, and floral evolution. (*See* Hickey 1984 [1115]; Kauffman 1984 [1023]; Tschudy 1984 [1132])

981. Bryan, J.R., and D.S. Jones. 1989. Fabric of the Cretaceous-Tertiary marine macrofaunal transition at Braggs, Alabama. *Palaeogeography, Palaeoclimatology, Palaeoecology* 69:279–302.

   Fifty percent of Cretaceous macroinvertebrates disappear at this Gulf coastal plain Cretaceous-Tertiary boundary. There is no evidence of gradual extinction. Species diversity remains high right up to the boundary event. Stratigraphic resolution is insufficient to give a precise picture of a short duration event, but the evidence is generally consistent with catastrophic extinction. (*See* Russell 1984 [1031] for additional cross references on species diversity and extinction.)

982. Channell, J.E., and J.P. Dobson. 1989. Magnetic stratigraphy and magnetic mineralogy at the Cretaceous-Tertiary boundary section, Braggs, Alabama. *Palaeogeography, Palaeoclimatology, Palaeoecology* 69:267–278.

   Examines the magnetic stratigraphy of shallow marine coastal plain sediments. Microfaunal and macrofaunal extinction events are not synchronous, which may be due to local changes in the sedimentary environment. The microfaunal Cretaceous-Tertiary boundary lies in a reversed magnetic polarity zone.

983. Chapman, C.R. 1989. Snowbird II: global catastrophes. *EOS, Transactions of the AGU* 70:217–218.

Summarizes the issues discussed at the Snowbird II conference on catastrophic extinction. The proceedings of this important conference were received as this book went to press (Sharpton and Ward 1990 [1153]). *See* Silver and Schultz (1982 [1088]) for the proceedings of the first Snowbird conference.

984. Cherfas, J. 1985. Extinction and the pattern of evolution. *New Scientist*, 3 October, 48–51.

We can identify five events that qualify as true mass extinctions. We can also determine several factors such as rarity, large body size and small population size, that make a given species prone to normal background extinction. Geographic distribution seems to be the primary factor, however, in surviving mass extinctions. (*See* Quinn and Signor 1989 [997] for additional cross references on distinguishing between mass extinctions and background extinctions.)

985. Donovan, S.K., ed. 1989. *Mass Extinctions: Processes and Evidence*, New York: Columbia University Press.

Twelve contributors analyze criteria for defining mass extinctions and review several mass extinction events, from the Precambrian to the Pleistocene. (*See* Orth 1989 [995]; Upchurch 1989 [1134]. *See also* Quinn and Signor 1989 [997] for additional cross references on distinguishing between mass extinctions and background extinctions.)

986. Elliott, D.K., ed. 1986. *Dynamics of Extinction*. New York: Wiley.

Contains twelve essays discussing mass extinction, including three articles on the Cretaceous-Tertiary boundary extinction (Part II, pp. 49–85).

987. Fouty, G. 1987. *Death of the Dinosaurs and Other Mass Extinctions*. Phoenix: Oryx Press.

An annotated bibliography of two hundred and seventy five items related to mass extinction. Focuses on the impact theory, and includes several references on extinction by humans. The scope is somewhat general, including popular magazines in addition to more scholarly works, and the work is suitable for high school or lower-level undergraduate students.

988. Hoffman, A. 1985. Patterns of family extinction depend on definition and geological timescale. *Nature* 315:659–662.

Our ability to separate mass extinctions from background extinctions is very limited. Depending on how we define mass extinctions, and which of several plausible timescales we use, the number and timing of extinction events can change dramatically. Such subjective criteria can result in the appearance of periodicity in extinction where none exists. (*See* Quinn and Signor 1989 [997] for additional cross references on distinguishing between mass extinctions and background extinctions.)

989. Hsü, K.J. 1986. *The Great Dying.* New York: Random House.

A well-written popular account of extinction theories, with an emphasis on catastrophic extinction. A good introduction to the conflicting extinction theories, but Hsü wanders off at the end into an odd critique of Darwinian theory in light of mass extinctions.

990. Jablonski, D. 1984. Keeping time with mass extinctions. *Paleobiology* 10:139–145.

Reports on a workshop to study the apparent 26 million year cycle of extinctions. No one has yet conclusively disproved the impact hypothesis, though some uncertainties remain. The evidence suggests that externally caused mass extinction events are both frequent and periodic.

991. Jablonski, D. 1986. Background and mass extinctions: the alternation of macroevolutionary regimes. *Science* 231:129–133.

There is a qualitative difference between background and mass extinction events. Marine bivalves and gastropods from the Atlantic coast show better survival when their larvae are mobile and disperse readily, and when the species are distributed over a wide geographic area. Clades with numerous species survive better than those with only a few species. At the Cretaceous-Tertiary boundary, however, survival was purely a function of wide geographic distribution. Adaptation *per se* is not important in surviving mass extinctions. (*See* McKinney 1987 [994]. *See also* Quinn and Signor 1989 [997] for additional cross references on distinguishing between mass extinctions and background extinctions.)

992. Lerbekmo, J.F., M.E. Evans, and H. Baadsgaard. 1979. Magneto-stratigraphy, biostratigraphy, and geochronology of Cretaceous-Tertiary boundary sediments, Red-deer Valley. *Nature* 279:26–30.

Terrestrial (dinosaur) extinctions in Alberta's Red Deer Valley correlate with marine (Foraminifera) extinctions at Gubbio, Italy. The extinctions are at the Cretaceous-Tertiary boundary. The base of magnetic anomaly 29 should be accepted as a worldwide approximation of that boundary.

993. Lerbekmo, J.F., C. Singh, D.M. Jarzen, and D.A. Russell. 1979. The Cretaceous-Tertiary boundary in south-Central Alberta—a revision based on additional dinosaurian and microfloral evidence. *Canadian Journal of Earth Sciences* 16:1866–1869.

The Nevis coal seam provides a stratigraphic marker of the Cretaceous-Tertiary boundary in Alberta.The apparent dinosaur fossils above the Nevis coal seam in Alberta do not correspond with regional approximations of the Cretaceous-Tertiary boundary. The specimens, originally reported by C.M. Sternberg, were incorrectly recorded as lying above the seam, but actually lie below it. (*See* Sloan et al. 1986 [1033] for additional cross references on the possibility that dinosaurs survived into the Paleocene.)

994. McKinney, M.L. 1987. Taxonomic selectivity and continuous variation in mass and background extinctions of marine taxa. *Nature* 325:143–145.

Sessile and planktonic organisms have much higher background extinction and mass extinction rates than mobile benthic organisms. During mass extinction events, only the intensity of the process varies, not the nature or the selectivity of the process itself. Background and mass extinctions are not qualitatively different from one another. *(See* Jablonski 1986 [991]. *See also* Quinn and Signor 1989 [997] for additional cross references on distinguishing between mass extinctions and background extinctions.)

995. Orth, C.J. 1989. Geochemistry of the bio-event horizons. In *Mass Extinctions: Processes and Evidence*, ed. S.K. Donovan, 37–72. New York: Columbia University Press.

Reviews, with a minimum of technical language, the methodologies used to probe the geochemistry of the Cretaceous-Tertiary boundary, and summarizes the development of the impact theory. Iridium anomalies must be interpreted cautiously. Orth looks at several bio-event horizons, from the Precambrian through the Pliocene, and discusses their geochemistry and possible causes.

996. Patterson, C., and A.B. Smith. 1989. Periodicity in extinction: the role of systematics. *Ecology* 70:802–811.

Arguments about the periodicity of extinctions have centered on the statistical interpretation of the data, but the quality of the data itself is questionable. At lower taxonomic levels (genera), the proportion of signal to noise in fossil census data declines 50% from the ratio in higher taxa (families). An analysis of fossil fish and echinoderms shows that only 25% of the data constitutes signal, while the remaining 75% is noise. Apparent peaks in the noisy portion of the data may be a result of periodicity in some taphonomic factor. *(See also* in the same issue [997]; Moses 1989 [1146].)

997. Quinn, J.F., and P.W. Signor. 1989. Death stars, ecology, and mass extinctions. *Ecology* 70:824–834.

While an astrophysical phenomenon might explain at least part of the Cretaceous-Tertiary boundary event, it does not explain other mass extinctions. Instead, a combination of ecological explanations is needed, based on a consideration of which clades survived and which did not. Mass extinctions are simply an extreme point in the continuum of background extinctions, and are not statistically different from background extinctions. Reviews methodological problems in measuring rates of extinction, the appropriateness of models based on higher-level taxa, and the calculation of periodicity. (*See also* in the same issue [996]; Moses 1989 [1146]. For additional references on distinguishing between mass extinctions and background extinctions, *See* Benton 1985 [978]; Cherfas 1985 [984]; Donovan 1989 [985]; Hoffman 1985 [988]; Jablonski 1986 [991]; McKinney 1987 [994]; Raup and Sepkoski 1986 [999]; Signor and Lipps 1982 [1006]; Newell 1982 [1027]].)

998. Raup, D.M. 1982. Biogeographic extinction: a feasibility test. In *Geological Implications of Impacts of Large Asteroids and Comets on the Earth*, ed. L.T. Silver and P.H. Schultz, 277–281. *Geological Society of America Special Paper* no. 190. Boulder: GSA.

Using a computer model, Raup digitizes all families of living terrestrial vertebrates, and all genera of living corals and echinoids. By introducing 105 random target points with varying lethal radii, the model allows a simulation of the extent of immediate extinctions from a wide range of impacts. Lethal areas greater than one-half the Earth's surface are necessary to create extinctions on the level seen in Phanerozoic extinctions. Given the high level of endemism resulting from widely separated continents and numerous dispersal barriers, it is even more unlikely that widespread biogeographic extinction would have resulted from regional catastrophic events. Mass extinctions must have had a global or near-global effect to create the patterns observed in the fossil record.

999. Raup, D.M., and J.J. Sepkoski jr. 1986. Periodic extinction of families and genera. *Science* 231:833–836.

Eight extinction events at the family level can be identified in the marine fossil record. These events were statistically significant from background extinctions ($P<0.05$,

Death of the Dinosaurs 333

for 2,160 families). Analysis at the generic level (11,800 genera) gives an even clearer picture. Time series analysis tends to support a 26 million year periodicity in extinctions. (*See* [1000]. *See also* Rampino and Strothers 1984 [1082]; Schwartz and Jones 1984 [1085]. *See* Quinn and Signor 1989 [997] for additional cross references on distinguishing between mass extinctions and background extinctions.)

1000. Raup, D.M.,and J.J. Sepkoski jr. 1988. Testing for periodicity of extinction. *Science* 241:94–96.

Responding to criticism of their 26 million year extinction cycle hypothesis, the authors point out that their analysis now extends to nearly 10,000 records at the genus level and 51 sampling intervals. The extended data set provides an even more precise fit to a 26 million year cycle [*See* 999].

1001. Robert, C., and H. Chamley. 1990. Paleoenvironmental significance of clay mineral associations at the Cretaceous-Tertiary passage. *Palaeogeography, Palaeoclimatology, Palaeoecology* 79:205–219.

Newly examined sections of the Cretaceous-Tertiary boundary show evidence of a major global geologic disruption prior to the boundary, accompanied by a sudden increase in erosional processes, and a substantial sea-level drop just after the boundary. Neither climatic changes nor a bolide impact can account for observed changes in the clay layer at the boundary.The two global events described would mask the mineralogic traces of either bolide impacts or volcanic eruptions in the boundary clay layer.

1002. Russell, D.A. 1979. The enigma of the extinction of the dinosaurs. *Annual Review of Earth and Planetary Sciences* 7:163–182.

Reviews the major extinction hypotheses prior to Alvarez's impact hypothesis, including temperature changes, supernovae, and volcanic eruptions. Russell concludes that supernovae are the most likely culprit. (*See* [1107–1110, 1112]. *See* Russell and Tucker 1971 [1111].)

1003. Russell, D.A. 1982. A paleontological consensus on the extinction of the dinosaurs? In *Geological Implications of Impacts of Large Asteroids and Comets on the Earth*, ed. L.T. Silver and P.H. Schultz, 401–405. *Geological Society of America Special Paper* no. 190. Boulder: GSA.

As yet there is no clear evidence that dinosaurs were declining in diversity at the time of the Cretaceous-Tertiary boundary event. Cautions against "putting all our dinosaur eggs in one polemical basket," and recommends an objective consideration of the evidence and problems of interpretation of the fossil record. (*See* Russell 1984 [1031] for additional cross references on species diversity and extinction.)

1004. Sepkoski, J.J. jr. 1982. Mass extinctions in the Phanerozoic oceans: a review. In *Geological Implications of Impacts of Large Asteroids and Comets on the Earth*, ed. L.T. Silver and P.H. Schultz, 283–289. *Geological Society of America Special Paper* no. 190. Boulder: GSA.

Mass extinction events are fairly frequent in the fossil record, with the Late Permian event being the most catastrophic. Reviews the timing and magnitude of fifteen extinction events in the marine fossil record.

1005. Sheehan, P.M., and T.A. Hansen. 1986. Detritus feeding as a buffer to extinction at the end of the Cretaceous. *Geology* 14:868–870.

Food chains that relied on living plant matter collapsed at the Cretaceous-Tertiary boundary. Scavengers, detritivores, and other animals in food chains that relied on dead plant matter fared much better. This is consistent with a temporary cessation of photosynthesis by a vast dust cloud, as predicted by the impact theory. The detritivore community had an ample larder on which to draw. (*See* Arthur et al. 1987 [1113].)

1006. Signor, P.W. III, and J.H. Lipps. 1982. Sampling bias, gradual extinction patterns, and catastrophes in the fossil record. In *Geological Implications of Impacts of Large Asteroids and Comets on the Earth*, ed. L.T. Silver and P.H. Schultz, 291–

296. *Geological Society of America Special Paper* no. 190. Boulder: GSA.

Evidence of an apparent decline in species diversity prior to the Cretaceous-Tertiary boundary does not necessarily mean that there was no catastrophic boundary event. Two types of sampling error could result in the observed patterns of declines in diversity. A reduced Late Cretaceous sample size would create an artificial pattern of declining diversity. The global unconformity created by Late Cretaceous marine regression would have artificially truncated the sedimentary record, leading to the appearance of declining diversity. The resulting sampling problems would create the illusion of declining diversity. The fossil record does not confirm either gradual or catastrophic extinction at the Cretaceous-Tertiary boundary. (*See* Quinn and Signor 1989 [997] for additional cross references on distinguishing between mass extinctions and background extinctions. *See* Russell 1984 [1031] for additional cross references on the relationship between species diversity and extinction.)

1007. Smit, J. 1982. Extinction and evolution of planktonic foraminifera at the Cretaceous/Tertiary boundary after a major impact. In *Geological Implications of Impacts of Large Asteroids and Comets on the Earth*, ed. L.T. Silver and P.H. Schultz, 329–352. *Geological Society of America Special Paper* no. 190. Boulder: GSA.

Only one species of Cretaceous Foraminifera, *Guembelitria cretacea*, survived beyond the Cretaceous-Tertiary boundary. All subsequent species of Foraminifera may have evolved from this single species. Examination of the biostratigraphy of the Gredero section in Spain shows that the extinction event occurred within a 50 year period, with up to 35,000 years before a stable planktonic community was reestablished. The interim period was characterized by high instability. The data is consistent with a punctuated equilibrium mode of evolution.

1008. Smit, J., and S. Van der Kaars. 1984. Terminal Cretaceous extinctions in the Hell Creek area, Montana: compatible with catastrophic extinction. *Science* 223:1177–1179.

The asteroid impact devastated terrestrial and marine environments. The Bug Creek and Hell Creek sites show no evidence of gradual extinction. Late Cretaceous material has been reworked and mixed with Paleocene sediments. Describes the stratigraphic correlations of the Hell Creek area, and reconstructs abandoned fluvial channels. (*See* Sloan et al. 1986 [1033] for additional cross references on the possibility that dinosaurs survived into the Paleocene.)

1009. Zachos, J.C., M.A. Arthur, and W.E. Dean. 1989. Geochemical evidence for suppression of pelagic marine productivity at the Cretaceous/Tertiary boundary. *Nature* 337:61–64.

Changes in $^{13}C/^{12}C$ ratios, barium levels, and $CaCO_3$ at the Cretaceous-Tertiary boundary in the North Pacific suggest a drastic decline in marine primary productivity. This reduction lasted for about half a million years. It is unlikely that a gradual environmental change could have triggered such an abrupt decline in productivity.

GRADUAL DECLINE

1010. Archibald, J.D. 1981. The earliest known Palaeocene mammalian fauna and its implications for the Cretaceous-Tertiary transition. *Nature* 291:650–652.

The earliest mammal sites in the Tertiary show a gradual transition, on the order of tens or hundreds of thousands of years. The Hell's Hollow site in Montana is unusual for having a good intact record immediately on either side of the Cretaceous-Tertiary boundary.

1011. Archibald, J.D. 1989. The demise of the dinosaur and the rise of mammals. In *The Age of Dinosaurs*, ed. K. Padian and D.J.

Chure, 162–174. *Geological Society of America Short Courses in Paleontology* no. 2. Knoxville: The Paleontological Society.

Summarizes principal extinction theories and the fossil record of dinosaur extinction. Archibald has been a major supporter of gradual extinction.

1012. Argast, S., J.O. Farlow, R.M. Gabet, and D.L. Brinkman. 1987. Transport-induced abrasion of fossil reptilian teeth; implications for the existence of Tertiary dinosaurs in the Hell Creek Formation, Montana. *Geology* 15:927–930.

Use of a tumbler to induce wear in five fossil teeth shows that sediment transport does not significantly abrade teeth. Abrasions are insufficient evidence that the fossils have been transported and reworked. The results neither confirm nor deny the possibility of Tertiary dinosaurs at Hell Creek. (*See* Sloan et al. 1986 [1033] for additional cross references on the possibility that dinosaurs survived into the Paleocene.)

1013. Carpenter, K., and B. Breithaupt. 1986. Latest Cretaceous occurrence of nodosaurid ankylosaurs (Dinosauria, Ornithischia) in western North America and the gradual extinction of the dinosaurs. *Journal of Vertebrate Paleontology* 6:251–257.

New ankylosaur discoveries from the Lance, Hell Creek, and Laramie Formations show that nodosaurid ankylosaurs survived at least to the Maastrichtian. Declining relative abundance of nodosaurids, and their apparent extinction well before the Cretaceous-Tertiary boundary, support declining dinosaur diversity in the Late Cretaceous and a gradual extinction of dinosaurs. (*See* Russell 1984 [1031] for additional cross references on the relationship between species diversity and extinction.)

1014. Charig, A.J. 1989. The Cretaceous-Tertiary boundary and the last of the dinosaurs. In Evolution and Extinction, ed. W.G. Chaloner, and A. Hallam. *Philosophical Transactions of the Royal Society of London B* 325:387–400.

Proof of catastrophic extinction requires world wide simultaneity of extinction, coincident with a causal disaster. We need to examine an unbroken geological record for some distance on either side of the Cretaceous-Tertiary boundary; such sedimentary beds are rare. Some dinosaurs may have survived into the Tertiary, but there are numerous difficulties in definitely proving the existence of Tertiary dinosaurs. There is much disagreement over the correlation of sedimentary layers between continents. Various methods of dating the Cretaceous-Tertiary boundary give different ages. Charig concludes that some dinosaurs survived into the Danian. (*See* Sloan et al. 1986 [1033] for additional cross references on the possibility that dinosaurs survived into the Paleocene.)

1015. Clemens, W.A. 1982. Patterns of extinction and survival of the terrestrial biota during the Cretaceous/Tertiary transition. In *Geological Implications of Impacts of Large Asteroids and Comets on the Earth*, ed. L.T. Silver and P.H. Schultz, 407–413. *Geological Society of America Special Paper* no. 190. Boulder: GSA.

The evidence for a global extinction of terrestrial flora and fauna, coincident with widespread marine extinctions, is questionable. The terrestrial fossil record is very incomplete, relative to the marine fossil record. Although terrestrial extinctions appear to be very quick, in terms of geological time, they are prolonged in terms of biological time. The fossil record is too scant to determine whether dinosaur diversity was actually stable or decreasing at the Cretaceous-Tertiary boundary. Problems of dating and correlation of sediments introduce a large element of uncertainty into calculations of the synchronicity of terrestrial animal and plant extinctions, and of terrestrial and marine faunal extinctions. The pattern of terrestrial faunal extinctions does not appear to correlate with any obvious ecological factor, and is probably due to multiple interrelated physical and biological factors. (*See* Russell 1984 [1031] for additional cross references on species diversity and extinction.)

1016. Clemens, W.A. 1983. Mammalian evolution during the Cretaceous-Tertiary transition; evidence for gradual, non-catastrophic change. In *Second International Symposium on*

Mesozoic Terrestrial Ecosystems, ed. Z. Kielan-Jaworska and H. Osmólska, p.55–61. *Acta Palaeontologica Polonica* 2 (1/2).

The gradual evolutionary change of river valley mammalian species at the Bug Creek, Montana, Cretaceous-Tertiary boundary contrasts with more abrupt changes in flood plain species. Regional patterns of extinction argue against a single global extinction event.

1017. Clemens, W., and D. Archibald. 1980. Evolution of terrestrial faunas during the Cretaceous-Tertiary transition. *Mémoires de la Société Géologique de France* 139:67–74.

The gradual record of mammalian and dinosaurian extinction at the Hell Creek and Tullock Formations challenges catastrophic extinction theories. These extinctions took place over a long period of time, and varied from site to site. Though a cataclysmic event might have occurred, it was not the primary force behind dinosaur extinction.

1018. Davies, K.L. 1987. Duck-bill dinosaurs (Hadrosauridae, Ornithischia) from the North Slope of Alaska. *Journal of Paleontology* 61:198–200.

A short description of hadrosaur bones from the Colville River. These are the first Alaskan dinosaur bones, and represent the farthest north (70°) that such bones have been found. The bones are on the Beringia land bridge between Asia and North America. The presence of dinosaurs so far north indicates that they could have coped with the low temperatures that might have resulted from an impact winter. (For additional references on polar dinosaurs and migration, *See* Rich and Rich 1989 [381]; Paul 1988 [439]; Hotton 1980 [727]; Brouwers et al. 1987 [1049].)

1019. Eaton, J.G., J.I. Kirkland, and K. Doi. 1989. Evidence of reworked Cretaceous fossils and their bearing on the existence of Tertiary dinosaurs. *Palaios* 4:281–286.

Reworked fossils of sharks and other marine fauna known to have gone extinct at the Cretaceous-Tertiary boundary are reported from a variety of Tertiary sites. Reworking of fossils may be more common than previously believed. (*See* Sloan et al. 1986 [1033] for additional cross references on the possibility that dinosaurs survived into the Paleocene.)

1020. Eberth, D.A. 1990. Stratigraphy and sedimentology of vertebrate microfossil sites in the uppermost Judith River Formation (Campanian), Dinosaur Provincial Park, Alberta, Canada. *Palaeogeography, Palaeoclimatology. Palaeoecology* 78:1–36.

A disconformity reflecting episodic tectonic activity divides two sedimentary facies at the Judith River Formation. Channels above the disconformity were tidally influenced, whereas those below it were not. Sedimentological data shows definite reworking of vertebrate microfossils near the Cretaceous-Tertiary boundary, casting doubt on the existence of Paleocene dinosaurs at this site. (*See* Brinkman 1990 [583]; Dodson 1987 [589] on the importance of microfossils. *See also* Sloan et al. 1986 [1033] for additional cross references on the possibility that dinosaurs survived into the Paleocene.)

1021. Fassett, J.E. 1982. Dinosaurs in the San Juan Basin, New Mexico, may have survived the event that resulted in the creation of an iridium-enriched zone near the Cretaceous/Tertiary boundary. In *Geological Implications of Impacts of Large Asteroids and Comets on the Earth*, ed. L.T. Silver and P.H. Schultz, 435–447. *Geological Society of America Special Paper* no. 190. Boulder: GSA.

Dinosaur bones in the Ojo Alamo sandstone lie above the palynological Cretaceous-Tertiary boundary. If such large animals survived the Cretaceous-Tertiary boundary event, that event could not have been a catastrophic asteroid impact. (*See* Sloan et al. 1986 [1033] for additional cross references on the possibility that dinosaurs survived into the Paleocene.)

1022. Hickey, L.J. 1981. Land plant evidence compatible with gradual, not catastrophic, change at the end of the Cretaceous. *Nature* 292:529–531.

Extinction rates of land plants at the Cretaceous-Tertiary boundary are moderate, and vary from place to place in their intensity and timing. They are not synchronized with dinosaur extinction, arguing against an asteroid impact and its consequent dust clouds.

1023. Kauffman, E.G. 1984. The fabric of Cretaceous marine extinctions. In *Catastrophes and Earth History: The New Uniformitarianism*, ed. W.A. Berggren and J.A. Van Couvering, 151–246. Princeton: Princeton University Press.

A major review of marine extinctions, exploring the patterns of ecological change that can be deduced from the fossil record. The pattern can be explained by a combination of normal environmental factors such as changes in temperature, salinity, and oxygen content of the ocean during a major eustatic sea-level rise, without resorting to "neocatastrophic" explanations. Rapid evolution of marine organisms occurs as the newly created niches are partitioned. Organisms adapted to warm, stable conditions take over, and are "set up for the kill" when numerous subsequent environmental changes disrupt this stable environment.

1024. Leahy, G.D. 1987. The gradual extinction of the dinosaurs: fact or artifact? In *Fourth Symposium on Mesozoic Terrestrial Ecosystems, Short Papers*, ed. P.J. Currie and E. Koster, 142–146. Drumheller, Alta.: Tyrell Museum of Paleontology.

Both Russell (1984 [1031]) and Sloan et al. (1986 [1033]) use varying estimates of dinosaur diversity to argue about possible declines in species diversity towards the end of the Cretaceous. Problems of sample size, sampling interval and preservation bias can significantly affect such diversity estimates. The author offers an independent estimate of dinosaur diversity that shows high diversity up to the Cretaceous-Tertiary boundary event. (*See* Russell 1984 [1031] for additional cross references on species diversity and extinction.)

1025. Mackal, R.P. 1987. *A Living Dinosaur: In Search of Mokelembembe*. Leiden: E.J. Brill.

Mackal searches darkest Africa for a possible living dinosaur. He doesn't find it. (*See* Sloan et al. 1986 [1033] for additional cross references on the possibility that dinosaurs survived into the Paleocene.)

1026. Mathur, U.B. 1987. Did the dinosaurs cross over to Tertiary in India? Current *Science* 56:606–607.

A brief review of evidence supporting the existence of Tertiary dinosaurs in India. (*See* Sloan et al. 1986 [1033] for additional cross references on the possibility that dinosaurs survived into the Paleocene.)

1027. Newell, N.D. 1982. Mass extinctions—illusions or realities? In *Geological Implications of Impacts of Large Asteroids and Comets on the Earth*, ed. L.T. Silver and P.H. Schultz, 257–263. *Geological Society of America Special Paper* no. 190. Boulder: GSA.

Extinction is a common occurrence; nearly all fossil taxa are extinct. Problems of sampling, sedimentary unconformities, and correlation in the fossil record introduce errors into any attempt to interpret patterns of extinction. Most mass extinctions actually occurred over a period of millions of years, following an extended period of declines in species diversity. (*See* Quinn and Signor 1989 [997] for additional cross references on distinguishing between mass extinctions and background extinctions. *See* Russell 1984 [1031] for additional cross references on species diversity and extinction.)

1028. Retallack, G., and G.D. Leahy. 1986. Cretaceous-Tertiary dinosaur extinction. *Science* 234:1170–1171.

One of a series of four letters in this issue (running through page 1175) debating the conclusion of Sloan et al. (1986 [1033]) that Paleocene dinosaurs existed in the Hell Creek area. Sloan is taken to task for not adequately accounting for the possibility that the fossils in question are simply reworked Cretaceous fossils, and for claiming that dinosaur diversity was decreasing at the end of the Cretaceous. Includes a three page rebuttal by Sloan and Rigby. (*See* Russell 1984 [1031] for additional cross references on species diversity and extinction. *See* Sloan et al. 1986 [1033] for additional cross references on the possibility that dinosaurs survived into the Paleocene.)

1029. Rigby, J.K. jr. 1989. The last of the North American dinosaurs. In *Dinosaurs Past and Present*, Volume II, ed. S.J. Czerkas and E.C. Olson, 118–135. Los Angeles: Natural History Museum of Los Angeles County.

Six Hell Creek sites have yielded the remains (mostly teeth) of Paleocene dinosaurs. The teeth are not reworked Cretaceous fossils; the nature of the clay-pebble conglomerate in which the fossils are found argues against it. Vertebrate fossils are rare in the overbank deposits, and when dinosaur fossils are found there are no associated Cretaceous mammals. (*See* Sloan et al. 1986 [1033] for additional cross references on the possibility that dinosaurs survived into the Paleocene.)

1030. Rigby, J.K. jr., K.R. Newman, J. Smit, S. Van der Kaars, R.E. Sloan, and J.K. Rigby. 1987. Dinosaurs from the Paleocene part of the Hell Creek Formation, McCone County, Montana. *Palaios* 2:296–302.

Six Hell Creek sites have yielded the bones of Tertiary dinosaurs. The absence of Cretaceous mammals in these sediments demonstrates that they are truly Paleocene. The presence of delicate fossils that would not survive reworking, in the same matrix as supposedly reworked dinosaur remains, argues against reworking of the Tertiary dinosaur fossils. Stratigraphic and pollen evidence are used to date several sites in the Hell Creek Formation. Palynological analysis demonstrates that the Hell Creek paleoenvironment was seasonally much drier than previously believed. An open canopy woodland was composed of savannas cut by streams with limited riparian habitats. (*See* Sloan et al. 1986 [1033] for additional cross references on the possibility that dinosaurs survived into the Paleocene.)

1031. Russell, D.A. 1984. The gradual decline of the dinosaurs—fact or fallacy? *Nature* 307:360–361.

Debates about declining dinosaur diversity in the Late Cretaceous are based on an inadequate sample. When older data is added, back to 210 million years ago, there is no apparent decline in diversity. Dinosaur diversity patterns match those of modern terrestrial mammals, plants, and marine invertebrates. (For additional cross references on species diversity and extinction, *See* Dodson 1990 [590]; Bryan and Jones 1989 [981]; Russell 1982 [1003]; Signor and Lipps 1982 [1006]; Carpenter and Breithaupt 1986 [1013]; Clemens 1982 [1015]; Leahy 1987 [1024]; Newell 1982 [1027]; Retallack and Leahy 1986 [1028]; Sloan et al. 1986 [1033]; Alvarez et al. [1040].)

1032. Russell, L.S. 1965. Body temperature of dinosaurs and its relationships to their extinction. *Journal of Paleontology* 39:497–501.

Uninsulated homeothermic dinosaurs would have been unable to adjust to the gradual climatic cooling that occurred toward the end of the Mesozoic. True endotherms and cold-blooded reptiles would have been able to survive this climatic transition.

1033. Sloan, R.E., J.K. Rigby jr., L.M. Van Valen, and D. Gabriel. 1986. Gradual dinosaur extinction and simultaneous ungulate radiation in the Hell Creek Formation. *Science* 232:629–633.

Final extinction of the dinosaurs did not take place until about 40,000 years into the Paleocene, following a continuing decline in species diversity. Ungulate radiation began well in advance of dinosaur decline, and the increased competition from mammalian herbivores hastened dinosaur extinction. Sloan suggests that climatic changes and consequent deterioration of the flora contributed to the demise of the dinosaurs. Even if the theorized asteroid impact did occur, it was not the sole cause of the dinosaurs' death, although, as Sloan points out, "we are convinced it did not help them." (*See* Retallack and Leahy 1986 [1028] for a series of critical letters responding to this article, followed by a rebuttal by Sloan and Rigby. *See* Russell 1984 [1031] for additional cross references on species diversity and extinction. For additional cross references on the possible survival of dinosaurs into the Paleocene, *See* Lerbekmo et al. 1979 [993]; Smit and van der

Kaars 1984 [1008]; Argast et al. 1987 [1012]; Charig 1989 [1014]; Eaton et al. 1989 [1019]; Eberth 1990 [1020]; Fassett 1982 [1021]; Mackal 1987 [1025]; Mathur 1987 [1026]; Retallack and Leahy 1986 [1028]; Rigby 1989 [1029]; Rigby et al. 1987 [1030].)

1034. Van Valen, L.M. 1988. Paleocene dinosaurs or Cretaceous ungulates in South America. *Evolutionary Monographs* 10:1–79.

Dinosaurs survived at least one to three million years into the Paleocene in South America. Dinosaurs occur with primitive Paleocene ungulates in Bolivia and Peru (El Molino and Vilquechico Formations). This co-occurrence is in sediments which are usually described as Upper Cretaceous, but which are actually Paleocene. Also reviews evidence from other areas for Paleocene dinosaurs.

1035. Whalley, P. 1988. Insect evolution during the extinction of the Dinosauria. *Entomologia Generalis* 13:119–124

The insect fossil record does not support catastrophic changes at the Cretaceous-Tertiary boundary. The dust clouds postulated by both volcanic and asteroid-impact hypotheses would have disturbed complex insect-plant interrelationships, and affected insect diapause cycles.

ASTEROIDS, COMETS, AND METEORS

1036. Alvarez, L.W. 1983. Experimental evidence that an asteroid impact led to the extinction of many species 65 million years ago. *Proceedings of the National Academy of Sciences* 80:627–642.

Because this paper is the text of a lecture presented at the NAS annual meeting it is a less formal and more intimate look at the development of the impact theory. Responds to criticism by Clemens, Archibald, and others.

1037. Alvarez, L.W., W. Alvarez, F. Asaro, and H.V. Michel. 1980. Extraterrestrial cause for the Cretaceous-Tertiary extinction: experimental results and theoretical interpretation. *Science* 208:1095–1108.

A seminal paper, initiating the ongoing debate over the asteroid-impact theory. Iridium abundance at the Cretaceous-Tertiary boundary in Italy (Gubbio), and Denmark (Stevns Klint) is far above normal terrestrial levels. The ratios of iridium isotopes and the lack of Plutonium (^{244}Pu) in the Gubbio sample argues against a supernova origin for the anomalies. A 10 km diameter asteroid would have generated an enormous ejecta plume, capable of shutting off photosynthesis, and devastating both aquatic and terrestrial food chains. Earth-crossing asteroids are common, and an asteroid of this size could be expected to collide with the Earth once every 100 million years.

1038. Alvarez, W., L. Alvarez, F. Asaro, and H.V. Michel. 1984. The end of the Cretaceous: sharp boundary or gradual transition? *Science* 223:1183–1186.

Criticizes work by Officer and Drake (1983 [1075]) to disprove the impact theory, and labels their attempt "pleasantly nostalgic" in its desire to "return to the time before the iridium anomaly was discovered."

1039. Alvarez, W., and F. Asaro. 1990. An extraterrestrial impact. *Scientific American* 263 (October):78–84.

A good non-technical review of the impact theory. The postulated asteroid would have released kinetic energy as heat in an explosion 10,000 times as massive as that of all the nuclear weapons in the world combined. The force of the explosion would have pushed the plume past escape velocity and into low Earth orbit, where the ejecta would slowly envelop the globe in a shroud of dust. A nuclear winter would ensue, with photosynthesis halted and temperatures plummeting. Global wildfires, volcanism, and acid rain triggered by the impact would have added to the environmental chaos created by the impact itself. Still to be determined are the location and number of impacts, and the effects such impacts have on biological evolution. Followed in this issue by an article from Courtiliot arguing for a purely terrestrial cause. (*See* Courtillot 1990 [1140]. *See also* Alvarez and Asaro 1990 [1039]; Crutzen 1987 [1052]; Griffis and Chapman 1990 [1060]; Prinn and Fegley 1987 [1081] for additional references on acid rain. *See* Wolfe 1991 [1096] for additional cross references on the impact winter.)

1040. Alvarez, W., E.G. Kauffman, F. Surlyk, L.W. Alvarez, F. Asaro, and H.V. Michel. 1984. Impact theory of mass extinctions and the invertebrate fossil record. *Science* 223:1135–1141.

Both gradualistic and catastrophic extinction play a role in evolution. Many of the marine invertebrates that disappear at the Cretaceous-Tertiary boundary had been in decline for some time, but reexamination of published data shows that four of these groups (ammonites, cheilostomate bryozoans, brachiopods, and bivalves) show an abrupt truncation at the Cretaceous-Tertiary boundary. (*See* Russell 1984 [1031] for additional cross references on species diversity and extinction.)

1041. Alvarez, W., and R.A. Muller. 1984. Evidence from crater ages for periodic impacts on the Earth. *Nature* 308:718–720.

Large impact craters show a 28.4 million year cycle. Within the limits of statistical error, this fits the phase of mass extinctions in the fossil record. The probability that this precise a fit could be random is one in a thousand.

1042. Berner, R.A., and G.P. Landis. 1988. Gas bubbles in fossil amber as possible indicators of the major gas composition of ancient air. *Science* 239:1406–1409.

Gas bubbles trapped in amber might be a time capsule for paleoatmospheres. Measured oxygen levels in Late Cretaceous amber bubbles are relatively high, 30% higher than today. Although the authors do not discuss the implications, an oxygen-rich atmosphere would have contributed to the global wildfires indicated by the soot layer at the Cretaceous-Tertiary boundary. (*See* Cerling 1989 [1050] for a critique. *See also*

Melosh et al. 1990 [1073] for additional cross references on the oxygen content of amber and global wildfires at the K-T boundary.)

1043. Bohor, B.F., E.E. Foord, P.J. Modreski, and D.M. Triplehorn. 1984. Mineralogic evidence for an impact at the Cretaceous-Tertiary boundary. *Science* 224:867–869.

Describes shocked quartz grains from a Montana claystone layer at the Cretaceous-Tertiary boundary. Planar features, traces of stishovite, reduced refractive index and asterism of the grains are similar to grains with shock metamorphoses in meteorite craters [*See* 1044].

1044. Bohor, B.F., P.J. Modreski, and E.E. Foord. 1987. Shocked quartz in the Cretaceous-Tertiary boundary clays: evidence for a global distribution. *Science* 236:705–709.

Shocked quartz grains are reported from the Cretaceous-Tertiary boundary at five European sites, the northern Pacific, and New Zealand. The grains show reduced refractive index, streaking in x-ray diffraction plates, and distinctive lamellae, all characteristic of shocked quartz. The grains are part of the ejecta cloud thrown up by the boundary impact event [*See* 1043].

1045. Bohor, B.F., D.M. Triplehorn, D.J. Nichols, and H.T. Millard jr. 1987. Dinosaurs, spherules, and the "magic" layer: a new K-T boundary clay site in Wyoming. *Geology* 15:896–899.

Describes a new Cretaceous-Tertiary boundary clay layer associated with the Lance Formation. The kaolinite claystone contains hollow goyazite spherules, covered by a smectitic layer with shocked minerals and an iridium anomaly. The spherules originated in the impact event.

1046. Boslough, M.B. 1991. Shock modification and chemistry and planetary geologic processes. *Annual Review of Earth and Planetary Sciences* 19:101–130.

Reviews the geochemical effects of meteorite impacts, including the shock metamorphosis of minerals.

1047. Bourgeois, J., T.A. Hansen, P.L. Wiberg, and E.G. Kauffman. 1988. A tsunami deposit at the Cretaceous-Tertiary Boundary in Texas. *Science* 241:567–570.

Describes an immense tsunami found near the Brazos River in Texas. An unusual sandstone bed shows evidence of a tidal wave 150 to 300 feet (50–100 m) high! This could have been caused by the postulated 10 km diameter bolide striking in deep ocean as much as 5,000 km away. (*See also* Florentin et al. 1991 [1054]; Hildebrand and Boynton 1990 [1061] for additional information on the tsunami. See Hildebrand and Boynton 1990 [1061] for additional cross references on proposed impact sites.)

1048. Brooks, R.R., R.D. Reeves, X.H. Yang, D.E. Ryan, J. Holzbecher, J.D. Collen, V.E. Neall, and J. Lee. 1984. Elemental anomalies at the Cretaceous-Tertiary boundary, Woodside Creek, New Zealand. *Science* 226:539–542.

Iridium and other siderophile elements at this New Zealand Cretaceous-Tertiary boundary site show a significant enrichment over non-boundary sediments. The elemental composition is very similar to that of Danish Cretaceous-Tertiary boundary shales.

1049. Brouwers, E.M., W.A. Clemens, R.A. Spicer, T.A. Ager, L.D. Carter, and W.V. Sliter. 1987. Dinosaurs on the North Slope, Alaska: high latitude, Latest Cretaceous environments. *Science* 237:1608–1610.

The "impact winter" predicted by Alvarez's asteroid theory would not have killed the dinosaurs. Abundant remains of herbivores and carnivores on the Alaskan North Slope shows that dinosaurs could thrive in colder climates with pronounced seasonal variation. The deltaic environment was dominated by mild to cold-temperate herbaceous vegetation, with deciduous coniferous trees and gymnosperms on higher ground. The deciduous vegetation would have posed an annual problem for herbivores, but the presence of juveniles argues against annual migrations. (*See* Wolfe 1991 [1096] for additional cross references on the impact winter. For additional references on polar dinosaurs and migration, *See*

Rich and Rich 1989 [381]; Paul 1988 [439]; Dodson et al. 1980 [591]; Dunham et al. 1989 [592]; Hotton 1980 [727]; Davies 1987 [1018]; Rich et al. 1988 [1083])

1050. Cerling, T.E. 1989. Does the gas content of amber reveal the composition of palaeoatmospheres? *Nature* 339:695–696.

Refutes Berner and Landis (1988 [1042]). Bubbles in amber do not accurately reflect the gas content of ancient atmospheres. The first crush yields a pulse of oxygen, which fades with further crushing. Oxygen may react chemically with intact and crushed amber. Measured oxygen levels under repeated crushing are actually lower, not higher, than normal atmospheric levels. (*See* Melosh et al. 1990 [1073] for additional cross references on the oxygen content of amber and global wildfires at the K-T boundary.)

1051. Croft, S.K. 1982. A first-order estimate of shock heating and vaporization in oceanic impacts. In *Geological Implications of Impacts of Large Asteroids and Comets on the Earth*, ed. L.T. Silver and P.H. Schultz, 143–152. *Geological Society of America Special Paper* no. 190. Boulder: GSA.

Uses a computer model to estimate the effect of an asteroid impact in the ocean. The amount of water vapor injected into the atmosphere increases as the square of the impact velocity. This is an entire order of magnitude higher than the amount of rock that would be vaporized by the same impact on solid ground. Much of this water vapor, in a point-source impact, would super-saturate the local atmosphere and immediately condense and fall back as rain. The model's predictions change substantially if the assumption of infinite ocean depth at the impact point is replaced by finite ocean depth. Because of the strong interdependence between asteroid size, composition, and velocity, and oceanic depth at the impact point, scenarios of climatic effects resulting from an asteroid impact are subject to a high degree of uncertainty. (*See also* Melosh 1982 [1072]; O'Keefe and Ahrens 1989 [1076] for oceanic versus terrestrial impacts.)

1052. Crutzen, P. 1987. Acid rain at the K/T boundary. *Nature* 330:108–109.

Nitric acid rain produced by the bolide impact would have destroyed the terrestrial biosphere and dissolved calcareous plankton. Reviews several studies on this phenomena, the greenhouse effect caused by increased atmospheric carbon dioxide, and the photochemical smog produced by the postulated global wildfires. (*See also* Alvarez and Asaro 1990 [1039]; Griffis and Chapman 1990 [1060]; Prinn and Fegley 1987 [1081] for additional references on acid rain. See O'Keefe and Ahrens 1989 [1076] for additional cross references on the greenhouse effect.)

1053. Dietz, R.S. 1991. Demise of the dinosaurs: a mystery solved? *Astronomy*, July, 30–37.

Provides a personalized account of the search for the Cretaceous-Tertiary boundary impact crater. Dietz discusses the merits of several candidates, including the Manson Impact Structure, Hildebrand's Colombia Basin crater (Hildebrand and Boynton 1990 [1061]), and reports from Cuba, Haiti, and Texas (Bourgeois 1988 [1047]). The latest discovery off the Yucatan coast, is the most likely impact structure yet reported. There has been some speculation that this Yucatan impact might have caused the vast arc of cenotes, large sinkhole structures that were used as sacred wells for Mayan sacrifices. (*See* Hildebrand and Boynton 1990 [1061] for additional cross references on proposed impact sites.)

1054. Florentin, J-M., R. Maurrasse, and G. Sen. 1991. Impacts, tsunamis, and the Haitian Cretaceous-Tertiary boundary layer. *Science* 252:1690–1693.

Describes the formation by impact of the complex structure of boundary sediments in Haiti's Beloc Formation. This bed contains the thickest ejecta layer and the largest microtektites discovered to date. Impact origin of the boundary layer bed is strongly supported by the simultaneous occurrence of shocked quartz, microtektites, and an iridium anomaly. Evidence suggests that giant tsunamis resulted from the Caribbean impact, possibly occurring in two successive sets.

(*See also* Bourgeois et al. 1988 [1047]; Hildebrand and Boynton 1990 [1061] for additional information on the tsunami. *See* Hildebrand and Boynton 1990 [1061] for additional cross references on proposed impact sites.)

1055. Ganapathy, R. 1980. A major meteorite impact on the earth 65 million years ago: evidence from the Cretaceous-Tertiary boundary clay. *Science* 209:921–923.

Nine noble metals appear in extraterrestrial concentrations in Danish clay at the Cretaceous-Tertiary boundary. The amounts are five to one-hundred times greater than normal terrestrial concentrations. A terrestrial origin might be acceptable, but only if iridium were enhanced and the other elements were not.

1056. Gerstl, S.A.W., and A. Zardecki. 1982. Reduction of photosynthetically active radiation under extreme stratospheric aerosol loads. In *Geological Implications of Impacts of Large Asteroids and Comets on the Earth*, ed. L.T. Silver and P.H. Schultz, 201–210. Geological Society of America Special Paper no. 190. Boulder: GSA.

Generates a computer model to calculate the effects on photosynthetic organisms of the sunlight deprivation that would be caused by an asteroid ejecta cloud. Impact from a 0.4 to 3 km diameter asteroid would deposit a total stratosphere aerosol load between 1 and 4×10^{16} grams. This would decrease photosynthesis to 10^{-3} of normal.

1057. Gilmore, J.S., J.D. Knight, C.J. Orth, C.L. Pillmore, and R.H. Tschudy. 1984. Trace element patterns at a non-marine Cretaceous-Tertiary boundary. *Nature* 307:224–228.

Raton Basin deposits from a Cretaceous-Tertiary boundary freshwater coal swamp show anomalous levels of iridium, scandium, titanium and chromium. The uniformity of the clay bed suggests that the fallout came from "a common source at a considerable distance." While the iridium levels could be explained by volcanic action, the chromium levels are far too high to be of volcanic origin.

1058. Grieve, R.A.F. 1987. Terrestrial impact structures. *Annual Review of Earth and Planetary Sciences* 15:245–270.

Describes the morphology, shock metamorphism, and formation of impact structures, and lists known impact craters. There is "good circumstantial evidence" for a large impact at the Cretaceous-Tertiary boundary. (*See* Hildebrand and Boynton 1990 [1061] for additional cross references on proposed impact sites.)

1059. Griffis, K., and D.J. Chapman. 1988. Survival of phytoplankton under prolonged darkness: implications for the Cretaceous/Tertiary boundary darkness hypothesis. *Palaeogeography, Palaeoclimatology, Palaeoecology* 67:305–314.

Modern planktonic organisms were subjected to long periods of darkness to simulate the dust shroud of the impact theory. Two species representative of Cretaceous organisms survived eight weeks of darkness. If the impact-related darkness was of two to three months duration, the hypothesis fits. If, however, the darkness lasted longer, the experimental and fossil data would not fit the hypothesis. (*See* [1060]. *See also* Wolfe 1991 [1096] for additional cross references on the impact winter.)

1060. Griffis, K., and D.J. Chapman. 1990. Modeling Cretaceous-Tertiary boundary events with extant photosynthetic plankton: effects of impact-related acid rain. *Lethaia* 23:379–383.

Four living species of phytoplankton, were tested for their response to acid rain. Their reaction to acidic conditions indicates that the hypothesized Cretaceous-Tertiary boundary acid rain was either not as long or not as severe as predicted. (*See* [1059]. *See also* Alvarez and Asaro 1990 [1039]; Crutzen 1987 [1052]; Prinn and Fegley 1987 [1081] for additional references on acid rain.)

1061. Hildebrand, A.R., and W.V. Boynton. 1990. Proximal Cretaceous-Tertiary boundary impact deposits in the Caribbean. *Science* 248:843–847.

The Colombian basin may hold the smoking gun of the impact theory. Seismic reflection shows a buried 300 km structure that may be the impact crater of the sought after Cretaceous-Tertiary boundary bolide. Boundary sediments on Haiti 50 centimeters thick are twenty-five times thicker than normal, indicating that the impact was within 1,000 km. Remains of a monstrous tsunami can be also identified in Cuba, where the boundary sediments are up to 450 meters thick. (For additional cross references on proposed impact sites, See Bourgeois et al. 1988 [1947]; Dietz 1991 [1053]; Florentin et al. 1991 [1054]; Grieve 1987 [1058]; Hildebrand and Penfield 1990 [1062]; Izett 1990 [1066]; Kunk et al. 1989 [1068]; Shoemaker 1983 [1086]; Sigurdsson et al. 1991 [1087]; Smit 1991 [1089].)

1062. Hildebrand, A.R., and G.T. Penfield. 1990. A buried 180 km-diameter probable impact crater on the Yucatan Peninsula, Mexico. *EOS, Transactions of the AGU* 71:1425.

Although abstracts are generally out of scope, this short note describes an important discovery soon to be published in more complete form. The authors describe a huge crater centered off the Yucatan coast near Chicxulub, with a thick ejecta blanket containing shocked quartz grains. The immense crater is the largest yet discovered. (*See also* Bourgeois et al. 1988 [1047]; Florentin et al. 1991 [1054] for additional information on the tsunami. See Hildebrand and Boynton 1990 [1061] for additional cross references on proposed impact sites.)

1063. Hsü, K.J. 1980. Terrestrial catastrophe caused by cometary impact at the end of the Cretaceous. *Nature* 285:201–203.

Cyanide from a cometary impact in the ocean killed calcareous marine plankton, and atmospheric heating from the falling comet killed the dinosaurs.

1064. Hsü, K.J. et al.1982. Mass mortality and its environmental and evolutionary consequences. *Science* 216:249–256.

Hsü joins nineteen (!) co-authors in analysis of Deep Sea Drilling Project samples. The data is consistent with a cometary impact. A sharp decrease in calcium carbonate in sediments at the Cretaceous-Tertiary boundary suggests a more acid ocean or decreased productivity. The decrease in oceanic carbon dioxide and consequent increase in atmospheric carbon dioxide could have created a greenhouse effect, with a temperature rise of 1.5–4 °C. This temperature increase would have led to extinction by thermal stress of any dinosaurs surviving the Cretaceous-Tertiary boundary. (*See* O'Keefe and Ahrens 1989 [1076] for additional cross references on the greenhouse effect.)

1065. Hut, P., W. Alvarez, W.P. Elder, T. Hansen, E.G. Kauffman, G. Keller, E.M. Shoemaker, and P.R. Weissman. 1987. Comet showers as a cause of mass extinctions. *Nature* 329:118–126.

Multiple cometary impacts could explain why mass extinctions seem to take place over long intervals of one to three million years, and proceed in a stepwise fashion. Collision with a comet would have the same effect as collision with an asteroid.

1066. Izett, G.A. 1990. The Cretaceous/Tertiary boundary interval, Raton Basin, Colorado and New Mexico, and its content of shock-metamorphosed minerals; evidence relevant to the K/T boundary impact-extinction theory. *Geological Society of America Special Paper* no. 249.

An impact layer and a lower boundary layer claystone can be identified in Raton Basin sediments. The claystone shows little evidence of impact or volcanic origin, other than a small amount of shocked mineral grains and mobile iridium. The impact layer contains extensive shocked mineral grains consistent with the impact theory. However, the thickness of the impact layer does not reflect distance from the impact site, nor is the layer as thick as previously believed. The claystone layer is not altered impact ejecta. This substantially reduces the 10 km size postulated for the asteroid, as well as the size of its impact crater. The Manson Impact Structure is the most likely impact site. (*See* Hildebrand and Boynton 1990 [1061] for additional cross references on proposed impact sites.)

1067. Izett, G.A., G.B. Dalrymple, and L.W. Snee. 1991. ^{40}Ar/^{39}Ar age of Cretaceous-Tertiary boundary tektites from Haiti. *Science* 252:1539–1542.

Argon dating of tektites from Haiti's Beloc Formation give an age for the Cretaceous-Tertiary boundary of 64.5 million years ago, plus or minus 0.2 my. These tektites are contemporary with the global iridium anomaly.

1068. Kunk, M.J., G.A. Izett, R.A. Haugerud, and J.F. Sutter. 1989. ^{40}Ar-^{39}Ar dating of the Manson Impact Structure: A Cretaceous-Tertiary boundary crater candidate. *Science* 244:1565–1568.

This 35 km diameter Iowa impact structure, the largest known in the United States, may be the Cretaceous-Tertiary boundary bolide impact site. Argon dating gives an age of 65.7 million years, plus or minus 1 my. (*See* Hildebrand and Boynton 1990 [1061] for additional cross references on proposed impact sites.)

1069. Kyte, F.T., and J.T. Wasson. 1986. Accretion rate of extraterrestrial matter: iridium deposited 33 to 67 million years ago. *Science* 232:1225–1229.

Iridium peaks only at the Cretaceous-Tertiary boundary in a nine-meter sample of Pacific abyssal clay. The peaks are far too small to support claims for comet showers at the Cretaceous-Tertiary boundary.

1070. Luck, J.M., and K.K. Turekian. 1983. Osmium-187/ Osmium-186 in manganese nodules and the Cretaceous-Tertiary boundary. *Science* 222:613–615.

The ratio between isotopes of osmium at the Stevns Klint (Denmark) and Raton Basin Cretaceous-Tertiary boundary suggest a meteoritic origin.

1071. McHone, J.F., R.A. Nieman, C.F. Lewis, and A.M. Yates. 1989. Stishovite at the Cretaceous-Tertiary Boundary, Raton, New Mexico. *Science* 243:1182–1184.

Stishovite is a form of silica associated with impact events. It does not occur at volcanic sites. Stishovite is found in mineral grains at the Raton Basin Cretaceous-Tertiary boundary.

1072. Melosh, H.J. 1982. The mechanics of large meteoroid impacts in the Earth's oceans. In *Geological Implications of Impacts of Large Asteroids and Comets on the Earth*, ed. L.T. Silver and P.H. Schultz, 121–127. *Geological Society of America Special Paper* no. 190. Boulder: GSA.

An oceanic impact would have different consequences from a terrestrial impact. An immense cloud of shock-vaporized water would be produced by an oceanic impact, generated by a steam explosion. A 10 km asteroid would have created a 500 km^3 steam bubble, driving a "violent vapor plume" of silica and water vapor several hundred kilometers into the atmosphere. This plume would have dispersed to form a global cloud. (*See also* Croft 1982 [1051]; O'Keefe and Ahrens 1989 [1076] for additional references on oceanic versus terrestrial impacts.)

1073. Melosh, H.J., N.M. Schneider, K.J. Zahnie, and D. Latham. 1990. Ignition of global wildfires at the Cretaceous/Tertiary boundary. *Nature* 343:251–254.

Reentry of ejecta is accompanied by the release of large amounts of thermal energy. Sharp increases in radiation flux following the bolide impact triggered global firestorms. Calculations show that for up to several hours following the impact, global temperatures may have reached the equivalent of a domestic oven set on broil! Wildfires would explain the layer of soot found at the Cretaceous-Tertiary boundary in several locations. (For additional references on the oxygen content of amber and global wildfires at the K-T boundary, *See* Berner and Landis 1988 [1042]; Cerling 1989 [1050]; Venkatesan and Dahl 1989 [1093]; Wolbach et al. 1985 [1095]; Tschudy et al. 1884 [1133]; Moses 1989 [1146].)

1074. Napier, W.M., and S.V.M. Clube. 1979. A theory of terrestrial catastrophism. *Nature* 282:455–459.

As the Sun passes through the spiral arms of the Milky Way Galaxy, planetesimals in the spiral arms may bombard the Earth. Impact frequencies in the fossil record reflect passages through these spiral arms. (*See also* Clube and Napier 1984 [1099].)

1075. Officer, C.B., and C.L. Drake. 1983. The Cretaceous-Tertiary transition. *Science* 219:1383–1390.

A combination of terrestrial phenomena, such as volcanism, regression of the inland seas and climatic change, can adequately account for the Cretaceous-Tertiary boundary faunal transition. The age and nature of that transition varies with the site studied and the methods used to examine it. High iridium levels are not necessarily due to extraterrestrial events. (*See* Alvarez et al. 1984 [1038] for a critique.)

1076. O'Keefe, J.D., and T.J. Ahrens. 1989. Impact production of CO_2 by the Cretaceous-Tertiary extinction bolide and the resultant heating of the Earth. *Nature* 338:247–249.

If the asteroid struck in shallow marine sediments rich in carbonates, the impact would have increased atmospheric carbon dioxide by a factor of two to ten times at a conservative estimate. This in turn would have increased global temperatures 2–10°K for about 10^5 years. The resulting greenhouse effect would have led to mass extinctions. (*See also* Croft 1982 [1051]; Melosh 1982 [1072] for oceanic versus terrestrial impacts. For additional cross references on the greenhouse effect at the Cretaceous-Tertiary boundary, *See* Crutzen 1987 [1052]; Hsü et al. 1982 [1064]; Pollack et al. 1983 [1080]; Prinn and Fegley 1987 [1081]; Wolfe 1991 [1096]; Hsü and McKenzie 1985 [1117]; McLean 1978 [1121]; Courtillot 1990 [1140]; McLean 1985 [1145].)

1077. Orth, C.J., J.S. Gilmore, J.D. Knight, C.L. Pillmore, R.H. Tschudy, and J.E. Fassett. 1981. Iridium abundance anomaly at the palynological Cretaceous/Tertiary boundary in northern New Mexico. *Science* 214:1341–1343.

The iridium anomaly in the Raton Basin measures up to 5,000 parts per trillion. Normal background levels at the site range from 2–40 ppt. This anomaly coincides with the disappearance of several Cretaceous pollens.

1078. Owen, M.R., and M.H. Anders. 1988. Evidence from cathodoluminescence for non-volcanic origin of shocked quartz at the Cretaceous/Tertiary boundary. *Nature* 334:145–147.

Cathodoluminescence studies of shocked quartz at the Cretaceous-Tertiary boundary show that the grains came from a variety of sedimentary, metamorphic, and igneous rocks. The grains show very little of the pale blue color typical of volcanic quartz, and are consistent with a bolide impact.

1079. Pal, P.C., and K.M. Creer. 1986. Geomagnetic reversals, spurts and episodes of extraterrestrial catastrophism. *Nature* 320:148–150.

Spurts in the frequency of geomagnetic polarity reversals occur at 30 million year intervals, and are associated with extinction events. The reversals are most likely due to turbulence in the Earth's core, due to extraterrestrial bombardment.

1080. Pollack, J.B., O.B. Toon, T.P. Ackerman, C.P. McKay, and R.P. Turco. 1983. Environmental effects of an impact-generated dust cloud: implications for the Cretaceous-Tertiary extinctions. *Science* 219:287–289.

Mathematical models of the effects of a large dust cloud show that oceanic extinctions could have been caused by the reduction or cessation of photosynthesis. The oceans would only have cooled a few degrees, but continents could have cooled up to 40°K. Reduced visibility and consequent inability to forage effectively, coupled with drastic cooling, would have annihilated larger land animals. The predicted cooling effect of the impact cloud contradicts other projections of a greenhouse warming effect. (*See* O'Keefe and Ahrens 1989 [1076] for additional cross references on the greenhouse effect. *See* Wolfe 1991 [1096] for additional cross references on the impact winter.)

1081. Prinn, R.G., and B. Fegley jr. 1987. Bolide impacts, acid rain, and biospheric traumas at the Cretaceous-Tertiary boundary. *Earth and Planetary Science Letters* 83:1–15.

Acid rain at the Cretaceous-Tertiary boundary might explain the observed patterns of extinction. Carbonate-buffered lakes and burrows would have acted as refugia. Either an asteroid or a comet impact would produce acid rain, although an asteroid impact would have a greater effect, with a resulting global pH of 4–5. Acid rain would have damaged plants, caused severe lung damage in animals, and led to toxic poisoning from the mobilization of heavy metals in the soil. Large terrestrial herbivores would have starved, and calcareous plankton and other calcareous organisms would have dissolved. Large amounts of carbon dioxide would have entered the atmosphere from the ocean. (*See also* Alvarez and Asaro 1990 [1039]; Crutzen 1987 [1052]; Griffis and Chapman 1990 [1060] for additional references on acid rain. *See* O'Keefe and Ahrens 1989 [1076] for additional cross references on the greenhouse effect.)

1082. Rampino, M.R., and R.S. Strothers. 1984. Terrestrial mass extinctions, cometary impacts, and the sun's motion perpendicular to the galactic plane. *Nature* 308:709–712.

Ized 30 million year cycle of mass extinction proposed by Raup and Sepkoski (1986 [999]; 1988 [1000]) fits the pattern of the Sun's vertical oscillation about the galactic plane, which takes about 33 million years, plus or minus 3 my. Encounters with vast interstellar dust clouds, which are concentrated along the galactic plane, could perturb comets and send them hurtling into the inner solar system. (*See also* Schwartz and James 1984 [1085].)

1083. Rich, P.V., T.H. Rich, B.E. Wagstaff, J. McEwen-Mason, C.B. Douthitt, R.T. Gregory, and E.A. Felton. 1988. Evidence for low temperatures and biologic diversity in Cretaceous high latitudes of Australia. *Science* 242:1403–1406.

Southeastern Australia was situated in polar latitudes during the Cretaceous. Mean annual temperatures were less than 5°C, with pronounced seasonality. The presence of a diverse dinosaur fauna indicates that dinosaurs could survive lengthy periods of low temperatures and low light levels (one to two months of darkness each year). This argues against cold and darkness being primary factors in dinosaur extinction. (For additional references on polar dinosaurs and migration, *See* Rich and Rich 1989 [381]; Paul 1988 [439]; Hotton 1980 [727]; Davies 1987 [1018]; Brouwers et al. 1987 [1049].)

1084. Schultz, P.H., and D.E. Gault. 1982. Impact ejecta dynamics in an atmosphere: experimental results and extrapolation. In *Geological Implications of Impacts of Large Asteroids and Comets on the Earth*, ed. L.T. Silver and P.H. Schultz, 153–174. *Geological Society of America Special Paper* no. 190. Boulder: GSA.

Experimental impacts of 0.635 cm aluminum projectiles into fine pumice dust allows detailed observation of the ejecta curtain. Extrapolates several experimental observations to estimate the possible effects of a large-size asteroid impact. The results suggest that only a small amount of the fine ejecta produced by the initial impact would be globally distributed. The reentry of high speed ejecta, however, would be "more than sufficient" to affect the photochemical balance of the atmosphere and reduce surface solar flux. (*See* Wolfe 1991 [1096] for additional cross references on the impact winter.)

1085. Schwartz, R.D., and P.B. James. 1984. Periodic mass extinctions and the Sun's oscillation about the galactic plane. *Nature* 308:712–713.

Stars in the disk oscillate about the galactic plane. One-half of the Sun's oscillation period is 31 million years, close to Raup and Sepkoski's (1986 [999]; 1988 [1000]) theorized 26 million year cycle. Changes in cosmic radiation with movement through the galactic plane might have caused dinosaur extinction. (*See also* Rampino and Strothers 1984 [1082].)

1086. Shoemaker, E.M. 1983. Asteroid and comet bombardment of the earth. *Annual Review of Earth and Planetary Sciences* 11:461–494.

The mean probability of collision with an Earth orbit-crossing asteroid is about one collision every 3.2 million years. Reviews the history of extraterrestrial impacts and impact craters, and demonstrates methods to calculate impact speed, impact energy, and cratering rates. The threshold size at which impacts would affect the biosphere is unknown. Objects the size of Alvarez's asteroid (10 km diameter) struck the Earth about once every 0.5×10^8 years during the Phanerozoic. The 20 km diameter asteroid 433 Eros has a 20% probability of hitting the Earth sometime in the next 400 million years. (*See* Hildebrand and Boynton 1990 [1061] for additional cross references on proposed impact sites.)

1087. Sigurdsson, H., S. D'Hondt, M.A. Arthur, T.J. Bralower, J.C. Zachos, M. van Fossen, and J.E.T. Channell. 1991. Glass from the Cretaceous/ Tertiary boundary in Haiti. *Nature* 349:482–487.

A thick layer of tektite-like glass near Haiti is evidence of a nearby impact event. The silica-rich glass, the oldest known impact glass, indicates that the impact occurred on the continental shelf. A high-calcium content glass was also produced by the fusion of marl sediment. Both the Yucatan and Manson impact structures could account for this evidence. The event is calculated to have released about 10^{15} moles of CO_2 from vaporized marl sediments. (*See* Hildebrand and Boynton 1990 [1061] for additional cross references on proposed impact sites.)

1088. Silver, L.T., and P.H. Schultz, eds. 1982. *Geological Implications of Impacts of Large Asteroids and Comets on the Earth. Geological Society of America Special Paper* no. 190. Boulder: GSA.

The proceedings of the "Snowbird Conference", held at Snowbird, Utah, in 1981, are a watershed for later developments in the debate over the impact scenario. Forty-eight papers from that conference comprise this GSA Special Paper, and several of these papers are analyzed in this section. *See* Chapman (1989 [983]) and Sharpton and Ward [1153] for information on Snowbird II.

1089. Smit, J. 1991. Where did it happen? *Nature* 349:461–462.
A short review of current efforts to locate the impact site of the Cretaceous-Tertiary boundary asteroid. The most likely candidate is the immense Chicxulub crater off the Yucatan coast. (*See* Hildebrand and Boynton 1990 [1061] for additional cross references on proposed impact sites.)

1090. Smit, J., and G. Klaver. 1981. Sanidine spherules at the Cretaceous-Tertiary boundary indicate a large impact event. *Nature* 292:47–49.
Spherules of once-molten potassium-feldspar sanidine appear in Cretaceous-Tertiary boundary clays at Caravaca, Spain. They provide evidence that an extraterrestrial impact occurred, but the potassium levels in the spherules are more consistent with a cometary impact than with a meteorite.

1091. Toon, O.B., J.B. Pollack, T.P. Ackerman, R.P. Turco, C.P. McKay, and M.S. Liu. 1982. Evolution of an impact-generated dust cloud and its effects on the atmosphere. In *Geological Implications of Impacts of Large Asteroids and Comets on the Earth*, ed. L.T. Silver and P.H. Schultz, 187–200. *Geological Society of America Special Paper* no. 190. Boulder: GSA.
Computer simulation of an optically thick dust cloud predicts that large amounts of dust would remain in the atmosphere for three to six months. Such a dust cloud would have created light levels too low for vision for one to six months, and light levels too low for photosynthesis for two months to one year. Terrestrial surface temperatures would have dropped below freezing for about four months to two years. Speculates on other physical and biotic effects of the hypothetical dust cloud. (*See* Wolfe 1991 [1096] for additional cross references on the impact winter.)

1092. Tredoux, M., M.J. De Wit, R.J. Hart, N.M. Lindsay, B. Verhagen, and J.P.F. Sellschop. 1989. Chemostratigraphy across the Cretaceous-Tertiary boundary and a critical assessment of the iridium anomaly. *Journal of Geology* 97:585–605.

Our understanding of the platinum-group elements (PGE), which includes iridium, is insufficient to use PGE's as evidence of a global impact event. The data are consistent with an impact in the Northern Hemisphere, but there is no solid evidence to support an exclusively extraterrestrial origin. Most studies do not examine the concentration and distribution of PGE elements other than iridium. Iridium predominance is an analytical artifact of Instrumental Neutron Activation Analysis (INAA), the most routinely used method. INAA has a much lower detection limit for iridium than for other PGE elements.

1093. Venkatesan, M.I., and J. Dahl. 1989. Organic geochemical evidence for global fires at the Cretaceous/Tertiary boundary. *Nature* 338:57–60.

Samples of Cretaceous-Tertiary boundary sediments from Gubbio (Italy), Stevns Klint (Denmark), and Woodside Creek (New Zealand) show high levels of PAH (polycyclic aromatic compounds). The nature of PAH compounds in the samples is consistent with the hypothesis that global wildfires occurred at the Cretaceous-Tertiary boundary. (*See* Melosh et al. 1990 [1073] for additional cross references on the oxygen content of amber and global wildfires at the K-T boundary.)

1094. Wallace, M.W., V.A. Gostin, and R.R. Keays. 1990. Acraman impact ejecta and host shales: evidence for low-temperature mobilization of iridium and other platinoids. *Geology* 18:132–135.

Iridium and other platinum group elements (PGE) show a significant diagenetic mobility in impact ejecta horizons in Australia's Late Proterozoic Bunyeroo Formation. The impact ejecta are definitely of meteoric origin. Iridium and other PGE's have been mobilized and enriched during diagenesis.

1095. Wolbach, W.S., R.S. Lewis, and E. Anders. 1985. Cretaceous extinctions; evidence for wildfires and search for meteoric material. *Science* 230:167–170.

Samples of Cretaceous-Tertiary boundary clay from Stevns Klint (Denmark), Caravaca (Spain) and Woodside Creek (New Zealand) contain a distinct layer of soot. The soot is estimated to be equivalent to the combustion of 10% of the amount of fixed organic carbon in the entire modern biosphere! The amount of soot involved would be far more effective in lowering global temperatures than the dust cloud generated by impact. (*See* Wolfe 1991 [1096] for additional cross references on the impact winter. *See* Melosh et al. 1990 [1073] for additional cross references on the oxygen content of amber and global wildfires at the K-T boundary.)

1096. Wolfe, J.A. 1991. Palaeobotanical evidence for a June 'impact winter' at the Cretaceous/Tertiary boundary. *Nature* 352:420–423.

Evidence of a brief impact winter from impact-generated dust clouds should be found in terrestrial environments. Leaves from a lily pond at the Cretaceous-Tertiary boundary at Teapot Dome, Wyoming, show evidence of freezing in June from an impact winter that lasted at least one to two weeks. A second impact followed about eight weeks later, burying the leaves killed by the freeze. The impact winter probably did not affect vegetation as profoundly as the wet greenhouse period that followed it. (*See* O'Keefe and Ahrens 1989 [1076] for additional cross references on the greenhouse effect. For additional references on the impact winter, *See* Alvarez and Asaro 1990 [1039]; Brouwers et al. 1987 [1049]; Griffis and Chapman 1988 [1059]; Pollack et al. 1983 [1080]; Schultz and Gault 1982 [1084]; Toon et al. 1982 [1091]; Wolbach et al. 1985 [1095]; Wolfe 1987 [1136].)

1097. Zahnle, K., and D. Grinspoon. 1990. Comet dust as a source of amino acids at the Cretaceous-Tertiary boundary. *Nature* 348:157–160.

Extraterrestrial amino acids at the Stevns Klint (Denmark) Cretaceous-Tertiary boundary were deposited after the boundary impact itself. The most likely source of the amino acids is dust from a comet, a portion of which actually impacted the Earth.

1098. Zhao, M., and J.L. Bada. 1989. Extraterrestrial amino acids in Cretaceous/Tertiary boundary sediments at Stevns Klint, Denmark. *Nature* 339:463–465.

Certain non-protein amino acids are rare on Earth, but common in carbonaceous chondrite meteorites. Two of these amino acids are present in the Cretaceous-Tertiary boundary sediments at Stevns Klint, a signature of an extraterrestrial impact.

NEMESIS, THE DEATH STAR

1099. Clube, S.V.M., and W.M. Napier. 1984. Terrestrial catastrophism—Nemesis or galaxy? *Nature* 311:635–636.

There are several astrophysical problems with the hypothetical orbit of Nemesis. The system as postulated is inherently unstable, and might not even survive a single revolution. (*See* Napier and Clube 1979 [1074].)

1100. Davis, M., P. Hut, and R.A. Muller. 1984. Extinction by periodic comet showers. *Nature* 308:715–717.

An unseen solar companion in an eccentric orbit is responsible for the periodic extinctions seen in the fossil record. The companion perturbs comets in the Oort cloud when it reaches perihelion. These comets fall inward toward the sun and some strike the Earth. Don't rush to complete your will, the solar companion won't return until about A.D. 15,000,000.

1101. Hills, J.G. 1984. Dynamical constraints on the mass and perihelion distance of Nemesis and the stability of its orbit. *Nature* 311:636–638.

Calculates the perturbation of the Oort cloud by Nemesis. The orbit of Nemesis is sufficiently eccentric to generate infalling cometary swarms in about 23% of its passages. A semimajor axis of 9×10^4 AU would result in cometary perturbation. There is also a distinct possibility that Nemesis itself could enter the planetary system, a result with a 0.15

probability over 177 computer model runs. This would generate "a catastrophe of truly cosmological proportions."

1102. Hut, P. 1984. How stable is an astronomical clock that can trigger mass extinctions on Earth? *Nature* 311:638–641.

    We cannot precisely calculate the timing of mass extinctions or the presumed orbit of Nemesis. Both calculations are fraught with uncertainties. Galactic tidal forces and the perturbations of passing stars makes it very difficult to predict the orbit of Nemesis.

1103. Muller, R. 1988. *Nemesis.* New York: Weidenfeld & Nicolson.

    A layman's guide to the development of the Nemesis hypothesis. Like Raup's book on this topic (Raup 1986 [1104]), gives a clear picture of what scientists do, and how scientific theories are shaped. Muller invented the Nemesis hypothesis, and his narrative introduces the reader to the human faces behind many of the papers in this chapter.

1104. Raup, D.M. 1986. *The Nemesis Affair: A Story of the Death of Dinosaurs and the Ways of Science.* New York: Norton.

    An excellent look at the human side of science, and its often stormy marriage with the press and the public. Raup's theories on the periodicity of extinction and the possible existence of the "death star" Nemesis are clearly explained. Gives students and laymen a look behind the scenes of the scientific enterprise, and explains how theories are formulated, tested, and debated [*See* 1103].

1105. Torbett, M.V., and R. Smoluchowski. 1984. Orbital stability of the unseen solar companion linked to periodic extinction events. *Nature* 311:641–642.

    We must look near the galactic plane for the orbit of Nemesis. Three-dimensional numerical modeling of possible orbits reveals that the orbit must be within 30° of the galactic plane, and that even this low-inclination orbit might be unstable.

1106. Whitmire, D.P., and A.A. Jackson IV. 1984. Are periodic mass extinctions driven by a distant solar companion? *Nature* 308:713–715.

Calculates the possible orbital axes and mass of Nemesis. The solar companion would have a mass in the black dwarf range, and should be observable in the infrared. This postulated companion is both smaller and more distant than the object considered in previous studies.

SUPERNOVAE

1107. Clark, D.H., W.H. McCrea, and F.R. Stephenson. 1977. Frequency of nearby supernova and climatic and biological catastrophes. *Nature* 265:318–319.

Interstellar gas clouds, of the type proposed to explain periodic extinction events, would need to be unusually compact to have the postulated effects. Such clouds are very rare, and it is most unlikely that the Sun would encounter them. The alternative hypothesis is a nearby supernova. Type II supernovae, the type most likely to be found in our passage through the galaxy's spiral arms, would occur on the average once every hundred years. A supernova would occur within 10 pc of the Sun once every 10^8 years, as the Sun crosses the spiral arms. The consequent destruction of the ozone layer would bathe the planet in lethal doses of ultraviolet radiation, and expose organisms to a hundred-fold increase in cosmic rays [*See* 1108].

1108. Hunt, G.E. 1978. Possible climatic and biological impact of nearby supernovae. *Nature* 271:430–431.

The reduction in ozone predicted by Clark et al. (1977 [1107]) as a consequence of a nearby supernova would create a pronounced cooling of the atmosphere. The estimated temperature drop, as suggested by Clark, would be sufficient to start an ice age.

1109. Ruderman, M.A. 1974. Possible consequences of nearby supernova explosions for atmospheric ozone and terrestrial life. *Science* 184:1079–1081.

Discounting direct surface effects, x-ray pulses and cosmic rays from a nearby supernova would temporarily deplete the ozone layer. This would result in a sharp increase in skin cancers, mutation rates, and possibly toxic levels of Vitamin D. Nocturnal animals (perhaps mammals?) would be relatively immune to these problems.

1110. Ruderman, M., and J.W. Truran. 1980. Possible transfer of lunar matter to earth due to a nearby supernova. *Nature* 284:328–329.

A Type I supernova explosion would yield an intense barrage of gamma rays. These gamma rays would not only directly harm terrestrial life, but also indirectly damage the biosphere. The explosion would be sufficient to blow off the uppermost layer of the lunar surface, some of which would be captured by Earth's atmosphere. This lunar soil should show enriched iridium content.

1111. Russell, D., and W. Tucker. 1971. Supernovae and the extinction of the dinosaurs. *Nature* 229:553–554.

A supernova should explode within a distance of 100 light years every 50 million years. Atmospheric disturbance from a supernova would disrupt thermal stratification in the ocean, and lead to several years of low global temperatures. (*See* Russell 1979 [1002].)

1112. Terry, K.D., and W.H. Tucker. 1968. Biologic effects of supernovae. *Science* 159:421–423.

One type II supernova occurs in our galaxy every 50 years. We would be exposed to a 50 r dose of cosmic radiation once every 50 million years. A shower of cosmic rays from a nearby supernova would kill animals, but have little effect on vegetation (except at extremely high dosage levels). Mutation rates would increase in the survivors.

CLIMATE AND VEGETATION

1113. Arthur, M.A., J.C. Zachos, and D.S. Jones. 1987. Primary productivity and the Cretaceous/Tertiary boundary event in the oceans. *Cretaceous Research* 8:43–54.

Marine primary productivity plummets at the Cretaceous-Tertiary boundary. Filter feeders and suspension feeders, who need an influx of living organisms to survive, became extinct. Detritus feeders had higher survival rates, with an enormous reservoir of dead organisms to feed upon. (*See also* Sheehan and Hansen 1986 [1005].) Low productivity might have lasted as long as 1.5 million years, which seems longer than the asteroid hypothesis would suggest. While an asteroid impact might explain these extinction patterns, some refugia must have existed for those filter feeders that survived.

1114. Gartner, S., and J.P. McGuirk. 1979. Terminal Cretaceous extinction scenario for a catastrophe. *Science* 206:1272–1276.

Two additional mechanisms for the Cretaceous extinction have been proposed since Russell's review (1979 [1002]): the greenhouse effect and the Arctic spillover model. Isolation of the Arctic sea created a large fresh to brackish water ocean. When this low salinity water spilled over into the Atlantic, it devastated the planktonic organisms. Reviews Cretaceous climates, and concludes that the climatic disturbance (drought or cooling) caused by the spillover drove the dinosaurs to extinction.

1115. Hickey, L.J. 1984. Changes in the angiosperm flora across the Cretaceous-Tertiary boundary. In *Catastrophes and Earth History: The New Uniformitarianism*, ed. W.A. Berggren and J.A. Van Couvering, 279–314. Princeton : Princeton University Press.

The observed pattern of floral change at the Cretaceous-Tertiary boundary boundary is just the opposite of what the various impact hypotheses predict. Northern latitude plants should have better resisted the predicted environmental changes than tropical plants; the fossil record shows that the reverse is true. The data are consistent with a model of climatic cooling toward the end of the Cretaceous.

1116. Hsü, K.J. 1986. Cretaceous/Tertiary boundary event. In *Mesozoic and Cenozoic Oceans*, ed. K. Hsü, 75–84. Washington: AGU.

Marine invertebrates maintained high levels of species diversity right up to the Cretaceous-Tertiary boundary. Siliceous planktonic species fared much better than calcareous plankton. Deep benthos species were only minimally affected. The destruction of calcareous plankton is probably due to acidic conditions in the ocean. A massive carbon influx into the ocean from dead organisms would have severely depleted oceanic oxygen. These conditions could be explained by either volcanic action or an asteroid impact. In light of the rapidly accumulating evidence, however, "only a stubborn few still cling to the hypothesis of catastrophic volcanism."

1117. Hsü, K.J., and J.A. McKenzie. 1985. A Strangelove ocean in the earliest Tertiary. In *The Carbon Cycle and Atmospheric CO_2: Natural Variation Archean to Present*, ed. E.T. Sundquist and W. Broecker, 487–492. *Geophysical Monograph Series* vol.32.

Carbon isotope anomalies across the Cretaceous-Tertiary boundary reflect the elimination of the surface to bottom oceanic carbon isotope gradient. An asteroid impact would have temporarily suppressed photosynthesis, and led to a "Strangelove ocean" devoid of plankton. The Strangelove ocean may have lasted for several thousand years. The consequent release of carbon dioxide from the ocean into the atmosphere would have led to global warming and an unstable Tertiary climate. (*See* O'Keefe and Ahrens 1989 [1076] for additional cross references on the greenhouse effect.)

1118. Johnson, K.R., D.J. Nichols, M. Attrep jr., and C.J. Orth. 1989. High-resolution leaf-fossil record spanning the Cretaceous/Tertiary boundary. *Nature* 340:708–711.

Megaflora fossils (leaves) from North Dakota are combined with palynological data across the Cretaceous-

Tertiary boundary. The 79% turnover in megaflora is consistent with an asteroid impact preceded by climatic warming in the latest Cretaceous.

1119. Knoll, A.H. 1984. Patterns of extinction in the fossil record of vascular plants. In *Extinctions*, ed. M.H. Nitecki, 23–68. Chicago: University of Chicago Press.

Extinction in vascular plants has not been studied as thoroughly as animal extinctions. Compared with animals, plants are less likely to suffer extinction from short term events, and can revegetate relatively rapidly. Dormancy, seeds, and other adaptations make it easier for plants to cope with environmental stress. Major extinctions of higher plant taxa tend to coincide with mass extinctions of marine invertebrates. Reviews the history of vascular plant extinctions, and concludes that plant extinctions at the Cretaceous/Tertiary boundary were only moderate in extent. The temporary dominance of ferns immediately after the boundary event is followed by a gradual angiosperm recolonization, probably from dormant plants, rootstocks and seeds. The evidence is consistent with an asteroid impact.

1120. Krassilov, V.A. 1981. Changes of Mesozoic vegetation and the extinction of dinosaurs. *Palaeogeography, Palaeoclimatology, Palaeoecology* 34:207–224.

Perhaps forests did in the dinosaurs. Dinosaurs favored open shrublands and marshes. Forestation at the end of the Cretaceous would have severely limited dinosaur habitats. Includes a discussion of dinosaur diet in relation to habitat, and the evolution of dinosaurian herbivory. Krassilov offers the interesting suggestion that skewed predator/prey ratios might be explained by the importance of small mammals in the diet of dinosaurian carnivores.

1121. McLean, D.M. 1978. A terminal Mesozoic greenhouse: lessons from the past. *Science* 201:401–406.

High levels of carbon dioxide in the Late Cretaceous atmosphere induced a greenhouse effect. Expulsion of oceanic carbon dioxide as temperatures rose would have created a feedback loop enhancing the greenhouse effect. Elevated temperatures could also explain the pronounced thinning of dinosaur eggshells during this period, a problem known to decrease reproductive success in modern birds. (*See* McLean 1985 [1145]. *See also* O'Keefe and Ahrens 1989 [1076] for additional cross references on the greenhouse effect.)

1122. Nichols, D.J., D.M. Jarzen, C.J. Orth, and P.Q. Oliver. 1986. Palynological and iridium anomalies at Cretaceous-Tertiary Boundary, south-central Saskatchewan. *Science* 231:714–7.

Palynological and iridium anomalies are found at the Morgan Creek Cretaceous-Tertiary boundary site. The high abundance of fern spores, with low species diversity, represents recolonization following the devastation of the angiosperm flora. Most plant taxa survived the transition, but new dominants emerged in the revived assemblages. (*See also* Spicer 1989 [1126].) No long-term climate changes are evident from the Late Cretaceous to the Early Tertiary.

1123. Rampino, M.R., and T. Volk. 1988. Mass extinctions, atmospheric sulphur and climatic warming at the K/T boundary. *Nature* 332:63–65.

The sharp decline in primary productivity at the Cretaceous-Tertiary boundary would have led to decreased production of dimethyl sulfide by marine algae. This compound is the primary condensation nuclei for marine clouds. Decreased cloud cover would have led in turn to higher temperatures. Temperatures increased as much as 6°C. Oxygen isotope data support the hypothesis that temperatures were significantly increased at (and after) the Cretaceous-Tertiary boundary.

1124. Retallack, G.J., and M.D. Spoon. 1987. Ecosystem changes across the Cretaceous-Tertiary boundary in eastern Montana. In *Fourth Symposium on Mesozoic Terrestrial Ecosystems, Short Papers*, ed. P.J. Currie and E. Koster, 191–196. Drumheller, Alta.: Tyrell Museum of Paleontology.

Paleosols from the Hell Creek Formation show distinct differences between Late Cretaceous and Paleocene layers.

Late Cretaceous paleosols suggest a closed canopy lowland forest, with a shallow water table. Paleocene soils feature early successional woodland species and wooded swamps.

1125. Saito, T., T. Yamanoi, and K. Kaiho. 1986. End-Cretaceous devastation of terrestrial flora in the boreal Far East. *Nature* 323:253–255.

Decline in angiosperm and gymnosperm pollen and a sudden increase in fern spores occurs at the Cretaceous-Tertiary boundary in Hokkaido, Japan. The ferns are followed by an invasion of pines, which are followed in turn by angiosperms. Coupled with similar evidence from North America, it seems that floral devastation was global in scope, and probably due to a catastrophic event.

1126. Spicer, R.A. 1989. Plants at the Cretaceous-Tertiary boundary. *Philosophical Transactions of the Royal Society of London B* 325:291–305.

Plants and plant communities are excellent indicators of temperature, precipitation, light levels and other physical factors. The fossil record at the Cretaceous-Tertiary boundary reveals a profound ecological catastrophe, particularly at lower and mid-latitudes in the Northern Hemisphere. Perhaps the dust cloud from the asteroid impact was limited mainly to the Northern Hemisphere. Floristic changes in India are minimal, and it is doubtful that the Deccan Traps volcanism had much effect on flora. Temperatures decline at the boundary, and precipitation increases. Broad-leaved evergreens fared particularly poorly. Plants that were formerly rare become dominant in the new floras. (*See also* Nichols et al. 1986 [1122].) Many extinctions were local, and some represent a "Lazarus effect", where species appear to go extinct but are found later on in the fossil record. The first Tertiary vegetation is dominated by ferns.

1127. Spicer, R.A., and J.T. Parrish. 1990. Latest Cretaceous woods of the central North Slope, Alaska. *Palaeontology* 33:225–242.

Conifer wood from the Prince Creek Formation in Alaska shows narrow growth rings, false rings, and high late wood to early wood ratios, indicating that the Late Cretaceous climate in this area was deteriorating. Together with a drastic decline in plant species diversity, these changes demonstrate a cooling and increasingly variable climate, with winter temperatures close to freezing on the North Slope.

1128. Stanley, S.M. 1984. Marine mass extinctions: a dominant role for temperatures. In *Extinctions*, ed. M.H. Nitecki, 69–117. Chicago: University of Chicago Press.

Most explanations of mass extinction among marine invertebrates are easily dismissed. These include salinity changes, anoxic episodes, regression of inland seas (species-area effects, i.e. reduction of "living space"), and competition or other purely biotic factors affecting the food web. Temperature change is the best explanation for marine extinction events. These would hit tropical species particularly hard; they are adapted to a relatively narrow range of temperatures. Reviews the entire history of marine extinctions, focusing on their relation to glaciation and temperature change.

1129. Swain, T. 1974. Reptile-Angiosperm coevolution. In *Secondary Metabolism and Coevolution*, ed. M. Luckner et al., 551–561. *Nova Acta Leopoldina* no. 7.

An unusual and challenging paper. Swain maintains that the decline in dinosaur diversity in the Late Cretaceous is a direct result of the rise to dominance of the angiosperms. Evolution of potent defensive secondary compounds, such as a switch from condensed to hydrolysable tannins and the production of toxic alkaloids, may have caused acute physiological distress or death. Dinosaurs may have succumbed to alkaloid poisoning [*See* 1130].

1130. Swain, T. 1976. Angiosperm-reptile co-evolution. In *Morphology and Biology of Reptiles*, ed. A. d'A. Bellairs and C.B. Cox, 107–122. *Linnean Society Symposium Series* no. 3. London: Academic Press.

A slightly more detailed treatment of Swain 1974 [1129], with a lengthy bibliography.

1131. Sweet, A.R., and T. Jerzykiewicz. 1987. Sedimentary facies and environmentally controlled palynological assemblages: their relevance to floral changes at the Cretaceous-Tertiary Boundary. In *Fourth Symposium on Mesozoic Terrestrial Ecosystems, Short Papers*, ed. P.J. Currie and E. Koster, 206–211. Drumheller, Alta.: Tyrell Museum of Paleontology.

Fossil pollen can be assigned to either wind pollinated or animal pollinated categories based on grain size, thickness of cell walls, and external features. The dominance of wind-pollinated species in the Late Cretaceous Alberta beds suggests an open vegetation structure. An open flood plain habitat could be maintained by herbivore disturbance and cropping. The marked disappearance of animal-pollinated species in early Paleocene sediments might indicate that pollinating animals were driven to extinction.

1132. Tschudy, R.H. 1984. Palynological evidence for change in continental floras at the Cretaceous-Tertiary Boundary. In *Catastrophes and Earth History: The New Uniformitarianism*, ed. W.A. Berggren and J.A. Van Couvering, 315–337. Princeton: Princeton University Press.

Reviews large-scale floral changes at the Cretaceous-Tertiary boundary, and concludes that normal evolutionary changes can explain the patterns observed. Angiosperm diversification reduced the numbers of gymnosperms, ferns, and their allies. Extinctions are confined mainly to the *Aquilapollenites* floral province in the Northern Hemisphere. Climatic change due to tectonic movements and sea-floor spreading can explain vegetation changes across the Cretaceous-Tertiary boundary.

1133. Tschudy, R.H., C.L. Pillmore, C.J. Orth, J.S. Gilmore, and J.D. Knight. 1984. Disruption of the terrestrial plant ecosystem at the Cretaceous-Tertiary boundary, western interior. *Science* 225:1030–1032.

Death of the Dinosaurs 377

Fern spores peak in abundance at two widely separated North American sites, the Hell Creek Formation in Montana and the Raton Formation in Colorado and New Mexico. The end-Cretaceous extinction spanned the continent. Angiosperms recovered rapidly. The absence of cuticular material and the presence of fusinite in boundary samples indicates a period of forest fires. (*See* Melosh et al. 1990 [1073] for additional cross references on the oxygen content of amber and global wildfires at the K-T boundary.)

1134. Upchurch, G.R. jr. 1989. Terrestrial environmental changes and extinction patterns at the Cretaceous-Tertiary boundary, North America. In *Mass Extinctions: Processes and Evidence*, ed. S.K. Donovan, 195–216. New York: Columbia University Press.

Late Cretaceous climates appear to have been warm and stable. Many Cretaceous indicator species stop at the Cretaceous-Tertiary boundary; on the other side of the boundary, fern spores increase dramatically. Reviews Mesozoic climates and floras. The floral evidence is consistent with rapid extinction due to a bolide impact. There is a sharp difference in extinction rates between food chains based on terrestrial plants and freshwater aquatic food chains, which have a significantly lower extinction rate. This is also consistent with catastrophic extinction.

1135. Van Valen, L.M., and R.E. Sloan. 1977. Ecology and the extinction of the dinosaurs. *Evolutionary Theory* 2:37–64.

Increases in gymnosperm abundance, the decrease in evergreen dicots and parallel increase in deciduous dicots, and the invasion of more northerly species, all support a transition from subtropical to temperate climates in the Late Cretaceous Hell Creek Formation. Dinosaurs might have found this new vegetation inedible, and the increasingly deciduous vegetation would have posed severe seasonal foraging problems. Diffuse competition from radiating small mammals, who could make better use of the resources of a temperate forest, also pressured dinosaur populations. A combination of circumstances resulted in the gradual replacement of the subtropical flora/dinosaur community by a temperate forest/mammal community, in a process of normal ecological succession.

1136. Wolfe, J.A. 1987. Late Cretaceous-Cenozoic history of deciduousness and the terminal Cretaceous event. *Paleobiology* 13:215–226.

The "impact winter" hypothesized for the Cretaceous-Tertiary boundary event strongly affected Northern Hemisphere floras but not Southern Hemisphere floras. Broad-leaved deciduous plants are not widespread in the Cretaceous. The Paleocene shows a high diversity of such plants, though only in the Northern Hemisphere. The lack of seasonal extremes at low to middle latitudes during the Late Cretaceous explains the low diversity of deciduous plants. The "impact winter" selected for the deciduous habit that became dominant in the early Tertiary in the Northern Hemisphere. (*See* Wolfe 1991 [1096] for additional cross references on the impact winter.)

1137. Wolfe, J.A., and G.R. Upchurch. 1986. Vegetation, climatic and floral changes at the Cretaceous-Tertiary boundary. *Nature* 324:148–152.

Vegetation changes at the Cretaceous-Tertiary boundary in the North American western interior show high levels of extinction in the south and low levels in the north, increases in precipitation, a short period of lower temperatures (consistent with an asteroid impact), and a major ecological disruption, with subsequent changes in vegetation that resemble normal ecological succession (quasisuccession). Deciduous species survived better than evergreen species, probably due to their superior response to lower temperatures [*See* 1138].

1138. Wolfe, J.A., and G.R. Upchurch jr. 1987. Leaf assemblages across the Cretaceous-Tertiary boundary in the Raton Basin, New Mexico and Colorado. *Proceedings of the National Academy of Sciences* 84:5096–5100.

Impact studies of Cretaceous-Tertiary boundary vegetation report only short-term effects, with a low rate of extinction. Leaf records from the Cretaceous-Tertiary boundary clay in the Raton Basin, however, show rapid extinction rates. Oddly, the pollen record shows only three genera going extinct, although leaf records reveal several extinct genera. Ferns dominate just above the Cretaceous-Tertiary boundary. Recovery of floral diversity was slow, an example of "quasisuccession", where long-term evolutionary change mimics short-term ecological succession. The data suggests a greater extinction of evergreen than deciduous species, and a marked increase in precipitation at the Cretaceous-Tertiary boundary that lasted through the early Paleocene. Plants with dormancy mechanisms triggered by darkness or low temperatures had higher survival rates.

VOLCANOS

1139. Axelrod, D.I. 1981. Role of volcanism in climate and evolution. *Geological Society of America Special Paper* no. 185.

A short monograph which surveys the extent and effects of planetary volcanism during the Cretaceous and Tertiary. Volcanic eruptions in the Late Cretaceous contributed to a global temperature decrease, which in turn had "a significant detrimental effect" on Cretaceous flora and fauna. Discusses the possible evolutionary changes that might accompany widespread volcanism.

1140. Courtillot, V.E. 1990. A volcanic eruption. *Scientific American* 263 (October):85–92.

There are few magnetic polarity reversals in Deccan Traps rocks; the deposits were laid down rapidly. Molten spherules, shocked quartz grains, and the iridium anomaly at the Cretaceous-Tertiary boundary could be explained by intense volcanic action. The effects on the environment of a major volcanic eruption and an impacting asteroid would be very similar. Sulfur from the volcanos would turn the ocean acid, triggering the massive release of carbon dioxide and a resulting greenhouse effect. The end-Cretaceous extinctions were due to "an episode of energetic mantle convection." (*See*

Alvarez 1990 [1039] in the same issue, defending the impact theory. *See also* O'Keefe and Ahrens 1989 [1076] for additional cross references on the greenhouse effect.)

1141. Courtillot, V., G. Féraud, H. Maluski, M.G. Moreau, D. Vandamme, and J. Besse. 1988. Deccan flood basalts and the Cretaceous/Tertiary boundary. *Nature* 333:843–846.

Argon dating of Deccan flood basalts shows a range of 65 –69 million years old. The bulk of the eruptions occurred within a short time, and may coincide with the Cretaceous-Tertiary boundary.

1142. Elliott, W.C., J.L. Aronson, H.T. Millard jr., and E. Gierlowski-Kordesch. 1989. The origin of the clay minerals at the Cretaceous/Tertiary boundary in Denmark. *Geological Society of America Bulletin* 101:702–710.

Stevns Klint Mg-smectite, previously believed to be the result of an impact, is actually reworked volcanic ash. Very little of the clay layer is impact debris. Iridium and other metals are mobile, and may have been concentrated by natural geochemical processes. Although the shocked quartz still suggests an impact, the clay layer supports explosive volcanism at the Cretaceous-Tertiary boundary.

1143. Hallam, A. 1987. End-Cretaceous mass extinction event: argument for terrestrial causation. *Science* 238:1237–1242.

A stepwise pattern is evident in extinctions which argues against a single asteroid impact. These patterns, however, can be explained by substantial volcanic eruptions. Each major argument in support of the impact theory can be explained equally well by massive volcanism. Volcanism also accounts for the strontium peak at the boundary, and the kaolinite pulse observed in Gubbio sediments.

1144. Henbest, N. 1989. Geologists hit back at impact theory of extinctions. *New Scientist*, 29 April, 34–35.

Although the impact theory has won several rounds of intense debate, terrestrial causes of dinosaur extinction are not down for the count. Some geologists think that the 'D' layer of the mantle might generate an episode of explosive volcanism every 20 to 30 million years.

1145. McLean, D.M. 1985. Mantle degassing unification of the trans-K-T geobiological record. *Evolutionary Biology* 19:287–313.

Deccan Traps (India) volcanism outgassed enormous amounts of CO_2. Coupled with other sources of CO_2 outgassing, this volcanism would have led to a global ecological disturbance, including a greenhouse effect. Both the Cretaceous-Tertiary boundary iridium anomaly and the reduction of marine $CaCO_3$ can be explained by this mantle outgassing. These extinction events occurred over a 50,000 year period for marine species. The record suggests a gradual evolutionary turnover rather than an asteroid impact at the Cretaceous-Tertiary boundary. (*See* McLean 1978 [1121]. *See also* O'Keefe and Ahrens 1989 [1076] for additional cross references on the greenhouse effect.)

1146. Moses, C.O. 1989. A geochemical perspective on the causes and periodicity of mass extinctions. *Ecology* 70:812–823

Although we cannot rule out the possibility of an asteroid impact, the Cretaceous-Tertiary boundary extinction can be readily explained by increased volcanism, sea-level changes and sea-floor spreading during the Late Cretaceous. Wildfires from volcanos would explain the soot layer at the boundary. The apparent periodicity of extinction events might also be due to unknown terrestrial cycles, perhaps a long-term convective cycle of mantle plumes. Provides an excellent table summarizing the principal literature relating to the physical and chemical nature of the Cretaceous-Tertiary boundary. (*See also* in the same issue Quinn and Signor 1989 [997]; Patterson and Smith 1989 [996]. *See* Melosh et al. 1990 [1073] for additional cross references on the oxygen content of amber and global wildfires at the K-T boundary.)

1147. Officer, C.B., and C.L. Drake. 1985. Terminal Cretaceous environmental events. *Science* 227:1161–1167.

Several sites show that iridium deposition took place over 10,000 to 100,000 years, supporting a volcanic rather than an extraterrestrial origin. Those sites with a sharper iridium peak are also characterized by a sedimentary discontinuity which makes it difficult to judge the amount of geologic time involved in creating the Cretaceous-Tertiary boundary layer. Sanidine spherules, osmium and strontium isotopes, and the presence of shocked quartz can be readily explained by volcanic action.

1148. Officer, C.B., A. Hallam, C.L. Drake, and J.D. Devine. 1987. Late Cretaceous and paroxysmal Cretaceous/Tertiary extinctions. *Nature* 326:143–149.

A thorough review (145 references) of the Cretaceous-Tertiary boundary extinctions. Intense volcanism explains the evidence advanced for an asteroid impact. Together with the major sea-level regression in the Late Cretaceous, volcanism accounts for the selective pattern of species extinction.

1149. Rampino, M.R. 1989. Dinosaurs, comets and volcanoes. *New Scientist*, 18 February, 54–58.

Both the impact and volcanic theories have their strengths and uncertainties, but perhaps both are valid. The force of the impact could have triggered flood basalt volcanism, of the type seen at Deccan Traps. Eleven such eruptions over the past 250 million years coincide with groups of impact craters and with extinction events.

1150. Rampino, M.R. 1982. A non-catastrophist explanation for the iridium anomaly at the Cretaceous/Tertiary boundary. In *Geological Implications of Impacts of Large Asteroids and Comets on the Earth*, ed. L.T. Silver and P.H. Schultz, 455–460. *Geological Society of America Special Paper* no. 190. Boulder: GSA.

The Cretaceous-Tertiary boundary clay is similar to locally derived clays on either side of the boundary, and is ultimately derived from changes in oceanic chemistry. Dissolution of calcium carbonates in the ocean, and subsequent deposition under reducing conditions, would concentrate iridium in the insoluble portion of the resulting limestone.

1151. Rampino, M.R., and R.C. Reynolds. 1983. Clay mineralogy of the Cretaceous-Tertiary boundary clay. *Science* 219:495–498.

Analysis of clays from the Cretaceous-Tertiary boundary by x-ray diffraction shows no evidence of exotic (extraterrestrial) mineralogy. Arguments about iridium anomalies are inconclusive, but the clays examined show only common minerals of local origin. Geochemical anomalies at the Cretaceous-Tertiary boundary can be explained by volcanic activity.

1152. Rampino, M.R., and R.B. Strothers. 1988. Flood basalt volcanism during the past 250 million years. *Science* 241:663–668.

Potassium-argon dating provides an independent chronology of major episodes of flood basalt volcanism. The estimated dates show a distinct cycle of 32 million years, matching the postulated periodicity of mass extinction events. Perhaps the volcanism was triggered by the impact of comets or asteroids.

1153. Sharpton, V.L., and P.D. Ward, eds. 1990. Global Catastrophes in Earth History. *Geological Society of America Special Paper* no. 247. Boulder: GSA.

As this book went to press, the proceedings of the Snowbird II conference were published. The fifty-eight contributions focus on the impact theory, and cover patterns of mortality, catastrophic volcanism, impact effects, the geological and biological record, and other mass extinction events. Like its predecessor, this volume is invaluable for anyone researching current theories of dinosaur extinction. (*See* Chapman 1989 [983] for a summary of the issues discussed at the conference. *See also* Silver and Schultz 1982 [1088] for the proceedings of Snowbird I.)

APPENDICES

MESOZOIC TIME CHART

PERIOD	EPOCH	AGE	MYA
	Upper Cretaceous	Maastrichtian	65.0
		Campanian	74.0
		Santonian	83.0
	(*Base Senonian*)	Coniacian	86.6
		Turonian	88.5
Cretaceous		Cenomanian	90.4
	Lower Cretaceous	Albian	97.0
		Aptian	112.0
	(*Base Gallic*)	Barremian	124.5
		Hauterivian	131.8
		Valanginian	135.0
	(*Base Neocomian*)	Berriasian	140.7
	Malm	Tithonian	145.6
		Kimmeridgian	152.1
		Oxfordian	154.7
	Dogger	Callovian	157.1
Jurassic		Bathonian	161.3
		Bajocian	166.1
		Aalenian	173.5
	Lias	Toarcian	178.0
		Pliensbachian	187.0
		Sinemurian	194.5
		Hettangian	203.5
	Late Triassic	Rhaetian	208.0
		Norian	209.5
Triassic		Carnian	223.4
	Mid Triassic	Ladinian	235.0
		Anisian	239.5
	Early Triassic	Spathian	241.1
	(*Scythian*)	Nammalian	241.9
		Griesbachian	243.4

STRATIGRAPHIC CORRELATIONS

	TRIASSIC	JURASSIC	CRETACEOUS
North America	Chinle Dockum Popo Agie	Morrison Navajo Kayenta	Judith River Oldman Two Medicine Hell Creek Edmonton Lance Kirtland Fruitland Aguja Cloverly Trinity St. Mary River Lakota Glen Rose Mesa Verde Ringbone
South America	Ischigualasto		Patagonia Beloc (Haiti) Lecho
Europe		Solenhofen Stonesfield Oxford	Wealden Transylvania
Africa	Red Beds	Madagascar Tendaguru	Madagascar Malawi Beds
Asia	Lufeng Maleri	Lufeng Kota	Nemegt Barun Goyot Khok Kruat Lameta Group

GLOSSARY

Two dictionaries are particularly useful for students of dinosaur biology:

Bates, R.L., and J.A. Jackson, eds. 1984. T*he Dictionary of Geological Terms,* prepared by the American Geological Institute. 3d ed. New York: Doubleday.

Lincoln, R.J., G.A. Boxshall, and P.F. Clark. 1982. *A Dictionary of Ecology, Evolution and Systematics.* Cambridge: Cambridge University Press.

aestivation—Seasonal dormancy, entering a state of torpor during the summer or dry season.

allometry—Differential growth and development of body parts, governed by the general equation $y=ax^b$. Volume, for example, increases as the cube of diameter with increasing body size, whereas surface area increases as the square of diameter.

altricial—Condition of offspring that are highly dependent on parental care at birth.

angiosperms—Flowering plants, possessing floral reproductive structures and enclosed seeds.

arboreal— Adapted for living in trees, as opposed to ground-dwelling (cursorial) organisms.

archosaurs—A taxonomic group ('ruling reptiles') containing dinosaurs, crocodiles, pterosaurs, and thecodonts.

behavioral thermoregulation—Regulating or altering body temperatures by behavior, for example by basking in the sun at a certain angle, or by entering the water or shade to cool down the body.

bioenergetics—The study of the energy flow through an ecosystem.

biogeography—The study of the distribution of plants and animals, and the evolution of that distribution over time.

biomass—The total weight of an organism, a population of organisms, or the organisms in a particular area, variously expressed as live weight, or dry weight; standing crop.

carnivores—Animals whose diet includes the flesh of other organisms. (*See also* secondary carnivory.)

carrying capacity—The upper limit on the number of organisms that can be supported in a given habitat, usually denoted as K.

character (trait)—A physical characteristic of an organism that can be inherited by its offspring. Carefully selected characters, or traits, form the basis for the systematic classification of organisms.

clade—Any branch of a cladogram; represents a monophyletic taxon.

cladistics—The classification of organisms based on evolutionarily derived characters. Any trait derived from a more primitive state can be used in cladistic analysis to unite taxa that share this trait. Derived characters are called apomorphic. If they are unique to one monophyletic taxon, they are called autapomorphic characters; if they are shared derived traits, they are called synapomorphic characters.

cladogram—A branching diagram showing the relationship between taxonomic groups. The pattern of branching is inferred from the distribution of shared derived character states.

coevolution—The reciprocal evolution of two species or groups of organisms, such as seed plants and seed dispersing animals, flowering plants and animal pollinators, etc.

cohort—A group of individuals recruited into the population at the same time, as for instance a group of juveniles born in the same breeding season.

coprolite—Fossilized fecal matter.

counterslab—The opposing slab, bearing the imprint of a fossil, which is often revealed when an imbedded fossil is cut from the rock matrix.

cursorial—Running; adapted for living on the ground, as opposed to arboreal.

deltaic—A habitat at or near the mouth of a large river; the deposition of sediments in a river delta.

density dependence—Any factor influencing natality or mortality that changes its effects on population growth with changes in the density of the population.

detritivores—Organisms such as microbes, fungi, and small invertebrates, which feed on dead or decaying organic matter.

diagenesis—The formation of rock from sediment, involving several physical and chemical changes.

diapsid—A group of reptiles having two openings in the skull, just behind the eye sockets. Includes dinosaurs, snakes, lizards, and crocodiles.

diphyletic—A taxonomic group derived from two separate ancestral lineages.

disturbance—Any factor such as fire, flood, or the passage of large herds of animals which alters the local physical environment.

ectotherm—Any organism which relies on body heat from an external source. Ectotherm body temperature depends on ambient environmental temperatures. Often used as synonymous with *poikilothermic* or *cold-blooded*.

endotherm—Any organism which relies on internal metabolic heat to maintain its body temperature. Endotherm body temperature is independent of ambient environmental temperature. Often used as synonymous with *homeothermic* or *warm-blooded*.

eustacy—Cycle of sea-level changes, such as the invasion of land by rising marine waters (transgression), or the retreat of the inland seas during periods of declining sea-level (regression).

fermentation—Metabolic process in which organic matter is broken down by anaerobic digestion.

flood plain—A habitat type in a lowland area, subject to frequent floods and high levels of sediment deposition.

fluvial—Pertaining to rivers or streams.

formation—Used to define a geological bed of any rock type, with well-defined boundaries and stratigraphic position.

fossorial—Adapted for burrowing or digging.

frugivores—Animals whose diet, in whole or in part, consists of fruit.

gait—The manner in which an animal walks or runs, such as a trot, gallop, etc.

gastrolith—Stomach stones, swallowed to assist in the grinding of food such as tough vegetable matter.

grade—A level of biological organization, usually characterized by a significant evolutionary advance, such as endothermy or placental birth; a group of species at the same level of organization.

gymnosperms—A taxon of higher plants characterized by naked seeds, often borne on cones. Includes pines, firs, spruces, ginkgos, and cycads.

habitat—The local environment in which an organism dwells, often characterized by a dominant species or physical attribute (for example, forest, flood plain, montane, deltaic, rain forest, wetland).

herbivores—Animals whose diet consists of vegetable matter.

Glossary

holotype—The original specimen upon which the classification of the genus and species was based.

homologies—Homologous structures are those structures that can be traced to a common ancestor, but which do not necessarily share a common function, for example the hand of a human, the wing of a bat, and the flipper of a dolphin. Only homologous structures are permitted in systematic classification.

ichnology—The study of fossil tracks and traces, such as footprints, eggshells, and coprolites; also *ichnotaxa, ichnospecies, ichnofauna.*

impact winter—The hypothesized decline in seasonal temperatures following the impact of a large asteroid at the Cretaceous-Tertiary boundary, supposedly caused by the presence of a large dust cloud thrown up by the impact.

inertial homeotherm—Large organisms that retain heat well, and shed heat slowly, due to the allometric relationship between surface area (skin) and volume (body).

K-selection—A suite of characteristics of organisms adapted for relatively stable environments. K-selected traits include large body size, delayed reproduction, and a few large offspring. (*See also* r-selection.)

lacustrine—Habitat created by the presence of a lake or pond; living in or on a lake or pond.

land bridge—A physical connection between two adjacent land masses, that forms a route for migration and dispersal of organisms.

life history traits—Strategies of reproduction or survival that characterize organisms during their life cycle, such as reproductive rate, size and number of offspring, and age at first reproduction.

lithosphere—The outer crustal plates of the Earth.

microfossil—A microscopic fossil, either a complete small organism, or small portions of larger organisms

monophyletic—A taxon which derives from a single common ancestor.

nanoplankton—Very small planktonic organisms, about 2–20μm in diameter.

niche—The combination of environmental characteristics suitable for the survival of a particular organism; the ecological role of a species in a community. Includes both the resources used by a species, as well as its interaction with other organisms.

paraphyletic—A classification based on plesiomorphic traits; a taxon which does not include all of the descendants of the most recent common ancestor.

phylogeny—The evolutionary interrelationship of organisms, often represented as a branching tree; the evolutionary history of a lineage of organisms.

plankton—Small aquatic organisms whose movement is controlled primarily by the movement of the water itself.

plesiomorphy—Any primitive trait. Plesiomorphic characters cannot be used as a basis for cladistic classification. A shared primitive trait is called a symplesiomorphy.

polyphyletic—A taxon derived from two or more separate ancestral lineages.

precocial—Condition of offspring that are relatively independent of the parent at birth.

predator/prey ratio—The ratio between the number of known predators in a given habitat, and the number of prey on which they feed. The ratio is different for ectothermic or endothermic communities.

primary productivity—The creation of new biomass by autotrophic organisms, usually by fixing carbon in photosynthesis.

r-selection—A suite of characteristics of organisms adapted for highly variable or unstable environments. These traits include small body size, rapid development, early age at first reproduction, and the production of numerous small offspring. Such organisms are good dispersers and colonizers. (*See* K-selection.)

refugia—Isolated habitats that maintain the environmental conditions that formerly characterized a much larger area, and provide a suitable habitat, or refuge, during times of environmental change for plants and animals adapted to those conditions.

resource partitioning—The sharing of limited resources by a group of species, which adapt to competition by using different resources, or by exploiting similar resources in a different and non-competitive way.

riverine—Habitat formed by the action of a river; lying adjacent to a river; living in or on a river.

secondary carnivores—Carnivores that eat other carnivores; may include cannibalism.

sessile—Organisms permanently attached to the substrate at their base.

sexual dimorphism—Organisms in which certain structures show physical differences characteristic of either sex, for example the presence of horns or sexual display structures in males.

sexual selection—The competition within a species for the opportunity to mate, based on physical or behavioral attributes.

shock metamorphism—Physical changes in rocks or minerals due to any significant physical shock, such as the impact of a large asteroid.

sister group—The two monophyletic taxa produced by a dichotomous branch in a cladogram.

stratigraphy—Study of the formation, distribution, physical attributes, and other characteristics of rocks as strata.

synapomorphy—A shared evolutionarily-derived trait, used as the basis for cladistic analysis.

synapsid—A group of reptiles which are characterized by a single opening in the skull, behind and below the eye socket. Includes the distant ancestors of mammals.

taphonomy—Processes that occur following the death of an organism, including diagenetic processes in fossil matrix rock.

taxon (taxa)—Any discrete taxonomic unit, such as an order, family, genus, or species.

taxonomy—The systematic classification of organisms based on a comparison of discrete physical characteristics.

tektites—A small glassy rock of extraterrestrial origin. Tektites may also be created when an extraterrestrial body impacts the Earth.

temperature-dependent sex determination—Control of the sex ratio in offspring by changes in nest temperatures.

thecodonts—Archosaurs in the Permian and early Triassic from which all more advanced archosaurs (such as dinosaurs), evolved.

thegosis—Sharpening of teeth by abrasion against other teeth; grinding of teeth.

therapsids—Also called mammal-like reptiles, a group of synapsid reptiles, mainly large herbivores and carnivores, which were dominant during the Permian and part of the Triassic.

tooth replacement—Process by which worn teeth are gradually replaced by new teeth growing behind or beneath them. Characteristic of some herbivorous dinosaurs.

trophic level—Any level in a "food chain", from primary producers (plants), to secondary consumers (top carnivores).

ungulates—A hoofed mammal.

upwelling—An upward movement of nutrient-rich cold water from the deep ocean.

zoogeography—Study of the geographic distribution of animals.

CLASSIFICATION OF DINOSAURS

Modern cladistic analysis has revolutionized the classification of dinosaurs. While Seeley's early classification into Ornithischia and Saurischia has been generally upheld, some recent discoveries, such as *Staurikosaurus* and *Herrerasaurus*, do not seem to belong to either taxa (Seeley 1887 [97]). The abbreviated classification below is adapted from Weishampel et al. 1990 [16].

SAURISCHIA
Staurikosaurus, Herrerasauridae,
Theropoda
Ceratosauria (*Ceratosaurus, Coelophysis, Syntarsus*)
Tetanurae
    Carnosauria (*Megalosaurus, Stokesosaurus*)
        Allosauridae (*Allosaurus*)
        Tyrannosauridae (*Tyrannosaurus, Albertosaurus, Daspletosaurus, Tarbosaurus*)
    Coelurosauria
        Ornithomimosauria
            Ornithomimidae (*Ornithomimus, Struthiomimus, Dromiceiomimus, Gallimimus*)
    Maniraptora
        Elmisauridae (*Chirostenotes, Elmisaurus*)
        Oviraptorosauria (*Oviraptor, Caenagnathus*)
        Troödontidae (*Troödon, Saurornithoides*)
        Dromaeosauridae (*Deinonychus, Dromaeosaurus, Velociraptor, Saurornitholestes*)
        Aves (*Archaeopteryx*, all birds as crown group)
Sauropodomorpha
Prosauropoda (*Thecodontosaurus, Anchisaurus, Massospondylus, Yunnanosaurus, Ammosaurus, Plateosaurus*)
Sauropoda (*Vulcanodon, Cetiosaurus, Apatosaurus, Brachiosaurus, Camarasaurus, Diplodocus, Alamosaurus, Titanosaurus, Mamenchisaurus*)
Segnosauria (*Segnosaurus, Erlikosaurus*)

ORNITHISCHIA
Lesothosaurus, Pisanosaurus, Technosaurus
Thyreophora
Scutellosaurus, Scelidosaurus
Stegosauria (*Kentrosaurus, Paranthodon, Stegosaurus*)
Ankylosauria
  Ankylosauridae (*Ankylosaurus, Euoplocephalus*)
  Nodosauridae (*Hylaeosaurus, Sauropelta, Panoplosaurus*)
Cerapoda
Ornithopoda
  Heterodontosauridae (*Lanasaurus, Lycorhinus, Heterodontosaurus*)
  Hypsilophodontidae (*Hypsilophodon, Thescalosaurus*)
    Tenontosaurus
  Dryosauridae (*Dryosaurus*)
  Iguanodontia
    Camptosauridae (*Camptosaurus*)
    Iguanodontidae (*Iguanodon, Ouranosaurus*)
  Hadrosauridae
    Hadrosaurinae (*Hadrosaurus, Maiasaura, Saurolophus*)
    Lambeosaurinae (*Corythosaurus, Lambeosaurus, Hypacrosaurus, Parasaurolophus*)
Marginocephalia
Pachycephalosauria
  Homalocephalidae (*Homalocephale*)
  Pachycephalosauridae (*Pachycephalosaurus, Stegoceras, Yaverlandia, Prenocephale*)
  Camptosauridae (*Camptosaurus*)
Ceratopsia
  Psittacosauridae (*Psittacosaurus*)
  Neoceratopsia
    Protoceratopsidae (*Protoceratops, Leptoceratops*)
    Ceratopsidae
      Centrosaurinac (*Centrosaurus, Pachyrhinosaurus Monoclonius, Styracosaurus*)
      Chasmosaurinae (*Pentaceratops, Torosaurus, Chasmosaurus, Triceratops*)

INDICES

INDEX OF CURRICULAR MATERIALS

Professors wishing to develop lectures on dinosaur biology at the high-school or undergraduate level, or even teach an entire course on the subject, will find this index particularly useful. I have tried to identify sources which could be assigned as student reading, or which would help introduce teachers to particular research problems related to dinosaurs. Students will also find that this material provides a good introduction to various topics for term paper assignments. I have concentrated on secondary readings from sources like *Scientific American* and *New Scientist*, as well as scholarly review articles from a variety of publications, useful textbooks, and core articles in critical areas of research. Textbooks that should be considered for a dinosaur course are listed under "suggested texts", and several titles useful for preparing slides for lectures are listed under "illustration sources".

angiosperms
    origin and evolution, 237, 257, 259, 620
    coevolution with dinosaurs, 611, 614, 656, 265
Archaeopteryx forgery claim, 880
bibliography (basic collection), 34
biogeography, 216, 219–220
birds
    feathers, 972
    origin and evolution, 934–935, 947, 949, 951, 963
    origin of flight, 958, 961, 966, 968–969, 971
    textbook of ornithology, 937, 954
carnivores
    dinosaurs, 663, 668
    social mammals, 657, 666, 669
census of dinosaurs, 590
cladistics, 833, 839, 841, 862, 867
climate, 224, 167
Cope–Marsh feud, 137, 142, 146, 150
course development, 57, 78
creationism, 36, 40, 52, 71
cursorial dinosaurs, 588
dinosaur census, 590
ecology, 580–581, 584, 594, 607,
    of modern animals, 636, 671
    and paleobiology, 598
    text, 701
ectothermy, 419–420, 428, 434, 440, 568
endothermy, 413, 416–417, 425, 435, 442, 445, 447
    and bone histology, 544, 546
    of mammals, 686, 690
eustacy, 192
    and Cretaceous climate, 205

extinction, 997
  asteroid, 1036–1037, 1149
  bibliography, 987
  crater site, 1053
  early theories, 1002
  gradual, 1011, 1017
  mass versus background, 984, 989, 1027
  Nemesis, 1103–1104
  Paleocene dinosaurs, 1014, 1033
  species diversity, 1031
  volcanos, 1146, 1149
fauna, Mesozoic, 594, 607
faunal replacement, 209, 580–581, 586
flight, evolution of, 970
future research needed, 24
gait and speed, 460, 464, 488, 490
geology of the Mesozoic, 167, 175
herbivores
  dinosaurs, 640, 655
  modern, 692–693
illustration sources, 8, 30, 37–38, 51, 54, 58, 68, 265
intelligence and brain size, 520–521
juveniles, 768, 790
life history traits, 592, 671
locomotion, 459
  and muscular control, 478
metabolism, diet, 618
nesting behavior, 41, 753, 766–767, 770
origin of dinosaurs, 816
Ornithischia, 856
  cladistics of, 865

paleontology, history, 95, 104, 109
phylogeny of dinosaurs, 839
plant evolution, 264
popular culture, 37
posture, weight, gait, 457, 459
predator/prey ratios, 447–448, 450
progressionism, 86
prosauropods, 814
reference book, 16
reproductive behavior, 753, 766–767, 770
  and sex determination, 754, 778
restoration, 30, 324, 379, 390
sauropods, 852
secondary text, 51, 66
sexual selection, 459, 715, 720, 726
  and mating systems, 719
size and ecology, 673, 697, 703
social behavior, 734–735, 740
suggested texts, 14, 16, 19, 22–23, 28, 33, 49–50, 56, 75
superiority of dinosaurs, 25
systematics, 825, 841
taphonomy, 578
thermoregulation in reptiles, 552, 556, 560
theropods, 840
time, discovery of, 83
tracks, ichnology, 500, 503–504, 508, 515
trophic structure, 579–580, 593
vertebrate evolution, 794–795, 799
Victorian dinosaur, 88, 425, 442
young adults text, 68

AUTHOR INDEX

Abercrombie, C.L., 555, 791
Ackerman, R.A., 742, 783
Ackerman, T.P., 1080, 1091
Adams, D., 270
Ager, T.A., 1049
Ahrens, T.J., 1076
Alexander, R.McN, 454–461
Alvarez, L.W., 1036–1038
Alvarez, W., 1037–1041, 1065
Anders, E., 1095
Anders, M.H., 1078
Anderson, A., 899
Anderson, J.F., 462–463
Anderson, R.A., 548
Anderson, T.H., 158
Ar, A., 742
Archibald, J.D., 1010–1011, 1017
Argast, S., 1012
Armstrong, E., 517
Armstrong, H.J., 160, 764
Armstrong, W.G., 271
Aronson, J.L., 1142
Arthur, M.A., 1009, 1087, 1113
Asaro, F., 1037–1040
Ash, S.R., 231, 263
Attrep, M. jr., 1118
Attridge, J., 272, 617, 834
Auffenberg, W., 549, 563
Averett, M.E., 159
Averett, W.R., 17, 159
Avery, R.A., 709
Avnimelech, M., 492
Axelrod, D.I., 232–233, 1139
Baadsgaard, H., 976, 992
Bacskai, J.A., 3
Bada, J.L., 1098

Baird, D., 493
Baker, A.J., 943
Bakken, G.S., 444
Bakker, R.T., 165, 413–417, 447, 464, 577, 591, 611, 825
Balda, R.P., 959
Bannikov, A.F., 338
Barron, E.J., 161, 189, 190
Barsbold, R., 273–276, 371
Bartlett, R.A., 99
Bartram, B.C.R., 657
Basabilvazo, G., 174
Batten, D.J., 234
Baur, G., 124
Baur, M.E., 418
Beardsley, T., 900
Bebout, D.G., 185
Beck, C.B., 235, 612
Beecher, C.E., 125
Begon, M., 671
Behrensmeyer, A.K., 18, 165, 578, 591
Béland, P., 448–449, 481, 579, 608, 977
Bell, C.J., 550
Belsky, A.J., 613
Bengston, P., 178
Bennett, A.F., 419, 551
Benton, M.J., 19, 84, 420, 580–582, 792, 801, 804, 812, 826–827, 919, 978–979
Berger, J., 710
Berggren, W.A., 980
Berman, D.S., 138, 277–278, 518, 737
Berner, R.A., 1042
Bertram, B.C.R., 711

403

Besse, J., 1141
Bibby, C., 85
Biewener, A.A., 473
Bird, R.T., 100
Bjork, P.R., 409
Blows, W.T., 279
Bock, B.C., 755
Bock, W.J., 957–958
Bogert, C.M., 553
Bohor, B.F., 1043–1045
Bolt, J.R., 531
Bonaparte, J.F., 208–212, 280–281, 805–806, 828, 950
Boslough, M.B., 1046
Boucot, A. J.,712
Bourgeois, J., 1047
Bouvier, M., 532
Bowler, P.J., 86, 126
Boynton, W.V., 1061
Bradbury, R., 20
Bralower, T.J., 1087
Brattstrom, B.H., 713
Breithaupt, B., 1013
Brenner, G.J., 236
Brett-Surman, M.K., 213, 829, 832, 920
Briggs, D.E., 21
Brink, A. S.,421
Brinkman, D.B., 282, 583
Brinkman, D.L., 1012
Brodkorb, P., 921–922
Broecker, W.S., 207
Brooks, R.R., 1048
Brouwers, E.M., 1049
Brown, B., 101–103
Bryan, J.R., 283, 981
Bryant, J.P., 616
Buckland, W., 79
Buehler, P., 874

Buffetaut, E., 151, 191, 214–215, 284, 658
Buffrénil, V. de,422–423
Bühler, P., 923
Bull, J.J., 743, 788
Bunnell, F.L., 682
Burchette, T.P., 516
Burggren, W.W., 552
Burghardt, G.M., 744, 755
Buscalioni, A.D., 394
Buss, I.O., 708
Calder, W.A. III, 672–673
Callison, G., 584, 745
Camp, C.L., 2
Campbell, H.W., 746
Caple, G., 959
Caraco, T., 659
Carpenter, K., 285–286, 585, 730, 830, 841, 1013
Carrier, D.R., 465
Carroll, R.L., 22
Carter, L.D., 1049
Case, E.C., 127
Case, T.J., 674, 747
Cavagna, G.A., 474–475
Cerling, T.E., 1050
Chabreck, R.H., 748–749
Chaloner, W.G., 620
Chamley, H., 1001
Channell, J.E.T., 982, 1087
Chao, S., 396–397
Chapin, F.S. III., 616
Chapman, C.R., 983
Chapman, D.J., 1059–1060
Chapman, R.E., 714, 831–832
Charig, A.J., 23, 216, 287, 294, 393, 586, 793–794, 833–835, 875–876, 1014

Chatterjee, S., 217–218, 288, 332, 807, 836, 901
Cheng, Z., 397
Chenggang, R., 513
Cherfas, J., 984
Chure, D.J., 6, 24, 56–57
Cita, M.B., 181
Clark, D.H., 1107
Clark, D.L., 199
Clark, J.L., 827
Clemens, E.T., 675
Clemens, W.A., 798, 1015–1017, 1049
Cloudsley-Thompson, J.L., 25
Clube, S.V.M., 1074, 1099
Cobabe, E.A., 289
Coe, M.J., 614, 676
Cohen, I.B., 128
Colbert, E.H., 26–28, 104–106, 162, 219, 290–291, 386, 497, 553, 795, 808
Cole, R.D., 163
Coley, P.D., 615–616
Collen, J.D., 1048
Conrad, K., 506, 602
Coombs, W.P. jr., 292–293, 316, 587–588, 660, 750–753, 837–838
Cooper, M.R., 192, 809
Cope, E.D., 129–135
Courtillot, V.E., 1140–1141
Cowles, R.B., 553
Cox, B., 8, 715
Cox, C.B., 220
Crabtree, D.R., 254
Cracraft, J., 839, 877, 924–929
Crane, P.R., 237–238, 252–253, 620
Crawford, E.C., 554

Creer, K.M., 1079
Crepet, W.L., 239, 245
Crichton, M., 29
Croft, S.K., 1051
Crome, F.H.J., 716
Crompton, A.W., 272, 294, 393, 424, 617, 834
Crooks, D.M., 176
Crowley, T.J., 193
Crowther, P.R., 21
Cruickshank, A.R.I., 810–812
Crutzen, P., 1052
Cui, K.H., 399
Cummings, D.H., 676
Currie, P.J., 295–296, 301, 411, 494–496, 661, 717, 840–842, 902–903, 918, 930,
Curtis, R.L., 202
Curwen, E.C., 80
Czerkas, S., 30, 297
D'Hondt, S., 1087
Dahl, J., 1093
Dalrymple, G.B., 1067
Dalzell, B., 419
Damuth, J., 677
Darrah, W.C., 107
Davidson, F.D., 412
Davies, K.L., 1018
Davies, N.B., 728
Davis, M., 1100
Dawson, W.R., 551
Day, M.H., 466
De Camp, C.C., 31
De Camp, L.S., 31
De Graciansky, P.C., 195
De Jong, W.W., 973
De Wit, M.J., 1092
Dean, W.E., 1009
DeCourten, F.L., 298

Deeming, C., 754
Deino, A.L., 168, 184
Delair, J.B., 152
Delaney, M.F., 555
DeMar, R.E., 531
Demment, M.W., 678
Deroo, G., 195
Desmond, A.J., 87–88, 425
Devine, J.D., 1148
Di Gregorio, M.A., 89
Diamond, J.M., 433
Dickson, D., 878
Dietz, R.S., 1053
Dilcher, D.L., 240, 258–259, 614
Dixon, D., 8, 32
Dmi'el, R., 484, 742
Dobson, J.P., 982
Dodson, P., 16, 164–165, 299–302, 426, 589–591, 717–718, 720, 778, 843–844
Doi, K., 1019
Dolly, E.D., 179
Donoghue, M.J., 238, 243
Donovan, S.K., 985
Douglas, J.G., 241
Douthitt, C.B., 1083
Downs, W.R., 172
Doyle, J.A., 238, 242–244, 247
Drake, C.L., 1075, 1147–1148
Dugan, B.A., 755
Dunbar, C.O., 153
Dunham, A.E., 592
Earle, M., 662
Eaton, J.G., 1019
Eberth, D.A., 184, 1020
Edinger, T., 519
Edwards, M.B., 497
Edwards, R., 497
Elder, W.H., 679

Elder, W.P., 1065
Eldredge, N., 839
Elliott, D.K., 986
Elliott, W.C., 1142
Elżanowski, A., 931–934
Emlen, S.T., 719
Enlow, D.H., 533
Erben, H.K., 756
Ethridge, F.G., 166
Evans, M.E., 992
Evans, S.E., 303, 845
Ewer, R.F., 813
Fairbridge, R.W., 9
Farlow, J.O., 33, 422–423, 427, 450–451, 498, 593, 614, 618, 663, 720, 1012
Fassett, J.E., 1021, 1077
Fastovsky, D.E., 167, 289
Fedak, M.A., 467–469, 475, 484
Feduccia, A., 428–429, 879, 904–905, 935, 960, 965
Fegley, B. jr. ,1081
Feldman, P., 977
Felton, E.A., 1083
Féraud, G., 1141
Ferguson, M., 754
Fiorillo, A.R.,757
Firth, B.T., 569
Flannery, T.F., 358
Fleury, B.E., 34
Florentin, J–M., 1054
Flores, R.M., 166
Folinsbee, R.E., 430
Foord, E.E., 1043–1044
Forster, C.A., 304, 592, 758
Foster, J., 977
Fouty, G., 987
Fowler, C.W., 680
Frakes, L.A., 194

Fraser, N.C., 594–595
Frederick, D.L., 283
Freeland, W.J., 619
Freidl, R.R., 418
Frey, E., 470
Frey, R.W., 35
Friis, E.M., 238–239, 245, 620
Fritz, P., 430
Gabet, R.M., 1012
Gabriel, D., 322, 1033
Gallup, M.R., 305
Galton, P.M., 221–222, 306–319, 359, 407, 596–597, 621–623, 714, 721, 759–760, 814, 825, 846, 906, 934
Ganapathy, R., 1055
Gardiner, B., 8, 847
Garland, T.jr. ,471–472
Garrick, L.D., 722–723
Gartner, S., 1114
Gates, D.M., 444, 566, 573
Gatesy, S.M., 473
Gault, D.E., 1084
Gauthier, J., 907, 936, 961
Geist, V., 724–725
Georgiadis, N.J., 692
Gerstl, S.A.W., 1056
Gerstner, P.A., 154
Gierl, A., 238, 255
Gierliński, G., 499
Gierlowski-Kordesch, E., 1142
Giffin, E.B., 320–322
Gill, F.B., 937
Gill, T., 136
Gillette, D.D., 500
Gilmore, J.S., 1057, 1077, 1133
Gingerich, P.D., 938
Gish, D., 36
Gittleman, J.L., 664

Glass, D.J., 183
Glut, D.F., 37–38
Golley, F.B., 624
Goodfield, J., 83
Goodwin, M.B., 168
Gorman, J., 41
Gostin, V.A., 1094
Gottlieb, O.R., 633
Gottsberger, G.,246
Gould, S.J., 520, 598, 880
Gouy, M., 238, 269
Gow, C.E., 323, 625
Greenaway, F., 876
Greenberg, M.H., 69
Greenberg, N., 556
Gregory, J.T., 4, 108
Gregory, R.T., 1083
Grieve, R.A.F., 1058
Griffis, K., 1059–1060
Grigorescu, D., 169
Grine, F.E., 761
Grinspoon, D., 1097
Hall-Martin, A., 462
Hallam, A., 170, 196–197, 223, 1143, 1148
Hallett, M.,324
Halstead, J., 39
Halstead, L.B., 39, 271
Hamley, T.L., 894–895
Hammond, J.K., 778
Hanks, J., 681
Hansen, T.A., 1005, 1047, 1065
Harestad, A.S., 682
Harlow, H.J., 557
Hart, R.J., 1092
Harvey, A.P., 15
Harvey, M.D., 166
Hass, G., 325
Hastings, R.J., 40

Haugerud, R.A., 1068
Hay, O.P., 1
Hays, J.D., 198
Heaton, M.J., 326
Hecht, M.K., 870, 881–882, 892, 908
Heglund, N.C., 467, 474–475, 485
Heilmann, G., 939
Heinrich, B., 431
Henbest, N., 1144
Henneman, W.W. III, 683
Herbin, J.P., 195
Herrera, C.M., 626
Herzog, H.A. jr., 723
Hickey, L.J., 244, 247, 262, 1022, 1115
Hildebrand, A.R.,1061–1062
Hill, A.P., 18
Hillman, S.S., 557
Hills, J.G., 1101
Hines, T., 791
Hirsch, K.F., 762–764
Hirst, S.M., 684
Hoefs, J., 756
Hoffman, A., 988
Hoffman, M., 557
Hoffman, M.A., 685
Hohnke, L.A., 432
Holzbecher, J., 1048
Hope, C., 791
Hopson, J.A., 521–523, 627, 686, 726
Horner, J.R.,41, 327–330, 765–770, 803, 848
Hotton, N. III, 599, 727
Houck, K.J., 603
Houde, P., 940
Houstan, D.C., 665

Howard, R.W., 109
Howe, H.F., 628–629
Howell, D.G., 171
Hsü, K.J., 989, 1063–1064, 1116–1117
Huey, R.B., 558–560
Hughes, N.F., 248
Hungate, R.E., 630
Hunt, A.P., 344
Hunt, G.E., 1108
Hunt, R.H., 771
Hunter, B., 461
Hut, P., 1065, 1100, 1102
Hutchinson, H.N., 90
Huxley, T.H., 91
Irvine, A.K., 706
Ishigaki, S., 501
Izett, G.A., 1066–1068
Jablonski, D., 9, 990–991
Jackson, A.A. IV, 1106
Jacobs, L.L., 42, 172
Jagger, J.A., 424
Jain, S.L., 331–332, 518, 772, 787
James, P.B., 1085
Janzen, D.H., 619, 631–632, 645
Jarzen, D.M., 614, 977, 993, 1122
Jayes, A.S., 461
Jenkins, F., 272
Jennings, C., 505
Jensen, J.A., 317, 410
Jerison, H.J., 524
Jerzykiewicz, T., 600, 1131
Jianjun, L., 513
Jimenez, S., 507
Johnson, K.R., 1118
Johnson, R.E., 322
Johnston, P.A., 534–535

Johnstone, R.C.B., 688
Jones, D.S., 981, 1113
Jordan, W.H jr., 43
Kaiho, K., 1125
Kappelman, J., 536
Karasov, W.H., 433, 548
Kauffman, E.G., 173, 1023, 1040, 1047, 1065
Kaufulu, Z.M., 172
Keays, R.R., 1094
Keller, G., 1065
Kemp, T.S., 849
Kennedy, W.J., 333
Kermack, D., 334
Kerourio, P., 789
Kessler, E., 883
Kidwell, S.M., 578
Kielan-Jaworowska, Z., 155, 211, 335
Kirkland, J.I.,1019
Kitchell, J.A., 199
Kitching, J.W., 761
Klaver, G., 1090
Klinger, H.C., 333
Knight, C.R., 336
Knight, J.D., 1057, 1077, 1133
Knoll, A.H., 1119
Kolata, G.B., 850
Kool, R., 476
Kosanke, R.M., 249
Kovach, W.L., 234
Krassilov, V.A., 250–251, 1120
Krebs, J.R., 728
Krouse, H.R., 430
Kubitzki, K., 633
Kucera, E.11
Kues, B.S.,7, 47, 337
Kuhn, O., 10
Kuhn-Schnyder, E., 11
Kunk, M.J., 1068
Kurochkin, E.N., 941
Kurtén, B., 44
Kurzanov, S.M., 338, 773, 909–911
Kushlan, J.A., 774–775
Kushlan, M.S., 775
Kutty, T.S., 332
Kyte, F.T., 1069
Lacasa, A., 950
Lambert, D., 12–13
Landis, G.P., 1042
Lang, J.W., 722–723
Langston, W. jr., 339–341
Lanham, U., 137
Latham, D., 1073
Laurie, A., 729
Laws, R.M., 687–688
Lawson, D.A., 342
Lawton, T.F., 174
Leahy, G.D., 1024, 1028
Learner, R.J., 45–46
Lee, A.K., 576
Lee, J., 1048
Lehman, T.M., 337, 343, 601, 851
Leidy, J., 110
Lerbekmo, J.F., 976, 992–993
Leunissen, J.A.M., 973
LeVene, C.M., 149
Lewis, C.F., 1071
Lewis, G.E., 111
Lewis, R.S., 1095
Li, W.H., 238, 269
Lidgard, S., 252–253
Lillegraven, J.A., 224
Lima, A.P., 776
Lindsay, N.M., 1092
Lipps, J.H., 1006

Liu, M. S., 1091
Lloyd, C.R., 200
Lock, J.M., 689
Lockley, M.G., 495, 500, 502–506, 513, 602–603, 730
Lommen, P.W., 444
Loveridge, J.P., 561
Lowe, P.E., 912
Lucas, S.G., 47, 174, 344, 604–605
Luck, J.M., 1070
Lutcavage, M., 562
Lutz, P.L., 562
Mc Clammer, J.U. jr., 254
McBee, R.H., 634
McCrea, W.H., 1107
MacDonald, D.W., 666
McDougall, I., 976
McDougall, K.A., 171
McEwen-Mason, J., 1083
McGinnis, H.J., 112
McGowan, C., 49–50, 434, 942–943
McGuirk, J.P., 1114
McHone, J.F., 1071
McIntosh, J.E.A., 681
McIntosh, J.S., 6, 138, 145, 277–278, 345, 591, 608, 852–853
McKay, C.P., 1080, 1091
McKenzie, J.A., 1117
McKinney, M.L., 994
McLean, D.M., 1121, 1145
MacLean, P.D., 599, 731
McLeod, R.M., 92
McLoughlin, J.C., 51
McMahon, T.A., 477–478
McNab, B.K., 563, 690
McNaughton, S.J., 635–636, 691–692, 159–160

McReynolds, E.S., 159–160
Mackal, R.P., 1025
Maderson, P.F.A., 962
Madsen, J.H. jr., 302, 346–347, 763
Magnusson, W.E., 776
Makela, R., 768
Maloiy, G.M.O., 461, 485, 675
Maluski, H., 1141
Mantell, G.A., 81
Marsh, O.C., 128, 139–141
Martin, J., 637
Martin, L.D., 884, 923, 944–945, 956, 963
Martin, M., 191
Martin, P.S., 632
Martin, R.D., 525
Martin, W., 238, 255
Marx, J.L., 435
Maryańska, T., 348–352, 638
Mash, R., 48
Mateer, N.J., 333, 353, 513
Mathur, U.B., 1026
Maurrasse, R., 1054
Meinke, D.K., 536
Melosh, H.J., 1072–1073
Mengel, J.G., 193
Meyer, C.A., 510
Michel, H.V., 1037–1038, 1040
Mikhailov, K.E., 773
Millard, H.T. jr., 1045, 1142
Miller, W.E., 763
Millet, J.S., 436
Milne, D.H., 52
Milner, A.C., 287, 835, 876
Milner, A.R., 225, 303
Modreski, P.J., 1043–1044
Molnar, R.E., 354–360, 732, 854, 885

Montadert, L., 195
Moody, R., 54
Moore, C.H., 185
Moratalla, J.J., 507
Moreau, M.G., 1141
Morris, W.J., 361–362
Mortimer, M., 671
Moses, C.O., 1146
Mossman, D.J., 508
Moullade, M., 175
Müller, C., 195
Muller, R.A., 1041, 1100, 1103
Murry, P.A., 790
Nadon, G.C., 495
Nairn, A.E.M., 175
Napier, W.M., 1074, 1099
Nations, J.D., 386
Neall, V.E., 1048
Nelson, M.E., 176
Newell, N.D., 1027
Newman, B.H., 363, 479
Newman, K.R., 1030
Niall, J.M., 605
Nicholls, E.L., 226, 364–365
Nichols, D.J., 260, 1045, 1118, 1122
Nield, T., 142
Nieman, R.A., 1071
Norberg, R.A., 964
Norford, B.S., 366
Norman, D.B., 14, 225, 639–640, 654–655, 777, 796, 855–857
Norris, G., 977
North, G.R., 193
Northrop, S.A., 7
Norton-Griffiths, M., 705
Novas, F.E., 815
Novellie, P., 694
Nturibi, J., 461

O'Connor, M.P., 564
O'Keefe, J.D., 1076
Officer, C.B., 1075, 1147–1148
Oliver, P.Q., 1122
Olsen, P.E., 480
Olshevsky, G., 858
Olson, E.C., 30, 55, 445
Olson, S.L., 946–947, 965
Oring, L.W., 719
Orth, C.J., 995, 1057, 1077, 1118, 1122, 1133
Osborn, H.F., 113–114, 143–144, 367, 606
Osmólska, H., 16, 349–352, 368–371, 638, 913
Ostrom, J.H., 145, 177, 372–377, 437–438, 641, 733–735, 797, 859, 886–888, 948–949, 966–969
Overall, K.L., 592
Owen, M.R., 1078
Owen, R., 93–94, 889
Owen-Smith, R.N., 693–694
Padian, K., 56–57, 378, 480, 536, 607, 798, 816, 936, 961, 970
Pal, P.C., 1079
Paladino, F.V., 564, 778
Parker, I.S.C., 688
Parker, L.R., 263
Parrish, J.T., 201–202, 1127
Patterson, C., 996
Paul, G.S., 213, 379, 439, 667–668, 817, 860, 920
Pawlicki, R., 537–538
Pedley, T.J., 695
Pellew, R.A., 696
Penfield, G.T., 1062
Perkins, B.F., 185
Perle, A., 276, 380

Peters, R.H., 697–699
Peterson, W.H., 189
Phillipson, J., 676
Pianka, E.R., 558–559, 565, 700–701
Pickett, S.T.A., 702
Pillmore, C.L., 1057, 1077, 1133
Pinshow, B., 468
Pirozynski, G., 977
Pittman, J.G., 509
Pittman, W.C. III, 198
Plate, R., 146
Platt, N.H., 510
Pledge, N.S., 360
Pollack, J.B., 1080, 1091
Pond, C.M., 779
Porter, W.P., 566, 592
Pough, F.H., 567–568
Powell, H.P., 318
Powell, J.E., 212
Prance, G.T., 246
Prange, H.D., 463
Preiss, B., 58
Prince, N.K., 603
Prinn, R.G., 1081
Quimby, H.M., 745
Quinn, J.F., 997
Raab, J.L., 486
Raath, M.A., 861, 914
Radinsky, L.B., 526, 799
Raelson, J.V., 698
Rahn, H., 463
Ralph, C.L., 569
Rampino, M.R., 1082, 1123, 1149–1152
Rand, A.S., 755
Rao, A., 68
Rao, C., 397
Ratkevitch, R.P., 59

Raup, D.M., 998–1000, 1104
Raven, P.H., 256
Rayner, J.V.M., 971
Reed, F.B., 271
Reeves, R.D., 1048
Regal, P.J., 257, 972
Reid, G., 977
Reid, R.E.H., 440, 539–544
Reif, W.E., 157
Reiss, M.J., 736
Retallack, G., 1028
Retallack, G.J., 258, 259, 1124
Reyment, R.A., 178
Reynolds, M.W., 179
Reynolds, R.C., 1151
Rhoades, D.F., 642
Riccardi, A.C., 180
Rich, P.V., 381, 527, 1083
Rich, T.H., 358, 381, 527, 1083
Richmond, N.D., 780
Ricqlès, A. de 423–424, 545–547
Ridley, M., 862
Rieber, H., 11
Rietschel, S., 890
Rigby, J.K. jr., 47, 337, 842, 1029–1030, 1033
Ritchie, A., 60
Robblee, A.R., 430
Robert, C., 1001
Robinson, D., 184
Robinson, P.L., 331
Rockwood, L.L., 643
Rodgers, D.H., 679
Rogers, K.L., 644
Romer, A.S., 5, 61–63, 147
Roniewicz, E., 370–371
Rosenthal, G.A., 645
Rosner, D.E., 427
Roth, E.C., 528, 599

Roth, J.J., 528, 599
Roth, P.H., 203
Rothschild, B.M., 382–384, 737
Rowe, T., 385–386, 818
Rowntree, V.J., 483
Roy, J.R., 977
Roy-Chowdhury, T.K., 331–332
Ruben, J., 891
Ruderman, M., 1109–1110
Rudwick, M.J.S., 95–96
Russell, A.P., 226, 364–365
Russell, D.A., 64–66, 291, 296, 298, 387–391, 448–449, 462, 481, 579, 608, 614, 863, 977, 993, 1002–1003, 1031, 1111
Russell, L.S., 115, 1032
Ryan, D., E. 1048
Saedler, H., 238, 255
Sahni, A., 227, 392, 781, 787
Saito, T., 1125
Sampaio, R.A., 776
Santa Luca, A.P., 393
Sanz, J.L., 394, 507, 950
Sarjeant, W.A.S., 67, 152, 156, 496, 508, 511–512
Satinoff, E., 529
Sattayarak, N., 215
Sattler, H.R., 68
Savage, R.J.G., 8
Savin, S., 204
Schaaf, A., 195
Schaefer, J., 74
Schafersman, S.D., 52
Schaller, G.B., 669
Schlanger, S.O., 181, 205
Schmidt, V.A., 158
Schmidt-Nielsen, K., 468, 484, 486, 703
Schneider, N.M., 1073

Schoener, T.W., 559
Schuchert, C., 116, 148–149
Schultz, P.H., 1084, 1088
Schwartz, R.D., 1085
Schwimmer, D.R., 283
Scott, R.W., 228
Scott, W.B., 117
Seagrave, R.C., 742
Seeherman, H.J., 469
Seeley, H.G., 97–98
Séguin, R., 391
Seisser, W.G., 283
Sellschop, J.P.F., 1092
Sen, G., 1054
Sepkoski, J.J. jr., 714, 999–1000, 1004
Sereno, P.C., 395–397, 864–868
Seymour, R.S., 441, 782–783, 789
Sharp, P.M., 238, 269
Sharp, R.M., 915
Sharpton, V.L., 1153
Sheehan, P.M., 1005
Shine, R., 570
Shoemaker, E.M., 1065, 1086
Shor, E.N., 150
Short, D.A., 193
Shounan, Z., 513
Sigal, J., 195
Signor, P.W., 997, 1006
Sigurdsson, H., 1087
Sikes, S.F., 704
Sill, W.D., 182
Silver, L.T., 1088
Silverberg, R., 69, 442
Silyn-Roberts, H., 915
Simpson, G.G., 118–120
Sinclair, A.R.E., 705
Singh, C., 993

Slatkin, M., 560
Sliter, W.V., 1049
Sloan, R.E., 842, 1030, 1033, 1135
Smallwood, J., 629
Smit, J., 1007–1008, 1030, 1089–1090
Smith, A.B., 996
Smith, B.J., 70
Smith, E.N., 571–572
Smoluchowski, R., 1105
Snee, L.W., 1067
Snell, E.H., 785
Soule, O.H., 573
Spicer, R.A., 260, 1049, 1126–1127
Spoon, M.D., 1124
Spotila, J.R., 443–444, 564, 573, 778, 784
Srivastava, S.K., 206
Stadtman, K.L., 763
Standora, E.A., 784
Stanley, S.M., 800, 1128
Stapel, S.O., 973
Stebbins, G.L., 261
Steel, R., 15
Stephenson, F.R., 1107
Sternberg, C.H., 121–122
Stevenson, R.D., 574
Stewart, J.D., 945
Stocker, G.C., 706
Stokes, W.L., 71, 646–647
Storer, J.E., 514
Stott, D.F., 183
Strothers, R.B., 1082, 1152
Sues, H.D., 229, 282, 319, 398, 738, 869
Sukumar, R., 707
Sun, A.L., 399

Sundquist, E.T., 207
Surlyk, F., 1040
Suteethorn, V., 215, 658
Sutter, J.F., 1068
Swain, T., 1129–1130
Sweet, A.R., 600, 1131
Swinton, W.E., 72, 82, 951
Tarsitano, S., 482, 870, 881–882, 892, 974
Taylor, C.R., 424, 467, 474–475, 483–486
Taylor, D.W., 262
Terry, K.D., 1112
Thomas, R.D.K., 445
Thomas, R.G., 184, 187
Thompson, C.V., 427
Throckmorton, G.S., 648
Thulborn, R.A., 400–404, 452, 487–490, 609, 649–651, 739, 819–822, 893–895, 916, 975
Thulborn, T., 515
Tidwell, W.T., 263
Tiffney, B.H., 264–265, 652, 656
Toon, O.B., 1080, 1091
Torbett, M.V., 1105
Tordoff, H.B., 961
Toulmin, S.E., 83
Tracy, C.R., 453, 785
Tredoux, M., 1092
Triplehorn, D.M., 1043, 1045
Trivers, R., 740
Troyer, K., 786
Truran, J.W., 1110
Tschudy, R.H., 1057, 1077, 1132–1133
Tucker, M.E., 516, 801
Tucker, W., 977, 1111–1112
Turco, R.P., 1080, 1091
Turekian, K.K., 1070

Turner, J.S., 569
Tweedie, M.W.F., 73
Tyson, H., 405
Upchurch, G.R. jr., 266, 1134, 1137–1138
Van Couvering, J.A., 980
Van der Kaars, S., 1008, 1030
van Fossen, M., 1087
Van Soest, P.J., 678
Van Valen, L.M., 1033–1034, 1135
Vandamme, D., 1141
Vanheerden, J., 823
Venkatesan, M.I., 1093
Ventress, W.P.S., 185
Verhagen, B., 1092
Versteeg, M., 973
Vézina, A.F., 670
Vianey–Liaud, M., 787
Visser, J., 187
Vogt, R.C., 788
Volk, T., 1123
Wade, M., 491, 739
Wagstaff, B.E., 1083
Waldman, M., 406
Walkden, G.M., 595
Walker, A.D., 896–897, 917, 952
Walker, C.A., 876, 953
Wall, W.P., 407, 714
Wallace, M.W., 1094
Ward, P.D., 1153
Washington, W.M., 190
Wassenberg, K., 699
Wasson, J.T., 1069
Watanabe, M.E., 771
Wattel, J., 973
Waugh, C.G., 69
Weaver, J.C., 446
Wedepohl, K.H., 756

Weigelt, J., 74
Weijermars, R., 186
Weishampel, D.B., 16, 157, 230, 408–410, 639–640, 653–655, 741, 769–770, 802–803
Weishampel, J.B., 230
Weissman, P.R., 1065
Welles, S.P., 824
Wellnhofer, P., 859, 898
Welty, J.C., 954
Wesley, A., 267
Whalley, P., 1035
Wheeler, P.E., 530
Whetstone, K.N., 945, 955–956
White, P.S., 702
White, T.E., 871
Whitehead, D.R., 268
Whitmire, D.P., 1106
Whybrow, P.J., 610, 876
Wiberg, P.L., 1047
Wieser, W., 575
Wilford, J.N., 75
Wilkins, T., 123
Williams, D.L.G., 789
Williams, G.E., 241
Willis, W.R., 959
Williston, S.W., 76
Wilson, K.J., 576
Wilson, M.C., 411, 918
Wing, L.D., 708
Wing, S.L., 656
Winkler, D.A., 172, 790
Witmer, L.M., 923
Wolbach, W.S., 1095
Wolf, L.L., 659
Wolfe, J.A., 260, 266, 1096, 1136–1138
Wolfe, K.H., 238, 269
Wolny, D.G., 159

Wood, J.M., 187
Wood, L., 271
Woodward, A., 791
Wyckoff, R.W.G., 412
Xijn, Z., 872
Yamanoi, T., 1125
Yang, X.H., 1048
Yang, Y.W., 269
Yates, A.M., 1071
Young, B.H., 730
Young, R.G., 188, 764
Zachos, J.C., 1009, 1087, 1113
Zahnie, K.J., 1073, 1097
Zardecki, A., 1056
Zhao, M., 1098
Zhiming, D., 77, 873
Zipko, S.J., 78

SUBJECT INDEX

Abelisauridae, evolution, 281
acceleration, mammals and birds, 467
acid ocean
  and extinction, 1064, 1116
  caused by volcanos, 1148
acid rain, extinction, 1039, 1052, 1060, 1081
acoustic display, hadrosaurs, 726
activity level
  and allometry, 703
  and thermoregulation, 431
advanced-mesotarsal ankle, 812, 836
aestivation
  heterodontosaurids, 403
  ornithischians, 627
  ornithopods, 651
aetosaurs, 801
Africa
  biogeography, 227
  Cretaceous fauna, 333
  dinosaur fauna, 172, 608
  expeditions, 104
  paleogeography, 161
  Tendaguru beds fauna, 608
African elephant. *See* elephant
African lion. *See* lion
aggregation
  alligators, 791
  juvenile ornithopods, 758
  and lizard thermoregulation, 556
aggression and injury from fighting in mammals, 710
Aguja Formation, fauna, 343
air sacs
  in birds and dinosaurs, 530
  thermoregulation, 414
Alamosaurus fauna, 601
Alamosaurus sanjuanensis, 337, 344, 604
Alaska
  Cretaceous floras, 260
  hadrosaurs discovered, 1018
  North Slope fauna, 1049
albedo
  climate, 194
  extinction, 1123
Alberta
  arid conditions, 600
  paleoecology carbon cycle, 207
Albertosaurus tracks, 730
Albertosaurus lancensis, 356
Alexornis antecedens, 922
Alexornis, 927
Alexornithidae, 922
alkaloids and extinction, 1129–1130
alligator. *See also* crocodile
  aggregation, 791
  behavior, 722, 723
  diet, 555
  juveniles and maternal behavior, 771
  maternal care, 774
  nest guarding, 775
  nest moisture, 749
  nest predation, 775
  nest spacing, 791
  nest temperature, 748
  thermoregulation, 553, 571, 573

allometric equation
  body size, 672, 697
  ecological traits, 672
  review of, 697
  size of birds and mammals, 673
allometry
  body size of vertebrates, 703
  bone length and body mass, 457
  brain/body size, 416–417, 520–522, 524
  birds and mammals, 525–526
  juveniles versus adults, 745
  metabolism/size, mammals and birds, 485
  pachycephalosaur domes, 321
  size and reproductive investment, 736
  size and locomotion, 478
  size and metabolism, 418
  surface and volume in small dinosaurs, 584
Allosauridae, range extended to Australia, 358
Allosaurus, evolution, 807
Allosaurus fragilis, osteology, 347
altricial habit, 674, 770
  and endothermy, 686
amber and gas content, 1042, 1050
Ambiortidae, 941
Ambiortus, 927
Ambiortus dementjevi, 941
Amblydactylus tracks, 494, 496
American alligator. *See* alligator
American Museum of Natural History collection, 26, 100

American West, exploration. *See* western interior basin, U.S.
amino acids
  dinosaur bone, 412
  extraterrestrial, 1098
  fossils, 271
  from cometary impact, 1097
  sequencing in avian phylogeny, 973
Ammosauridae, 290
Ammosaurus, 312, 493
amphibians in Mesozoic fauna, 607
Anchiceratops, 341
Anchisauridae, 823
Anchisauripus, tracks, 733
Anchisaurus, 312, 622
angiosperms. *See also* herbivory
  ancestral appearance, 262
  aridity and evolution, 197
  biogeography, 201, 220
  cause of dinosaur extinction, 1129–1130
  cladistics, 243
  coevolution with dinosaurs, 417, 611, 614, 620, 654–656
  coevolution with mammals, 224. *See also* grasses and grazers, coevolution
  colonizing species, 237, 258
  competitive displacement, 252
  Cretaceous, collections of, 254
  DNA sequencing, 238, 255, 269
  eustacy and evolution, 258
  extinction, 1125–1126
  initial dispersal of, 201, 236
  Mesozoic flora, 265

Subject Index

molecular clock, 238, 255, 269
monocot and dicot divergence, 269
monophyletic, 247, 242
origin of, 235-236, 242, 244, 246–248, 250–253, 256, 260–262, 620
   coastal, 237, 258–259
   pre-Cretaceous, 255, 269
   tropical uplands, 232
poleward dispersal of, 232, 236, 260
pollination of, 239, 257
polyphyletic, 250, 251
radiation, 240, 611
secondary compounds, 642
   and mammalian herbivores, 619
   plant defense, 615-616, 633, 645
seeds and seed dispersal, 257, 261
animal pollinators, extinction of, 1131
anisognathous jaw, 653
ankle joints, 821–822, 860
   thecodonts, 836
Ankylosauria systematics, 830
Ankylosauridae
   cladistics, 855
   evolution, 837
   phylogeny, 348
ankylosaurs. *See also* individual taxa
   armor, 285
   Australia, 357
   diet, 325
   evolution, 820
   fossorial habit, 292–293
   juveniles, 752
   pelvic structure, 293
   skull, 325
   species diversity, 1013
Anomoepus pienkovskii, tracks, 499
anoxic oceanic events, 195, 203
Anserimimus planinychus, 275
Antarctica, paleogeography, 161
Anthodon serrarius, 316
Apatosaurus
   blood pressure, 432
   ecology, aquatic or terrestrial habit, 577
   skull and systematics, 138, 277
apparency model, plant defenses, 615–616
Apparent Digestibility Coefficient, 557
Aquatilavipes swiboldae, 930
Aquilapollenites, extinction, 1132
Araeoscelidia, 845
Araraquara fauna, 208
arboreal origin of flight. *See* flight, origin of, arboreal
Archaeopteryx, 425, 874–875, 879, 882, 884–885, 887–889, 892, 895, 898, 901, 905, 935, 958, 960, 963, 968
   ancestral to modern birds, 950
   not ancestral, 912
   beach habitat, 881–882
   brain, 521, 897
   contemporary with carinate birds, 941
   as dinosaur, 893–894
   Eichstätt conference, 874

Archaeopteryx, (cont'd)
  endothermy, 429, 879
  feathers, 904
  flight, 891, 964–965, 967, 969–971, 974
  forgery claim, 876, 878, 880, 890, 898
  habits, 895
  homologies with Syntarsus, 914
  misclassified specimen, 886
  new species, 883
  origin from thecodonts, 881
  origin of birds, 908
  pubis, 274
  as reptile, 891–892
  review of Ostrom's work, 877
  as scavenger, 882
  skull and pelvic structure, 896
  systematics, 929
  and theropod pelvic types, 380
Archosauria, 51
  cladistics, 826–827, 849, 860
  phylogeny, 847
  taxonomy, 825
Archosauromorpha, 845
archosaurs
  competition with therapsids, 586
  evolution, 793–794
  Mesozoic fauna, 607
Arctic Ocean, Cretaceous, 199
Arctic spillover model, extinction, 1114
Argentina, El Brete, fauna, 212
Argentina
  fauna, 208, 212–213, 282
  Triassic beds, 182
arid habitats, 600

aridity
  affects on early angiosperms, 197
  Jurassic and Cretaceous, 197
  Triassic, 191
Arizona, 493
armadillos, bloating, 286
Armatosauria, 872
armor, sauropods, 394
Arrhinoceratops brachyops, 405
arthritis, 384
artwork. *See* illustration sources; dinosaurs in art
Asian elephant. *See* elephant
assimilation efficiencies, ectotherms and endotherms, 449
asteroid, comets, and meteors as causes of extinction, 1036–1098
asteroid impact
  climatic effects, 1051, 1137
  computer model, 1051, 1056
  extinction, 1116
  fires, 1073
  impact energetics, 1086
  impact site, 1047, 1053–1054, 1061–1062, 1066, 1068, 1087, 1089
  impact structures, review, 1058
  impact winter, 1049, 1059, 1080, 1084, 1091, 1096, 1136–1137. *See* also polar dinosaurs
  laboratory experiments, 1084
  ocean impact, 1051, 1072, 1076
  probability of impact, 1086

Subject Index

shock metamorphism, 1046, 1058
shocked quartz, 1043–1044, 1078. *See also* shock; siderophiles; smectite; clay layer; tektites; tsunami
  size of, 1066
  volcanism, 1149
astragalus, birds, 942, 945
Atlascopcosaurus loadsi, 381
atmosphere, Cretaceous, 1042
  amber gas content, 1050
  atmospheric modeling, 190, 202
Australia
  Cretaceous flora, 241
  Early Cretaceous, 381
  ornithischian fauna, 357
  paleogeography, 161
Aves. *See* birds
Aviales, 907
avian evolution, 933
Avimimus
  pelvic structure and taxonomy, 910
  similarity to birds, 909, 911
Avisaurus archibaldi, 213, 920
axial tilt, and climate, 233, 241
background extinction versus mass extinctions. *See* extinction, background level
Barapasaurus tagorei, 332
Barosaurus, systematics, 277
Barun Goyot Formation, fauna, 348, 369
Baryonychidae, 287, 835
Baryonyx walkeri, 287, 835
Bearpaw Sea, Montana, 803, 206
Bearpaw Shale, fauna, 327

behavior. *See* social behavior; specific behaviors such as display, herding, hunting, sexual selection, parental care, migration, etc.
behavior in fossil record, 712
behavioral ecology, 728
behavioral thermoregulation. *See* thermoregulation, behavioral
bending moment, 457
bentonites
  Judith River Formation, 184
  Cretaceous-Tertiary boundary, 976
bibliographic essay on dinosaur books, 34
bibliography, 1–6
  extinction, 987
  geology, 156
Bighorn Basin, fauna, 304
biogeography, 208, 230. *See also* land bridges
  Americas, 281
  birds, 220, 925, 931
  computer model, extinctions, 998
  Cretaceous, 216
  hadrosaurs, 829
  Indochina, 215
  Jurassic, 170, 221, 385
  land bridge, hadrosaurs, 1018
  Mesozoic, 220
  ornithopods, 225
  sauropods, America, 344
  Thailand, 284
  theropods, 920
  Triassic, 217
  vertebrate evolution, 447
bioindicators

eggshells, 430
fauna and climate, 437
biomechanics of thecodont and theropod locomotion, 482
bipedal stance and locomotion
  biomechanics of, 482
  birds, 468
  evolution of, 793
  flight, 958
  hadrosaurs, 307
  of mammals
    and birds, 469
    energy expenditure of, 483
  rhea, compared with quadrupeds, 484
  gaits, 489
Bird, Roland T., 100
birds
  abundance in Cretaceous, 933, 941
  altricial young, 686
  astragalus, 942, 945
  biogeography, 925, 931
  biology of, 937, 954
  carinate, evolution of, 941
  cladistics, 907, 919, 926–927, 929, 936, 946
  coracoid, primitive condition of, 905
  descent from dinosaurs. *See* origin of, from dinosaurs; similarities to dinosaurs
  diving
    in Cretaceous, 933
    taxonomy, 934
  eggshell development, 915
  endothermy, 421
  evolution of, 937, 951, 973
  fenestra pseudorotunda, 955
  flightless, 953
    evolution of, 973
    in Cretaceous, 933
  fossil trackway, 930
  Huxley's views on, 89, 91
  Mesozoic taxa, 944
  opisthopubic pelvis, 917
  origin of, 19, 899–900, 903, 908, 918, 928, 947, 961, 975
    from crocodiles, 897, 917, 943–944, 952, 955–956, 963
    from dinosaurs, 417, 480, 874, 885, 887, 894, 899, 901–902, 905–907, 914–915, 927, 936, 938, 942, 945, 948–949, 966
    from mammals, 919
    from thecodonts, 881–882, 892, 912, 921, 939
    from theropod dinosaurs, 368, 911, 913
  pelvic structure, 917
  periotic sinus, 902
  phylogeny, 825, 927, 946
  pretibia, 942
  prokinesis, 923
  pterygoid, 923
  pubis, 917
  radiation, Tertiary, 944
  rarity of terrestrial fossils, 933
  scapulocoracoid, primitive condition of, 905
  similarities to dinosaurs, 411, 902, 905, 907, 909, 911, 913, 916, 918, 936, 942
  systematics, 916, 925, 928, 935
  teeth, 945

Subject Index

bloating and preservation, 286
blood pressure, 441
  giraffe, 695
  mammals and sauropods, 432
body size. *See* size
body temperature, 431
  allometry, 703
body weight. *See* weight
bone
  circumference, and body weight, 462
  growth rings, 545–547
  microscopy, 537–538
  primary and secondary in reptiles, 533
  remodeling, 533, 540
  bone histology, 414–416, 440, 532, 544, 546–547
bone loading, 463, 466
bone war, 124–150. *See also* E.D. Cope and O.C. Marsh
bone, Haversian. *See* Haversian system; bone, histology
Bothriospondylus, bones, 547
bottleneck, evolution, 803
Brachiosauridae, 853
Brachiosaurus, 446
  blood pressure of, 432
Brachyceratops, 844
Brachylophosaurus goodwini, 330
brain
  evolution, 731
  metabolic requirements, mammal, 517
  size of brain
    endothermy and behavior of reptiles and dinosaurs, 521
    evolution of reptilian, 524

  intelligence, 517, 530
  metabolism and longevity, mammals, 685
brain/body size allometry, 416–417, 520–522, 524
  mammals and birds, 525–526
braincase
  pachycephalosaurs, 321
  sauropod, 518
brains, bibliography of paleoneurology, 519
braking, mammals and birds, 474
Brazil, fauna, 208, 290
Bristol fissures, reptile fauna, 582, 594–595
British Columbia, bird footprints, 930
Brontosaurus. *See Apatosaurus*
Brown, Barnum, 100–101, 111, 120
browse line, coevolution of with dinosaurs, 614
Buckhorn Conglomerate, stratigraphy, 176
Buckland, William, 152
buffalo, locomotion, 461
burst running, and evolutionary constraints in tetrapods, 465
Caenagnathidae, 296
Caenagnathiformes, 924
Caenagnathus, 368
Caenagnathus collinsi, 924
Caenagnathus sternbergi, 924
calcium carbonate and acid ocean, 1064
Camarasauridae, 853
Camarasaurus, relation to *Apatosaurus* and *Diplodocus*, 277

Camelotia borealis, 314
Camptosaurus, sternal plate, 302
Camptosaurus, 222, 299
Camptosaurus prestwichii, 318
Canadian dinosaurs, 64, 66
cancer from supernova, 1109
cannibalism
  reptile, alligator, 555
  secondary carnivory, 450, 453
canopy trees, angiosperms, 237, 266
carbon dioxide and climate, 194, 207. *See also* greenhouse effect, extinction
cardiovascular system. *See also* circulatory system
  allometry, 703
  giraffe, 695
  mammals and dinosaurs, 432
  reptiles, 552
Careless Creek
  fauna, 300
  juveniles, 757
Carnatosaurus sastrei, 281
Carnegie Museum dinosaur collection, 112, 346
carnivore size
  and home range, 682
  and population density, 698
carnivores and carnivory, 450, 453, 657, 670, 1120. *See also* hunting; predation; pack hunting
  birds, mammals, 665
  body size, mammals, 664
  comparison with modern, 416
  lions, 659
  lizards, 576–567
  mammals, 705
  and social behavior, 662, 666
  prey size, 670
  secondary carnivore, 450, 453.
carnosaurs
  diet, 663
  evolution, 281, 805, 807
  hunting behavior, 667
  systematics
    and ecology, 668
    and phylogeny, 291, 808, 818
  of Triassic species, 834
carrying capacity, and rainfall, 676
cassowary
  frugivory and behavior, 716
  seed dispersal, 706
casts and molds, tracks, 500
catalog of dinosaurs, 858
  of North American genera, 863
catastrophic extinction, 976–1009. *See also* specific theories; extinction
Caytoniales, 250
Cedar Mountain Formation, stratigraphy, 176
Cenomanian, Turonian Black Shale Horizon, 195
cenotes, and impact site, 1053
census
  of tracks, 602
  data, problems, 590
center of mass, 457
  mammals and birds, 467
Central Atlantic Seaway, Jurassic, 223
Centrosaurinae, 851
Centrosaurus, 339–340, 844

Subject Index

social behavior, 717
Ceratopsia, systematics, 751
ceratopsians, 395. *See also*
   individual taxa
   cladistics, 844
   defense and ischial curvature, 270
   diet, 374
   ecology, 164, 583
   evolution, 797
   frill
      morphology and function, 386
      size 851
   function of shield, 374
   herbivory, 797
   herding behavior, 187, 717
   horn and frill function, 720
   jaw mechanics, 374
   juveniles, 300–301, 343
   sexual dimorphism, 718, 720
   sexual selection, 732
   stress fracture, 382
   systematics, 851
   taxonomy, 289
Ceratopsidae, taxonomy, 405
Ceratopsoidea, 872
Ceratosauria, cladogram, 385
ceratosaurs, phylogeny, 818
Cerra Cóndor, fauna, 208
Cetiosauridae, 853
Cetiosaurus
   foraging, 637,
   systematics, 277
Chaoyoungosauroidea, 872
Chasmosaurinae, 851
Chasmosaurus canadensis, 343
Chasmosaurus mariscalensis, 343

cheeks and cheek teeth
   heterodontosaurids, 403
   ornithischians, 621
cheetah
   as predator, 669
   social behavior, 657
Chicxulub, crater, 1062, 1089
China
   dinosaurs, 60, 70, 77, 399
   Lower Jurassic fauna, 399
   paleogeography, 161
Chinle Formation, geology, 188
Chirostenotes, 913
Chirostenotes pergracilis, 296
chromium, 1057
circulatory system, 438, 441
   reptiles, 568
cladistics, 839, 841
   angiosperms, 243
   analysis using computer models, 850
   application to dinosaurs, 867
   archosaurs, 826, 849, 860
   birds, 907, 919, 926–927, 929, 936, 946
   ceratopsians, 844
   Diapsida, 826, 845
   dinosaurs, 282, 816
   hadrosaurs, 848
   Ornithischia, 817, 855, 864–865
   ornithopods, 225, 304, 796, 857
   recommended textbook on, 862
clay layer, Cretaceous-Tertiary boundary, 1001, 1045, 1057, 1066, 1150-1151
clay layer, volcanic, 1142–1143

climate, 189–207. *See also* temperature
 and angiosperm evolution, 266
 Cretaceous, 180–181, 190, 194, 197–198, 200–201, 204, 226, 232, 241, 266, 1127
 Cretaceous-Tertiary boundary, 1001
 effect on modern herbivore biomass, 676
 and extinction, 601, 778, 1001, 1033, 1083, 1113–114, 1135, 1138
 by supernova, 1111
 of ectothermic dinosaurs, 1032
 of plants, 1132
 Jurassic, 170, 194, 197, 231
 Late Cretaceous, 193, 601
 Mesozoic, 167, 207, 224
 and birds, 925
 methodologies, 201
 Pangea, 197
 sea, floor spreading, 194
 seasonality, 193
 South America, Cretaceous, 180
 and supernova, 1107–1108
 Triassic, 191, 194, 231
 volcanic effects, 194, 1139, 1148
 warming and plant extinction, 1118
climate space, 566, 573
Cloverly Formation
 fauna, 165, 177, 286, 304
 stratigraphy, 177
 taphonomy, 165
clutch size, 782
Cnemidophorus tigris, ecology, 548
Coelophysis, taxonomy, 378
coelurosaurs, 212, 291, 936. *See also* birds, similarities to dinosaurs
 competition with crocodiles, 952
 evolution, 805, 808
 phylogeny, 818
 systematics, 808
 similar to birds, 936, 948
Coelurus, 377
coevolution
 brain size, mammal, 526
 dinosaurs and angiosperms. *See* angiosperms, coevolution with dinosaurs
 fossil record, review, 712
 of grasses and grazers. *See* grasses and grazers, coevolution
 of insects and angiosperms, 239–240
 of mammals and angiosperms, 224
 of seed dispersal by vertebrates, 626
Colbert, Edwin H., 26, 42, 105–106
cold-blooded dinosaurs. *See* ectothermy
Cole method, reproductive traits and body size, 683
collagen, fossils, 271
collection bias, and predator/prey ratios, 448

Subject Index

collection development, libraries, 34
colonial behavior, 41
colonial nesting, 770
  birds and reptiles, 753
  hadrosaurs and hypsilophodonts, 766
  hadrosaurs, 644
  hypsilophodonts, 767
  ornithopods, 765
  reptiles, interaction, 755
colonization hypothesis, seed dispersal, 629
colonizing species. *See also* r-strategist
colonizing species, angiosperm, 237, 242, 244, 247, 258–259, 261, 264
color, and reptile behavior, 713
Colorado, field trips, 17
Columbosauripus ungulatus, tracks, 514
combat, mammals, risk, 710
comets. *See also* asteroid impact; Nemesis
  amino acids, 1097
  extinction, 1063–1065, 1069, 1082, 1090
  impact and volcanism, 1152
community ecology
  Dinosaur Provincial Park, 579
  importance of lactation, 779
  Oldman Formation, 593
  Juan Basin, 604
  ungulates, 684
community evolution, 55
community structure, 55
Como Bluff, O.C. Marsh collections, 145

compensatory growth, herbivory, 613
competition, 728. *See also* faunal replacement; mammals
  diapsids and mammal, like reptiles, 792
  dinosaurs and therapsids, 617
  faunal replacement competitive, 581
  hadrosaurs, 361
  lizards, 560, 570
  mammals and dinosaurs, 416, 424, 639, 1120, 1135
  models, 671
  therapsids and mammals, 690
  therapsids and archosaurs, 586
  Triassic, fauna, 801
conifers. *See also* gymnosperms
  competition with angiosperms, 237, 252
  Late Cretaceous cooling, 1127.
Connecticut State Dinosaur Park, theropod tracks, 660
constraints, evolution of gait, 465
continental drift, 219
  Mesozoic, and avian biogeography, 925
cooperative behavior, 728
  and deceptive behavior, 740
Cope's Rule, 800
  and angiosperm evolution, 264
Cope, E.D., 114, 126, 144
  attack on O.C. Marsh, 132–133, 135
  bibliography, 144
  biographical sketch, 136, 143
  response to O.C. Marsh, 130
  temperament, 127
Cope, Marsh feud, 124–150

Cope, Marsh feud (cont'd)
  bibliography, 137
  books about, 137, 146, 150
  popular account, 142
  summary of, 147
coprophagy, 634
coprocoenoses, and endothermy, 436
coprolites
  India, 772
  review, 609
coprophagy, transfer of microbes, 644
Coraciiformes, phylogeny, 922
coracoid in birds, primitive condition of, 905
Cordilleran, 601
Corythosaurus, 362
Corythosaurus casuarius, 843
cosmic rays, extinction, 1085, 1107, 1109
Cossack dancer syndrome, 491
courtship behavior, 734–735
  birds and reptiles, 753
cranial anatomy, ornithischians, 621
cranial kinesis, and ornithopod herbivory, 796
craters
  Caribbean impact, 1061
  Chicxulub, 1062
  Haiti, 1054, 1087
  Iowa Impact Structure, 1068
  Manson Impact Structure, 1066, 1068
  morphology of, 1058
  rates of cratering, 1058, 1086
  review, 1058
  Yucatan, 1053, 1062, 1089

creationism, 36, 40, 52, 71
crests, hadrosaurs, 326, 366, 372–373
  function of, 351–352, 610, 741
Cretaceous, Alaskan floras, 260
Cretaceous
  angiosperms, 254
  and climate, 266
  atmosphere in amber, 1042, 1050
  biogeography, 216
  climate, 181, 190, 194, 197, 200, 226, 232, 241, 601, 1127
  Late Cretaceous, 193
  eustacy, 232
  geology, 178
    United States, 173
  marine communities, 228
  oceans, 181
  paleogeography, 161, 200
  polar climate, 233
  South America, geology, 180
Cretaceous-Tertiary boundary. *See also* specific elements and minerals; asteroid impact
  age, 1067
  Beloc Formation, 1054, 1067
  Canada, Alberta, 976, 992–993
  carbon isotope gradient, 1117
  clay layer, 1001, 1045, 1057, 1066, 1150-1151
  correlation and date, stratigraphy, 992
  Denmark, Stevns Klint, 1037, 1048, 1055, 1070, 1093, 1095, 1142

Subject Index

determination, methodology, 995
dinosaur survival. *See* Paleocene dinosaurs
Europe, 1044
geochemistry, 1094
Italy, Gubbio, 992, 1001, 1037, 1093
Gulf coastal plain, 981–982
Haiti, 1054
Hell Creek Formation, 1133
paleosols, 1124
Hell's Hollow, 1010
Iowa, 1068
Japan, Hokkaido, 1125
Judith River Formation, 1020
Lance Formation, 1045
magnetostratigraphy, 992
Montana, 976, 1016, 1043
Nevis seam, 993
New Mexico, San Juan Basin, 47
New Zealand, 1044, 1048, 1093, 1095
Pacific Ocean, 1044
physical and chemical changes, 1146
radiometric age, 976
Raton Basin, 1057, 1066, 1070, 1077, 1133
Red Deer Valley, 992
Saskatchewan, 976, 1122
South Atlantic Ocean, 1001
Spain, Caravaca, 1090, 1095
temperatures, 204
Tunisia, El Kef, 1001
Wyoming, Teapot Dome, 1096
crocodile. *See also* alligator
ancestral to birds, 897, 917, 943–944, 952, 955–956, 963
behavior, 722
cladistics, 827
competition with coelurosaurs, 952
crocodile-normal, crocodile-reverse, ankle joint, 811, 836
crocodiloid ankle joint, 821
gait comparison with dinosaurs, 470
juvenile social behavior, 744
Mesozoic fauna, 607
nesting
behavior, plasticity of, 746
competition with iguanas, 755
temperatures, 776
teeth, 945
thermoregulation, 561, 572
cropping, lizards, 648
Ctenosaurus similis, locomotion, 472
cursorial habit, adaptations, 588
cursorial origin of flight. *See* flight, origin of, cursorial
cycadophytes
competition with angiosperms, 252
Jurassic, 267
cynodonts, thermoregulation, 421
Czekanowskiales, 250
D layer and cycles of mantle volcanism, 1144
Dakota Formation, fauna, early work, 131
Dakota sandstone, 263
Davenport Ranch, Texas track site, 733

Deccan Traps, volcanism, 1126,
  1140–1141, 1145, 1149
deciduous habit
  extinction, 1137–1138
  impact winter, 1136
decompression syndrome,
  reptiles and mammals, 383
defoliation, effect on vegetation,
  643
Deinocheirus mirificus, 370
Deinonychosauria, 291
Deinonychus antirrhopus
  described, 375
  preying on a sauropod, 305
  revised description, 376
deltaic plain habitat, 605
demographics, 592
  of elephants, 681
density dependence
  and life history, 680
  elephants, 681
dentition. *See* teeth
deposition and ichnofauna, 506
Dermochelys coriacea
  metabolic rate, 562
  thermoregulation, 564
detritivores, extinction, 1005,
  1113
Devonian controversy, 96
Diademodon, endothermy, 421
Diapsida, cladistics, 792, 826,
  845, 847, 870
Diclonius, 838
dicots, evolution of, 269
Dicraeosaurus, systematics, 277
Dicroidium flora, faunal
  replacement, Triassic, 209
dictionary, popular work, 12, 38
dicynodonts, 924

diet, 618
  carnosaurs, 663
  hadrosaurs, 641
  lizards, 557, 567, 570, 576
  relation to habitat, 1120
  sauropods, 646
  stomach stones, 647
digestion
  and body size, 678
  digestion, evolution of, 436
  mammals and reptiles, 433
digital width, tracks, 507
Dinamation, 43
dinosaur courses, development
  of, 57, 78
Dinosaur Provincial Park. *See
  also* Oldman Formation
  age and stratigraphic
    correlations, 184
  fauna, 295
  paleoecology, 579
Dinosaur Triangle, 159
  field trips, 17
  geology of, 163, 188
  Jurassic eggs, 764
  location of fossil sites, 160
  stratigraphy, 176
Dinosauria, as a Class, 825, 833
Dinosauria, naming of, 93
dinosauroid, intelligent, 390–391
dinosaurs, list of taxa, 858, 863,
  871
dinosaurs, superiority of, 25
dinosaurs in art, 30, 37
Diplodocidae, 853
  revision of family, 277
Diplodocus
  Cope, Marsh controversy, 134,
    138

Subject Index

posture and gait, 457
skull and systematics, 138, 277
Dipsosaurus dorsalis, digestive efficiency, 557
directed dispersal hypothesis, seed dispersal, 629
Dirhopalostachyaceae, 250
dispersal
　dinosaurs, island hopping, 214
　hadrosaurs, 829
　post, breeding birds and reptiles, 753
　primitive angiosperms, 201
display behavior, reptiles, 713
display structures
　horns, mammals, 724
　sexual selection, 715
disturbance
　ecological effects of, 702
　effect of elephants, 687-688, 708
diversity of vertebrates, 798
diversity of species. *See* species diversity
Djadokhta Formation, fauna, 369
DNA sequencing
　and angiosperm origin, 238, 255, 269
　avian phylogeny, 973
Dockum Formation, 217
　biogeography, 218
dominance hierarchies, mammals, 724
dormancy, plants, extinction, 1119
Dromaeosauridae, 355, 375
　systematics, 398, 869
Dromaeosaurus albertensis, 291
Dromiceiomimus, 364, 389

Dromiceiomimus brevitertius, speed, 481
drought
　extinction, 1114
　effects on flora and fauna, 585
Dryosaurus, 221-222, 311
dugong thermoregulation, 528
duplex ankle joint, 821
dust cloud
　computer model, 1091
　effect of, extinction, 1005, 1059
　foraging effects, 1080
duty factor
　birds, 473
　mammals, 455-456
dynamic similarity of gaits, 456, 458, 460, 471
Dysalotosaurus lettow-vorbecki, 221
early discoveries of dinosaurs, 79-83, 152
ecology, 33, 577-610
　and mating systems, 719
　and paleobiological theory, 598
　dinosaurs, general, 65
　general text, 701
　lizards, 559
　modern birds and animals, 671-708. *See also* specific animals
ectohydric eggs, 785
ectothermy
　advantages of, 580
　dinosaur ecology, 579
　evolution, reptiles, 568
　and extinction, 1032
　and life history, 747

ectothermy (cont'd)
  mathematical model, 443–444
edentates, thermoregulation, 528
Edmonton Formation,
  paleoecology, 206
Edmontonia, 830
efficiency, metabolic, 575
eggs, 500, 770. *See also* nests,
  eggs, and juveniles, 742–791
  birds and reptiles, 753
    Egg Island and Egg
      Mountain, 767, 770
  endohydric and ectohydric,
    785
  gas conductance, 782
  hypsilophodonts, 767, 790
  India, 772
    paleoecologicy, 781
    sauropods, 781
  Jurassic, 764
  manipulation, 767
  Mongolia, 773
  preservation bias, 762
  reptile
    heat and water exchange,
      742
    water content, 785
  sauropod, structure, 787, 761
  water conductance, 789
eggshells
  birds, crocodiles, and
    dinosaurs, 430
  development, 915
  thickening
    hypsilophodont, 756
    pathologically thickened,
      763
  thinning
    and temperature, extinction,
      1121
    hypsilophodont, 756
    not pathological, 782, 789
    taxonomy and shell structure,
      762
ejecta cloud
  laboratory experiments, 1084
  thermal energy, 1063
El Brete, Argentina, fauna, 212
elastic recoil, mammals and
  birds, 467
elastic similarity, 458, 471, 477–
  478
elasticity. *See also* dynamic
  similarity, elastic similarity
elasticity, and locomotion, 475
elephant, 446
  ecology and life history traits,
    693, 704, 707–708
  effect on habitat, 687–688,
    707–708
  energetic model for dinosaurs,
    448
  herbivory, 675
  locomotion, 461
  population regulation, 681
  thermoregulation, 679
Elmisauridae, 296
  systematics, 913
Elmisaurus elegans, 295
Elmisaurus rarus, 913
embryonic dinosaurs, 769–770,
  777
embryos, fossil bird, 932
Enaliornis, braincase, 934
Enantiornithes, 953
encephalization quotient, 522,
  526

Subject Index

encyclopedia, popular, 8, 14, 16
endemism and eustacy, 196
endocast, 521, 524, 527
   compared with modern reptiles, 523
endothermocentric fallacy, 556
endothermy versus ectothermy, 73, 413–576. *See also* insulation
   affects stance restoration, 482
   Avimimus, 909
   brain size, 521–522
   feathers, 972
      of *Archaeopteryx*, 879
   evolution of, 426, 428, 686
      in mammals, 424, 690
   fermentation heat, 618
   hadrosaur anatomy, 326
   life history, 592
   migration, 727
   parental care, birds and reptiles, 753
   polar habitats, 439
   reproductive costs, 575
   set points, 431
   dinosaurs, 916
   juvenile ceratopsians, 750
   mammals, 421
   mathematical model, 450
   Oldman Formation community, 593
   parietal, pineal complex, 528
   terms defined, 428
   therapsids, 424
   unites birds and dinosaurs, 825
   zoogeographic evidence for, 438
energy budget, lizards, 576

environmental gradients, Dinosaur Provincial Park, 579
epiphyseal complex, and endothermy, 528
EQ. *See* encephalization quotient
Erlikosaurus, 817
Erlikosaurus andrewsi, 276
escape hypothesis, seed dispersal, 629
Eubrontes
   social behavior, tracks, 733
   swimming tracks, 660
Euoplocephalus
   forelimb musculature, 292
   juvenile, 752
   pelvic structure, 293
   skull, 325
Euoplocephalus tutti, 285
Euparkeria, 821
   ancestral to birds, 921
Euparkeria capensis, 813
Europe, paleogeography, 161
Euskelosaurus brownii, taxonomy, 314
eustacy
   Cretaceous, 192, 198, 232
   effect on evolution, 192, 196, 803
   effect on extinction, 980, 1023, 1148
   models (Jurassic), 196
   and origin of angiosperms, 232, 258–259
evergreen habit, extinction, 1126, 1137–1138
evolution, 792–803. *See also* taxonomy and phylogeny; cladistics;

evolution (cont'd)
See also as subhead under specific topics
  archosaur hindlimb and pelvis, 793
  dinosaurs, general, 65
  effects of volcanos, 1139
  initial radiation, 804
  rates, Mesozoic flora and fauna, 655
  speculative, popular work, 32
  vertebrates, 22
evolutionary constraint, gait, 465
extinction. See also asteroids, comets, meteors, Nemesis, Cretaceous-Tertiary boundary
extinction, catastrophic, 976–1009, 1134. See also specific theories, asteroid, volcanos, supernova,etc.
  acid rain, 1039, 1052, 1060, 1081
  albedo, 1123
  and sex determination, 754
  angiosperms
    and dinosaurs, 614
    alkaloids, effect of, 1129–1130
    effects of herbivore extinctions, 656
  Arctic spillover model, 1114
  background level, 979, 984–985, 988, 994, 997, 991
  benthic organisms, 994
  bibliography, 987
  biogeography, 998
  carbon pulse from, 1116
  Carnian, 617

  climate, 420, 444, 601, 778, 1001, 1018, 1083, 1114, 1118, 1132, 1135
    and ectothermy, 1032
    and supernova, 1111
  comets, 1063–1065, 1069, 1090
  computer model, 998
  cyanide, 1063
  deciduous habit, 1136–1138
  detritivores and scavengers, 1005
  dimethyl sulfide,1123
  drought, 1114
  dust cloud, 1091
    and photosynthesis, 1005
  Early Cretaceous, 344
  early theories, 103, 977, 1002
  eustacy, 980, 1023, 1148
  fires, 1039, 1042, 1050, 1073, 1093, 1095, 1133
    from volcanos, 1143, 1146
  galactic plane oscillation, 1082, 1085
  galaxy, passage through, 1074
  gradual, 1010–1035
    marine, 1023
    plants, 1022
  greenhouse effect, 1039, 1052, 1064, 1076, 1080–1081, 1117, 1121
    volcanic, 1140, 1145
  heavy metals, 1081
  impact sites reviewed, 1053, 1089
  impact winter, 1049, 1059, 1080, 1084, 1091, 1096, 1136–1137
  iridium anomaly. See iridium

Late Triassic, 978
Lazarus effect, 1126
macrofauna, 982
magnetic polarity reversals, 1079, 982
mammalian, 1011, 1016
  gradual, 1010
  compared with dinosaurs, 1017
marine. *See* marine extinctions
mass, 985–986, 989, 1004
microfauna, 982
of animal pollinators, 1131
oxygen isotopes, 1123
periodicity, 978, 988, 990, 996–997, 999–1000, 1041, 1079
  from galactic passage, 1074, 1082
  from galactic plane, 1085
  from volcanism, 1144, 1146, 1152
photosynthesis, 1091
plankton, 994, 1059–1060, 1081, 1116–1117
plants, 1077, 1118–1119, 1132, 1137
supernova effects on, 1112˙
primary productivity, 1009, 1123
quasisuccession, 1137–1138
r versus K-strategists, 605
rate, 192, 979
refugia, 998
  at Cretaceous-Tertiary boundary, 1113
sampling bias in record,1006, 1027
selectivity, 991, 994, 997

sessile organisms, 994
Snowbird I Conference, 1088
Snowbird Conference II, 983, 1153
species diversity. *See* species diversity, extinction
Strangelove ocean, 1117
supernova, 1002, 1107–1112
survival of dinosaurs. *See* Paleocene dinosaurs
tectonics and eustacy, 1001
temperature changes, 784, 1002, 1023, 1049, 1080, 1091, 1115, 1121, 1123, 1128
Triassic, 804
tsunami, 1047, 1054, 1061
volcanos. *See* volcanos, extinction
patterns in fauna, 1015
Fabrosauridae, 846, 868
aestivation, 627
as archetypal ornithischian, 400
cranial anatomy, 796
dental morphology, 323
taxonomy, 323
Fabrosaurus, 393
  dentition and jaw mechanics, 649
Fabrosaurus australis, 402, 868
  and Scelidosaurus, 404
  dentition, 651
  skull, 400
faunal interchange
  Cretaceous, Americas, 210
  South America, 280

faunal replacement
  not competitive, 581
  therapsids and archosaurs, 586, 580
  Triassic, 182, 209, 617, 623, 792–794, 801, 804
feathers, 935, 958
  and endothermy, 972
  Archaeopteryx, 879, 888, 893, 966, 891
    for dinosaurs, 439
    asymmetry, 960, 964
  Archaeopteryx, 895
  Avimimus, 909, 911
  evolution of, 962, 972
  functions of, 975
    as insulation, 879, 904, 963, 974–975
  on theropod juveniles, 975
feeding behavior, 734–735
female choice, 740. *See also* sexual selection
fermentation
  efficiency, 678
  endotherms, 618
  herbivores, 592, 618
  in juvenile reptiles, 786
  transfer of microbes to young, 644
  ungulate herbivory, 675
ferns, dominance at Cretaceous-Tertiary boundary, 1122, 1125–1126, 1133–1134, 138
fibro-lamellar bone, 539–541, 543–545
fictional works, 20, 29, 48, 69
field guides, 12–13
filter feeders, extinction, 1113

fires, extinction, 1039, 1042, 1050, 1073, 1093, 1095, 1133
  amber gas content, 1042
  volcanos, 1143, 1146
first discoveries of dinosaurs, 79, 83, 152
Fischer cycles, ocean, 203
flexible body mass, of predators, 662
flight 879, 904, 957–975
  adaptations, vertebrate, 466
  Archaeopteryx, 895
  Avimimus, 909
  birds, 957, 975
  evolved from flightless birds, 973
  energetics, 463
  gliding, 874, 882, 971
  origin of, 893, 899, 932, 935–936, 951, 971–972
    arboreal, 881, 944, 957–958, 961, 963, 966, 970, 974
    Archaeopteryx, 891
    cursorial, 888, 911, 959, 961, 963, 966–970
  physics of, 959
  preadaptation for, 957–958, 966, 968, 971
  in pterosaurs, 970
  role of feathers in, 960, 964, 974
  in vertebrates, 971
flightless birds, 933, 953, 973. *See also* ratites; ostrich; rhea; flight
  evolution of, 940, 973
  locomotion, 473
flood basalt volcanism, 1141

Subject Index

flood plain, habitat, 604–605
flower types and floral features, evolution of, 245
flowering plants. *See* angiosperms
fluvial channels, taphonomy, 166–167
fluvial sedimentology, 166
foliage, as fruit, 631
food intake convergence, ectotherms and endotherms, 449–450
food selection, ungulates, 694
foot pad impressions, ornithopods, 495
foraging
  and body size, 672
  carnosaurs, 663
  lizards, 548–549
  mammals, 705
  ungulates, 684
Foraminifera, extinction, 1007
fossilization, 18, 74
fossils. *See also* microfossils
  first American discovery, 118
Fourth Crossing, Texas track site, 733
frill, ceratopsians. *See* ceratopsians, frill
frontals, theropods, 661
Froude number, 454, 456, 460
  birds, 473
  mammals, 455, 458
frugivory, *Struthiomimus*, 365
fruit
  and vertebrate seed dispersal, 626
  Cretaceous, 652
  evolution of, 245

Fruitland Formation
  fauna, 337, 604–605
  flora, 263
Fulengia, 868
Fulengia youngi, 303
Fulgurotherium australe, 381
fur, as dinosaur insulation, 439. *See also* insulation
future research, suggestions for, 24
gait, 413–417, 419, 440, 457, 459–460, 463–464, 466, 490–491. *See also* stance; posture; speed; running
  birds, 473
  and bone structure, 546
  consistent with ectothermy, 434
  and evolutionary constraint, 465
  from tracks, 476, 494, 515
  mammals, 456, 458
  and birds, 468, 474
  ratites similar to dinosaurs, 480
  stride and gait, 477
galactic plane, extinction, 1082, 1085
galactic spiral arms
  extinction in transit, 1074
  supernova, 1107
Gallimimus, 364
Gallimimus bullatus, 371
gallop, 489
  mammals and birds, 474
gamma rays, supernova, 1110
gastroliths, 647
gazelles, herbivory, 691
genera, number of valid, 590

geochemistry, iridium
  methodologies, 995. *See also*
  iridium
geography. *See* paleogeography
geologists, bibliographic index
  of, 156
geology of the Mesozoic, 158–
  188
  Cretaceous, 173, 178
    South America, 180
  history of, index to, 156
  Jurassic, 170
    Gulf Coast, 185
    North America, 171
geometric similarity, 471, 477
Geranosaurus, 294
Geranosaurus atavus, 403
Gething Formation, bird
  footprints, 930
gigantothermy, turtles and
  dinosaurs, 564
ginkgophytes, Jurassic, 267
giraffe, 446
  blood pressure, 695
  ecology, 693
  feeding ecology, 696
gliding flight. *See* flight
Gobi Desert, 335
Gobipteryx, 927
Gobipteryx minuta, 932, 931
gomphotheres, and seed dispersal
  628, 632
Gondwanaland, 219, 920
  Triassic land bridge with
    Laurasia, 218
  biogeography, 214
  fauna, 211
Good Reptile model, 416, 443–
  444

Gorgosaurus, 356
goyazite, 1045
gradual extinction, 1010–1035
Grallator, tracks, 733
Grallator (Eubrontes)
  soltykovensis, tracks, 499
Grallator, (Grallator) zvierzi,
  tracks, 499
grasses and grazers
  African, ecology, 692
  coevolution, 613, 635–636,
    691
  relationships, ungulates, 684
graviportal, 588
Gravitholus albertae, 407
Great Surveys, American West,
  99
greenhouse effect
  extinction, 1039, 1052, 1064,
    1076, 1080–1081, 1117,
    1121
  volcano, 1140, 1145
gregariousness, 733
group size, lions, 659
growth rates, 747
  and bone structure, 541–543,
    545–547
growth rings
  bone, 545–547
  teeth, 531, 534–536
guilds, herbivory, 656
gular flaps and endothermy, 530
Gulf Coast
  geology, Jurassic, 185
  coastal plain, extinction, 981–
    982
Gulf of Mexico, geology, 158
gut microflora, transfer to
  juvenile reptiles, 786

gymnosperms, 265
  competition with angiosperms, 264
  extinction, 1125
  Jurassic flora, 267
  Late Cretaceous, 1127
  origin and evolution, 612
habitats
  arid and semiarid, 600
  floodplains, 604–605
  loss, extinction, 1120
  preferences, Dinosaur Provincial Park, 579
  relation to diet, 1120
Hadrosauridae, 169, 605
  neck and posture, 638
  systematics, 330, 848
Hadrosaurinae, 372
hadrosaurs. See also individual taxa
  Alaska, 1018
  Asian, reviewed, 352
  biogeography, 829
  cladistics, 330, 848
  cranial anatomy, 351, 372, 408, 796
  crests, 366, 372, 726, 732
    function of, 326, 351–352, 373, 610, 741
  dental battery, 372
  dentition and jaw mechanics, 653
  diet, 610
  display behavior, 329
  ecology, 164, 641
  embryos, 769–770
  endothermy, 326
  evolution, 328
  jaws, 372
  juveniles, 300, 327, 768
  monophyly, 832
  nasal cavity
    homologies, 408
    lambeosaurines, 408
    nasal salt glands, 610
  nervous system, 530
  nesting, 766
  Pacific coast, 361
  parental care, 768
  phylogeny, 328, 829
  posture, 307
  sensory apparatus, 372
  sexual selection, 726, 732
  social behavior, 730
  speed, 481, 487
  taxonomy, 832, 838, 843
  thermoregulatory function, 530
  terrestrial or aquatic habit, 641
  tracks, 494, 496, 730
  vocalization and behavior, 326, 741
Hadrosaurus, 327
Haemothermia, 847, 849, 919
Haiti
  Cretaceous-Tertiary boundary, 1067, 1087
  tsunami, extinction, 1061
harems, birds and reptiles, 753
Harlan, R., 154
Hatcher, John B., 116
Hateg Basin, paleoecology, 169
Haversian system, 414–416, 532–533, 538, 540–541, 543–546
Hayden, Ferdinand V., 99
head butting
  pachycephalosaurs, 319, 321, 721, 732, 738

head butting (cont'd)
  ceratopsians, 732. See also
    ceratopsians
  hadrosaurs, 726, 732
  mammals, 724
heat exchange
  model, 574
  reptiles, 552
heat load and endothermy, 413
heat storage capacity, 444
heat transfer, 566, 574
heavy metals and extinction, 1081
height, methodologies from tracks, 515
heliothermy, 428
Hell Creek Formation, 1028
  extinction pattern, 1017
  fauna, 213, 319–320, 322, 355
  Paleocene dinosaurs, 1008, 1012, 1029–1030, 1033
  paleosols near Cretaceous-Tertiary boundary, 1124
herbivory, 265, 417, 446, 611–656, 1131. See also angiosperms
  African biomass and rainfall, 676
  African grazing animals, 692
  caloric value of vegetation, 624
  cassowaries, 716
  ceratopsians, 797
  cheeks, 621
  coevolution of grasses and grazers, 613, 635–636, 691
  disturbance, 1131
  Cretaceous mammals, 639
  early dinosaurs, 617, 623
  effect on angiosperm evolution, 611
  effect on vegetation, 643
  elephants, 708
    effect on habitat, 687–688, 707
  evolution, 639
    of skull, 796
  gazelle and wildebeest, 691
  gut microbes, 630, 634
    transfer to juveniles, 786
  gymnosperms, 612
  insects, 642
  jaw mechanisms, 639
  lizards, 557, 567, 576, 648
  mammals, 693, 705
    plant defenses, 619
  Mesozoic fauna, 655
  ornithopod jaws, 802
  pioneer plants, 615
  plant defenses, 633, 642, 645
  plants and dinosaurs, 265
  quality of plant food, 678
  rise of angiosperms, 656
  ruminant or nonruminant, 678
  size
    and home range, 682
    and population density, 677, 698
  stealthy or opportunistic, 642
  thegosis, 650
  ungulates, 675, 684, 694
herding behavior, 489, 591
  sauropods, 454, 503, 587
  trackways, 509
  ceratopsians, 187, 717
  hadrosaurs, 730
    juvenile tracks, 496
  ostrich, 711

sauropods 454, 503
  track sites, 733
Herrerasauridae, 815, 823
  cladogram, 282
Herrerasaurus, 823
Hesperornis, 923
Hesperornithes, and prey, 933
Hesperornithiformes, 884, 923, 927
  systematics, 929
Heterodontosauridae, 806
heterodontosaurs, 856
  tooth replacement, 625, 627
Heterodontosaurus tucki, 294, 393
  dentition, 627
  invalid synonym, 401
heterothermy, 428
hippopotamus
  ecology, 693
  herbivory, 675
  effects of, 689
Holyoke Ma., track site, 733
Homalocephale calathoceros, 349
home range and body size, 682, 698
homeothermy, 428, 547
Hoplitosaurus marshi, 279
horns
  ceratopsians. *See* ceratopsians
  mammals, 724
  taxonomic utility, 859
  Triceratops, 859
Howe Quarry, 101
hunting. *See also* pack hunting, predation, carnivory
  carnosaurs, 667–668
  strategies of mammals, 664

Huxley, Thomas H., 85, 88–89 91
hyena
  as predator, 669
  social behavior, 657
Hylaeosaurus, 93, 279
Hypacrosaurus, 362
Hypselosaurus priseus, 756
hypsilophodonts, 856. *See also* individual taxa
  Australia, 357, 359
  cranial anatomy, 796
  embryos, 769–770
  habits, 596–597
  in North America, 317
  nesting, 766–767, 770, 790
  pelvic musculature, 306
  taxonomy, 846
Hypsilophodon foxii, 91
  pathological changes in eggs, 756
Hypsilophodontidae, systematics, 311, 401
ice age, supernova, 1107–1108
ichnofauna
  in ecological studies, 602
  preservation of, 506
ichnology, 35, 67
  development and methodologies, 508
  review, 504
  symposium, 500, 502
Ichthyornis, 884
Ichthyornithes, and prey, 933
Ichthyornithoformes, 927
iguana
  eating, 648
  transfer of gut microflora, 786
  juvenile social behavior, 744

iguana (cont'd)
  nesting competition with crocodiles, 755
  nests compared with hadrosaurs, 644
iguanid lizards, locomotion, 472
Iguanodon, 81, 93, 299
  discovery of, 82, 152
  in North America, 317
  posture and gait, 457
  systematics, 848
Iguanodon lakotaensis, 409
Iguanodon prestwichii, 318
Iguanodontidae, 169, 856. *See also* individual taxa
  evolution, 819
  as grade, 846
  systematics, 299, 857
  Australia, 357
  cranial anatomy, 796
Iliosuchus, 309
illustration sources for slides, 30, 37–38, 51, 54, 58, 68, 265
impact effects of asteroid. *See* craters; asteroid impact
impact winter, 1059. *See* also polar dinosaurs
  and extinction, 1049, 1080, 1084, 1091, 1096, 1136–1137
incubation, and sex ratios in reptiles, 743, 754
India
  biogeography, 227
  egg sites, 772
  Jurassic fauna, 331
  Late Cretaceous fauna, 781
  list of dinosaur taxa, 772
Indochina, biogeography, 215

Indosaurus matleyi, 288
Indosuchus raptorius, 288
inertial homeotherms, 416, 419–420, 434, 444, 542, 550, 574
  mathematical model, 443
  lizards, 563
  turtles, 564
insectivores, and prey size, 670
insectivory, Triassic fauna, 594–595
insects, extinction, 1035
insulation
  dinosaurs and therapsids, 542
  and endothermy, 413
  feathers. *See* feathers, function, as insulation
  fur and feathers, 439
  hatchling dinosaurs, 452
  and thermoregulation, 564, 566
intelligence. *See also* brain
  energetic cost of, 517
  dinosauroid model, 390–391
interdigital angulation, tracks, 507
Intertrappean Formation, fauna, 787
intestinal microbes, and digestion, 630, 634
intraspecific combat
  injury risk, mammals, 710
  pachycepahalosaurids, 319, 321
  sauropods, 737
intrinsic rate of natural increase. *See* r, demographics
Irenesauripus, tracks, 494
iridium, 1038, 1048, 1055, 1057, 1069, 1075, 1077, 1092, 1094, 1122

Subject Index

geochemistry, 995
Instrumental Neutron
  Activation Analysis, 1092
  lunar soil, supernova, 1110
  terrestrial origin, 1150
  volcanic origin, 1140, 1143,
    1145, 1147–1148, 1151
ischial curvature, ceratopsians,
  270
Ischigualasto Formation, fauna,
  282
Ischisaurus, 823
Isle of Wight, fauna, 279
isognathous jaw, 653
jackal, as predator, 669
jaw. *See also* herbivory;
  angiosperms, coevolution
  anisognathous, 639
  evolution of, 924
  hadrosaurs jaw mechanics, 653
  isognathous, 639
  mechanics, evolution, 802
Jerusalem, tracks, 492
Judith River Formation
  age and stratigraphic
    correlations, 168, 184
  fauna, 300–301, 319, 330, 392,
    589
  paleoecology, 583
  taphonomy, 187, 1020
  theropods, 842
Jurassic
  biogeography, 170, 221
  molluscs, 223
  climate, 170, 194, 197, 231
  eustacy, 196
  evolution, gaps in fossil record,
    798
  geology, 170

Gulf Coast, 185
gymnosperm flora, 267
non-dinosaurian fauna, 594
stratigraphy, 170
  gaps in record, 798
vegetation, 231
Jurassic dinosaurs, O.C. Marsh
  studies on, 139–141
juveniles, 1049
alligators, parental care, 774
altricial, 773
ankylosaurs, 752
behavior, 770
  alligator, 771
  extant reptiles, 744
  hypsilophodonts, 767
  tracks, 494
body size and proportion, 745
brain, 527
Camarasaurus, 591
carnosaurs, behavior and diet,
  663
ceratopsian, 300–301, 343, 750
cohorts
  hypsilophodonts, 790
  ornithopods, 758
  Psittacosaurus, 751
crocodile thermoregulation,
  561
diet of reptiles, 555
dispersal of alligators, 771
distinguished from adults, 745,
  759
feathered theropods, 975
hadrosaur, 300, 327, 496, 768
hypsilophodonts, 790
Kentrosaurus, 759
lowland nesting site, 757
Maiasaura, 769–770

juveniles (*cont'd*)
  migration of, 757
  mortality of elephants, 681
  ornithopods, 758
  Orodromeus, 769–770
  polar dinosaurs, 381
  prosauropods, 303, 334
  Psittacosaurus mongoliensis, 751
  rarity of, 103, 164, 584, 843, 780
  stegosaurs, 752, 759–760
  turtles, metabolic rate, 562
  misclassification of, 844, 857, 868
K-selection, 700. *See also* r-selection
  and allometric equation, 672
  dinosaurs, 779
  extinction, 605
  scarcity of juveniles, 780
Kaiparowits Formation
  fauna, 410
  and biogeography, 298
Kakuru kujani, 360
kaolinite, 1057, 1143
Khok Kruat Formation, biogeography, 215
Khorat Group, fauna, 284
Khorat Plateau, psittacosaurs, 215
kinetic energy, mammals and birds, 467
killing, methods of predators, 667–668. *See also* pack hunting
King, Clarence, 99, 123
kinship theory, 740
Kirtland Formation
  fauna, 337, 604
  flora, 263
Knight C.R, 336
Komodo dragon, 451
  ecology, 549
  thermoregulation, 563
Koonwarra, fauna, 381
Kota Formation, fauna, 331
kritosaurs, social behavior, 726
Labocania anomala, 354
Lacertidae
  behavior, thermoregulation, and metabolism, 709
lactation, 779
lagosuchid thecodonts, 815
Laguna Manantiales, fauna, 208
Lake Eanes, Texas track site, 733
Lake Malawi, fauna, 172
Lakota Formation, similar to Wealden fauna, 279
Lambeosauridae, systematics, 330, 848
Lambeosaurinae
  true narial crests, 372
  taxonomy, 843
Lambeosaurus, 327
Lambeosaurus clavinitialis, 843
Lambeosaurus lambei, 843
Lambeosaurus laticaudas, 362
Lameta Formation, fauna, 787
Lameta Group, fauna, 288
Lanasaurus scalpridens, dentition, 625, 627, 651
land bridge, 829. *See also* biogeography
  Americas, 210
  angiosperm dispersal, 201
  biogeography, 1018

Subject Index

Europe, North America,
  Cretaceous, 409
  Jurassic, 221–222, 280, 309, 318
  Late Cretaceous Mongolia, North America, 295
  Late Jurassic, Europe and North America, 317
  Triassic, 217, 219
  Cretaceous, 213, 216, 227, 229
Laramide strata, age, 174
Late Cretaceous faunal communities, 601
lateral variation, communities, 604
Laurasia, 219, 920
  biogeography, 214
  fauna, 211
law of acceleration, E.D. Cope, 126
Lazarus effect, extinction, 1126
Leaellynasaura amicagraphica, 381
leaf macrofossil record, 253
Lecho Formation, Argentina, fauna, 213
Leidy, Joseph, 110, 113–114
leopard
  as predator, 669
  social behavior, 657
Lepidosauromorpha, 845
lepidosaurs
  cladistics, 826
  evolution, 465
  Mesozoic fauna, 607
  systematics, 870
Leptoceratops, 601
Leptoceratops gracilis, 388
Leptopleuron, 84

Lesotho, fauna, 402
Lesothosaurus, systematics, 866
Lesothosaurus diagnosticus, 323, 868
library collection development, 34
life history, 592
  African herbivores, 692
  density dependence, 680
  ecology, 671
  scarcity of juveniles, 780
  theory of, 728
  traits
    and ectothermic dinosaurs, 747
    of elephants, 707
    and lizard thermoregulation, 556
    of lizards, 548–549, 559, 565, 570
  mammals, 683
  reptiles, mammals, birds, 674
limbic system, evolution, 731
Limnornis corneti, 883
lion
  ecology and life history, 669
  social behavior, 657
Lithornis cohort, ancestral to ratites, 940
living dinosaurs, 1025
lizards. *See also* iguana
  behavior, 709
  diet, 557
  ecology, 548–549, 559, 565, 570
  metabolism, 709
  panting and thermoregulation, 554

lizards (cont'd)
  prey selection, 567, 576
  thermoregulation, 556–557,
    560, 563, 576, 709
    behavioral, 558
  locomotion, 416, 477
    and evolutionary constraint,
      465
    bioenergetics, 469
    dynamics, 478
    ground birds, 473
    improvements, competition
      with therapsids, 586
    mammals, 458
    mammals and birds, 475, 485
    reptiles, 472
    stress and body size, 461
Louisiana, as model
  paleoclimate, 592
Lufeng Formation, fauna, 303
Lufengosaurus huenei, 303
lunar soil, supernova deposition,
  1110
Lycorhinus angustidens, 401, 403
  dentition, 627
Lycorhinus consors, 403, 625
Lycorhinus tucki, 403
Lyell, Charles, 84
Macrophalangia, 913
Macrophalangia canadensis, 296
Madagascar, biogeography, 227,
  229
magnetic polarity reversal and
  extinction, 1079, 982, 1140,
  1143
Magnolia, 240, 258, 262
Maiasaura, embryos, 777
Maiasaura peeblesorum, 769–
  770
  juveniles, 768
  osteology, 328
Majunga District, fauna, 229
Majungatholus atopus, 229
Malawi, fauna,172
Maleri Formation, India,
  biogeography, 218
Mamenchisaurus, systematics,
  277
mammal-like reptiles. *See*
  therapsids
mammals
  altricial young, 686
  brain size, 685
  competition with dinosaurs,
    416, 424, 639, 1120, 1135
  egg laying, 686
  evolution of endothermy, 424,
    426, 690
  extinction of
    Cretaceous-Tertiary
      boundary, 1017
    gradual, 1016
  gait and speed, 455–456, 460
  large herbivores, 693
  longevity, 685
  Mesozoic fauna, 607
  metabolic rate and brain size,
    685
  radiation, 1011
  relation to birds, 919
Manson Impact Structure, 1066,
  1068
Mantell, Gideon, 80, 82, 84, 152
map turtles, sex determination,
  temperature, 788
Marginocephalia, 395, 866
marine communities, Cretaceous,
  228

Subject Index

marine extinctions, 980–982, 991–992, 994, 998–999, 1004, 1007, 1009, 1023, 1040, 1059–1060, 1063–1064, 1081, 1113–1114, 1116–1117, 1123, 1128, 1150
  versus terrestrial, 1015
  volcanic, 1145, 1148
marine sediments, dinosaurs in, 327
Marsh, Othniel C., 114, 128, 145
  and Apatosaurus, 277
  biography and bibliography, 125, 148–149
  defense of, 124
Marsh, Cope feud. *See* Cope, Marsh feud
mass extinction. *See* extinction, mass; extinction, catastrophic
mass. *See* size
Massospondylus, 622
  skull, 272
mating systems, 719, 728
Megalosauridae, 280
  systematics, 406
Megalosaurus, 79, 93, 406
  discovery of, 152
Megapode birds, mound nests, 783
megaspores, Cretaceous Tertiary catalog, 234
Melanosauridae, taxonomy, 314
Menefee Formation, flora, 263
Mesaverde Group, flora, 263
mesotarsal ankle joint, 821
Mesozoic
  biogeography, 220

  of birds, 925
  climate, 207, 224
    and birds, 925
  fauna, introduction to, 27
  geography, 224
  geology, 170, 175, 183
    North America, 171
  non-dinosaurian fauna, 607
  paleogeography, 171
    and birds, 925
  stratigraphy, 183
metabolic heat, birds, 484
metabolic rate, 618
  and set points, 431
  brain size and longevity, mammals, 685
metabolism
  allometry, 703
  mammals and reptiles, 433
  reptile, 551
metatarsus, theropods, 411
meteor craters. *See* craters, asteroid impact
microbial digestion, ruminants, 630, 634
microfossils, 1020
  as ecological markers, 583, 589
microvertebrate fossils, hydrodynamic sorting, 187
migration, 233, 439, 591–592, 1049
  and endothermy, 727
  biogeography, 216
  ceratopsians and hadrosaurs, 210
  effects on predators, 665
  juveniles, 757
Milankovitch cycles, 203

modern birds and mammals,
ecology of, 671–708. *See
also* specific animals
Mokele mbembe, living
dinosaurs, 1025
molecular clock
and ratite phylogeny, 973
angiosperm origin, 238, 255,
269
molluscs, Jurassic biogeography,
223
Mongolia, 335
arid conditions, 600
eggs, nests, 773
fauna, 369
hatchling ceratopsians, 750
expeditions, 104, 155
monitor lizards, 451
ecology, 549
Monoclonius, 844
monocots, evolution of, 269
monophylesis, ratites, 973
monophyly, 393
archosaurs, 860
birds, 901, 907
Diapsida, 845, 870
dinosaurs, 274, 806, 812, 815,
821, 833, 860, 907
hadrosaurs, 832
ornithischians, 400, 819
Morrison Formation
fauna, 165, 591
field trips, 17
geology, 188
taphonomy, 165, 302, 591
trackways, 603
mosasaurs in Mesozoic fauna,
607
motor control, musculature, 478

mound nesting, birds and
reptiles, 783
Moyenisauropus karaszevskii,
tracks, 499
Mt. Tom, track site, 733
muscles, 466
mammals and birds, 467, 475
mechanics and metabolism,
478
museums
exhibits, 12–13
list of, 21
restoration, 324, 336–367, 379,
390
mutation rates, supernova, 1109,
1112
N.C. Wickramasinghe, and
Archaeopteryx forgery
claim, 878, 880
Nanosaurus agilis, 868
nasal apparatus, hadrosaurs, 373
nasal salt glands in hadrosaurs,
610
National Museum, Washington,
collection, 145
Navahopus falcipollex, tracks,
493
neck anatomy, hadrosaurs and
Saurolophus, 638
Nemegt Formation, fauna, 369
Nemegtosaurus, systematics, 277
Nemesis, 1099–1106
Neodiapsida, 845
Neognathae, systematics, 929
neomammalian formation, 731
Neornithes, 884
systematics, 929
neoteny, birds from dinosaurs,
975

neotetrapods, 794
nesting, 766
  hadrosaurs, 644
  ornithopods, 765
  site of nests
    Proctor Lake, Texas, 790
    upland vs lowland, 757
nests, 41, 500, 753, 770. *See also*
    nests, eggs, and juveniles,
    472–791
  birds and reptiles, 753
  competition between iguanas
    and crocodiles, 755
  crocodiles, 746
  guarding by alligators, 771,
    775
  hypsilophodonts, 767, 790
  Mongolia, 773
  moisture, alligator, 749
  predation, alligator, 775
  spacing
    alligators, 791
    hypsilophodonts, 767
  temperature
    alligator, 748
    crocodiles, 776
    and sex determination in
      reptiles, 743, 754, 778,
      784
  underground, 782, 789
  birds and reptiles, 783
Neugen, fauna, 208
Neusticosaurus, embryos, 777
New Mexico
  bibliography, 7
  extinction, 1077
  geology, 174
  paleontology, 47
Noasaurus leali, 212

noble metals, 1055
nocturnal habit, mammals, 413,
    690
  and endothermy, 424
Nodosauridae. *See also*
  individual taxa
  evolution, 837
  species diversity, 1013
  systematics, 830
nonruminants, efficiency of, 678
Nopcsa, F., 157
North America. *See* western
    interior basin; specific
    locations and geological
    formations
Northern Malawi, geology and
  fauna, 172
nuclear winter. *See* impact winter
nutrition model, 592
oceans
  acidic conditions, 1116
  circulation in Cretaceous, 203
  Cretaceous, 181
  currents, Mesozoic, 189
  impact, asteroid and extinction,
    1072, 1076
  lithosphere, production rate,
    186
  stagnation, Cretaceous, 195
  upwelling, 190, 199, 202–203
Odontoholcae, 884
Odontornithes, early work, 128
Oldman Formation
  fauna, 285, 579
  ecology, 593
  paleoecology, 448, 450
  taphonomy, 164, 387
olfactory system,
    pachycephalosaurs, 321

Oligosauroidea, 872
Omosaurus phillipsi, 760
ontogenetic stage, model, 745
Oort cloud. *See* comets; Nemesis
opisthopubic pelvis
  Archaeopteryx, 896
  birds, 917
  theropods, 274
opportunistic herbivore, 642
optimal foraging theory
  ungulates, 694
  lions, 659
organic-rich rocks, upwelling, 202
origin of angiosperms, 231–269. *See also* angiosperms, origin
origin of birds. *See* birds, origin
origin of dinosaurs, 804–824, 916. *See also* thecodonts; faunal replacement; archosaurs
Ornatotholus browni, 319
Ornithischia, 872. *See also* specific taxa
  Australia, 357
  Britain, review, 404
  cladistics, 817, 855, 864–865
  dentition, 627
    and cranium, 621
    and tooth replacement, 649
  evolution, 806, 817, 819
  named, 97
  herbivorous adaptations, 623
  jaw mechanics, 649
  monophyly, 400
  origin, 400, 402
  pubis, 906
  radiation of, 580
  speed 481, 487
  systematics, 866, 907, 916
  Triassic fauna, 808
Ornitholestes, 377,
  adaptations, 606
ornithomimids. *See also* individual taxa
  habits, 389, 606
  Mongolia, fauna, 371
    compared with American, 275
  speed, 481
  systematics, 389
  taxonomy, 364
Ornithomimus, 364, 389
Ornithomimus elegans, 295–296
Ornithomimus velox, 298
ornithopods, 856. *See also* individual taxa
  aestivation, 651
  biogeography, 225
  catalog of, 230
  brain, 527
  cladistics, 304, 796, 857,
    and vicariance, 225
  colonial nesting, 765
  dentition, 651
  jaw evolution, 802
  juveniles, 758
  nesting site fidelity, 765
  phylogeny, 400
  sexual selection, 732
  systematics, 403, 866
  taxonomy, 846
  tracks, 507, 510, 603
Ornithosuchia, systematics, 912
Ornithosuchus, not a dinosaur, 805
Ornithotarsus immanis, 129
Ornithurae, 884, 907, 950

Subject Index

Orodromeus embryos, 777
Orodromeus makelai, 769-770
Orthomerus, 169
osmium, 1070
  extinction, volcanic, 1147
osteoarthritis, 384
osteocytes, 537-538
osteology of reptiles, 61, 76
ostrich. *See also* flightless birds; ratites
  evolution of, 940
  phylogeny, 973
  predator defense and social behavior, 711
ostrich mimics. *See* Ornithomimidae and specific genera
Ostrom J.H., reviewed, 877
Ouranosaurus, 299, 848
overcompensation and herbivory, 613
Oviraptor, 296, 368
oviraptoroids, habits, 296
Owen, Richard, 84, 87-88, 92, 94
  proposes Dinosauria, 93
oxygen consumption, locomotion, mammals and birds, 485-486
ozone layer, supernova, 1107-1109
Pachycephalosauria, new suborder, 349
Pachycephalosauridae
  North American species, 319
  systematics, 407
pachycephalosaurs, 395. *See also* individual taxa
  cranial anatomy, 407
  domes, 407
  allometry, 320
  behavior, 714
  function of, 721, 732, 738
  habits, 349
  sexual dimorphism, 349, 714
  sexual selection, 721, 732, 738
  social behavior, 319, 321
  taxonomy, cranium, 714
Pachycephalosauroidea, 872
Pachycephalosaurus, 322
Pachycephalosaurus wyomingensis, 320
Pachyrhinosaurinae, 339
Pachyrhinosaurus, 341
Pachyrhinosaurus canadensis, 339-340
pack hunting, 663
  and body size, mammals, 662
  carnosaurs, 667, 668
  Deinonychus, 375
  mammals, 666
Palaeopoda, 823
  systematics, 808
Palaeosauridae, 290
palaeosaurs, evolution, 808
Palaeoscincus africanus, 316
palaeotetrapods, 794
paleobehavior
  and ecological theory, 598
  in fossil record, review, 712
paleobiology, 33
  encyclopedic work, 21
Paleocene dinosaurs, 993, 1008, 1012, 1014, 1019-1021, 1026, 1028-1030, 1033-1034
  living species, 1025
paleoclimate. *See* climate

paleoecology, 33, 55
  and taphonomy, 578
paleogeography
  Cretaceous, 200
  Mesozoic, 167, 171, 224
  birds, 925
Paleognathae, systematics, 929
Paleognathiformes, systematics, 926
paleomammalian formation, 731
paleoneurology, 153
  bibliography, 519
paleontologists, bibliographic index, 156
paleontology. *See also* vertebrate paleontology
  encyclopedia, 9
  history, 84, 86, 88, 92, 95–96, 104, 108–109, 118, 119–20, 151, 153–154
  popular work, 15
paleopathology, 382–383
Paluxy River tracks, creationism, 40, 52. *See also* creationism
palynology
  Late Cretaceous, 249
  Tertiary, 249
Pangea, 219
  breakup, 186
  climate, 197
Panoplosaurus, 285, 327, 830
panting, thermoregulation, lizard, 554
Parahesperornis, 923
Paranthodon africanus, 316
Paranthodon oweni, 316
Parasaurolophus, 410
Parasaurolophus community, 604–605

parent-offspring interaction, 740
parental care
  alligator, 771, 774
  brain size, 520
  birds, 779
    and mammals, 686
    and reptiles, 753
  ceratopsians, 750
  dinosaurs, 779
  effects of body size, 674
  endothermy, reptiles, mammals, birds, 674
  hadrosaurs, 768
  hypsilophodonts, 790
parental investment, 728, 740
parietal foramen, and endothermy, 528
Patagonia
  fauna, 208, 280–281
  faunal interchange, 210
  expeditions to, 104
Patagosaurus fariasi, 280
patch dynamics, and disturbance regimes, 702
Peabody Museum, Yale, collection, 145
Pectinodon, 903
pelvic girdle, 274
pelvic structure, three saurischian types, 380
Pentaceratops, 386
Pentaceratops sternbergii, 343
periodicity of extinction, 978, 988, 990, 996–997, 999–1000, 1041, 1079
  galactic plane, 1082, 1085
  Nemesis, 1103
  passage through galactic arms, 1074

volcanos, 1144, 1146, 1152
periotic sinus, birds, 902
persistent plants, herbivory, 615
phenetic taxonomy, 831
photosynthesis, extinction, 1005, 1091, 1056
phylogeny, 825, 839, 873
   and evolution of birds, 919, 956
   catalog of genera, 863
   dinosaurs, 816
   Triassic dinosaurs, 393
Phytosauria, 284
Piatnitzkysaurus floresi, 280
Piciformes, phylogeny, 922
pictorial works. *See* illustration sources
Pinacosaurus, taxonomy, 348
pineal body
   and endothermy, 528
   thermoregulation, 569
Pisanosaurus mertii, 806, 821, 868
piscivores, and prey size, 670
plankton
   extinction, 1059–1060, 1081, 1116–1117
   rate of evolution Cretaceous, climate, 204
plant apparency model, 615–616
plant matter, caloric value, 624
plant succession, extinction, 1135
plants. *See also* angiosperms; gymnosperms; herbivory
   chemical defenses, 615–616, 619, 633, 642, 645
   extinction of, 1115, 1118, 1120, 1022, 1077, 1124, 1127, 1131, 1138

Jurassic and Triassic, 231
   quality as food, 678
   seed dispersal, 628, 632
   supernova effects, 1112
plate tectonics, Asia, 284
Plateosauridae, 823
plateosaurs, evolution, 808
Plateosaurus, skull, 272
platinum group elements, 1092, 1094
plesiosaurs, locomotion, 459
Pleurocoelus, hind foot, 305
pleurokinesis, 796
pleurokinetic hinge, ornithopods, 639
poems, 45, 46
Poicilopleuron valens, 110
poikilothermy, 428
Polacanthoides ponderosus, 279
Polacanthus foxi, 279
polar climate, Cretaceous, 233, 241
polar dinosaurs, 233, 381, 439, 1018, 1049, 1083. *See also* impact winter
   Australia, 241
Polish-Mongolian expeditions, 335
pollen
   grains, Cretaceous and Tertiary catalog, 234
   types, evidence of extinction, 1131
pollination. *See also* wind pollination
   and success of angiosperms, 256–257
   evolution, 239–240, 246

polyandry, polygamy, and polygyny, 719
Polysacralosauroidea, 872
Popo Agie, ichnofauna, 602
Poposauridae, 807
popular culture, 37
popular works, 31, 39, 44, 54, 58, 72–73
   Victorian era, 90, 98
population density
   and species body size, 677
   elephants, 681
   large mammals, 680
population ecology, 671
population regulation, mammals, 683
Postosuchus kirkpatricki, 807
posture, 457, 464. *See also* stance; gait; speed; running
   alligator thermoregulation, 553
   and evolutionary constraint, 465
   birds, 473
   in restoration, 482
Potomac Group, angiosperms, 247
Powell, John W., 99, 107
powered flight. *See* flight
precocial habit, 674, 767, 770, 933
   ceratopsians, 750
predation, 658, 663. *See also* carnivory; pack hunting; carnosaurs; specific predators
   attacks in water, 494
   carnosaur behavior, 667–668
   effect on ungulate population, 657
   escape into water, 641, 660
   and gaits, 491
   and hadrosaur herds, 730
   lion group size, 659
   lizards, 560
   and size, 567, 576
   mammals, 664, 669
   models, 671
   prey
      interactions with, 728
      stampede of prey, 739
   and prey group size, ostriches, 711
   and running speed, 490
   and scavenging, 665
   trackways, 509
predator size and prey size, 698–699
   and home range, 682
predator wastage, 449
predator/prey ratios, 414–417, 440, 447–453, 593, 603, 1120
   lizards, 451
predators
   defense against, 734–735
   group size, 662
prehistoric life, popular work, 13
premaxillary teeth, 846
Prenocephale, 322
Prenocephale prenes, 349
prepubic pelvis, 274
preservation, 74
   bias, and predator/prey ratios, 449. *See also* sampling bias
   ichnofauna, 506
pretibia, birds, 942, 945
prey selection
   and body size, mammals, 664

Subject Index

by lizards, 533, 540–541, 543, 567, 576,
primary productivity, extinction, 1009, 1123
primitive metotarsal, PM joint, 836
Proctor Lake, nesting site, 790
progenesis
  and angiosperm origin, 242
  birds from dinosaurs, 975
progressionism, 84, 86–87
prokinesis, birds, 923
Prosauropoda, 823, 828
  evolution, 805
  systematics, 808, 834
prosauropods
  diet, 272
  evolution, 809–810, 817
  first herbivores, 622
  habits, 312
  juveniles, 303, 334
  origin and systematics, 814
  systematics, 312
  trackway, 493
protein extraction, dinosaur bone, 412
proteins in fossils, 271
Proterosuchia, 824
Protoavis texensis, 899–901
Protoceratops, taxonomy, 348
Protoceratops andrewsi, sexual dimorphism, 718
protoceratopsians, phylogeny of Asian, 350
Protoceratopsidae, 388
protoreptilian formation, 731
pseudosuchian thecodonts, 819, 824
  ancestral to ankylosaurs, 348

evolution, 807
Psittacosauridae, systematics, 751
Psittacosauroidea, 872
psittacosaurs
  China, 397
  Thailand, 215
Psittacosaurus, taxonomy, 348
Psittacosaurus meileyingensis, 397
Psittacosaurus mongoliensis, 397
  hatchlings, 750
  juveniles, 751
Psittacosaurus xinjiangensis, 396
Pteranodon, 425
  early work, 98
pteridophytes, 265. *See also* ferns, dominance at Cretaceous-Tertiary boundary
  competition with angiosperms, 252
  Jurassic, 267
pterodactyls, 425
  early work, 98
pterosaurs
  and flight, 970
  brain, 521
  locomotion, 459
  Mesozoic fauna, 607
pterygoid, birds, 923
pubis
  birds, 917
  similar in birds and dinosaurs, 906
punctuated equilibrium, 417
  marine extinctions, 1007
Purgatoire Valley, trackways, 603

quadrupedal locomotion
    compared with bipedal, 484
    mammals, 468–469
    evolution of, 793, 809
Quaesitosaurus orientalis, 338
quartz, Cretaceous-Tertiary
    boundary. *See* shocked
    quartz
quasisuccession, extinction,
    1137–1138
Queensland, stampede site, 739
r, demographics, 683
r-selection, 700. *See also*
    colonizing species
    and allometric equation, 672
    angiosperms, 264, 656
    extinction, 605
    and K-selection, size of
        dinosaurs, 584
    mammals, 779
Rabbit Valley, discoveries in,
    159
radiation, evolution, and eustacy,
    196
rafting, 829. *See also*
    biogeography
rainfall, effect on large herbivore
    biomass, 676
rain forest, evolution, 266
rate of extinction. *See* extinction,
    rate; *See also* extinction,
    mass; extinction,
    catastrophic; extinction,
    background level
ratites, 905. *See also* ostrich;
    flightless birds
    and dinosaur eggshells, 915
    evolution of, 940

gait similar to dinosaurs, 480,
    491
model for dinosaur ontogeny,
    745
phylogeny
    and evolution, 926
    molecular clock, 973
similar to ornithomimids, 389
similar to *Hypsilophodon*, 306
similarity to theropods, 942
systematics, 929
Raton Basin, extinction, 1138
reconstruction, 324, 336, 367,
    379, 390. *See also*
    restoration
    mounting, sauropod neck, 637
    museum, 43
    stance, 482
reference works, 8, 16
refugia
    at Cretaceous-Tertiary
        boundary, 1113
    in mass extinctions, 998
regression, oceanic. *See* eustacy;
    sea-floor spreading
relative stride length, 490
religion, 71. *See also* creationism
reproductive age, 592, 747
reproductive behavior, 41
reproductive investment. *See also*
    parental investment
    and body size, 736
    ectotherms versus endotherms,
        575
reptiles
    anatomy, 61
    osteology, 61, 76
    systematics, 421
reptilian brain, in mammals, 731

reptilian thermoregulation. *See* thermoregulation, reptiles
Resistant-Fit Theta-Rho-Analysis, 831–832
resource availability, plant defenses, 616
resource partitioning, 285
   African herbivores, 692
respiration
   allometry, 703
   and evolutionary constraint, 465
restoration, 30, 324, 336, 367, 379, 390. *See also* reconstruction
   and stance, 491
Revueltosaurus callendri, 868
reworked fossils. *See* Paleocene dinosaurs
Rhabdodon, 169
rhea
   gait similar to dinosaurs, 480
   locomotion energetics, 484
rhinoceros
   behavioral ecology, 729
   ecology, 693
   herbivory, 675
rhynchosaurs, 801
Ringbone Formation, 174
river channels, taphonomy of, 166-167
Roca Blanca, fauna, 208
Rocky Hill, Ct. track site, 733
Romania,
   fauna, 169
   Cretaceous birds, 883
ruminants
   efficiency, 678
   intestinal fauna, 630, 634
running, 460, 463, 477, 489–490, 498, 588. *See also* gait; stance; speed
   birds
      energy expenditure, 484
      and mammals, 468–469
   mammals, 455, 471, 486
      energy expenditure, 483
Russia, paleogeography, 161
Saichania chulsanensis, 348
salt glands, 610
Saltasaurus loricatus, 212
sample size, alpha taxonomy, 854
sampling bias, fossil record, 1006. *See also* preservation bias
San Juan Basin, fauna, 604–605
   fauna, 337, 386
   flora, 263
   history of discoveries, 120
   paleontology, 47
sanidine spherules, 1090
   volcanic, 1147–1148
satire, speculative, 48
Saurischia, 872. *See also* individual taxa
   named, 97
   origin, 805
   systematics, 834, 907, 916
   three pelvic structure types, 380
   Triassic fauna, 808
Sauriurae, 884
Saurolophinae, pseudo-narial crests, 372
Saurolophus, neck and posture, 638
Saurolophus angustirostris, 352

Sauropelta edwardsi, 286
Sauropoda, systematics, 808, 852
sauropodomorhs, 805
Sauropodomorpha, systematics, 834
sauropods, 280. *See also* individual taxa
  Africa, 333
  anatomy, 852
  aquatic or terrestrial, 338, 587, 591
  armored, 394
  biogeography, 332
  blood pressure, 432
  bones, 543, 547
  braincase, 518
  diet, 446
  feet, 305
  habits, 305
  hiatus, western interior, 344
  eggs, 787
  eggshell structure, 761
  evolution, 809, 828
  India, eggs, 781
  neck and tail, 457
  origin, 810
  predation, 658
  quadrupedality, 809
  sexual dimorphism in tails, 737
  social behavior, 591
  speed from tracks, 503
  stomach contents, 646
  swimming, 501, 577
  systematics, 853
  teeth, 337
  tracks, 100, 102, 603
sauropterygians, Mesozoic fauna, 607
Saurornithidae, systematics, 869

Saurornithidae, Saurornithidae, 902, 918
  systematics, 869, 903
Saurornithoides junior, 273
Saurornithoides mongoliensis, 273
Saurornithoididae, new family, 273
Saurornitholestes langstoni, 398
Scabby Butte, fauna, 341
scales, evolution into feathers, 962. *See also* feathers
scandium, 1057
scapulocoracoid, birds, primitive condition of, 905
scavengers
  birds, mammals, 665
  effect on avian populations, 933
  extinction, 1005
Scelidosauridae
  cladistics, 855
  systematics, 820
Scelidosauroidea, 872
Scelidosaurus, ancestral to ankylosaurs, 837
Scelidosaurus harrisonii, 820
  redescribed, 363
  reexamined, 404
scientific creationism, 36, 40, 52, 71
Scott, W.B., 117
sea turtles. *See also* turtles
  temperature-dependent sex determination, 784
sea-floor spreading
  climate, 194
  Cretaceous, 192, 198

Subject Index

sea-level drop, Cretaceous-Tertiary boundary, 1001
seasonality
  and climate, 193
  and migration, 591
secondary bone, 533. *See also* bone
secondary carnivory, 450, 453. *See also* carnivory
  lizards, 567
  reptile, alligator, 555
secondary compounds, 642. *See also* angiosperms
  mammalian herbivores, 619
  plant defense, 615–616, 633, 645
secondary productivity, Oldman Formation, 593
sedimentology
  Mesozoic, 183
  preservation of tracks, 516
seed dispersal
  angiosperms, 245, 257
  cassowaries, 706
  elephants, 708
  herbivores, 631
  Late Cretaceous, 652
  review, 629
  vertebrates, 626, 628, 632
seed ferns, as ancestral angiosperms, 242
seeds
  Cretaceous, 652
  extinction, 1119
  production, effects of defoliation, 643
segmented frill of hadrosaurs, 329
Segnosauria, defined, 276

Segnosauridae, 276
Segnosaurus, 817
Segnosaurus galbinensis, 276
selectivity of extinctions, 991, 994, 997
semiarid habitats, 600
Serengeti, ecosystem dynamics, 635–636, 705
set points, thermoregulation, 431
sex chromosomes, reptiles, 743, 754
sex determination, temperature, 754, 778
  dinosaurs, 784
  map turtles, 788
  reptiles, 743, 754
  sea turtles, 784
sex ratios, 740
sexual dimorphism, 343
  ceratopsians, 718, 720, 851
  hadrosaurs, 726
  pachycephalosaurids, 714
  sauropod tails, 737
  stegosaurs, 759
  Syntarsus, 861
sexual selection, 417, 459, 715, 728
  ceratopsians, 720
  hadrosaurs, 726
  lizards, 559
  mammals, 724
  and mating systems, 719
  ornithopods, 732
  pachycephalosaurids, 320
shield, ceratopsians. *See* ceratopsians
shock metamorphism, 1046, 1058

shocked quartz, 1043-1044, 1078
  volcanic, 1140, 1143, 1147–1148
short-filled ceratopsians, 851
siderophiles, 1048
silica, extinction, 1071
Sinclair expedition, 101
site fidelity. *See also* nesting; nests
  birds and reptiles, 753
  nesting ornithopods, 765
size, 418
  allometric relationships, 697, 703. *See also* allometric equation; allometry
  birds and mammals, 672
  bone loading, 462
  bone structure, 546
  carnivore, and prey size, 670
  diet, lizards, 567, 576
  digestive type, 678
  ecology, large mammals, 693
  evolution, 800
  gut size, 678
  home range, 682, 698
  and life history, birds and mammals, 673
  and locomotion, 464, 477–478
    mammals, 456
    and birds, 467, 475
  and locomotion stress, 461
  mammals
    and birds, 474
    endothermy, 690
    and pack hunting, 662
    and reproductive rate, 683
  and parental care, mammals, birds, reptiles, 674. *See also* parental investment; reproductive investment
  population density, 677, 698–699
  reproductive investment, 736
  predictive allometric model, 745
  relation of predator and prey, 662
    in mammals, 664
  small dinosaurs, 584
  thermoregulation, 444, 542, 550
    alligators, 553, 573
    crocodiles, 561, 572
    reptiles, 563, 571, 574
skeletal structure, allometry, 703
skin impressions
  dinosaurs, 101, 103
  ornithopod foot pad, 495
Sloan Canyon, ichnofauna, 602
small dinosaurs, 584
smectite, 1045
smog, extinction, 1052
snakes, juvenile social behavior, 744
Snowbird I Conference, extinction, 1088
Snowbird Conference II, extinction, 983, 1153
social behavior
  advantages, lions, 659
  aggression, pachycephalosaurids, 319, 321
  alligator, 722–723
  basis for in herbivorous dinosaurs, 786
  bioenergetics, 459

Subject Index

and brain size, reptiles and
dinosaurs, 521
carnosaurs, 667–668
cassowary, 716
ceratopsians, 187, 717–718,
720, 732
dinosaurs, 734, 735
elephants, 687–688, 708
from tracks, 496, 508, 733
gregariousness, 603
sauropods, 591
hadrosaurs, 326, 726, 730, 732
display, 329
herding, 187, 489, 496, 509,
591, 711, 717, 730, 733
sauropods, 454, 503, 587
mammals, 724
carnivores, 666
modern animals, 715
modern reptiles, juveniles, 744
nesting birds and reptiles, 753
ostrich, 711
pachycephalosaurs, 714, 721,
732, 738
pack hunting, 375, 663
reproduction, 41
reptiles, evolution, 713
rhinoceros, 729
sauropods, 587
theropods, 861
ungulates, 725, 732
zebra and onager, 710
soot. *See also* fires, extinction
extinction, 1095
volcanos, 1143
South Africa, fauna, 353
South America
biogeography, 208

Cretaceous climate and
geology, 180
faunal replacement, 209
paleogeography, 161
Triassic beds, faunal
replacement, 182
Southeast Asia, fauna, 284
southwestern U.S.A.
Mesozoic fauna, museums, 59.
See also New Mexico
speciation, rates, 192
species, number of valid, 590
species diversity, 590, 1028
African herbivores, 692
extinction, 981, 1003, 1006,
1015, 1024, 1027, 1031
marine, Cretaceous, 228
vertebrates, 798
species recognition, ceratopsians,
720
speed, 454, 459–460, 464, 469,
481, 487–490, 498, 588,
603. *See also* running;
stance; gait; posture
birds, 484
from tracks, 494, 476, 515
from stampede, 739
ground birds, 473
mammals, 455, 461, 471
and birds, 467–469, 474–475
vertebrate oxygen
consumption, 468
Sphenosuchus, 952
Spitzbergen, fauna, 497
spores, Cretaceous and Tertiary,
catalog, 234
St.Mary River Formation, 803
fauna, 341

stampede, West Central Queensland, 739
stance
 evolution, 793
 methodologies from tracks, 515
 ratites similar to dinosaurs, 480
stance, gait, and speed, 419, 454–491
static stress similarity, 477
Staurikosauridae, 823
Staurikosaurus, 823
 cladogram, 282
Staurikosaurus pricei, 290
stealthy herbivore, 642
Stegoceras, skull cap, 721
Stegoceras browni, 407
Stegoceras edmontonense, 320
Stegoceras validus, 714
 function of dome, 738
Stegosauridae
 cladistics, 855
 systematics, taxonomy, 315
Stegosaurinae, 873
Stegosauroidea, 872
stegosaurs, 279. *See also* individual taxa
 evolution, 820
 jaw, 278
 juvenile, 752, 759–760
 ontogeny, 759
 plates, 422–423, 427
  single row, 297
 posture and gait, 457
 sexual dimorphism, 759
 systematics, 873
Stenonychosaurus, 903
 systematics, 273

Stenonychosaurus inequalis, 387, 391, 902, 918
 foot, 411
Stenotholus kohleri, 322
step length
 birds, 473
 mammals, 455
Sternberg, C.H., 115, 120–122
stishovite, 1043, 1071
stochastic models, phylogeny, 850
Stokesosaurus clevelandi, 309, 346
stomach stones, 647
Strangelove ocean, 1117
stratigraphy, 169
 and catastrophism, 980
 Jurassic, 170
 gaps in record, 798
 Mesozoic, 183
strength, 416, 459
streptostyly, 653
stress fracture, ceratopsian, 382
stride frequency
 birds, 473
 mammals, 455
stride length
 and speed, 454
 birds, 473
 mammals, 456
strontium, extinction, volcanic, 1143, 1147
Struthiomimus, 389
 habit, 365, 606
 systematics, 912
Struthiomimus altus, 364
 forelimb and pectoral girdle, 365
Stygimoloch spinifer, 319

Subject Index

Styracosaurus, 340, 341, 844
subcursorial, 588
succession, 803
  extinction, 1135
superiority of dinosaurs, 25
supernova, extinction, 1103, 1107–1112
surface, volume allometry, small dinosaurs, 584
suspension feeders, extinction, 1113
Svalbard, fauna, 497
Swanage site, Dorset,U.K., track site, 733
swimming
  hadrosaurs and ceratopsians, 164
  sauropods, 501, 587
  theropods, 660
Synapsida, evolution, 421
Syntarsus and the evolution of birds, 914
Syntarsus kayentakatae, 385
Syntarsus rhodesiensis, 861
  systematics, 841
tail frill, hadrosaurs, 329
tail fusion, sauropods, 737
Talarurus, taxonomy, 348
taphonomy, 18, 55, 74, 167, 169
  ecology, 578
  fluvial sediments, 166
  ichnofauna, 506
  scarcity of mammals, 436
  skin impressions, 495
  tracks, 504, 516
Tarchia kielanae, 348
tarsus
  evolution, 815
  taxonomy, 836

thecodont, 824, 836
theropod, 824
Tawasaurus, 868
taxa, number of valid, 590
taxonomy, 825, 873
  difficulties with dinosaurs, 854
  handbook, 10-11
  reference, 16
Technosaurus, 868
tectonic events, Cretaceous-Tertiary boundary, 1001
tectonics
  Gulf of Mexico, 158
  history, 186
teeth
  abrasion, 1012
  birds and crocodiles, 945
  early dinosaurs, 623
  growth rings, 531, 534–536
  heterodontosaurids, 627
  ornithischians, 621
  sediment transport, 1012
  taxonomy, 838, 842, 846, 869, 903
  theropod systematics, 869
tektites, Cretaceous-Tertiary boundary, Haiti, 1087
Telerpeton, 84
temperature. *See also* climate
  and asteroid impact, 1091
  Cenozoic, 204
  Cretaceous, 204
  extinction, 784, 1018, 1023, 1049, 1080, 1115, 1121, 1123, 1128
  and sex determination, 754, 778
  dinosaurs, 784
  map turtles, 788

temperature, and sex
  determination (cont'd)
  reptiles, 743, 754
  sea turtles, 784
Tendaguru beds, African fauna, 608
Tennessee, first dinosaur discovery, 283
Tenontosaurus, 299
Tenontosaurus, sternal plate, 302
Tenontosaurus tilletti, 304
  juveniles, 758
tension circle, ceratopsians, 270
Teratosauridae, 290
terrestrial birds, 933
territorial behavior
  birds and reptiles, 753
  mammals, 724
  reptiles, 713
tetanurines, phylogeny, 818
Tethys Sea
  biogeography, 214
  currents, 189
Tetrapodosaurus borealis, 286
tetrapods, early niches available, 580
textbooks, recommended
  dinosaurs, 14, 16, 23, 28, 33, 49–50, 56, 75
  paleontology, 19
  vertebrate paleontology, 22
Thailand
  Cretaceous fauna, 215
  fauna, 284
Thecodontosaurus antiquus,
  juveniles, 334
thecodonts, 819
  ancestral to birds, 881–882, 912, 921, 939
  ancestral to dinosaurs, 813
  ancestral to Saurischia, 916
  ankle joints, 812, 821, 836
  biomechanics of locomotion, 482
  evolution of, 792–794, 804–805
  faunal replacement, 581
  relation to dinosaurs, 812, 821, 824
  systematics, 815
  taxonomy, 836
thegosis, ornithischians, 650
therapsids
  competition with archosaurs, 209, 586, 801
  ecology, 599
  endothermy, 424
  evolution, 690, 794
  faunal replacement, 580–581
  thermoregulation, 542
thermal conductance, 563
thermal evolution, mammals, 421
thermal time constant, 550, 571
thermoregulation
  alligators, 571, 573
    posture, 553
  behavioral, 419, 444, 569, 574
    alligator, 553
    crocodile, 561, 572
    elephants, 679
    lizards, 556–558, 560, 563, 576, 709
    panting of lizards, 554
  bioenergetics, reptiles, 556
  brain cooling, 530
  crocodile, 561, 572
  hadrosaur crests, 352
  and internal fermentation, 618

Subject Index

and life history traits, lizards, 556
mammals and birds, 421
mathematical model, 444
migration, 727
physiological control, 529, 569
reptiles, 548, 576
set points, 431
size, 542
Stegosaurus plates, 422–423, 427
terms defined, 438
turtles, 562, 564
theropods. *See also* individual taxa; birds, origin from dinosaurs
biogeography, 214, 920
biology and systematics, 840
biomechanics of locomotion, 482
cranial anatomy, 661
dentition, 869
evolution, 274, 824
feathered, 975
phylogeny, 818, 894
sexual dimorphism, 861
South Africa, 353
systematics, 808, 834–835, 903, 907
taxonomy, 854, 861
teeth, 842
tracks, 507, 510
in Wealden Beds, 308
Thescelosaurus, ecology, 583
Thescelosaurus edmontonensis, 310
Thescelosaurus neglectus, 310
thigmothermy, 428
Thyreophora

cladistics, 855
systematics, 865-866
Tianchungosauroidea, 872
tibiotarsal anatomy, evolution, 815
time, discovery of, 83
tinamous, systematics, 929
titanium, 1057
Titanosauridae, 853
titanosaurids, 212
biogeography, 214
India, 781
Africa, 333
Titanosaurus, 169
armor, 394
phylogeny, 337
tooth replacement
aestivation, 651
Fabrosaurus, 649
heterodontosaurids, 403, 625
ornithischians, 627
tooth wear, hadrosaurs, 653
Tornillo Group, age of, 342
Torosaurus, 405
evolution, 797
Torosaurus utahensis, 342
Trachodon mirabilis, 838
trackways and tracks, 35, 459, 464, 489, 492–516
Albertosaurus, 730
basic textbook, 515
birds, 930
in British Isles, bibliography, 511
casts and molds, 500
in China, 513
and creationism, 40, 52
in Dinosaur Triangle, 505
in ecological studies, 602–603

trackways and tracks (cont'd)
  in Glen Rose Formation, 509
  in Gulf Coastal Plain, 509
  hadrosaurs, 730
  interpretation, 67, 504
  methodologies for recording, 512
  in Peace River Canyon, 496, 508
  sauropods, 100, 102
  statistical analysis, 507
  taphonomy, 495, 504, 506, 516
  taxonomic utility, 67, 507
transgression, oceanic. See eustacy; sea-floor spreading
Transylvania, dinosaur fauna, 169
trees. See also angiosperms; gymnosperms; plants; herbivory
  effect of defoliation, 643
  first angiosperms in canopy, 266
Triassic
  climate, 191, 194, 231
  extinction, 978
  non-dinosaurian fauna, 594–595
  vegetation, 231
Triassic-Jurassic boundary, defined, 162
Triceratops, 601
  diet, 374
  evolution, 797
  jaw mechanics, 374
  posture and gait, 457
  systematics, 859
tripodal stance, 491
triune brain, 731

Troödon, ecology, 583
Troödontidae
  dubious family, 273
  systematics, 903
  trophic relationships
    Cretaceous, 579
    Oldman Formation, 593
tropical vegetation, caloric value, 624
trot, 489
tsunami, extinction, 1047, 1054, 1061
Tullock Formation, extinction pattern, 1017
  juvenile social behavior, 744
  thermoregulation, 562, 564
Twin Mountains Formation, nesting site, 790
Two Medicine Formation, nest sites, 644, 767
Tylocephale gilmorei, 349
Tyrannosauridae, evolution, 281
Tyrannosaurus
  evolution, 807
  gait and stance, 479
  posture and gait, 457
Tyrannosaurus rex, 342
tyrannosaurs, 450
  adaptations, 606
  evolution, 288
  secondary carnivory, 453
Ugrosaurus olsoni, 289
ultraviolet radiation from supernova, 1107–1108
Uncompahgre Uplift, 159
underground nesting, 782, 789
  reptiles, 783
ungulates
  comparison with modern, 416

Subject Index

ecology, 684
herbivory, 675
as models for ornithopod crests and horns, 732
optimal foraging model, 694
social behavior and ecology, 725
upwelling zones, 190, 203
Arctic, Cretaceous, 199
computer models, 202
Uromastix aegyptius, eating, 648
Utah, field trips, 17
varanid lizards, 570
Varanus, 451
Varanus komodoensis, 563
variation in taxonomy, 854
vascularization, bone, 538
Vectisaurus valdensis, 313, 857
vegetation. *See* climate; plants; angiosperms; gymnosperms
vertebrate paleontology, 19, 22, 42, 53, 62–63, 795. *See also* paleontology
vertebrates
evolution, 795, 799
species diversity, 798
vicariance
Cretaceous, 211
model, ornithopods, 225
Victoria
Cretaceous flora, 241
fauna, 381
Victorian era
dinosaur model, 84, 98, 442, 464, 491
paleontologists, 88
scientists, glossary of, 85
visual display, hadrosaurs, 726
viviparity, evolution of, 686

vocalization, 459
alligators, 771
hadrosaurs, 326, 741
volcanos
acid ocean, 1148
climate, 194, 1139, 1148
effect on evolution, 1139
extinction, 1002, 1039, 1057, 1075, 1078, 1116, 1139–1152
fire, 1143
greenhouse effect, 1140, 1145
iridium, 1140, 1143, 1145, 1147–1148
magnetic polarity reversal, 1140, 1143
osmium and strontium, 1147
shocked quartz, 1140, 1143, 1147–1148
and periodicity of extinction, 1144, 1146, 1152
sanidine spherules, 1147–1148
Volkheimeria chubutensis, 280
Vulcanodon, 823, 828
evolution of, 809
Vulcanodon karibaensis, 810
Vulcanodontidae, 853
waif dispersal, 829
Walkeria maleriensis, 218
warm-blooded dinosaurs. *See* endothermy
wastage, by predators, 449
water loss, eggs, 782, 789
Wealden Beds
fauna, 287
faunal similarity to American fauna, 279
ornithopods, 313
theropods, 308

weight, 457, 459, 463-464
  and bone size, 462
  mammals, 471
western interior basin, U.S.
  fauna and flora, Late
    Cretaceous, 641
  marine communities, 228
  Mesozoic geography, 179
  stratigraphy, 171
  early discoveries,99, 110, 123
  geology, 173
  road logs, 173
Western Interior Seaway, 163,
    226
Wheeler, George M., 99
wild dogs, social behavior, 657
wildebeest, herbivory, 691
wildfires, extinction. *See* fires,
    extinction
wind
  patterns, computer models, 202
  pollination, 257, 268
    extinction of animal
      pollinators, 1131
  polar, 190
woody angiosperms, evolution,
    246
Xiaosaurus dashanpensis, 868
Yaverlandia bitholus, 721
young adults, dinosaur textbook,
    68
Yucatan, crater, 1053, 1062,
    1089
Yunnanosaurus, 622
zebras, intraspecific aggression,
    710
zoogeography, evidence for
    endothermy, 438